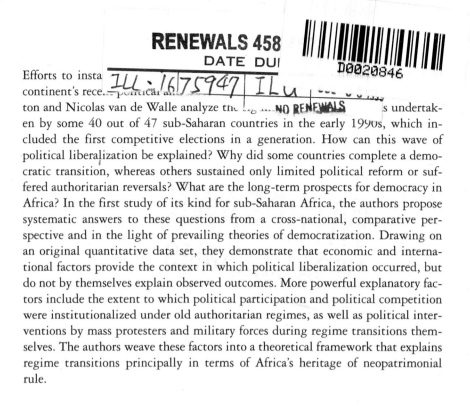
Efforts to insta... continent's rece... political and ... ton and Nicolas van de Walle analyze the ... ... s undertaken by some 40 out of 47 sub-Saharan countries in the early 1990s, which included the first competitive elections in a generation. How can this wave of political liberalization be explained? Why did some countries complete a democratic transition, whereas others sustained only limited political reform or suffered authoritarian reversals? What are the long-term prospects for democracy in Africa? In the first study of its kind for sub-Saharan Africa, the authors propose systematic answers to these questions from a cross-national, comparative perspective and in the light of prevailing theories of democratization. Drawing on an original quantitative data set, they demonstrate that economic and international factors provide the context in which political liberalization occurred, but do not by themselves explain observed outcomes. More powerful explanatory factors include the extent to which political participation and political competition were institutionalized under old authoritarian regimes, as well as political interventions by mass protesters and military forces during regime transitions themselves. The authors weave these factors into a theoretical framework that explains regime transitions principally in terms of Africa's heritage of neopatrimonial rule.

DEMOCRATIC EXPERIMENTS
IN AFRICA

CAMBRIDGE STUDIES IN COMPARATIVE POLITICS

General Editor
PETER LANGE   Duke University

Associate Editors
ELLEN COMISSO   University of California, San Diego
PETER HALL   Harvard University
JOEL MIGDAL   University of Washington
HELEN MILNER   Columbia University
RONALD ROGOWSKI   University of California, Los Angeles
SIDNEY TARROW   Cornell University

OTHER BOOKS IN THE SERIES

DEMOCRATIC EXPERIMENTS IN AFRICA

Regime Transitions in Comparative Perspective

MICHAEL BRATTON

Michigan State University

NICOLAS VAN DE WALLE

Michigan State University

CAMBRIDGE
UNIVERSITY PRESS

PUBLISHED BY THE PRESS SYNDICATE OF THE UNIVERSITY OF CAMBRIDGE
The Pitt Building, Trumpington Street, Cambridge CB2 1RP, United Kingdom

CAMBRIDGE UNIVERSITY PRESS
The Edinburgh Building, Cambridge CB2 2RU, United Kingdom
40 West 20th Street, New York, NY 10011-4211, USA
10 Stamford Road, Oakleigh, Melbourne 3166, Australia

First published 1997

Printed in the United States of America

Typeset in Garamond #3

Library of Congress Cataloging-in-Publication Data
Bratton, Michael.
Democratic experiments in Africa : regime transitions in
comparative perspective / Michael Bratton, Nicolas van de Walle.
p.   cm. — (Cambridge studies in comparative politics)
Includes bibliographical references.
ISBN 0-521-55429-2 (hardcover). — ISBN 0-521-55612-0 (pbk.)
1. Democracy—Africa, Sub-Saharan.   2. Africa, Sub-Saharan—
Politics and government—1960–   I. Van de Walle, Nicolas, 1957–
II. Title.   III. Series.
JQ1879.A15B73   1997
321.8¢0967—dc20   96-34885
                                                             CIP

*A catalog record for this book is available from
the British Library*

ISBN 0 521 55429 2 hardback
ISBN 0 521 55612 0 paperback

For
Nicholas and Emily,
Nadia and Juliette

CONTENTS

FIGURES AND TABLES

Figures

Tables

PREFACE

This book offers a systematic account of political regime changes in Africa, 1990–94. Through it, we hope to reinsert the study of African politics into the mainstream of comparative political analysis, from which it has been marginalized for too long.

In many respects – empirically, theoretically, and methodologically – scholarly studies of democratization have yet to become fully comparative. Empirically, entire world regions are excluded: Whereas most contemporary studies of democratization focus on Latin America or Southern Europe and latterly on Eastern Europe, Africa has received far less attention. In this book, we examine experimental efforts to install democratic regimes in Africa in the early 1990s. Although many of these experiments did not succeed, the opening of authoritarian regimes did mark the return of politics to the continent, a breakthrough welcomed not only by African citizens eager to exercise long-denied civil rights but also by political scientists anxious for something consequential to study in Africa. At its most modest, this book seeks to fill an empirical gap by chronicling African efforts – in all their initial euphoria and subsequent disillusionment – to displace incompetent dictatorships with accountable forms of government.

At a more ambitious level, we wonder whether widely accepted bodies of theory on the breakdown of authoritarian regimes and the global wave of democratization are useful in interpreting recent political trends in Africa. Although scholars of democracy have devised concepts that travel quite well, African experiences challenge some aspects of regime transition theories. In particular, theories based on the demise of bureaucratic forms of authoritarianism cannot fully account for transitions from more personalistic forms of rule. As an alternative, we propose an approach that explains the dynamics and outcomes of transitions in terms of the institutional heritage of previous regimes, a heritage in Africa enveloped by the neopatrimonial practices of political "big men." This approach is elaborated and tested against rival explanations in the pages that follow.

As far as possible, we employ comparative methods. Because of the influence of anthropology and history in area studies, accounts of African politics – including studies of contemporary regime transitions – are dominated by thick descriptions of individual country cases. What are usually missing are systematic, theoretically driven, empirically based accounts of patterns of political change across African countries. In this book, we take advantage of the large number of country cases in Africa – well over 40 in the sub-Saharan region alone – to engage in cross-national analysis. Only for critical cases that exemplify broad trends do we employ detailed accounts of events in particular countries; more commonly, we summarize clusters of country experience at a middle-range level of analysis; and where possible, we test propositions from the theoretical literature using aggregate indicators and statistical methods. To the latter end, the book reports on an original set of quantitative data on political institutions and regime transitions that we compiled for all countries in sub-Saharan Africa. The objective of our comparative inquiry is to probe the underlying causes of regime transition; we seek to document not only "what" but also "why."

Over the three years that it took to complete this project, research was funded principally by the National Science Foundation through grant No. SBR 9309215. During this period, the project also benefited from the authors' involvement in research projects on political reform in Cameroon (funded by the McArthur Foundation) and Zambia (funded by the U.S. Agency for International Development). At an early stage of developing our politico-institutional framework, we received a small amount of support from the World Bank through the Global Coalition for Africa for its comparative research project on democratic transitions in Africa. We are grateful to all donors and sponsors.

Our work has benefited from the comments of valued colleagues. Special thanks are due to those who read and evaluated the entire manuscript, including Paul Abramson, Joel Barkan, Michael Chege, Christopher Clapham, Stephen Ellis, Peter Lewis, Jean-François Médard, and the two anonymous reviewers appointed by Cambridge University Press. They helped us to rethink and amend the presentation of key ideas. A large number of colleagues have provided assistance with individual country cases or have suggested corrections and reinterpretations to parts of the text. For these contributions we are grateful to Tessy Bakary, Boubacar Barry, Robert Bates, Ruth Collier, Michael Coppedge, Larry Diamond, David Gordon, E. Gyimah-Boadi, Axel Hadenius, John Heilbrunn, Mark Jones, Richard Joseph, Robert Kauffman, Terry Karl, Atul Kohli, Carol Lancaster, Aileen Marshall, Thandika Mkandawire, Célestin Monga, Gerardo Munck, Joan Nelson, and Donald Rothchild. Comments from participants at panel presentations at the American Political Science Association, the African Studies Association, the International Political Science Association, the Latin American Studies Association, and at seminars at Princeton and Stanford Universities also helped to refine and improve our arguments.

For help on statistical procedures we recognize Philip Alderfer, Darren Davis, Jim Granato, and Larry Heimann, all of Michigan State University. Collection of data was undertaken by research assistants Kimberly Butler, John Uniack Davis, Soo Chan Jang, Sangmook Kim, Kimberly Ludwig, and Yu Wang. The two Kimberlys especially went well beyond the call of duty to ensure that our data and documentation were accurate and consistent. As authors, however, we take full responsibility for any errors that remain.

Earlier versions of parts of the manuscript have appeared elsewhere. We acknowledge several publishers who kindly provided clearance to reprint extracts of copyrighted material. Parts of Chapters 2 and 5 first appeared in *World Politics* (Johns Hopkins University Press) in July 1994. Chapter 3 is an updated and expanded version of a piece that first appeared in Hyden and Bratton's edited volume on *Governance and Politics in Africa* (Lynne Reinner Publishers, 1992) and in *Comparative Politics* in July 1992. And a first draft of some of the material in Chapter 6 was published initially in a collection of papers on *The Democratic Challenge in Africa,* edited by Richard Joseph under the aegis of the Carter Center in May 1994.

The book is organized as follows. In the Introduction, we provide a brief overview of political trends in Africa's period of regime transition in the first half of the 1990s.

Chapter 1 surveys the prodigious literature on democratization and the different approaches that have been used to explain the success and failure of democratization attempts. We develop our own *politico-institutional* approach, which puts emphasis on the institutional characteristics of preceding political regimes and on patterns of political behavior during transitions, on the basis of a discussion of the strengths and weaknesses of existing theories.

Chapter 2 extends and illustrates this theoretical framework by discussing the nature of African political institutions, both formal and informal. It portrays regimes in Africa as *neopatrimonial,* noting that the institutional characteristics of such regimes have distinctive implications for the process of democratization. Transitions in Africa are likely to diverge, not only from those in the more bureaucratized states elsewhere in the world but also among themselves, depending on the institutional arrangements for different types of neopatrimonial rule.

Chapter 3 describes in detail the beginning, internal dynamics, and outcomes of recent political transitions across the continent. Through careful empirical analysis of actual events, this narrative highlights key patterns and deviations.

The book then shifts from description and characterization to explanation. Chapters 4, 5, and 6 test our politico-institutional approach with the help of a comprehensive base of quantitative data that includes variables on each country's socioeconomic status, legacy of political institutions, and transition trajectory. Extensive use is also made of critical and comparative case studies. Chapter 4 focuses on political protests, Chapter 5 on explaining political liberalization, and Chapter 6 on understanding democratic and other outcomes. Generally speaking, we find that economic conditions do not convincingly account for transition trajectories, as has sometimes been suggested. International factors prove somewhat more helpful. The most compelling explanation, however, centers on political and institutional legacies, some of which derive from the structure of previous regimes and others from more contingent actions of mass protesters and military officers. By molding these factors into multivariate statistical models and illustrating their various dimensions with references to key African countries, these chapters present the core of our empirical analysis.

Chapter 7 examines the prospects for democracy in Africa as of the mid-1990s. It distinguishes between the reversal, survival, and consolidation of fragile democratic regimes, paying particular attention to the institutional underpinnings of these longer-term outcomes. We ask whether democratic innovations outweigh the institutional continuities of neopatrimonial rule, and we arrive at sobering conclusions. The Conclusion recaps the argument and assesses its implications for the study of comparative politics.

Michael Bratton
Nicolas van de Walle
East Lansing,
January 1997

African Countries and Principal Cities, 1991

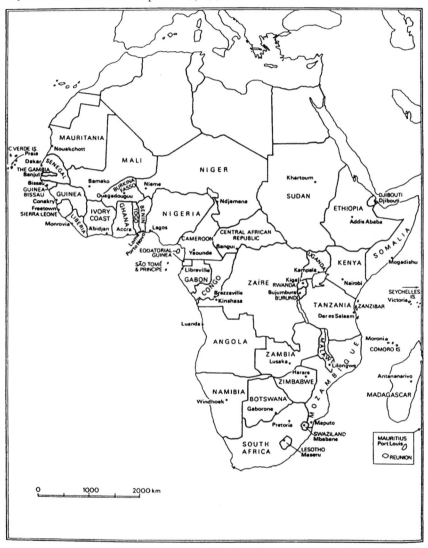

"Like development, democratization is not something that one people does for another. People must do it for themselves or it does not happen."

Claude Ake, *Journal of Democracy,* 1991, p. 38.

"Montesquieu observed that, at birth of new polities, leaders mold institutions, whereas afterwards institutions mold leaders."

Robert Putnam, *Making Democracy Work,* 1993, p. 26.

"The goat eats where it is tethered."

Cameroon proverb quoted by Jean-François Bayart,
The State in Africa, 1993, p. xvii

INTRODUCTION

In January 1989, students marched out of classes at the national university in Cotonou, the capital city of the West African country of Bénin.[1] They demanded that the government immediately disburse long-delayed scholarships and restore guarantees of public sector employment for university graduates. By July, civil servants and schoolteachers also took to the streets with threats of a general strike to protest having gone without salaries for months.

The government of Bénin could not respond to these demands because it was bankrupt. Tax revenues had been slumping for years, capital flight was increasing, and top public officials were embroiled in embarrassing financial scandals. Unhappy with the government's failure to put into effect an economic austerity program, foreign donors withheld disbursements of the budgetary support that was keeping the government afloat. In response to this economic quandary and to the mass street protests, Bénin's military-installed president Mathieu Kérékou began to make political concessions. In August 1989, he invited a prominent human rights activist and legal reformer into the Cabinet; in September, he announced a broad amnesty for political exiles and released some 200 political prisoners.

The protesters were not assuaged, however, escalating their demands to include an end to the ill treatment of political detainees and a clampdown on corruption. Endeavoring to recapture the political initiative, Kérékou surprised his compatriots with a landmark announcement on December 5, 1989, that the People's Revolutionary Party of Bénin (PRPB) would abandon both its ideological commitment to Marxism–Leninism and its monopolistic grip on political affairs. Four days later, he accepted the principle of a return from single-party to multiparty politics. Most important, the president created a commission to prepare a "national reconciliation conference" to which political and trade union organizations, religious associations, and Béninois living abroad would be invited to discuss the country's future.

Perhaps sensing the leader's weakness, key elements in the ruling coalition began to defect. Senior military officers distanced themselves from Kérékou, de-

1

claring the army politically neutral and agreeing to withdraw from public life and return to the barracks. Led by teachers and postal workers, trade unionists broke away from the government-chartered National Federation of Workers' Unions of Bénin (UNSTB). Demonstrations grew apace with as many as 40,000 citizens paralyzing downtown Cotonou at the end of 1989. In an attempted show of strength, Kérékou walked among the protesters but was booed and jostled. For the first time, government-controlled television screened pictures of demonstrators holding placards with slogans hostile to the regime.

By the time the National Conference of Active Forces was convened in a downtown Cotonou hotel on February 19, 1990, Kérékou had clearly lost control of political events. Declaring "I will not resign, I will have to be removed," he apparently hoped the national conference would provide a last-ditch opportunity to retain office.[2] Yet the 488 conferees soon declared themselves sovereign, suspended the republic's constitution, dissolved the national assembly, created the post of prime minister, and appointed to it Nicéphore Soglo, a former World Bank official. The nine-day proceedings of the national conference turned into a devastating personal indictment of Kérékou and his cronies for mismanaging the economy and pillaging the public treasury. Although retaining the offices of head of state and army, the fatally wounded strongman had no choice but to support a new constitution that allowed for presidential term limits and multiparty elections, and to accept the installation of an interim government composed of independent technocrats.

Following a massive "yes" vote for the new constitution by 96 percent of eligible Béninois in December 1990, competitive elections were planned for the legislature in February 1991 and the presidency in March 1991. A total of 24 political parties contested parliamentary seats, and 13 candidates, including both Soglo and Kérékou, vied for the presidency. Despite polling irregularities in several northern parliamentary departments and violent ethnic clashes during the second round of presidential balloting, the elections were certified by domestic and international observers to have been generally free and fair. Soglo's loose electoral coalition, called the Union for the Triumph of Democratic Renewal, not only won the largest bloc of assembly seats, but Soglo himself trounced Kérékou in the presidential race by a two-to-one margin.

Following this decisive electoral defeat, Matthieu Kérékou asked forgiveness for abusing power during his tenure in office and vowed his "deep, sincere, and irreversible desire to change."[3] In a parting act, the interim government agreed not to prosecute the outgoing dictator for any crimes he may have committed previously. Kérékou responded by pledging loyalty to the new government and asking the people of Bénin to rally behind its program for national development.

A PERIOD OF REGIME TRANSITION

As an isolated event, the demise of a local strongman in a West African backwater would normally attract little attention. But Bénin was among the first of a much larger number of countries in Africa that went on to experience a regime transition; Kérékou's downfall was simply an early harbinger of unprecedented political changes soon to follow all over the continent. Moreover, the emblematic drama that unfolded in Cotonou's public arenas combined in one country's experience the core attributes of a landmark transition to democracy, however fragile the institutions of this type of regime subsequently proved to be. In Allen's words, "Bénin may lay claim to the most extensive and impressive peaceful political transformation of any formerly one-party African state in the present period."[4]

The general objective of this study is to understand what happened politically to African countries in the early 1990s. Why did political protesters rise up? Why did incumbent leaders accede to the demands of their opponents? Why, in some countries, were dictators displaced in multiparty elections? Why, in other countries, did they survive and continue governing according to well-established authoritarian methods?

The first half of the 1990s saw widespread political turbulence across the African continent, which can be summarized with reference to a few key political trends. Transitions away from one-party and military regimes started with political protest, evolved through liberalization reforms, often culminated in competitive elections, and usually ended with the installation of new forms of regimes. While not unfolding uniformly and to the same extent everywhere, these movements and institutional rearrangements were evident to some degree in almost all African countries. Together, they amounted to the most far-reaching shifts in African political life since the time of political independence 30 years earlier. Linked in a rough sequence, they delineate a period of regime transition in Africa that lasted for approximately five years between the beginning of 1990 and the end of 1994.

These political trends are depicted graphically in Figures 1 to 4. Data is derived from two main sources: an original data handbook on African political transitions[5] and a standard, time-series data set on civil liberties and political rights worldwide.[6] Starting in 1990, the number of political protests in sub-Saharan Africa rose dramatically, from about twenty incidents annually during the 1980s to a peak of some 86 major protest events across 30 countries in 1991 (see Figure 1).[7] The following year marked the pinnacle of a trend of increased political liberty in which African governments gradually introduced reforms to guarantee previously denied civil rights (see Figure 2).[8] There was also a marked upswing in the number of competitive national elections, from no more than two annually in the 1980s to a record 14 in 1993 (see Figure 3).[9] That the general direction of change was toward democracy is evidenced by the gradually increased availability of basic political rights, which climbed steadily from a low point in 1989 to a peak in 1994 (see Figure 4).[10] There is thus little doubt that Africans experienced a broad and pronounced ferment of political change in the early 1990s.

These data point to several noteworthy features about regime transition in Africa. First, key political events occurred sequentially, peaking at roughly one-year intervals: Whereas the frequency of political protests crested in 1991, liberalization reforms reached their apex in 1992; whereas most electoral activity oc-

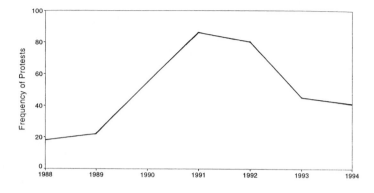

Figure 1   Trends in Political Protest, Sub-Saharan Africa, 1988–1994

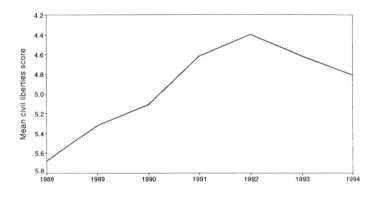

Figure 2   Trends in Political Liberty, Sub-Saharan Africa, 1988–1994

curred in 1993, indicators of democracy were still rising in 1994. The succession of transition events strongly suggests that one trend precipitated the next. In other words, increases in mass protests may have directly contributed to elite decisions to undertake political reform; subsequently, the extent of reform measures may have in turn influenced the convening of competitive elections, some of which led to democratic transitions. Thus connective patterns seem to underly what otherwise appear to be highly contingent political processes.

Second, African regime transitions happened rapidly. No more than four years elapsed between the beginning of the political protest movement in 1990 and 1993's feverish round of elections. Indeed, for the 35 sub-Saharan African countries that underwent regime change by December 1994, the median interval between the onset of transition and the accession to office of a new govern-

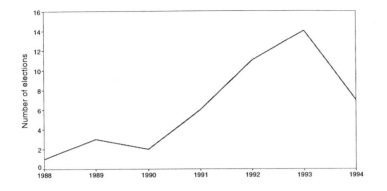

Figure 3   Trends in Competitive Elections, Sub-Saharan Africa, 1988–1994

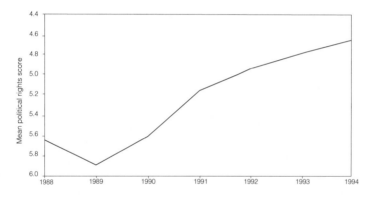

Figure 4   Trends in Democracy, Sub-Saharan Africa, 1988–1994

ment was just 35 months (and just 9 months in Côte d'Ivoire). Compared with the recent experiences of Poland and Brazil, where democratization evolved gradually over periods of at least a decade, African regime transitions seemed frantically hurried. Insofar as democratization involves the institutionalization of procedures for popular government, precious little time was available for such procedures to take root, implying that the consolidation of democratic institutions in Africa will be problematic in years to come.

Finally, trends in African regime transitions were not linear. Recent peaks in key transition events were followed by descents toward new valleys. In part, curvilinear trends reflect the nature of the political phenomena under study. Street protests are naturally episodic because protesters can rarely sustain high levels of mobilization over a long duration, especially if they attain their objectives. Elections occur intermittently after fixed intervals; following a rash of polls, one would expect their frequency to decline until the next electoral cycle. But the liberalization or democratization of political regimes are less bound by such intrinsic rhythms; trends in these phenomena are more likely to depict secular political changes.

Declining mean civil liberties scores for African countries after 1992 therefore amounted to a genuine setback in political liberalization. They reflect not only the reclosing of some political regimes after promising initial openings but also the incidence of major human rights catastrophes in countries like Somalia and Rwanda. Indeed, the entire wave of regime transition in Africa passed its zenith during 1993, as the emergence of fragile democracies in a few countries began to be offset by a rehardening of political regimes elsewhere. Continued gains in democratization through 1994 (see Figure 4), an apparent exception to the downturns in other trends, is probably an artifact resulting from the cumulative effect of the installation by competitive election of four new regimes – in South Africa, Malawi, Guinea-Bissau, and Mozambique – in that year. The observation of sequential linkages among transition trends leads us to expect that the mean political rights scores for African countries will also turn downward in the near future.[11]

A POLITICAL WATERSHED?

Did the period of regime transition in the early 1990s mark a watershed in African politics? Unfortunately, this question does not have a clear and definitive answer. African transitions led to widely divergent outcomes that were expressed through the installation or restoration of a broad range of authoritarian, democratic, or mixed regimes (see Chapter 3). In other words, the political processes of the period displayed a combination of *both* change *and* continuity. Among other objectives, this book seeks to distinguish the innovations introduced into African political life in the early 1990s from underlying institutional foundations that remained very much the same.

Political change certainly occurred. For the first time in the postcolonial era, the trend toward the centralization of political power at the apex of the state was halted and partially reversed. In almost all African countries, autocratic leaders were forced to acknowledge that they could not monopolize and direct the political process and that they would have to divide and redistribute some of the excessive powers they had accumulated. Several major, general innovations occurred in African politics during the period of transition in the early 1990s as compared with the earlier postcolonial era.[12]

The first was increased political competition; African citizens came to enjoy a measure of choice in who would govern them. To the extent that elections were held in Africa before 1990, these were largely noncompetitive affairs in which, by foregone conclusion, a dominant ruling party won all available elective seats. In the five years (1985 to 1989) prior to the onset of the current wave of regime transitions, competitive elections were held in only nine sub-Saharan African countries, measured as elections in which an opposition party obtained a presence in the national legislature. These countries included a group of multiparty regimes – Botswana, Gambia, Mauritius, Sénégal, and Zimbabwe – that had evolved a measure of experience with political competition by allowing a limited space for opposition parties to organize. In the four remaining countries – Liberia, Madagascar, South Africa, and Sudan – competitive elections were not only irregular but seriously compromised by electoral malpractice, a restrictive franchise, or continued military interference in civilian politics.

This record changed dramatically after 1990. In the five years that followed, the number of African countries holding competitive legislative elections more than quadrupled to 38 out of a total of the 47 countries in the sub-Saharan region. Opposition parties won legislative seats in 35 of these elections, and the average share of legislative seats held by opposition parties rose from a paltry 10 percent in 1989 to a somewhat more robust 31 percent by 1994.[13] Of the elections held in 38 African countries from 1990 to 1994, 29 can be considered as founding elections in the sense that they paved a route away from the monopoly politics of authoritarian regimes.[14] In an early evaluation, Wiseman depicted these elections as "an important and non-ephemeral alteration in the way a significant number of African states are, and will be, governed."[15] Discussion and further assessment of these elections is provided in Chapters 3 and 6.

A second innovation was leadership turnover. The postcolonial era in Africa saw the consolidation of personal rule, by which incumbent heads of state concentrated power in their own hands and constructed procedural defenses against being voted out of office. Political succession occurred relatively infrequently, and then only when the military staged a coup or an ailing civilian strongman installed a handpicked successor.[16] Before 1990, more than nine out of ten incoming national leaders were appointed to their posts by military or party elites.[17] The small minority who won office through election invariably did so as candidates of a dominant political party that already held power. On only one occasion before 1990 was a sitting chief executive displaced by means of election; the independence leader of Mauritius, Sir Seewoosagur Ramgoolam, was swept from office in 1982 in the landslide victory of an opposition alliance headed by Aneerood Jugnauth.[18]

The March 1991 election in Bénin therefore marked the first instance on mainland Africa when a national political leader was peacefully supplanted as a consequence of the expressed will of the people. Unexpectedly, at least 10 more such democratic leadership transitions occurred in sub-Saharan Africa in the five short years between 1990 and 1994. In three additional cases, the incumbent did not run in the election, but a new leader was elected anyway. Compared with previous patterns of political succession in Africa, the electoral turnover of presidents was a novelty.

Africa's period of transition was marked not only by greater electoral competition and the ouster of incumbents but sometimes by fundamental changes in the rules of the political game. The range of political regimes on the sub-Saharan subcontinent was altered during this period. At the turn of the decade, the predominant types of regime in Africa were military oligarchies, civilian one-party states, or hybrids of the two (see Chapter 2). The most common institutional formation was a plebiscitary system in which a personalistic leader, who had come to power by a military coup, had constructed a single ruling party that periodically ratified its limited political legitimacy through ritualistic, noncompetitive elections. In 1989, 29 African countries were governed under some kind of single-party constitution, and one-party rule seemed entrenched as the modal form of governance in Africa; only 11 African countries were ruled directly by the military without the pretense of political party institutions (see Table 3).

By 1994, a transformation had taken place: Not a single *de jure* one-party state remained in Africa. In its place, governments adopted new constitutional rules that formally guaranteed basic political liberties, placed limits on tenure and power of chief political executives, and allowed multiple parties to exist and compete in elections. To all appearances, the African one-party state was not only politically bankrupt but – at least as a legal entity – extinct.

At the same time, it should be emphasized that in many other respects the Africa of 1994 was not markedly different from the Africa of a decade before. The enduring institutional characteristics of the continent's politics continued to condition the longevity and success of democratic experiments. In other words, the watershed changes just noted were offset by significant continuities.

For example, despite leadership alternation in some countries, long-standing incumbent leaders in other countries managed to survive competitive elections. Notably, in open presidential contests after 1990, just as many incumbents (15) were reelected as were replaced (14). Henry Bienen and Jeffrey Herbst interpret the reported election results as meaning that "political liberalization is less successful in promoting leadership transition in Africa than is usually assumed and less than elsewhere in the world."[19] Indeed, incumbent leaders seemed to soon learn from the electoral defeats of African colleagues that participatory politics constituted a threat to be controlled. Moreover, even when the faces of top leaders changed, the new rulers were often drawn from the same social and political classes as before, including an aging generation of old-guard politicians who had previously served the postcolonial regime. The election of recycled leaders engendered doubts about whether they would govern any differently than the men they replaced.

Few political institutions were strengthened by regime transition. The state's ability to respond to citizens' needs, either by ensuring law and order throughout the territory or by providing basic services to low-income populations, was still seriously deficient in many countries. National judicial and legislative institutions remained weak. Moreover, past practices of clientelism, rent-seeking, and fraud remained deeply ingrained in certain administrations. The election of new leaders did not mean that they would cease to search for the spoils of political office; on the contrary, the advent of elections marked a scramble for political positions and an intensification of tendencies to quickly make the most of the benefits of office-holding. And just because one-party rule was legally defunct did not, *de facto,* mean that dominant parties would resist using large electoral majorities to revive monopolistic styles of rule. Finally, even though non-state institutions were reinvigorated by the transitions, they remained on the whole weak. Serious doubts soon emerged whether opposition parties, a free press, labor unions, and various other civic, religious, and professional associations would prove strong enough to enforce the accountability and transparency needed for democratic governance. These benefits were far from guaranteed in most countries, making it difficult to resist the view that the consolidation of democratic rule in the region would be difficult and exceptional (see Chapter 7).

These and other tendencies soon became evident in Bénin. Despite a peaceful transfer of power (amidst much public celebration) and the resumption of foreign aid, the Soglo-led democratic government faced daunting economic and political challenges. If anything, the state of the economy had worsened during the uncertain transition, making a tough economic reform program more urgent than ever. Emboldened by its ability to oust Kérékou, much of the political class was wary of presidential prerogatives and keen to assert the power of a revitalized legislature. By late 1993, Soglo's relationships with the 12 parties represented in the legislature were contentious and polarized. When the legislature rejected the government's 1994 austerity budget proposals, thereby triggering a major political crisis, some observers predicted the return to the kind of institutional paralysis that had discredited the country's first attempt at multiparty rule in the early 1960s.[20] The regime's legitimacy was also undermined by persistent accusations of corruption and arrogance in the president's inner circle, which Soglo had packed with family members.

In a startling turn of events in the scheduled presidential elections of March 1996, Béninese voters punished Soglo by bringing back the previously discredited Kérékou.[21] The second leadership turnover in Bénin – a landmark institutional development that restored a previously discredited leader – raised fresh and fascinating questions about the complex amalgamations of political continuity and change that characterize Africa's democratic experiments.

DEFINING DEMOCRATIC TRANSITIONS

Before proceeding, we define some of the key concepts used in this study, beginning with regimes, regime transitions, and democracy.

Political *regimes* are sets of political procedures – sometimes called the "rules of the political game" – that determine the distribution of power. These rules prescribe who may engage in politics and how.[22] The relevant rules may be formally codified in constitutions and other legal statutes; or they may be informal, embodying customs and habits to which all participants are attuned. Differences among types of regimes are captured in the first instance by the contrast between democracy and authoritarianism, and, more finely, by further distinctions among subsets within these broad categories.

A regime *transition* is a shift from one set of political procedures to another, from an old pattern of rule to a new one. It is an interval of intense political uncertainty during which the shape of the new institutional dispensation is up for grabs by incumbent and opposition contenders. For this reason, a regime transition can be depicted as a struggle between competing political forces over the rules of the political game and for the resources with which the game is played. Regime transition may occur by means of a short, sharp transformation – for example, when a coercive autocracy collapses and gives way to an elected democracy. Or a transition may unfold incrementally, as when a personal dictatorship gradually relaxes controls on its political opponents and introduces a softer, more liberalized form of authoritarian rule. The direction of transitions is nonetheless multivalent, potentially unfolding toward harder, more authoritarian regime types. It is also reversible, as when new regimes are installed but political innovations fail to take root, and older forms of rule reassert themselves.

To what extent can any new regime be described as a *democracy?* And to what extent do processes of regime change resemble *democratization?* We believe that these concepts can be applied to Africa, and we disagree vigorously with the view that their usage in sub-Saharan contexts is "both arbitrary and terribly premature."[23] We argue instead that the efforts of African citizens to hold their leaders accountable for providing for the common good are, at heart, a quest for democracy. We further contend that the innovative trend to install leaders by means of competitive elections, while far from the be-all and end-all of democratization, is an indispensable first step. Moreover, to view recent African political developments through a lens of democratization provides a useful point of comparison both within the continent and to other world regions. Indeed, instead of adding to Africa's marginalization by asserting its cultural uniqueness, we see value in situating our study within the ambit of mainstream analysis. In considering African cases of regime transition in the context of the rich literature on democratization, we are able to highlight their singularity – but also their similarity – in relation to political reforms that have swept the rest of the late-twentieth-century world.

Democracy is a contested term. Various authors have endowed it with assorted meanings, including "a distinctive set of political institutions and practices, a particular body of rights, a social and economic order, a system that ensures desirable results, or a unique process of making collective and binding decisions."[24] Influential contemporary interpretations of democracy range from a tight focus on the electoral procedures for choosing political elites[25] to expansive visions of citizen participation in political parties, community groups, and workplace organizations.[26]

The etymology of the term *democracy* reveals its roots: It refers to rule by the people.[27] Democracy is a form of regime whose legitimacy derives from the principle of popular sovereignty: Namely, that ordinary citizens are equally endowed with the right and ability to govern themselves. We recognize that the notion of rule by the people contains intrinsic ambiguities. For example, Robert Dahl has asked how "the people" are designated.[28] Rustow has proposed that democracy cannot be installed unless the inhabitants of a state share a sense of national unity: "The people cannot decide until somebody decides who are the people."[29] And what constitutes "rule"? One could argue, following the ancient Greeks, that rule by the people is possible only under conditions of direct democracy when citizens gather and make decisions in a face-to-face assembly. Alternatively, one could accept Montesquieu's more practical standard that democracy inevitably requires citizens to sacrifice some of their rights of decision-making to representatives who will speak and act on their behalf.[30]

These dilemmas need not detain us long, even for contemporary Africa. To be sure, the scope of the *demos* is problematic on a continent where the boundaries of the modern state rarely coincide with the sense of nationhood felt by its various peoples. Nevertheless, since colonial times, African political leaders have claimed authority and subdued communal identities by asserting the legitimacy of inherited state boundaries.[31] That strong centrifugal tendencies persist is attested by Eritrea's secessionist independence from Ethiopia in 1992, as well as by continuing civil wars in Sudan and the Western Sahara. But Africa's political reformers have generally aimed to change the rules of politics *within* the state rather than to alter the state's parameters. Like the nationalist movements of the 1950s, the prodemocracy movements of the 1990s articulated a view of "the people" that was consistent with state citizenship.

Furthermore, modern democracy has inexorably come to mean representative democracy. Even if the small-scale political communities of precolonial Africa displayed attributes of direct democracy, which is debatable, such communities have long been superseded. Traditional political practices often allowed for public discussion of community issues before a male elder announced a "consensus" position. But the principle of direct democracy was compromised to the extent that leaders could exercise authority arbitrarily to shape the public agenda and interpret the group will. Moreover, whether in state or stateless societies, political norms tended to limit the number of decision makers, with male elders accumulating political authority at the expense of women, younger people, slaves, and strangers.

The enlarged size of the postcolonial political community and the complexity of development policy issues necessitate representative forms of governance. At the same time, citizen control of elected representatives is imperfect in all modern democracies. It is particularly elusive in Africa, where many citizens have limited levels of formal education and live in remote rural areas; not surprisingly, they tend to regard central government as remote and inscrutable. Democratic principles can be expressed in a variety of institutional forms, including forms that embody cultural preferences derived from African traditions. But for ordinary people – in Africa as elsewhere in the world – the challenge of democracy concerns how to obtain accountability from officials of the state. According to John Dunn, "those best placed to represent themselves in African countries are the denizens of the higher reaches, civil and still more military, of its state apparatuses.... it is exceptionally difficult for their fellow citizens to impede them from collectively representing themselves."[32]

In our view, debates over the meaning of democracy boil down to two core definitional issues. First, is the nature of democracy best distinguished according to the form of its *procedures* or the *substance* of its results? We prefer a procedural definition precisely because political regimes are best understood as sets of rules. As Ake notes, "It is the involvement in the process rather than the acceptability of the end decision, which satisfies the right to participate."[33]

We recognize that citizens often judge the performance of regimes in terms of the substantive benefits they receive from the government in power. But various types of political regimes can perform equally well (or badly) on valued policy matters such as economic growth, the distribution of income, and the provision of public services. Indeed, the extensive literature probing the effects of regime type on policy performance reaches no firm conclusions about whether political democracy promotes or inhibits economic growth and income equality.[34] In any event, to judge democracy by the substance of policy outcomes runs the risk of confusing political regimes with the extent of state intervention in the economy or with the capacity of economic institutions. The distinctive feature of democracy is not that it is better than authoritarian rule at raising or equalizing living standards but that it provides political access to decision making for ordinary citizens. Thus, our understanding of democracy refers to a set of political *procedures,* or rule *by* the people; we disassociate it from rule *for* the people, which implies, substantively, a distributive socioeconomic order.

Second, does the definition of democracy embody a *minimal* set of essential requirements? Or does it provide a *comprehensive* characterization that exhausts the phenomenon's full complexity? This study prefers an approach that captures basic elements as most useful in distinguishing political regimes, especially in situations where democratization has only just begun. The flowering of any type of regime undoubtedly requires the mature development of a system of interlocking political institutions and sets of widely shared political values. But to define democracy in terms of the full realization of ideal forms is to risk finding few actual democracies or none at all. Robert Dahl reserved the term "democracy" for "a hypothetical system ... [that is] completely responsive to all its citizens" and resorted to the awkward neologism of "polyarchy" to refer to responsive regimes in the less than perfect real world.[35] On balance, we prefer to use the common currency of "democracy" but to strictly specify its referents to a few essential attributes.

The task of adducing a definition of democracy is now simplified. By what *minimal* set of political *procedures* are citizens in a modern state able to govern themselves? The most basic requirement for democracy is that citizens be empowered to choose and remove leaders. Thus, democracy is defined in this study as a form of political regime in which citizens choose, in competitive elections, the occupants of the top political offices of the state. According to this definition, a transition to democracy occurs with the installation of a government chosen on the basis of one competitive election, as long as that election is freely and fairly conducted within a matrix of civil liberties, and that all the contestants accept the validity of the election results. Note that this approach to democracy does not depend on proving that contestants for power are "true" democrats. It does not pressuppose the existence of a political culture of democracy among either elites or masses. It requires only that incumbents and opponents acknowledge, however reluctantly, the acceptability of electoral contests for leadership.

One aspect of this definition requires further discussion. We emphasize that elections must be conducted within a matrix of civil liberties. In practice, civil liberties guarantee that politics will be genuinely competitive. Before elections, all potential candidates must have the opportunity to offer themselves for office, to express their political views openly, and to form political associations to aggregate support behind their bid for power. At the same time, citizens must be equally free to obtain political information to move without hindrance to political meetings, and to opt for political associations of their choice. As we demonstrate in Chapter 6, democratization presupposes political liberalization, that is, the provision of civil liberties. Since Schumpeter's time, definitions of democracy based on a "procedural minimum" have included the requirement of respect for civil liberties as a means of ensuring that elections are not merely formalistic exercises in the uncontested ratification of incumbents. Importantly, Collier and Levitsky consider that "efforts to standardize terminology" in the comparative politics literature have led to "a substantial consensus ... around a procedural minimum or expanded procedural minimum definition."[36]

Although we hew to this definitional consensus, we recognize that elections alone are not a sufficient condition of democracy. We do not wish to commit the "fallacy of electoralism" by ignoring that the consolidation of democracy in the long run involves the permanent establishment of many other valued institutions, such as civilian control over the military, independent legislatures and courts, viable opposition parties and voluntary associations, plus a free press.[37] But no other democratic institution precedes elections, either in timing or importance. In our view, elections are the principal and necessary condition of democracy, the first step without which democracy cannot otherwise be born. Furthermore, we apply the term "democratic" only to the immediate outcome of regime transitions, that is, to signify whether a new regime is *installed* by electoral means. To designate that a transition is "democratic" is only to record the inauguration of an elected government; no judgment is passed on whether the new regime can survive in the short, medium, or long term. We consider regime survival and consolidation, which concern the durability of democracy, to be analytically separate questions, albeit important ones, that we address at the end of this book.

ENDNOTES

1. In this study, accounts of regime transitions in African countries were assembled from primary journalistic sources, digests of political events, and secondary academic analyses. For the Bénin story, lively narratives can be found in Chris Allen, "'Goodbye to All That': The Short and Sad Story of Socialism in Bénin," *Journal of Communist Studies* 8, (June 1992): 63–81; Francis Laloupo, "La Conférence Nationale du Bénin: un Concept Nouveau du Changement de Régime Politique," in *Année Africaine, 1992–93,* ed. Dominique Darbon (Bordeau, France: Centre d'Etudes d'Afrique Noire, 1993), pp. 89–114; Théophile Vittin, "Crise, Renouveau Démocratique et Mutations du Paysage Médiatique au Bénin," *Afrique 2000* 9 (1992): 37–58; and Richard Westebbe, "Structural Adjustment, Rent Seeking, and Liberalization in Bénin," in *Economic Change and Political Liberalization in Sub-Saharan Africa,* ed. Jennifer A. Widner (Baltimore: Johns Hopkins University Press, 1994), pp. 80–100. An interesting debate over the relative strengths of state and social forces in the Bénin transition is found in John Heilbrunn, "Social Origins of National Conferences in Bénin and Togo," *Journal of Modern African Studies* 31 (1993): 277–99; and Katherine Nwajiaku, "The National Conferences in Bénin and Togo Revisited," *Journal of Modern African Studies* 32 (1994): 429–47.
2. *Africa Research Bulletin,* March 1990; see also *Agence France Presse,* 15 February 1990; *Radio France Internationale,* 27 February 1990.
3. *Africa Research Bulletin,* March 1991; see also *Le Soleil,* 11 March 1991, *Le Monde,* 13 March 1991.
4. Allen, "Goodbye to All That," p. 64.
5. Michael Bratton and Nicolas van de Walle with Kimberly Butler, Soo Chan Jang, Kimberly Ludwig, and Yu Wang, "Political Regimes and Regime Transitions in Africa: A Comparative Handbook." For machine-readable format see University of Michigan, International Consortium for Political and Social Research, 1996; for hard copy see Michigan State University, *MSU Working Papers on Political Reform in Africa,* no. 14 (East Lansing: Department of Political Science, Michigan State University, 1996).
6. *The Comparative Survey of Freedom* (New York: Freedom House, 1989–1995). Freedom House reports scores for a country's compliance with standard lists of civil liberties (13 items) and political rights (nine items) as estimated by a panel of expert reviewers. It summarizes the quality of different regimes on a seven-point scale, with one representing the "most free" and seven the "least free." The Freedom House data has been criticized and defended over the years. See Kenneth Bollen, "Liberal Democracy: Validity and Method Factors in Cross-National Measures," *American Journal of Political Science.* 34, no. 4 (November 1993): 1207-30 versus Muller and Seligson, "Civic Culture and Democracy: The Question of Causal Relationships," *American Political Science Review* 88, no. 3 (September 1994): 637. In practical terms, the survey provides the best coverage of any data set on liberties and democracy currently available. The data are derived in a reasonably systematic manner, presented in a quantitative form, and are complete, both cross-sectionally (for 186 countries in recent years) and over time (from 1973 to the present).

7. Political protest is defined as mass action directed at political goals. Its incidence was counted from the annual editions of a single document of record: *Africa South of the Sahara* (London: Europa Publications, 1989–1995).

8. Political liberty is operationalized as the average civil liberties score for all 47 sub-Saharan African countries as measured in *The Comparative Survey of Freedom* (1989–1995).

9. See the elections listed in Table 7, plus all other competitive, direct legislative elections, 1988–1994. The data include all 47 sub-Saharan African countries, including existing multiparty regimes. They also cover elections to constituent assemblies (in Ethiopia and Uganda in 1994), but exclude indirect elections (in Uganda in 1989 and Swaziland in 1993).

10. Democracy is operationalized as the average political rights score for all 47 sub-Saharan African countries as measured in *The Comparative Survey of Freedom* (1989–1995).

11. Contrary to this hypothesis, the data on political rights for 1995 showed no such decline, with the African average continuing to rise to a new high of 4.53 on the Freedom House scale. See *Freedom Review,* January–February 1996: 15–17.

12. Again, the quantitative data for this study are drawn from the data set described in the Appendix and published in Michael Bratton and Nicolas van de Walle et. al., "Political Regimes and Regime Transitions in Africa" (1996).

13. Only in Djibouti did one party capture all the seats, mainly because opposition parties, by boycotting the election, chose not to compete. Uganda's constituent assembly election and Swaziland's national assembly election were conducted on a no-party basis, making it impossible to ascribe shares of seats to parties.

14. In founding elections, the position of head of government is openly contested following a period in which such political competition had been denied. For Africa, the figure of 29 founding elections excludes three categories: elections in the five countries that were already putative democracies; legislative elections in the presidential regimes of Djibouti in December 1992 and Equatorial Guinea in November 1993; and elections for temporary constituent assemblies in Uganda in March 1994 and Ethiopia in June 1994. In the latter two categories the position of head of government was not contested (see Table 7).

15. John A. Wiseman, "Early Post-Redemocratization Elections in Africa," *Electoral Studies* 11 (1992): 279.

16. On leadership longevity in Africa, see Henry Bienen and Nicolas van de Walle, "Time and Power in Africa," *American Political Science Review* 93 (1989): 19–34.

17. A study of 101 cases of political succession in Africa from 1963 to 1987 reports that 57 percent of new leaders were designated by the military, 31 percent by civilian incumbents, and only 8 percent by election. See Rodger Govea and John Holm, "A Report from a New Data Set on African Succession," paper presented at the annual meeting of the African Studies Association, Seattle, November 1992. For earlier analyses, see Victor T. Levine, "The Politics of Presidential Succession," *Africa Report* 28 (1983): 22–6, and Arnold Hughes and Roy May, "The Politics of Succession in Black Africa," *Third World Quarterly* 10 (1988): 1–22.

18. See Larry W. Bowman, *Mauritius: Democracy and Development in the Indian Ocean* (London: Dartmouth, 1991), 208. The 1967 elections in Sierra Leone are some-

times cited as another example of leadership turnover. See Henry Bienen and Jeffrey Herbst, "Authoritarianism and Democracy in Africa," in *Comparative Political Dynamics: Global Research Perspectives,* ed. Dankwart A. Rustow and Kenneth P. Erickson (New York: Harper Collins, 1991), p. 212. In this case an opposition party led by Siaka Stevens did obtain a majority of seats in the house of representatives. But as the election results came in, the loyalist army chief Brigadier David Lansana staged a coup d'état that prevented Stevens from assuming office. Because no new government was installed, this political transition was never completed.

19. See Institute for Policy Reform (Washington, D.C.), "The Relationship Between Political and Economic Reform in Africa," paper prepared for the U.S. Agency for International Development, under Cooperative Agreement No. 0095–A–00–1126–00 (1995), p. 24.

20. See Curt D. Grimm, "Increasing Participation in the Context of African Political Liberalization: the Bénin Budget Crisis of 1994 and Its Implications for Donors," paper presented to the Special Program of Assistance for Africa Working Group on Economic Reform in the Context of Political Liberalization (Washington, D.C., January 18–19, 1995).

21. With 78 percent of registered voters going to the polls in the second round of voting, Kérékou defeated his rival 53 to 47 percent. "Joie et protestation au Bénin apres l'annonce de l'élection de l'ancien dictateur Mathieu Kérékou," *Le Monde,* March 26, 1996; and "Au Bénin, rigeur démocratique et couleur Africaine pour l'investiture de l'ancien dictateur," *Le Monde,* April 6, 1996.

22. Robert Fishman draws useful analytic distinctions between regimes, governments, and states. Regimes are "the formal and informal organization of the center of political power, and of its relations with the broader society. A regime determines who has access to political power, and how those in power deal with those who are not.... Regimes are more permanent forms of political organization than specific governments, but they are typically less permanent than the state. The state, by contrast, is a (normally) more permanent structure of domination and coordination including a coercive apparatus and the means to administer a society and extract resources from it." Fishman, "Rethinking State and Regime: Southern Europe's Transition to Democracy," *World Politics* 42 (April 1990): 428.

23. Michael G. Schatzberg, "Power, Legitimacy and 'Democratisation' in Africa," *Africa* 63 (1993): 457.

24. Robert Dahl, *Democracy and Its Critics* (New Haven: Yale University Press, 1989), p. 5. For a lucid discussion of the origins and range of competing definitions of democracy, see David Held, *Models of Democracy* (Stanford: Stanford University Press, 1987). This discussion is curtly summarized by Georg Sorenson, *Democracy and Democratization: Processes and Prospects in a Changing World* (Boulder, Colo.: Westview, 1993), p. 10.

25. In his classic definition, Joseph A. Schumpeter holds that democracy is an "institutional arrangement for arriving at political decisions in which individuals acquire the power to decide by a competitive struggle for the people's vote." See Schumpeter, *Capitalism, Socialism, and Democracy* (1942; reprint, London: Allen and Unwin, 1976), p. 260. For 50-year retrospective reflections on Schumpeter's arguments about democracy's relationships to capitalism and socialism, see the special issue of *The Journal of Democracy* 3 (1992).

26. See C. B. Macpherson, *Democratic Theory: Essays in Retrieval* (Oxford: Clarendon Press, 1973) and *The Life and Times of Liberal Democracy* (Oxford: Oxford University Press, 1977). Held summarizes Macpherson's scheme as follows: "A substantial basis would be created for participatory democracy if parties were democratized according to the principles and procedures of direct democracy, and if these 'genuinely participatory parties' operated within a parliamentary or congressional structure complemented and checked by fully self-managed organizations in the workplace and local community. Only such a political system, in Macpherson's view, would actually realize the profoundly important liberal democratic value of 'the right to equal self-development.'" Held, *Models of Democracy*, p. 258.

27. The term *demokratia,* as first used in Greek city–states in the fifth century B.C.,was derived from the words *demos* (the people) and *kratia* (authority). Dahl, *Democracy and Its Critics,* p. 3; and Held, *Models of Democracy,* p. 2.

28. Dahl, *Democracy and Its Critics,* p. 3.

29. Dankwart A. Rustow, "Transitions to Democracy: Toward a Dynamic Model," *Comparative Politics* 2 (April 1970): 351, quoting W. Ivor Jennings, *The Approach to Self-Government* (Cambridge: Cambridge University Press, 1956), p. 56.

30. See Charles-Louis de Secondat (Baron de Montesquieu), *De l'esprit des lois* (Paris: Editions Garnier Frères [1748], 1961).

31. See Carl H. Rosberg and Robert G. Jackson, "Why Africa's Weak States Persist," *World Politics* 33 (1982): 1–24.

32. Dunn, "The Politics of Representation and Good Government in Post-Colonial Africa," in *Political Domination in Africa,* ed. Patrick Chabal (Cambridge: Cambridge University Press, 1986), p. 163. Dunn considers that effective representation is possible only when social interests are coherently organized; yet, Africa displays "comparatively weak institutionalization of its civil society at the level of the territorial state" (p. 160).

33. Claude Ake, "The Unique Case of African Democracy," *International Affairs* 69 (1993): 143.

34. See Alex Inkeles and Larry Sirowy, "The Effects of Democracy on Economic Growth and Inequality: A Review," in *On Measuring Democracy: Its Consequences and Concomitants,* ed. Alex Inkeles (New Brunswick, N.J.: Transaction Publishers, 1991), pp. 149–50. See also Adam Przeworski and Fernando Limongi, "Political Regimes and Economic Growth," *Journal of Economic Perspectives* 7 (Summer 1993): 51–69. For a review of these issues in Latin America, see Karen Remmer, "The Political Economy of Elections in Latin America, 1980–1991," *American Political Science Review* 87 (June 1993): 393–406. For Africa, see John Healey and Mark Robinson, *Democracy, Governance, and Economic Policy: Sub-Saharan Africa in Comparative Perspective* (London: Overseas Development Institute, 1992).

35. Robert A. Dahl, *Polyarchy: Participation and Opposition* (New Haven: Yale University Press, 1971), p. 3.

36. David Collier and Steven Levitsky, "Democracy with Adjectives: Strategies to Avoid Conceptual Stretching" (paper presented at the annual meeting of the Latin American Studies Association, Washington, D.C., October, 1995), pp. 2, 5.

37. See Philippe Schmitter and Terry Lynn Karl, "What Democracy Is ... and Is Not," *Journal of Democracy* 2, (1991): 75–88. The fallacy of electoralism has

sometimes bedeviled policymakers. For the pitfalls of judging a country's democratic credentials on the basis of adherence to the formalities of an election, with illustrations from U.S. foreign policy in Latin America, see Abraham F. Lowenthal, ed., *Exporting Democracy: The United States and Latin America* (Baltimore: Johns Hopkins University Press, 1991); and Thomas Carothers, *In the Name of Democracy: U.S. Policy Toward Latin America in the Reagan Years* (Berkeley: University of California Press, 1991).

1

APPROACHES TO
DEMOCRATIZATION

The theoretical literature on democratization offers a wide array of competing explanations about regime change. Analysts have long been fascinated about whether, how, and why democracies are installed and consolidated. The debates generated by these inquiries raise paradigmatic issues that lie at the heart of social and political theory.

The first set of issues concerns the relative impact on political change of structural factors versus individual actions and events. Are regime transitions a function of underlying preconditions at the level of the deep formations of economy and society? Or does political change depend on the preferences and choices of leaders and on their skills at mobilizing resources, counteracting opponents, and taking advantage of opportunities? There is more at stake in this debate than the old dilemma of whether history unfolds deterministically as a result of the tectonic shifts of social forces or capriciously through the deeds of great men. A complete theory of political agency would also attend to the endeavors of ordinary citizens, the interplay between elite and mass actions, and the unintended as well as the planned consequences of political events.

The second debate concerns the degree to which political change is determined by national rather than international forces. The choice is this: Are the trajectories of regime transition best apprehended by paying attention to the separate and distinctive domestic histories of each country? Or should we adopt a more holistic perspective that locates countries as parts of larger international systems, subject to powerful influences from beyond their own borders? These questions seem particularly germane for small, indebted countries on the margins of an increasingly global economy in a post–Cold War world.

The last controversy involves the relative explanatory importance of political versus socioeconomic factors. On the one hand, political processes can be regarded as epiphenomena whose characteristics derive principally from prevailing socioeconomic conditions. Alternatively, political scientists like to think that politics is *sui generis,* that is, an autonomous institutional realm in which the exercise of power gives shape to the social and economic worlds. Stated differently, this debate concerns whether politics is the dependent or independent variable. Differences of opinion on this issue do not deny the utility of the interdisciplinary study of political economy but highlight the question of whether politics or economics is in command.

This chapter reviews the various approaches to these issues taken in the literature on regime transitions. It compares and evaluates the arguments developed by influential writers who favor contrasting interpretations of democratization, whether structural or contingent, economic or political, international or domestic. And it summarizes efforts, all of which are to some degree plausible, to apply these frameworks to Africa.

We then lay out our own *politico-institutional approach.* This analytic framework is based partly on hard choices among the available perspectives and partly on theoretical synthesis. To anticipate our case, we argue for an approach based on *domestic political factors,* with attention given to both their *structural and contingent* dimensions. We do so by discussing of the notion of *structured contingency,* asking precisely how political agents and political institutions interact to affect one another. In short, we interpret the recent democratic experiments in Africa as the product of purposive political action in a context of inherited political regimes.

STRUCTURAL VERSUS CONTINGENT EXPLANATIONS

STRUCTURAL APPROACHES

Structural analysts consider that the prospects for political change are embedded in the architecture of social systems. From this perspective, democracy is the political expression of the social order of modern industrial society. The process of democratization is the analogue in the realm of political authority of the breakdown of feudal systems of economic production and aristocratic social status, representing a general trend toward the inclusion of previously excluded groups in large-scale institutions. The driving forces of these systemic changes are impersonal forces such as technological innovation and its application to production, the spread of market-based social relations, and the emergence of new social identities. Theorists who favor a structural perspective – regardless of whether they rely empirically on cross-national statistical data or comparative historical case studies – study aggregate phenomena. Their explanations of contemporary political trends always return to a foundation of macrolevel structures that solidified during the past; they consider that "social patterns, once forged, often persist beyond their original conditions."[1]

Ever since Marx, Weber, and Durkheim, social scientists have noted an affinity between capitalist industrialization and political democracy. Writers in both the liberal and materialist intellectual traditions have traced the sources of democracy to structural changes arising during Western Europe's transformation from an agrarian to industrial society. In our era, the touchstones of this thesis are the now-classic works of Seymour Martin Lipset and Barrington Moore.[2] Lipset highlights the formative role of economic development – manifest in rising levels of wealth and education and increased rates of industrialization and urbanization – in creating conditions conducive to stable elected government. Consistent with other modernization theorists, Daniel Lerner in particular, Lipset argues that industrialization draws rural dwellers into towns, where opportunities for literacy give rise to citizen demands for participation in government.[3] Moore draws attention to the metamorphosis of the social class structure – notably the economic and political demise of the landed aristocracy and the emergence of an independent commercial bourgeoisie – in bringing about representative democracy in Britain, France, and the United States. In his view, the protagonists of democratization were not so much the newly urbanized masses as the entrepreneurial middle classes who sought to advance personal freedoms and property rights.

To varying degrees, structuralist propositions have been internalized into the conventional wisdom of political science. Larry Diamond shows that the observed correspondence between economic wealth and political democracy has generally withstood the tests of time and rigorous empirical reanalysis.[4] Bollen and Jackman express the established consensus that "the level of economic development appears to be the dominant explanatory variable" in determining political democracy.[5] Even Rueschemeyer and colleagues, who question the inevitability of democracy under capitalism, note that "democracy by any definition is extremely rare in agrarian societies."[6] Expanding on this observation, Huntington considers that "the correlation between wealth and democracy implies that transitions to democracy should occur primarily in countries at the middle levels of economic development. In poor countries democratization is unlikely, in rich countries it has already occurred."[7] Applying this logic to Africa, with its low levels of GNP per capita and paltry growth rates, he contends that "economic obstacles to democratization in sub-Saharan Africa will remain overwhelming well into the twenty-first century."[8]

The proposition that middle classes foster democratic political reform has gained less wholehearted acceptance. Neo-Marxist writers generally discount the possibility that the bourgeoisie will fulfill its historic mission as an agent of democratic revolution under conditions of dependent development.[9] Liberal writers have been preoccupied as much with cultural and gender cleavages as with socioeconomic ones and have tended to accept as an article of faith Moore's glib epigram: "no bourgeois, no democracy."[10]

Yet middle classes have sometimes revealed themselves as halfhearted advocates, or even outright opponents, of democratization. Some structural analysts expect that "middle classes would favor their own inclusion (in political decision making) but would be ambivalent about the further extension of political rights."[11] In Latin America in the 1960s and 1970s, for example, business interests called upon military forces to take over governments in order to manage economic downturns and labor unrest.[12] Only later in the 1980s, as threats to property rights receded and military regimes laid waste to human rights, middle classes in Latin America reverted to the side of social movements supporting democratic restorations.[13] Africanists noted related trends. Martin Kilson attributes the decline of competitive politics in Africa in the 1960s and 1970s to self-interested class behavior: Because "democracy ¼ has a long run tendency to secularize popular consciousness, the African bourgeoisie scuttles democracy or competitive politics, closing off by force and stealth the avenues available to the masses to power."[14]

Viewing the big picture of political change through the wide-focus lens of socioeconomic structures has both advantages and drawbacks. It assumes correctly that, once constructed, institutional edifices have inertia – and social trends have momentum – that generally exceed human intent and control. It demonstrates that opportunities for political innovation are often constrained by the deadweight of inherited establishment. And because structural analysis starts with the concrete and enduring features of society – features that can be observed, described, and measured – it lends itself to empirical analysis. Indeed, testable hypotheses can be drawn directly from the mainstream literature: Like anywhere else in the world, one would expect that the prospects for democracy would be best in those parts of Africa with the highest rates of urbanization, education, and industrialization. Contrary to the assumption that the continent is universally poverty-stricken, there are considerable variations across African countries in terms of their material, infrastructural, and human endowments, variations that provide a basis for comparatively testing relationships between socioeconomic structures and experiences with democratization.

Nevertheless, any supposed socioeconomic "preconditions" of democracy are remote from the dynamic political processes of democratization itself. Important as the size of the industrial sector and the extent of class formation may be, these foundational features are *too* deeply embedded in the society and economy to explain much on their own. To be convincing, an account of the political role of the middle class as an agent for or against democratization, for example, must be stretched over several intermediate steps; it must show that members of this class share a common political interest, that they act cohesively to express it, and perhaps most important, that they possess political instruments – like business associations or political parties – through which to articulate and aggregate preferences. The role of relevant political institutions that intervene in the day-to-day political struggles of regime transitions needs to be determined. Because such institutions lie close to the surface of politics, they are likely to have a more direct impact upon political outcomes than deep structures have. For their part, deep structures are better held in reserve as background factors. Although they can do some of the heavy lifting required for basic analysis, they are usually insufficiently nuanced to explain divergent political paths in countries of similar socioeconomic status.

Structural analysis also imposes a static view of the political world. As a result, it is better suited to understanding political continuities that prevail over long periods than accounting for the occurrence of short, sharp interludes of rapid change. When applied to processes of democratization, structural analyses do best at explaining the protracted processes of regime legitimation and consolidation (see Chapter 7). It is no accident that comparative historical sociologists are concerned about *la longue durée* over which regime continuities take shape and that modernization theorists study the *stability* – read, longevity – of democratic regimes.[15] Structural analysis is less appropriate to predicting revolutionary breaks with an established past. Even Stephen Krasner's insightful model of "punctuated equilibrium," which posits long periods of institutional stasis interrupted by short-lived changes, does not use a consistent theoretical apparatus to account for *both* continuity and change. As Krasner notes, "Different kinds of causal variables are appropriate for explaining the creation, as opposed to the maintenance, of state institutions."[16] Thelen and Steinmo argue that a model based on structural continuities cannot explain change without undermining its own logical predicates.[17]

We suspect that a structural approach therefore is useful in explaining no more than the outer parameters of political transitions. For example, it may help to answer whether an old authoritarian regime will endure, or help to predict the kind of political equilibrium that will prevail after a transition is over. But a structural approach can never account for the cut and thrust of events during interludes between regimes, or play more than a partial role in foreseeing whether any given transition attempt will result in the installation of a democratic government.

Finally, because of a tendency to determinism, structural approaches lead analysts to overlook opportunities for innovation and to be overly pessimistic about the prospects for installing democracies. In Di Palma's words, "It is a dismal science of politics ¼ that passively entrusts political change to exogenous and distant social transformations ¼ applied to the future of democracy, such a science translates instinctively the structurally improbable into the politically impossible."[18] Indeed, leading democratic theorists have been uniformly cautious. Robert Dahl considers that "it is unrealistic to suppose ¼ that there will be any dramatic change in the number of polyarchies within a generation or two"; Samuel Huntington echoes that "with a few exceptions, the limits of democratic development in the world may well have been reached."[19] From the perspective of the mid-1990s, and without any reference to eventual durability, recent efforts to install democratic regimes in Africa would seem to belie these prognoses. We therefore agree with Myron Wiener's assessment that "perhaps it is time to recognize that [empirical] democratic theory, with its list of conditions and prerequisites, is a poor guide to action."[20]

CONTINGENT APPROACHES

Rather than adopting a macroscopic perspective on the abiding features of societies, other analysts have focused on the decisions and behaviors of individual political agents. Rooted in the classic liberal tracts of Smith and Popper, this approach grants conceptual primacy to the freedom of individuals to make choices, whether among goods in a marketplace or through open political expression, association, and voting.[21] In our times, this approach has reached its fullest expression in the discipline of microeconomics and in rational-choice approaches to the study of political behavior and public decision-making.[22] According to these modes of analysis, variations in political outcomes are best addressed by starting with the motivations, preferences, and calculations of self-interested actors.

A focus on individual agents produces a contingent model of change in which the outcomes of political conflicts are not predetermined by the weight of structural precedent. According to Guiseppe Di Palma, "Hard facts do not mean necessity ... unless relevant circumstances cumulate in the extreme, the end result is not inescapable."[23] Guillermo O'Donnell and Philippe Schmitter echo these sentiments when they write that regime transitions are abnormal periods of "undetermined" political change in which "there are insufficient structural or behavioral parameters to guide and predict the outcome."[24] Instead, regime transitions are shaped by the willful strategic choices of principal political agents. Take, for instance, Spain's unexpectedly successful passage from military dictatorship to parliamentary democracy, which featured influential interventions by the constitutional monarch and reformers from within the Franco regime. In addressing this case, structural analysts suffered from blind spots: They were "inadequately prepared for the intervening role of political actors; ... to perceive the extent to which innovative political action can contribute to democratic evolution; ... [and] to give account of the notion that democracies can be made (and unmade) in the act of making them."[25] One clear implication is that democracy "may operate with success even in countries and regimes whose predicament would not otherwise be favorable."[26]

A contingent model of change assumes that one agent's initiative prompts another actor's response and that political events cascade iteratively from one to another.[27] Compared with the orderliness of authoritarian rule, the interludes between regimes are marked by frenzied partisan disputes and by uncertainty about the nature of resultant regimes. Contingency theorists find little evidence that processes of transition are shaped by preexisting macroeconomic conditions and class interests, or even by inherited political institutions. Instead, individual behavior hinges on subjective perceptions of the actions of others and calculations of the potential risks and benefits of aligning with political incumbents or opposition movements. In the heat of political combat, formerly cohesive social classes and political organizations tend to splinter, making it impossible to deduce the alignments or actions of any protagonist. Rather, political outcomes are driven by the immediate reactions of strategic actors to unfolding events.

From a contingent perspective, political outcomes emanate from interaction and bargaining. Implicit is a notion of democracy, not so much as a model set of political ideals but as a second-best compromise. Here, the key to democratic transition is the ability of participants to arrive at arbitrated agreements that grant everyone at least part of what each wants. Juan Linz and Alfred Stepan have described this process as political "crafting."[28] The crafting of democratic solutions to problems of political conflict pays particular attention to three main facets of change: the nature of the "crafters," that is, the political alliances that coalesce for and against change; the process of "crafting," namely, the dynamics of contestation and decision making among these groups (for example, the forging of reformist pacts); and the finished "craftwork," that is, the rules and institutions that all parties come to agree on. The emphasis throughout is on the strategies and tactics of the principal players and the processes of struggle and accommodation through which they interact. Curiously, regime transitions have received little attention from rational-choice theorists, despite the apparent suitability of the interactive struggles between incumbent leaders and opposition movements to modeling within a game theoretic framework.[29]

In the literature on African politics, the independent influence of individual political preferences has been acknowledged most often in studies of political leadership. The agenda for African nationalism was set by larger-than-life political leaders whose influence was studied within the Weberian framework of charismatic authority.[30] For the postcolonial period, Robert Jackson and Carl Rosberg identified the distinctive practices of personal rule, through which "princes," "autocrats," "prophets," and "tyrants" rode roughshod over constitutional constraints or institutional offices.[31] With the notable exception of Robert Bates, few efforts have been made in studies of African politics to account for political behavior explicitly in terms of rational-choice precepts.[32] Nonetheless, that much political behavior in Africa can be understood as resulting from the purposeful quest for personal enrichment is a thesis that runs through the Africanist literature.

Efforts to understand regime transitions in Africa have raised the analytic profile of what Goran Hyden has called "the actor dimension."[33] Hyden draws attention to "the creative potential of politics," especially "the ability of leaders to rise above the ordinary, to 'change the rules of the game,' and to inspire others to partake in efforts to move society forward in new and productive directions."[34] He defines governance as the conscious management of regime structures and identifies the need for reciprocal interactions among political actors that lead to covenants about the distribution of political power. Naomi Chazan observes that there is no grand design to the political reform process; instead, "individuals, groups, and government leaders constantly [alter] their course of action in the light of specific events and conditions in other sectors."[35] In our own earlier work – and in Chapter 3 of this book – we draw attention to the contingent trajectory of political interactions during regime transitions, conceiving of popular protest and political reform as "a series of dynamic exchanges in which strategic actors take their cues from the behavior of adversaries."[36]

A contingent approach to explaining regime transitions has several evident strengths. Most obviously, it provides analytic tools to penetrate and dissect the internal dynamics of the transition period itself. It reveals that contenders for political power react situationally to initiatives taken by opponents and that political change is often an unintended consequence of unplanned chains of events. From this perspective, the prospects for change hinge less on the constraining conditions inherited from the past than on the skills of individuals at seizing opportunities. Because contingent approaches make room for political agency, they free the analyst from the deterministic lockstep inherent in inquiries that begin with preexisting structures. In so doing, contingency analyses allow the possibility that transitions will lead to innovative outcomes that break with habit and routine.

On the other side of the coin, the weaknesses of contingent analysis derive from its excessive voluntarism.[37] For purposes of argument, we wish to state this problem in extreme form: If political actors are held to enjoy unconstrained choice, then any one political outcome is just as likely as any other. Under these circumstances, a construct of contingency would be unable to perform the theory's basic parsimonious function – namely, to simplify and summarize reality. For example, it could not distinguish the sort of patterned sequence of transition phases that we propose in the Introduction and Chapter 3. Moreover, to the extent that outcomes of political struggles were truly uncertain, a contingency theory would lack explanatory and predictive power. It could not demonstrate *why* one actor or a set of actors ever prevailed over another in any given political struggle. Because any temporary equilibrium within an ongoing process of change would be potentially reversible by opposing action, outcomes would be difficult, if not impossible, to foresee. One could not predict with any confidence, for example, whether a given regime transition was headed toward or had finally arrived at democracy.

This portrayal of contingency analysis is obviously overdrawn. But it points to the main shortcomings of the approach. However uncertain the processes of regime transition may be – and they are highly uncertain – they are never purely random. Instead, political transitions display regularities. These regularities are expressed in many ways: in common processes by which transitions begin, unfold, and end; in similar sequences of innovation and reaction during transitions; in patterns of victory and loss by different categories of actor; and in common prospects for the installation of particular types of regime, including democracies. These regularities do not derive from the free play of unconstrained action; indeed, they are counteracted by them. Instead, the patterning of transition trajectories is traceable to the context in which political actors operate. Ironically, therefore, a contingency theory can gain analytic purchase only when placed on some kind of structural scaffolding that imparts a motif to political action.

Take one example: The institutional position of participants in political transitions – usually incumbent government officials and opposition social movements – shapes their differential access to power resources, including ideology, organization, and finances.[38] Whereas incumbents can readily use their occupancy of political office to draw on the material and coercive resources of the state, opposition movements often hold the ideological advantage, being able to mobilize civic action through a human rights or prodemocracy message. Both sides deploy the resources at their disposal in the political struggles that occur in the interval during the breakdown of authoritarian regimes. It stands to reason that the institutional location of protagonists and their differential access to resources tilt the power balance in favor of some actors and against others.

Contingent approaches also suffer from a myopia of the moment. By "heavily discounting the past," they create a problem of "presentism."[39] Immersion in the dynamics of political transitions leads analysts to grant undue importance to current events and lose track of longer-term trends in political development. The gains of immediacy and liveliness achieved by contingent analysis are offset by a foreshortening of historical perspective. A contingency approach also reinforces the tendency, inherent in voluntarism, to underestimate the obstacles that political actors confront in obtaining their desired goals. A dose of optimism is a welcome antidote to cheerless historicism. But the optimism of the will inherent in contingent analysis can be exaggerated; its proponents may mistakenly assume that democratization is easier and more likely than it actually is.

INTERNATIONAL VERSUS DOMESTIC EXPLANATIONS

We turn now to another key debate in the study of democratization. Does the impetus for regime transition originate at home or abroad?

INTERNATIONAL APPROACHES

States and regimes are not isolated entities. They exist in an international system that both undergirds them and exposes them to change. Most social scientists take the nation–state as the prime unit of comparative analysis. But they frequently discover that explanations of domestic political dynamics require reference to influences emanating from an outside environment. In the extreme, some analysts even grant causal primacy to the international system, treating it as an all-embracing whole in which states – and the regimes devised by their rulers – are merely parts. One unfortunate consequence is that all too often internal political developments are reduced to mere functions of international relations.

The most drastic account of domination from abroad is found in theories of international dependency or, in Africanist vocabulary, neocolonialism. According to this approach, the evolving interests of capital at the core of the global economy either entirely block, or at best permanently subordinate, the development prospects of poor countries.[40] Because dependency analysts were mainly interested in capital accumulation and class formation at the periphery, they paid relatively little attention to political arrangements. Some such writers recognized that Africa's emergent bourgeoisie was a political class that owed its control of economic means to the occupancy of state office.[41] Others drew attention to the fact that dependent states displayed weak organizational capacities.[42] While most neo-Marxist scholars considered that national development was not a top priority of the political class, others like Richard Sklar identified "developmental dictatorship" as the political regime most commonly associated with the neo-colonial state in Africa.[43] In a context in which the principal focus was on economic accumulation for consumption by state elites, analysts neglected the legitimation of states or the democratization of their political regimes.[44]

Yet international factors clearly impinge on the formation and consolidation of states. Jackson and Rosberg record the paradoxical persistence of Africa's weak states, whose international boundaries have remained intact despite the evident incapacity of some central governments to enforce public authority throughout their territories.[45] Arguing for a juridical rather than empirical conception of statehood, these authors trace the endurance of African states to an international consensus on the norm of state sovereignty. International law grants equal protection to all states – regardless of size or strength – against outside interference in internal political affairs. In this regard, African states benefited from achieving independence during a period when internationalism reached a high-water mark; these states derived sovereign rights from global organizations like the United Nations, the Commonwealth, and Francophonie.[46] At the same time, the Cold War often enabled African political leaders to attract resources, and obtain protection for their chosen regimes by playing one superpower off against another. In comparison to the states of early modern Europe, forged internally out of feudalism and absolutism, African states and regimes were in large part the creation of a postimperial international order. Charles Tilly has noted that "the later the state-making experience ... the less likely ... internal processes ... are to provide an adequate explanation of the formation, survival or growth of a state."[47]

The issue of whether international systems provide support or impose restraints on the development of new states is complicated by the fact that these global systems are themselves changing. Analysts are only just beginning to understand the nature and implications of the momentous events and trends that accompanied the end of the Cold War. These include the collapse of Soviet bloc communism, the universalization of free markets, the mobility of financial capital, the global information revolution, the rise of social movements, and the emergence in international affairs of a hegemonic Western bloc headed by the United States. These novelties combined to challenge the political status quo throughout the world, dramatically increasing the likelihood that authoritarian regimes would have to undertake at least a measure of political liberalization. The current ascendancy of the ideology of liberal democracy has led some commentators to lapse into jingoistic triumphalism.[48] Other, more cautious voices warn against assuming that liberal values are gaining universal acceptance, pointing to the persistence of indigenous political values and the limited capability of Western powers to promote democracy abroad.[49] Nevertheless, to the extent that political protesters and embattled leaders in the early 1990s came to cast their appeals in the language of liberal democracy, they reflected the influence of powerful ideas emanating from Western arenas.

Although most analysts therefore acknowledge some role for international forces in democratization in the late twentieth century, a small literature elevates these factors to pride of place. Geoffrey Pridham argues for postwar Western Europe, Southern Europe in the 1970s, Latin America in the 1980s – and especially for Eastern Europe at the end of the Cold War – that "a favourable or supportive geostrategic environment has been essential, even perhaps crucial" for successful transitions to constitutional democracy.[50] Also with reference to Eastern Europe in the spring of 1989, Kumar finds that "the causes of the revolutions and the conditions of their success were largely external (changes in Soviet policy); the ideas were mainly derived from external sources (Western liberal ideas going back to the Enlightenment and the French Revolution)."[51] According to this interpretation, Mikhail Gorbachev's decision to withhold Soviet military protection from discredited communist governments in Eastern Europe was a signal to opposition forces there that prodemocracy sentiments could prevail.[52]

This literature refines the umbrella concept of "the international context" by unpacking such components as background conditions, decisive events, influential actors, and forms of influence. Two principal forms of international influence on democratization have been identified: first, the policy conditions for democratic reform imposed by international donor and financial agencies, which are backed by the threat of material sanctions on weak states. This factor is particularly compelling to observers of Africa who note the continent's debt crisis and doubt the commitment and capacity of its governments to political reform. Barry Munslow's view that "the move for democratisation is being driven primarily from outside the African continent" coincides with Tom Young's that "the recent wave of democratisation is largely externally engineered."[53] According to *Africa Confidential,* "the principal cause of Africa's wind of change is the World Bank and the donor countries ... [who] are explicitly demanding political change as a condition for further loans to Africa."[54] With reference to francophone Africa, Kathryn Nwajiaku contends that "the French Ministry of Cooperation has been able to virtually supervise the democratization process in certain countries helped by the pressures that can be brought to bear on [sic] the World Bank and International Monetary Fund."[55] Such Western pressures were reinforced by retreat from the East. Jeffrey Herbst notes that the withdrawal of Soviet, Eastern European, and Cuban technical advisors in the late 1980s undermined left-leaning African regimes from Ghana to Zimbabwe.[56]

A second form of international influence consists of the demonstration effects of opposition political movements, which diffuse spontaneously through civil society as citizens jump on the democracy bandwagon. An international perspective raises the prospect of a "domino theory" of regime transitions whereby political events in one country evoke effects across international borders. Variously described as "contagion," "diffusion," or "snowballing," these effects suggest why political phenomena commonly occur in "waves." Usually, contagion theories have been used to understand the international spread of violence and military coups.[57] The toppling of hard-line regimes in East Germany and Bulgaria, for example, led both incumbent and opposition groups in Czechoslovakia to recognize and act upon the vulnerability of their own regimes. This type of international diffusion can occur within regions undergoing regime transitions as well as from dominant cores to dependent peripheries. Important in these processes are breakthroughs in communications technology that have increased contact among ordinary people, facilitating the spread of political ideas. To take just one example, Chinese students in Tiananmen Square used fax machines and satellite television coverage as tools of ideological dissemination and political organizing. The exposure of citizens to multiple information sources and the free exchange of ideas poses a direct challenge to the structures of political control imposed by autocrats. In this light, some commentators see a direct connection between the mass demonstrations that hauled down Lenin's statues in Leipzig and Prague and the rise of African protest movements. Georg Sorenson contends that "it is clear that the rapid changes in Eastern Europe were an important catalyst in Africa."[58] And Samuel Decalo notes, "One cannot exaggerate the psychological effect of pictures of the trial and execution of [Romanian president Nikolai] Ceausescu.... Africans could clearly see that their own country's 'departures from democratic standards' ... closely parallel defects exposed in Eastern Europe."[59]

The case for an externally inspired process of political change might seem particularly persuasive for Africa. After all, the rash of political openings in African countries from 1990 onward occurred almost simultaneously, implying a shared response to a common external stimulus, such as the collapse of communism or the end of superpower rivalry. Yet we would argue that mere synchronicity does not demonstrate an external origin to these transitions; political outcomes would also have to be consistent. That regime transitions were widely divergent across African countries, with outcomes ranging from the installation of democracy to the deepening of military dictatorships, suggests that major explanatory variables intervene between the international context and the transition processes. Even if one accepts that external factors help to mold democratization processes and outcomes, they do not fully explain them. As Fishman notes, "To emphasize the distinctiveness of specific cases in no sense implies that the comparative enterprise has been abandoned. It simply avoids the false assertion that there is one comprehensive causal constellation accounting for significantly different outcomes and processes."[60]

DOMESTIC APPROACHES

International factors have clear limitations in explaining the recent global wave of democratic transitions, even if African cases constitute a trailing edge. Unlike democratization after World War II, new regimes have generally been installed in the contemporary era without resort to military conquest and foreign occupation. Furthermore, although the Cold War was a landmark event for democratization in Eastern Europe and Africa, it cannot account for earlier cases in Southern Europe and Latin America, which occurred in the 1970s long before the ascendance of liberalism was anywhere in sight. And, despite the growing influence of international financial institutions over economic policy in aid-receiving countries, outsiders remain constrained by international law and administrative capacity from supplanting the *de facto* governments of sovereign states.[61]

We therefore propose that the prospects for regime transition derive in the first instance from the actors, organizations, and institutions that inhabit the national arena. In this light, the key analytic questions are: Is there a domestic constituency for political reform? If so, can it prevail over domestic political forces of resistance and reaction?

An account of political transitions that emphasizes the internal aspects of national politics can be justified as follows. Political regimes are sets of rules that prescribe a given distribution of power between the holders of public office and the collectivity of citizens. A change of regime involves a fundamental realignment of these rules, transforming the composition of the players included in processes of public decision making. A political transition therefore has direct, tangible consequences for domestic political actors and organizations because it reconfigures the allocation of political power and, by implication, all the perquisites that flow from it. Thus, one would expect that such processes would be extremely hard fought among domestic stakeholders who, after all, have a great deal to gain or lose from transition outcomes. Although the incumbents of state office and their domestic political opponents may call on international support or be buffeted by external influences, they remain the prime movers of, and principal protagonists in, struggles over state power.

The case for a domestically driven account of political development has been eloquently made by Tony Smith. He argues that international systemic perspectives "deprive local histories of their integrity and specificity, thereby making local actors little more than the pawns of outside forces."[62] In his view, the development prospects of countries in the South derive from the organization of the states, the social interests of the elites that control them, and their substantially autonomous political and policy choices. Even in colonial situations, "natives invariably wielded significant power," forming local and informal "constellations of interest in accommodating or opposing foreign rule that made for many of the significant differences in the pattern of postwar decolonization."[63] Decolonization in turn led to the existence of an indigenously controlled state that rested on the aggregation of at least some local interests and that "insulate[d] the local society from the international system."[64] Citing the corporatist aspirations of state elites and their reliance on patron–client political ties, he discerns "domestic factors ... as the predominant force behind the creation of authoritarian states."[65] To address these issues, Smith calls for historically grounded analysis of "the relative autonomy of the various Third World countries which comes from the real strength of local traditions and institutions."[66]

Even under conditions of extreme financial dependence, dominant national actors retain political autonomy and decision-making discretion. Jean-François Bayart notes that "African governments exploit, occasionally skilfully, the resources of a dependence which is, it cannot ever be sufficiently stressed, astutely fabricated as much as predetermined."[67] In other words, African leaders capitalize on external connections, deriving sustenance from positions as intermediaries to the international system. As Christopher Clapham says of incumbent rulers, "All of them are basically concerned to use external resources – from armaments on the one hand, to famine relief on the other – as a means of consolidating their own hold on power."[68] Tony Smith elaborates these points into a general insight: International factors obtain their greatest influence, "not from an active threat of intervention so much as from a threat of withdrawal, which could abandon ... dependent regimes to civil and regional conflict."[69] Dependency theory is thus stood on its head. Far from undermining the prospects for the political development of poor states, connections to the international system are a vital source of wherewithal for the construction of states and regimes.

Indeed, Africans continue to resist international pressures. Donors have encountered considerable difficulty in ensuring that African governments adhere to economic reform agreements, with many structural adjustment programs remaining unimplemented, to the point that bilateral assistance agencies are withdrawing and multilateral conditionality is becoming much less exacting. There is no reason to expect recipient governments to comply any more fully with externally imposed political reform commitments. Africans are likely to perform in concert with the preferences of foreign powers only when such actions coincide with their own identities and interests.

This internal logic of African politics extends to contemporary regime transitions. As Bayart argues, "External dynamics played an essentially secondary role in the collapse of authoritarian regimes.... demands for democracy in Africa are not exceptional and, just as with the logic of authoritarianism, they are grounded in their own historicity."[70] We can expect that political leaders will adapt to changing international circumstances by seeking new methods for obtaining or retaining power. In an international context where liberal ideas are hegemonic, all political leaders – regardless of their true beliefs and objectives – will attempt to cloak themselves in the legitimating mantle of democracy and make themselves available as candidates for elected office. But political rhetoric of born-again political reformers should not obscure the fact that their actions are driven consistently by an indigenous political logic. This logic, which centers on political struggle for state office and its attendant privileges, provides a more solid foundation for the analysis of regime transition in Africa than the shifting winds of change that blow in intermittently from abroad.

We suspect that global power shifts provide the occasion – but not the basic cause – for new or dormant domestic forces to bubble to the surface after prolonged periods of repression. In the 1990s, the remission of superpower rivalry led to a reduction, reallocation, and in some cases elimination of sources of external economic and political support for authoritarian regimes. But the impact of new international conditions was always mediated through domestic state–society relations. Shifts in the resource base of an extant regime altered the balance of power between state and civil society, creating new constraints for political incumbents and fresh opportunities for opposition social movements. As Keohane and his colleagues suggest, "When the structure of politics – that is, the resources available to actors and therefore their capacity to exercise influence – is transformed, state strategies and the characteristics of institutions can be expected to change as well."[71] The trajectory of subsequent political change then depends on whether domestic political actors adapt to an altered resource base and changed circumstances. As Spalding contends, we should probe whether protest movements can succeed, especially in the light of new opportunities in "the openness of the political opportunity structure and the organizational resources available."[72]

Indeed, arguments based on domestic factors have seemingly won the day in the transitions literature. Philippe Schmitter reports as one of his "firmest conclusions" that "transitions from authoritarian rule and the immediate prospects for political democracy were largely to be explained in terms of national forces and calculations."[73] Laurence Whitehead concurs: "Internal forces were of primary importance in determining the course and outcome of the transition attempt, and international factors played a secondary role."[74] Working independently, Samuel Huntington distinguishes between the preconditions and processes of transition: "While external influences often were significant causes of third wave democratizations, the processes themselves were overwhelmingly indigenous."[75] In our view, these observations place international factors where they belong – namely, to the fore of deep socioeconomic structures but behind domestic political forces.

In sum, international factors – like changes in the international balance of power, the international diffusion effects of protest movements, or pressures from international donors – cannot on their own account for regime change, let alone for the installation and consolidation of democracy. Instead, the trajectory of political transitions is most directly affected by domestic factors such as the relative strength and cohesion of incumbent and opposition forces. In particular, democratization requires a homegrown constituency for political reform.

ECONOMIC VERSUS POLITICAL EXPLANATIONS

ECONOMIC APPROACHES

Economic explanations of political change are as old as social science itself. All involve the general proposition that changes in material conditions lead directly to changes in political life, defined as authoritative allocation processes and their symbols. A full exploration of the relationship between the economic and the political realms is unnecessary for our purposes.[76] Nor will we discuss approaches based on deep economic structures of the kinds reviewed in an earlier section. Instead, we review the work of writers who trace regime change to more immediate economic trends, crises, and policy reforms.

Early modernization theorists typically assumed, in Robert Packenham's formulation, that "all good things go together," in which case economic growth would naturally engender a progressive and unproblematic transition to democratic politics.[77] Such views could not withstand the sharp increase in political instability that broke out in the developing world during the 1960s, in particular the slew of military coups in Africa and Latin America.[78] Other theorists thus posited that, on the contrary, rapid economic change was inherently destabilizing. Samuel Huntington argued that economic growth would cause a sharp increase in social aspirations and economic inequality, and that the weak political institutions in emerging states would not be able to control or channel the resulting explosion in political participation.[79] Far from creating a harmonious context in which democracy might blossom, governments would find it hard to maintain political order. Analysts have since retained the insight that developing countries owed their instability at least in part to rapid changes in economic conditions. Thus, Gurr theorized that social violence resulted from a "revolution of rising expectations" brought on by modernization.[80] Popkin linked the rise of revolutionary peasant movements in Asia to the breakdown of traditional authority systems due to economic change, and Bates traced the rise of ethnic conflict in Africa directly to modernization.[81]

Nonetheless, by focusing on the need for viable political institutions to absorb the participatory upsurge, Huntington emphasized the primacy of politics, thus switching analytic attention to the political management of economic change. The policies of governments and their ability to promote economic growth have since been viewed as key to the maintenance of political stability. Many observers of Third World politics thus posit a causal link between short-term swings in economic performance, the popularity of governments, and their ability to remain in power. More specifically, it is suggested that citizens are likely to blame the government for negative economic conditions and attempt to punish incumbents, either by voting them out of office, or when that is not possible, by engaging in various types of protest. High levels of inflation and recessions have typically been viewed as the economic conditions least likely to be tolerated by the citizenry. Thus, a number of studies link bouts of high inflation with regime breakdown in Latin America in the 1970s.[82]

But what exactly is the connection between poor economic performance and regime change? In Latin America during the 1960s and 1970s, recession or inflation may have spurred popular mobilization, but it was the military that typically engineered changes of regime in order to put into place less, not more, participatory practices. Indeed, the "second wave" of democratization that followed World War II was terminated and reversed in a rash of military coups. A number of statistical analyses have demonstrated an increased chance of military coups in a context of either inflation or slow growth.[83] Such coups are interpreted as resulting from the unhappiness of army officers with rising economic stress and their fears of a populist explosion that would disrupt public order and the social status quo.[84]

These arguments concern transitions from democratic rule, rather than from authoritarian rule. Haggard and Webb contend, however, that many of the early "third wave" democratizations were also precipitated by economic crisis.[85] The failure of Latin American military regimes to bring about economic growth, they argue, sapped governments of their primary claim to legitimacy and paved the way for a return to popular government. In Africa as well, the disastrous economic decline of many states throughout the 1980s led to widespread predictions that the region would soon witness a rise in political instability. When the current wave of democratic transitions began, country case studies typically focused on the region's downward economic spiral. In a typical analysis, Richard Westebbe links the emergence of popular protest in Bénin to that country's deep economic crisis.[86] More generally, Claude Ake notes that "the demand for democracy in Africa draws much of its impetus from the prevailing economic conditions within."[87] He goes on to suggest that political behavior in Africa is driven by an instrumental view of democracy: "Ordinary Africans do not separate political democracy from economic democracy or for that matter from economic well-being. They see their political empowerment, through democratization, as an essential part of the process of getting the economic agenda right at last and ensuring that the development project is managed better and its rewards more evenly distributed."[88]

We can distinguish another important set of economic analyses that explain regime change with reference not so much to prevailing economic conditions but to the policies of governments. For instance, a large literature assesses the political impact of attempts to impose austerity-inducing economic reform policies.[89] It assumes that threats to political stability will arise from popular rejection of short-term economic hardship. For others, however, the danger comes from elites. In an influential analysis, Guillermo O'Donnell links the rise of "bureaucratic-authoritarian" regimes in Latin America to the need of governments, at a specific stage of industrialization, to pursue economic policies that would increase economic inequalities, thus requiring the repression of popular participation.[90] Similarly, John Sheahan argues that the turn to authoritarian governments in Latin America in the 1970s was directly related to the need to impose austerity policies.[91]

Such analyses are prevalent for Africa, too: Many scholars argue that structural adjustment reforms destabilized the region's authoritarian regimes in the late 1980s.[92] Their reasons vary, however. For some, economic liberalization helped to pave the way by weakening rent-seeking autocrats who relied on state control over the economy to avoid popular accountability.[93] For others, it was the intense austerity demanded of populations by the adjustment programs sponsored by the international financial institutions that made regime delegitimation and unrest inevitable. As Lubeck and Watts write of Nigeria, "Predictably the SAP has shattered the living standards among the wage and salaried groups ... and reduc[ed] educational, social and health expenditures so far that universities have collapsed, cholera is widespread (the highest reported globally) and malnutrition, destitution, and unemployment are common. In turn, each tightening of the screw has stimulated widespread rioting led by students, unemployed workers, market women and a burgeoning urban lumpenproletariat.[94] The insight is a valuable one, even if the authors conflate the effects of the economic crisis and the reform measures designed to overcome it, a recurring analytical weakness of this literature.

Interestingly, many of these authors view democracy and economic reform as incompatible. Either they argue that austerity is incompatible with participatory democracy, or that the policy regime that results from the donors' reform agenda is likely to generate a degree of social inequality that will require nondemocratic forms of repression to sustain itself.[95]

Economic explanations for political change hold much attraction for Africa, because of the obviously powerful impact the economic crisis was having on most African polities when the transitions began. As we will show in Chapter 3, transitions were spurred at their outset by protest against austerity and adjustment programs. Moreover, these explanations can easily be tested empirically, since there are plenty of quantitative indicators of economic conditions.

Nonetheless, such explanations pose as many questions as they answer. First, like structural explanations, they describe the context in which the transitions took place, but they provide little information on the how and when of transitions. Africa's economic crisis had begun as early as the first oil crisis and reform programs sponsored by the IFIs had often started as early as the late 1970s. Economic approaches cannot explain why regime transitions began around 1990, rather than, say, 1985, or 2005 for that matter. Economic crises were ubiquitous in Africa yet, as we will show, popular unrest emerged in only about two thirds of the region's polities.

Nor, by themselves, do economic explanations shed much light on the internal dynamics of transition; every plausible scenario mapping out the exact link between economic crisis and regime transition can be counterbalanced by a logical argument, buttressed by empirical evidence, against such a link. As Share and Mainwaring note, "A favorable economic situation may give authoritarian elites the confidence necessary to begin a transition, but it may also provide a justification for remaining in power. An economic crisis often creates problems for transition to democracy, but it can also contribute towards the erosion of authoritarianism."[96] Similarly, the rise of popular protest against authoritarian regimes such as those in Portugal and Spain in the 1970s or in Taiwan and Korea in the 1980s, followed not decline but economic miracles of rapid sustained economic growth. As Huntington notes, rapid economic growth "raises expectations, exacerbates inequalities, and creates stresses and strains in the social fabric that stimulate political mobilization and demands for political participation."[97]

Almost invariably, economic approaches are compelling only if and when they are embedded within a political approach. For example, African populations' reactions to the economic crisis and reform attempts were almost certainly mediated by perceptions of the government's competence and legitimacy and by the fairness of its efforts to address the crisis. Ideological and organizational factors almost invariably matter; they shape objective material conditions into political forces. Economic explanations should not be dismissed; instead, they need to be integrated within a political economy approach in which politics is in command.

POLITICAL APPROACHES

By political, we have in mind approaches that place analytical primacy on the institutions that allocate power. We distinguish such approaches from the purely contingent approaches already discussed. We identify three nested levels of institutional analysis in the literature that analyze political traditions, political regimes, and political institutions. Although there is some overlap among these categories, distinctions are heuristically useful.

We define political *traditions* as long-standing cultural legacies that over time come to suffuse political institutions and societal attitudes and thus achieve an autonomous capacity to influence political outcomes. A number of scholars have posited the political power of such traditions. Perhaps its most famous exemplar is Weber's linkage of Protestantism with the rise of capitalism.[98] Similarly, analyses of China and the Soviet Union emphasize the impact of the "Confucian" and "Tzarist" traditions on Communist regimes there.[99] Generalizing from Italy, Robert Putnam argues that community associations and institutions with roots stretching back hundreds of years can create a civic spirit that dramatically enhances the efficacy of modern democratic government.[100] The message is clear: The daily practices of organizations build institutions, which over time foster the emergence of political traditions, which in turn serve to maintain and strengthen them. In sum, "attitudes and practices constitute a mutually reinforcing equilibrium."[101]

In Africa, the absence of democracy before 1989 has often been blamed on such long-standing political traditions. For Chazan, for example, the lack of democratic political experiences and the weakness of "linkage mechanisms between state and society" have "an important bearing on the meaning and influence of democratic norms on the continent."[102] Schatzberg considers that cultural norms in Africa are likely to undermine democratic reforms and their impact on African political systems.[103] Most compelling is Bayart's account of the politics of the belly[104] which is embedded in well-established customs, values, and informal relationships. He argues that the political behaviors practiced by Africans are distinctively derived from the continent's material poverty: Where resources are scarce, the object of political contestation is to secure economic consumption, which in turn is best guaranteed by capturing state power. These politics are a life-and-death struggle over private access to limited public resources; the zero-sum nature of the struggle compels would-be political leaders to enrich themselves in order to wield influence over followers and competitors. And because a "goat eats where it is tethered," private consumption of public resources under-mines and enfeebles state institutions. For Bayart and colleagues, belly politics expresses itself in political rhetoric, in popular humor and imagery, as well as in the workings of the continent's formal institutions.[105]

Other observers argue, on the contrary, that precolonial political systems were largely participatory and inclusive, thus representing a democratic tradition on which Africa could usefully build.[106] Some extend this argument to reject "imported" Western forms of liberal democracy in favor of specifically African forms derived from indigenous traditions.[107] For example, to explain the survival of democracy in Botswana, several scholars turn to the precolonial Tswana pub-lic assemblies, called *kgotla,* as a tradition on the basis of which modern consti-tutional institutions could be modeled and legitimated.[108] Following a similar logic, Eboussi-Boulaga suggests that the African National Conferences of 1991 and 1992 owed their success to their resemblance to traditional African modes of consensus building and *palaver.*[109] Other observers have been considerably less sanguine about the democratic heritage of precolonial Africa.[110] For many, the nature of precolonial institutions is in any event an academic issue rendered ir-relevant by the transformative impact of Western colonialism.

The colonial state is argued to have instituted an antidemocratic ethos that continues to pervade politics to the present day. For Crawford Young, for in-stance, the external origins and often brutally coercive practices of the colonial state have constituted its own powerful legacy, which was projected forward into the postcolonial period. Thus, the postcolonial state inherited "its structures, its quotidian routines and practices, and its more hidden normative theories of gov-ernance" from its colonial predecessor.[111] Chabal and others suggest that the ab-sence of domestic political accountability has been a key legacy of colonialism that shapes politics and inhibits reform to this day.[112] Ellis interprets Africa's re-cent round of protests as a popular revolt against the dominant political culture and a demand for a new mode of accountability.[113] These authors do not distin-guish between colonial powers and instead identify a single colonial state. On the other hand, Collier and Widner have made differences between the practices of the different European occupants a key variable in explanations of the evolution of African political regimes after independence and their ability to democratize after 1989.[114] Nonetheless, in both cases, the argument is less a culturalist one than one about *political regimes,* to which we now turn.

We remind you of the definition of political regimes offered earlier in this book: Regimes are the sets of procedures that determine the distribution of power. At any moment, regimes represent the concrete embodiment of authori-ty traditions and over time help to create or reinforce those traditions. In a clas-sic essay, Juan Linz distinguishes different types of authoritarian regimes, based on their degree of inclusiveness, the degree of popular mobilization, and the po-litical values they express.[115] Linz's analysis suggests that regimes have a lasting impact on politics that extends beyond their own life, and that their characteris-tics predispose them to evolve in distinctive ways.

Dahl presents an even more precise and insightful characterization of political regimes, which we employ.[116] He distinguishes political regimes along two
dimensions: the degree of political *competition* and the degree of political *participation*. First, regimes vary in the extent of permissible public opposition to
government policies. The dimension of political competition, or contestation,
distinguishes monopolistic regimes, in which political power is concentrated in
the hands of a narrow elite controlling a handful of organizations, from pluralistic regimes, in which power is dispersed among numerous institutions and
groups. The second independent dimension of all regimes is the extent of political participation allowed. This is defined as the breadth of popular involvement
in public life, or "the proportion of the population which is entitled to participate on a more or less equal plane."[117] On this dimension, regimes range from
inclusionary to exclusionary, depending on the proportion of the population that
plays a part in decision making. For example, regimes that restrict the electoral
franchise on the basis of race, gender, ownership of property, or any other distinction are more exclusive than regimes that include all prospective voters without discrimination.

Dahl's approach allows us to classify a wide range of regimes in a highly parsimonious manner in order to study the impact of regime type on specific political processes, notably transitions. Is there in fact a relationship between regime
type and the likelihood, nature, and extent of political transition? Scholars have
so far only scratched the surface in understanding political transitions in terms of
the structure of the preceding regime. Huntington's analysis of "third wave" democratic transitions in 35 countries found little overall relationship between the
nature of the incumbent authoritarian regime and the pattern of political transition. He contended that, whereas political transitions are most likely to be initiated from the top down, such dynamics are equally likely in transitions from one-
party, military, or personalistic regimes. Nevertheless, leaders of one-party and
military regimes are somewhat more likely than personal dictators to engage the
opposition in a negotiated transfer of power. By contrast, personalistic regimes
are more susceptible than other regime types to collapse in the face of a popular
protest; dictatorial leaders usually refuse to give up power voluntarily and try to
stay in office as long as they can.[118]

Other analysts have been somewhat more open to regime-based explanations of regime change. Early on, Rouquié argued that, because soldiers saw
themselves holding power temporarily, they were more likely to permit democratization than civilian governments.[119] Karen Remmer's work is particularly suggestive. She has argued that, once one recognizes the "enormous range
of variation concealed within the authoritarian [and democratic] categor[ies],"
political outcomes vary systematically with regime type.[120] From recent Latin
American experience she proposes that inclusionary democracies tend to collapse as a result of intrigue among the political elite, whereas exclusionary
democracies are more likely to succumb to pressure from below. Moreover, once
inclusionary regimes have held power, the reimposition of an exclusionary

regime requires heavy doses of state coercion. It is unclear, however, whether Remmer's generalizations can apply to the demise of autocracies as well as to the breakdown of democratic rule.

At the beginning of the independence era, Africanist scholarship was preoccupied with regimes and regime typologies that were based on often superficial and spurious distinctions – for instance, the types of party systems in existence. Excessively formalistic and Eurocentric in their uncritical importation of Western institutional constructs into African politics, such perspectives soon lost favor, and analysts, with the notable exception of Ruth Collier, moved away from regime based analysis. Instead, they favored either sociological approaches derived from Weber, which mostly ignored formal authority structures, or Marxian and dependency approaches, which tended to lump all African states in the same general category. This book seeks to restore political regimes as a viable analytical construct.

Finally, political regimes are themselves constituted by combinations of political *institutions*. An influential definition sees institutions as "sets of constraints on behavior in the form of rules and regulations; a set of procedures to detect deviations from the rules and regulations; and finally, a set of moral, ethical, behavioral norms which define the contours that constrain the way in which the rules and regulations are specified and enforcement carried out."[121] As such, political institutions can be highly abstract notions, such as constitutional principles, or they can be expressed concretely in actual organizations, such as trade unions, political parties, or the military. They include key aspects of formal politics, like the judiciary, but also informal customs such as patronage, clientelism, seniority principles, or lobbying.

If regimes are nested within broader political traditions, political institutions are nested within regimes. Political institutions both express the values and power configuration of regimes and traditions and help to reproduce them over time. It is now widely recognized that specific institutions condition politics through their powerful impact on the incentives faced by individuals. Under the rubric of the new institutionalism, a large literature has emerged in recent years that seeks to demonstrate this (for a fuller discussion, see next section). It includes efforts to examine the political consequences of electoral laws,[122] to explain why some states adopt policy ideas faster than others,[123] or to assess the manner in which states respond to external economic shocks.[124]

Political institutions should have a powerful impact on political transitions. Many observers have noted that democratization in Africa is problematic because of the absence, weakness, or politicization of key institutions, which are a legacy of past practices. To discern the contemporary impact of formal institutions we need to probe the following sorts of questions for each African country: How professional and neutral is the army? How plural is the party system and how well organized are its component parties? How dense and autonomous are voluntary associations within civil society?[125] It makes sense to believe that these institutions cannot recover easily from past repression and that in the meantime their absence or debility marks politics on the continent. On the other hand, the informal institutions that result from and simultaneously sustain Bayart's politics of the belly must surely condition individual incentives and shape political outcomes in Africa.

A POLITICO-INSTITUTIONAL APPROACH

As should now be abundantly clear, we favor an explanation of regime transitions based on *domestic political* considerations. We have argued that, as analytical instruments, macroeconomic and international factors are too blunt to discriminate among the particular political histories of countries undergoing regime transition. Instead, they constitute contexts that shape political structures and precipitate political action. But because of their essentially secondary or supporting role in relation to the explanation of regime transitions, we choose to downplay economic and international factors in our explanatory model, which concentrates on the processes and institutions internal to existing political regimes. Except that it is often overlooked, the point is so obvious that it hardly seems necessary to make: A country's political prospects derive directly from its own inherited practices.

THE INSTITUTIONAL POLITICS OF REGIME TRANSITION

A "new institutionalist" approach has brought together methodological individualists and historical materialists around a common concern with the interactions of political institutions and processes. Starting from rational-choice assumptions, Douglass North concludes that "history matters ... because the present and the future are connected to the past by the continuity of today's institutions. Today's and tomorrow's choices are shaped by the past."[126] Embarking from quite different roots in historical sociology, Terry Karl argues that "historically created structures, while not determining which one of a set of a limited set of alternatives political actors may choose, are 'confining conditions' that restrict, or in some cases enhance, the choices available to them."[127] To the extent that North's "path dependency" and Karl's "structured contingency" illuminate the contribution of domestic political factors to regime transitions, we find value in these approaches.

A convincing institutionalist synthesis has been forged by Kathleen Thelen and Sven Steinmo, who assert that "political struggles are mediated by the institutional setting in which [they] take place" because "institutions shape the goals that political actors pursue and ... structure power relations among them, privileging some and putting others at a disadvantage."[128] Unlike earlier institutionalists, these writers are less concerned with the formal-legal characteristics of institutions for their own sake, than with the ways in which "institutions structure [political] battles and in so doing, influence their outcomes."[129] The core characteristics of this approach are: an "emphasis on intermediate institutions that shape political strategies, the ways institutions structure relations of power among contending groups in society, and especially the focus on the *process* of politics and policy-making within given institutional parameters."[130]

A core insight of this approach is that the interactions between structure and action are reciprocal. Political behavior is not just the consequence of structural precedent but also an independent social force and analytic factor in its own right. Political actors regularly struggle, commonly over the content of policies but, more important, over the design of institutions. In this interpretation, the architecture of political institutions – of both state and civil society – is largely a product of the purposive initiatives of goal-oriented actors (as well as the unintended consequence of their interactions). Thelen and Steinmo propose that "institutional change results from deliberate political strategies to transform structural parameters in order to win long-term political advantage."[131] Political actors try to configure political institutions because they know that institutions create authoritative precedents that can relieve them of the burden of constantly fighting the same old political battles over and over again. They seek to change the rules of the political game so that they will work more consistently in their own favor.[132] From this perspective, political institutions become not only instruments for guiding and controlling political behavior but also arenas of tenacious partisan contention, particularly during periods of turmoil.

Thus, a politico-institutional approach is unusually well suited to the analysis of regime transitions. As is argued throughout, the prospects for political change in any country are partly predetermined by its distinctive institutional heritage. The structural characteristics of previous political regimes therefore constitute a reasonable starting point for analysis of transition processes. For Africa, we consider that the monopolistic political institutions constructed by autocratic leaders have affected the resource endowments and habitual practices of all key political actors. This approach has several merits. It shifts attention from the background of macrosocial class interests and ethnic identities to the political foreground of electoral, party, military, parastatal, and voluntary organizations through which political struggles are actually waged. And it allows in principle that formal political institutions are thoroughly steeped in, and penetrated by, informal personal networks. This insight is highly germane to Africa, where considerations of clan and clientage corrupt the bureaucratic operations of formal-legal institutions, creating a distinctive set of opportunities and constraints for political reform (see Chapter 2).

A politico-institutional approach also usefully stresses the importance of the rules that govern political interactions. In many respects, political transitions center on struggles over the rules of the political game, with alternate clusters of rules representing opposing regime options. Actors in transitions exert considerable effort in structuring political rules in their own favor: On one hand incumbent leaders seek to retain powers of arbitrary discretion over rule changes, and on the other opposition forces call for the introduction of more universalistic legal standards.

Transition struggles regularly come to center on constitutional rules that determine the distribution of power among formal political institutions, or electoral laws, under which founding elections will be conducted. Outcomes of rule disputes are never completely predetermined; while incumbents can often lay down the law, opposition forces can sometimes force rule changes. Yet outcomes are usually meaningful; especially in regimes where political offices provide economic rents, rules can determine who gets what, when, where, and how. A concern with rules, and struggles over them, thus enable analysts to address a full range of questions about regime transition, installation, and consolidation.

A final advantage of a politico-institutional approach is that it situates the analyst at an intermediate location from which middle-range theory can potentially be constructed. It builds numerous "analytical bridges": between actors as agents and objects of history; between formal state institutions and informal societal processes; and between grand generalization and narrower national cases.[133] We grant relatively less emphasis to macroeconomic and international explanations of domestic political phenomena partly because these grand theories are too highly pitched; they employ large-scale concepts to aim at broadly inclusive generalizations. By contrast, an institutional perspective using a set of simple political variables at an intermediate level of explanation promises several advantages: to close the gap between causes and outcomes by focusing on explanatory factors that are proximate to the object of study; to illuminate *both* regularities *and* variations across countries; and to account for *both* continuities *and* changes across time.[134]

Obviously, existing institutional approaches are not without weaknesses. To begin with, the new institutionalism has not fully overcome the constitutional bias of the old institutionalism. Thelen and Steinmo acknowledge that institutions may appear in informal guises, but institutionalists still usually study entities that are formally organized and legally incorporated.[135] In countries that are governed according to a rule of law and the precepts of bureaucratic rationality, this choice of subject matter would be largely unproblematic. Under such circumstances, it is pertinent to inquire – according to the most lively debate in the new institutionalist literature – whether presidential or parliamentary constitutional forms are better suited to the consolidation of democracy.[136] In countries where the rule of law is only weakly routinized and where constitutional rules are easily changed by political leaders or flouted by state functionaries or armed dissidents, however, such debates are hardly relevant. This is not to say that politics in countries lacking an entrenched tradition of constitutional governance is, as in Aristide Zolberg's famous portrayal, "an almost institutionless arena with conflict and disorder as its most prominent features."[137] Routine procedures of politics to which participants are acutely attuned do exist. But many of the most important rules are informal; they are not written down and they are not justiciable in a court of law.

As Chapter 2 will argue, the real institutions of politics in Africa are the informal relations of loyalty and patronage established between "big men" and their personal followers. The unwritten rules of neopatrimonial politics shape the decisions of leaders, engender compliance from citizens, and pervade the performance of bureaucratic organizations. Formally, the domination of political patrons and the subordination of their clients is expressed in the monopolistic political organizations of military oligarchies and civilian one-party states. The constitutional and electoral rules decreed by personalistic leaders, as well as the systems of party and civic organizations that they permitted, embody and express the constrained expectations of the African political game. While taking such formal institutions into account, institutional analysis in an African context must also supersede them, pragmatically addressing the actual opportunities and constraints confronting political actors. To become truly comparative, institutional analysis must make good on its claims to incorporate both formal and informal institutions into the framework of analysis. This book attempts a modest step in that direction. The nature of Africa's neopatrimonial regimes and their expected implications for political transitions are the subjects of the next chapter.

Another problem with institutional analysis is that the quest for middle-range conceptualization generates an unparsimonious framework. Thelen and Steinmo operate with an unwieldy shopping list of relevant institutions that stretches to encompass "the rules of electoral competition, the structure of party systems, the relations among various branches of government, and the structure and organization of economic actors like trade unions."[138] In some instances, generalization may be possible only within the restricted horizons of a single institution such as an electoral law or an institutional arena such as a party system. But to stop short at this level is to run the risk of generating a series of partial and unconnected insights that do not amount to an integrated theory. For all their virtues, middle-range investigations sometimes overlook conceptual economies that can be obtained by notching up analysis to more generic levels.

As stated earlier, we regard *political regimes* as aggregate clusters of interlocking institutions. Because leaders try to apply a consistent set of political rules across institutional arenas, regimes tend to cohere into a mutually reinforcing syndrome of governance. Following a military coup, for example, military leaders often suspend politics simultaneously throughout the polity, including in the legislature, in the party system, and in civil society. In the presence of such systemic regularities, it is theoretically more efficient to focus on political regimes than on individual institutions. Thus, where possible and relevant, this study conducts analysis in terms of regime types, with special reference to distinctions between civilian and military regimes and between plebiscitary and competitive civilian one-party regimes.

Furthermore, beyond political regimes lies an even more general level of analysis that concerns overarching *institutional dimensions*. As presented here (and in Chapter 2), regime types can be distinguished according to the broadly comparative dimensions of *political participation* and *political competition*. For example, whereas multiparty democracies display high levels of both these attributes, personal dictatorships are deficient on both counts. Thus, wherever the opportunity is appropriately presented, this study seeks to generalize about political institutions at the level of their operating principles. We wish to know, for example, whether a country's previous experience with institutionalized precedents of political participation and political competition have any bearing on the onset, dynamics, and outcomes of contemporary regime transitions.

THE STRUCTURE OF POLITICAL CONTINGENCY

Our presentation so far says little about the relative merits of structural and contingent models of explanation, the topic on which this chapter now ends. We resist making a forced, dichotomous choice in this instance; we insist instead on having the best of both worlds. An approach that is neither overly deterministic or excessively voluntaristic seems the most defensible epistemological position for social science analysis.[139] It retains an analytical focus on human agency, conflict, and choice, the elements that distinguish the social from the physical sciences. But it presupposes that patterns of regularity can be discerned within the tumult of historical events that can make human behavior, however fleetingly and conditionally, susceptible to scientific investigation. Attention to a *structured contingency* approach allows, on the one hand, that structural precedents impart shape to current events and, on the other, that today's private decisions change even durable public institutions. To paraphrase a classic statement, it allows that people can make their own history, even if not under conditions of their own choosing. We think that such a mixed perspective is well suited for viewing the panoramic drama of political actors who are both the agents and objects of history.

Contingent political events may be structured in several alternate ways. First, inherited rules and institutions impose limits on the range of choices available to actors and predispose them to opt for certain courses of action over others. As Crawford Young convincingly contends, "A regime develops a logic of its own, whose ultimate aim is the reproduction over time of its particular configuration of institutional arrangements and dominant ideas."[140] Hence, the choices made by political actors during turbulent periods of regime transition may be traced back, in important part, to a framework of political institutions implanted during earlier eras. One would expect, for example, that political actors face different structures of constraint and opportunity and hence behave differently during regime transitions according to their positions within official and informal hierarchies. One would also expect political behavior to vary depending on whether the authoritarian regime that is undergoing reform is personalistic or bureaucratic, military or civilian, participatory or competitive.

Second, events may be structured through regularities and patterns of their own. Although regime transitions may seem unruly and unpredictable, they may also over time adhere to an inner logic. Early choices or events give shape to later choices and events. And just as political institutions mold behavior, so regular patterns of behavior congeal into institutions. It seems plausible that momentous decisions by incumbent leaders – for example, to allow civil liberties or permit competitive elections – create new political situations in which old options are foreclosed and fresh responses are required. To take another example, the way a regime transition proceeds – say by violence or negotiation – affects not only how the transition itself ends but also the prospects for the consolidation of the subsequent regime. As Krasner comments, "Once a critical choice is made it cannot be taken back ... it canalizes future development ... [and] forecloses other options ... because of the vested interests it creates."[141] Thus, structured contingency allows not only that present paths depend on past precedents but also that contemporary events have intrinsic patterns and that these patterns can in turn model subsequent developments.

Third, structure and contingency connect by alternate means: incrementally or dialectically. To date, the former mechanism has received greatest attention in the literature. Because structural analysis regards social innovation as deriving from paths established by earlier precedents, it emphasizes institutional continuities, that is, the recurrent patterns by which institutions are gradually reproduced. There is much merit to the theme of institutional continuity, and we use it repeatedly in this study to explain why the *consolidation* of democracy is so difficult in Africa. But too great an emphasis on gradualism and continuity can lead inexorably down a deterministic cul de sac according to which, for example, only countries with some sort of past democratic political experience are capable of democratizing in the present. If this were the case, then democratic *transitions* would never have begun anywhere in the world.

Instead, the possibility exists that actions and events can be a *reaction against* a prevailing institutional tradition. Indeed, a dialectical, conflict-based trajectory of political change is highly germane to democratization, which invariably involves popular demands for political representation directed against elite-dominated regimes. The notion that the structures of society can evoke unanticipated political conflicts is well captured in the argument by Reuschemeyer and the Stevenses that "capitalist development is associated with democracy because it transforms the class structure, strengthening the working and middle classes and weakening the landed upper class. It was not the capitalist market nor capitalists as the new dominant force, but rather the contradictions of capitalism that advanced the cause of democracy."[142] Krasner applies this argument to the political realm, noting the "disjunctures and stress within any given political system ... structures do not exist because they perform certain functions, and functions do not necessarily give rise to corresponding structures."[143] Rather, political life is fraught with tensions and conflicts that periodically erupt in "strife and uncertainty about the rules of the political game."[144]

With reference to Africa, we note that performance of political regimes can be so contradictory as to sometimes call their own viability into question. With reference to postcolonial developments in Sénégal, Catherine Boone finds that "consolidating power and promoting economic growth proved to be contradictory imperatives.... [R]egimes seem to use state prerogatives in ways that erode the bases of their own power."[145] State elites in Africa have sought political power primarily to obtain and defend economic benefits, to the point that they have blocked private accumulation by independent groups in society, thus undermining the entire project of economic development. Joel Migdal makes a similar point with reference to both African and non-African cases but in more singularly political terms. He points to the pathological paradox whereby incumbent rulers fear to increase the capacity of state institutions out of concern that they can be turned against them by local strongmen. While political elites may wish to maintain political order, they cannot do so because "the politics of survival" prevent them from creating an administrative apparatus that is capable of enforcing rules.[146]

In time, such self-serving political strategies become autodestructive. The *modus operandi* of such regimes create not only grievances that inspire movements of political opposition but also weak state institutions that are incapable of managing inevitable popular disaffection. Applying this line of reasoning to regime transitions in Latin America, Malloy and Seligson argue that "the shift from one type of regime to another usually occurs because of the failures of the preexisting regime ... one regime emerges in response to the incapacity of another."[147]

Where, then, does the notion of structured contingency lead? The insight that structure and agency exist in a relationship of reciprocal influence could be held to provide unclear operating instructions. In wanting to have it both ways, analysts cannot determine *a priori* the primacy of institutional precedent or human initiative in any specific instance of political change. Under what conditions will structure shape action? Under what conditions will the opposite hold true? The answer to this dilemma, in our view, is not to revert arbitrarily to a univariate model applied universally. Rather, there is good reason to expect that the relative importance of structure and contingency will be determined situationally. Some circumstances lend themselves to politics as usual, and others to political innovation.

Fortunately, the existing literature on democratization is very clear about when to expect structural continuities or agent-led innovations. The literature reviewed in this chapter makes it clear that scholars favor contingent explanations for *regime transitions* and structural explanations for *regime consolidation*. Following this established intellectual consensus, our analysis of regime transitions begins with reference to the interplay of purposive political actors (see Chapter 3), thus solving the immediate problem of where to start. But because we suspect that a contingent approach tells only part of the story, the bulk of this book (see Chapters 4, 5, and 6) searches for patterns of institutional regularity within the processes of regime transition in Africa.

We are troubled by the fact that to date analysts have found it necessary to resort to entirely separate and largely incompatible models of explanation to account for different phases of democratization. We accept that certain explanatory factors might rise and fall in importance as transitions unfold. But to acknowledge that regime transitions are highly contingent processes is not to accept that they are entirely unstructured or that different phases of transition are unstructured to the same degree. We surmise instead the existence of some measure of underlying institutional continuity or institutionally driven conflict within regime transitions. We expect that an approach based on the institutions of postcolonial African politics can help us to understand – at one and the same time – the nature of old regimes, the dynamics of regime transitions, and the prospects for the consolidation of new regimes. It is to these general propositions that this book is dedicated.

ENDNOTES

1. Dietrich Rueschemeyer, Evelyne Huber Stephens, and John D. Stephens, *Capitalist Development and Democracy* (Chicago: University of Chicago Press, 1992), p. 7.

2. Seymour Martin Lipset, *Political Man: The Social Basis of Politics* (New York: Doubleday, 1960), especially Ch. 2; Barrington Moore Jr., *The Social Origins of Dictatorship and Democracy: Lord and Peasant in the Making of the Modern World* (Boston: Beacon Press, 1966), especially Ch. 7.

3. Daniel Lerner, *The Passing of Traditional Society* (Glencoe, Ill.: Free Press, 1958). See also Karl W. Deutsch, "Social Mobilization and Political Development," *American Political Science Review* 55 (1961): 493–514.

4. Larry Diamond, "Economic Development and Democracy Reconsidered," *American Behavioral Scientist* 35, (1992): 450–99. Diamond discovers that "the relationship between economic development has weakened somewhat in the last 30 years as the number of democracies, especially in the middle ranges of development, has grown" (p. 460). Nonetheless, a general index of development (the United Nations' Development Program's Human Development index – a composite measure of adult literacy, life expectancy, and [the log of] per capita GDP) is even more strongly correlated with democracy than per capita GDP alone.

5. Kenneth Bollen and Robert Jackman, "Political Democracy and the Size Distribution of Income," *American Sociological Review* 50 (1985): 438–57.

6. Rueschemeyer et al., *Capitalist Development and Democracy*, p. 2.

7. Samuel P. Huntington, *The Third Wave: Democratization in the Late Twentieth Century* (Norman: University of Oklahoma Press, 1991), p. 60.

8. Ibid., p. 312.

9. Fernando Henrique Cardoso and Enza Faletto, *Dependency and Development in Latin America* (Berkeley: University of California Press, 1979); Peter Evans, *Dependent Development: The Alliance of Multinational, State and Local Capital in Brazil* (Princeton: Princeton University Press, 1979).

10. On communal solidarities see Crawford Young, *The Politics of Cultural Pluralism* (Madison: University of Wisconsin Press, 1976), and Donald Horowitz, *Ethnic Groups in Conflict* (Berkeley: University of California Press, 1985). On gender identities, see Georgina Waylen, "Women and Democra-

tization: Conceptualizing Gender Relations in Transition Politics," *World Politics* 46 (1994): 327–54; Jane Jacquette, *The Women's Movement in Latin America: Participation and Democratization* (Boulder, Colo.: Westview, 1994); and Jane Parpart and Kathleen Staudt, *Women and the State in Africa* (Boulder, Colo.: Lynne Rienner, 1989); Moore, *Social Origins of Dictatorship and Democracy,* p. 418.

11. Rueschemeyer et al., *Capitalist Development and Democracy,* p. 6.

12. José Nun, "The Middle-Class Military Coup," in *The Politics of Conformity in Latin America,* ed. Claudio Veliz (New York: Oxford University Press, 1967). See also Guillermo O'Donnell, *Modernization and Bureaucratic Authoritarianism: Studies in South American Politics* (Berkeley, Calif.: Institute for International Studies, 1973).

13. James M. Malloy and Mitchell Seligson, *Authoritarians and Democrats: Regime Transition in Latin America* (Pittsburgh, Penn.: University of Pittsburgh Press, 1987), p. 6.

14. Martin Kilson, "The Anatomy of African Class Consciousness," in *Studies in Power and Class in Africa,* ed. Irving Leonard Markovitz (New York: Oxford University Press, 1987), p. 62.

15. Preoccupation with the long-term continuities in human societies over many centuries is most pronounced in the Annales school of history, notably the work of Fernand Braudel. For studies on Africa along these lines, see Jean-François Bayart, *L'Etat en Afrique: la politique du ventre* (Paris: Fayard, 1989); and Achille Mbembe, *Afrique indociles: Christianisme, pouvoir et Etat en societé postcoloniale* (Paris: Karthala, 1988). For a recent statement in the modernization tradition, see Robert Jackman, *Power Without Force: The Political Capacity of Nation–States* (Ann Arbor: University of Michigan Press, 1994).

16. Stephen Krasner, "Approaches to the State: Alternative Conceptions and Historical Dynamics," *Comparative Politics* 16 (1984): 223–46. See also Timur Kuran, "Now Out of Never: The Role of Surprise in East European Revolutions, 1989," *World Politics,* 44, (1991): 7–48 and Susanne Lohmann, "The Dynamics of Informational Cascades," *World Politics,* 47, 1 (1994): 42–101.

17. Kathleen Thelen and Sven Steinmo, "Historical Institutionalism in Comparative Politics," in *Structuring Politics: Historical Institutionalism in Comparative Analysis,* ed. Thelen, Steinmo, and Frank Longstreth (Cambridge: Cambridge University Press, 1992), p. 15.

18. Guiseppe Di Palma, *To Craft Democracies: An Essay on Democratic Transitions* (Berkeley: University of California Press, 1990), p. 4.

19. Robert Dahl, *Polyarchy: Participation and Opposition* (New Haven: Yale University Press, 1971), p. 208; Samuel P. Huntington, "Will More Countries Become Democratic?" *Political Science Quarterly* 99 (1984): 218.

20. Myron Wiener, "Empirical Democratic Theory and the Transition from Authoritarianism to Democracy," *PS: Political Science and Politics* 20 (1987): 862–3. See also Albert Hirschmann, "The Search for Paradigms as a Hindrance to Understanding," *World Politics* (1970): 329–43. Both sources are cited by Di Palma, *To Craft Democracies,* p. 5.

21. Adam Smith, *The Wealth of Nations* (1776; reprint, New York: Modern Library, 1937); Karl Popper, *The Poverty of Historicism* (Boston: Beacon Press, 1957).

22. For example, Anthony Downs, *An Economic Theory of Democracy* (New York: Harper & Row, 1957); James Buchanan and Gordon Tullock, *The Calculus of Consent* (Ann Arbor: University of Michigan Press, 1962); Mancur Olson, *The Logic of Collective Action* (Cambridge: Harvard University Press, 1965); Robert Axelrod, *The Evolution of Cooperation* (New York: Basic Books, Macmillan, 1984).

23. Di Palma, *To Craft Democracies,* p. 4.

24. Guillermo O'Donnell and Philippe C. Schmitter, *Transitions from Authoritarian Rule:Tentative Conclusions about Uncertain Democracies* (Baltimore: Johns Hopkins University Press, 1986), p. 3.

25. Di Palma, *To Craft Democracies*, p. 8.

26. *Ibid.,* p. 12.

27. Di Palma sees transitions as "open processes of interaction." *Ibid.,* p. 10.

28. Juan J. Linz and Alfred Stepan, "Political Crafting of Democratic Consolidation or Destruction: European and South American Comparisons" (paper presented at the Conference on Reinforcing Democracies in the Americas, the Carter Center, Atlanta, Georgia, November 17–18, 1986).

29. A useful overview is Adam Przeworski, "The Games of Transition," in *Issues in Democratic Consolidation: The New South American Democracies in Comparative Perspective,* ed. Scott Mainwaring, Guillermo O'Donnell, and J. Samuel Valenzuela (Notre Dame: University of Notre Dame Press, 1992). See also Przeworski, *Democracy and the Market: Political and Economic Reforms in Eastern Europe and Latin America* (New York: Cambridge University Press, 1991); Barbara Geddes, *Politician's Dilemma* (Berkeley: University of California Press, 1994); Josep M. Colomer, "Transitions By Agreement: Modeling the Spanish Way," *American Political Science Review* 85 (1991): 1282–1302; and Scott Gates and Brian D. Humes, *Games, Information and Politics: Applying Game Theoretic Models to Politics* (Ann Arbor: University of Michigan Press, 1996), esp. Ch 5.

30. See Victor T. Levine, *Political Leadership in Africa* (Stanford: Stanford University Press, 1967); Henry Bretton, *The Rise and Fall of Kwame Nkrumah* (New York: Praeger, 1966); and Irving L. Markovitz, *Léopold Sédar Senghor and the Politics of Négritude* (New York: Atheneum, 1969). For a more general framework, see Ann Ruth Willner, *Charismatic Political Leadership: A Theory* (Princeton, N.J.: Center of International Studies, 1968). For updated works that build on this tradition, the relevant titles are John R. Cartwright, *Political Leadership in Africa* (London: Croom Helm, 1983); and John A. Wiseman, ed., *Political Leaders in Black Africa: A Biographical Dictionary* (Brookfield, Vt.: E. Elgar, 1991).

31. Robert H. Jackson and Carl G. Rosberg, *Personal Rule in Black Africa: Prince, Autocrat, Prophet, Tyrant* (Berkeley: University of California Press, 1982).

32. Robert H. Bates, *Beyond the Miracle of the Market: The Political Economy of Agrarian Development in Kenya* (New York: Cambridge University Press, 1989), and *Markets and States in Tropical Africa: The Political Basis of Agricultural Policies* (Berkeley: University of California Press, 1981). For an appreciation and critique of this contribution, see Ernest J. Wilson III and Howard Stein, "The Political Economy of Robert Bates: A Critical Reading of Rational Choice in Africa," *World Development* 21 (1993): 1035–53.

33. Goran Hyden, "Governance and the Study of Politics," in *Governance and Politics in Africa,* ed. Goran Hyden and Michael Bratton (Boulder, Colo.: Lynne Rienner, 1992), pp. 8–10.

34. Goran Hyden, "Governance: A New Approach to Comparative Politics" (paper presented at the annual meeting of the African Studies Association, Chicago, October 28-31, 1988), pp. 4, 16.
35. Naomi Chazan, "Liberalization, Governance, and Political Space in Ghana," in *Governance and Politics in Africa,* ed. Goran Hyden and Michael Bratton (Boulder, Colo.: Lynne Rienner, 1992), p. 123.
36. Michael Bratton and Nicolas van de Walle, "Toward Governance in Africa: Popular Demands and State Responses," in *Governance and Politics in Africa,* ed. Goran Hyden and Michael Bratton (Boulder, Colo.: Lynne Rienner, 1992), p. 30.
37. Nancy Bermeo, "Rethinking Regime Change," *Comparative Politics* 22 (1990): 359–77; Daniel Levine, "Paradigm Lost: Dependence to Democracy," *World Politics* 40 (1988): 377–94.
38. For an elaboration of this line of reasoning, see Michael Bratton, "Civil Society and Political Transitions in Africa," in *Civil Society and the State in Africa,* ed. John W. Harbeson, Donald Rothchild, and Naomi Chazan (Boulder, Colo.: Lynne Rienner, 1994), pp. 51–81.
39. Ernest J. Wilson III, "Creating a Research Agenda for Studying Political Change in Africa," in *Economic Change and Political Liberalization in Sub-Saharan Africa,* ed. Jennifer A. Widner (Baltimore: Johns Hopkins University Press, 1994), 260; Rueschemeyer et al., *Capitalist Development and Democracy,* p. 7.
40. For Africa, the crude version of the dependency thesis is expressed in Walter Rodney, *How Europe Underdeveloped Africa* (Dar es Salaam, Tanzania: Tanzania Publishing House, 1972). More nuanced class-analytic accounts can be found in Giovanni Arrighi, "International Corporations, Labor Aristocracies, and Economic Development in Tropical Africa," in *Imperialism and Underdevelopment,* ed. Robert I. Rhodes (New York: Monthly Review Press, 1970); Samir Amin, *Unequal Development: An Essay on the Social Formations of Peripheral Capitalism* (New York: Monthly Review Press, 1976); Colin Leys, *Underdevelopment in Kenya: The Political Economy of Neocolonialism* (London: Heinemann, 1975); and Claude Ake, *A Political Economy of Africa* (London: Longman, 1981).
41. Issa Shivji, *Class Struggles in Tanzania* (New York: Monthly Review Press, 1976); Irving L. Markovitz, *Power and Class in Africa* (Englewood Cliffs, N.J.: Prentice-Hall, 1977); Richard L. Sklar, "The Nature of Class Domination in Africa," *Journal of Modern African Studies* 17 (1979): 531–2.
42. Immanuel Wallerstein, *The Capitalist World Economy* (New York: Cambridge University Press, 1979); and Peter C. Gutkind and Wallerstein, eds., *The Political Economy of Contemporary Africa* (London: Sage, 1976).
43. The term originates with A. James Gregor, *Italian Fascism and Developmental Dictatorship* (Princeton: Princeton University Press, 1979). Its application to Africa is owed to Richard L. Sklar, "Democracy in Africa," *African Studies Review* 36 (1983): 11–24. Under this regime, the political class "embraced statist nationalism in order to mobilize all talents and resources for a program of forced and rapid industrialization."
44. On the rise and fall of developmental goals in the politics of non-Western states and the preoccupations of comparative analysts, see Samuel P. Huntington, "The Goals of Development," in *Understanding Political Development,* ed. Myron Wiener and Huntington (Boston: Little, Brown, 1987), Ch. 1.
45. Robert H. Jackson and Carl G. Rosberg, "Why Africa's Weak States Persist," *World Politics* 35 (1982): 1–24.

46. *Ibid.,* 278.

47. Charles Tilly, ed., *The Formation of National States in Western Europe* (Princeton: Princeton University Press, 1975), p. 46.

48. Francis Fukuyama, "The End of History?" *The National Interest* (Summer 1989): 3–18; Joshua Muravchik, *Exporting Democracy: Fulfilling America's Destiny* (Washington, D. C.: American Enterprise Institute, 1991); Henry Kissinger, *Diplomacy* (New York: Simon & Schuster, 1994).

49. On cultural alternatives to liberal democracy, see Samuel P. Huntington, "The Clash of Civilizations?" *Foreign Affairs* 72 (1993): 22–49. For a persuasive treatise on the tensions between liberal democracy and the political values prevalent in African countries, see Peter P. Ekeh, "Historical and Cross-Cultural Contexts of Democratization in Africa: A Challenge to Democratic Theory" (paper presented at the annual meeting of the American Sociological Association, Miami, August 13–17, 1993). See also Tony F. Smith, "Making the World Safe for Democracy," *The Washington Quarterly* 16 (1993): 197–214. On this theme, see also Brad Roberts, ed., *The New Democracies: Global Change and U.S. Foreign Policy* (Cambridge: Massachusetts Institute of Technology Press, 1990); and James Schlesinger, "Quest for a Post–Cold War Foreign Policy," *Foreign Affairs* 72 (1993): 17–28.

50. Geoffrey Pridham, "The International Dimension of Democratization: Theory, Practice, and Inter-Regional Comparisons," in *Building Democracy? The International Dimension of Democratization in Eastern Europe,* ed. Pridham, Eric Herring, and George Sandford (London: Liecester University Press, 1994), p. 7. See also Geoffrey Pridham, ed., *Encouraging Democracy: The International Dimension of Democratization in Southern Europe* (London: Liecester University Press, 1991).

51. Krishna Kumar, "The 1989 Revolutions and the Idea of Europe," *Political Studies* (September 1992): 441.

52. The causal direction of this relationship could be inverted – that is, with democratization as the engine of change. In the former Soviet Union and Eastern Europe, the end of the Cold War looks as much like an effect as a cause of political opening and electoral transition. As Larry Diamond and Marc Plattner write, "most dramatically of all, the democratic revolutions of 1989–91 precipitated the collapse of communism in Eastern Europe and the former Soviet Union and thus brought an end to the Cold War that had been the central feature of international relations for almost half a century." Diamond and Plattner, "Introduction," in *The Forum for Democratic Studies* (Washington, D.C: National Endowment for Democracy, August 1994).

53. Barry Munslow, "Democratization in Africa," *Parliamentary Affairs* 46 (1993): 483; Tom Young, "Elections and Electoral Politics in Africa," *Africa* 63 (1993): 299.

54. *Africa Confidential* 31 (1990): 3.

55. Kathryn Nwajiaku, "The National Conferences in Benin and Togo Revisited," *Journal of Modern African Studies* 32 (1994): 430.

56. Jeffrey Herbst, "The Fall of Afro-Marxism," *Journal of Democracy* 1 (1990): 92–101.

57. See Samuel P. Huntington, "Patterns of Violence in World Politics," in *Changing Patterns of Military Politics,* ed. Huntington, *International Yearbook of Politi-*

cal Behavior Research, vol. 3 (New York: Free Press, 1962); Robert D. Putnam, "Toward Explaining Military Intervention in Latin American Politics," *World Politics* 20 (October 1967): 83–110; Egil Fossum, "Factors Influencing the Occurrence of Military Coups d'Etat in Latin America," *Journal of Peace Research* 4 (1967): 238–51; Manus Midlarsky, "Mathematical Models of Instability and a Theory of Diffusion," *International Studies Quarterly* 14 (1970): 60–84. For Africa, see Stuart Hill and Donald Rothchild, "The Contagion of Political Conflict in Africa and the World," *Journal of Conflict Resolution* 30 (1986): 716–35; see also Richard P.Y. Li and William R. Thompson, "The 'Coup Contagion' Hypothesis," *Journal of Conflict Resolution* 19 (1975): 63–88.

58. Georg Sorenson, *Democracy and Democratization: Processes and Prospects in a Changing World* (Boulder, Colo.: Westview, 1993), p. 36.

59. Samuel Decalo, "The Process, Prospects and Constraints on Democratization in Africa," *African Affairs* 91 (1992): 14. The quotation within refers to Douglas C. Anglin, "Southern African Response to Eastern European Developments," *Journal of Modern African Studies* 28 (1990): 448. In fairness, we must note that Decalo goes on to say that "the spillover effect, though it definitely crystallized and catalyzed pro-democracy demonstrations in Africa does not tell the whole story. The continent was already *ripe* for upheaval."

60. Robert Fishman, "Rethinking State and Regime: Southern Europe's Transition to Democracy," *World Politics* 42 (1990): 440.

61. Commenting on the extreme case of the U.S.–led reinstallation of Jean Bertrand-Aristide in Haiti in 1994, Robert Fatton considers that, even here, where "international factors impinge[d] massively upon both productive capacity and the structure of governance ¼ they cannot obliterate the internal logic of the country." Robert Fatton, "From Predatory Rule to Democratic Governance: The Ambiguities and Paradoxes of Haiti's 'Extrication' from Dictatorship" (paper presented at the annual meeting of the American Political Science Association, Chicago, August 31 – September 3, 1995).

62. Tony Smith, "The Underdevelopment of the Development Literature," in *The State and Development in the Third World,* ed. Atul Kohli (Princeton: Princeton University Press, 1986), pp. 35–6.

63. *Ibid.,* p. 38.

64. *Ibid.,* p. 39.

65. *Ibid.,* p. 45.

66. *Ibid.,* p. 66.

67. Bayart, *L'Etat en Afrique,* p. 28.

68. Christopher Clapham, "The *Longue Durée* of the African State," *African Affairs,* 93 (1994): 436.

69. Smith, "Underdevelopment," p. 29.

70. Bayart, *L'Etat en Afrique,* pp. x–xi.

71. Robert Keohane, Joseph Nye, and Stanley Hoffman, eds., *After the Cold War: International Institutions and State Strategies in Europe, 1989–1991* (Cambridge: Massachusetts Institute of Technology Press, 1993), p. 2.

72. Nancy Spalding, "Resource Mobilization in Africa: The Role of Local Organizations in the Tanganyika Independence Movement," *Journal of Developing Areas* 28 (1993): 92, 94.

73. Philippe C. Schmitter, "An Introduction to Southern European Transitions from Authoritarian Rule," in *Transitions from Authoritarian Rule: Southern Europe*, ed. Guillermo O'Donnell, Philippe C. Schmitter, and Laurence Whitehead (Baltimore: Johns Hopkins University Press, 1986), p. 5.

74. Laurence Whitehead, "International Aspects of Democratization," in *Transitions from Authoritarian Rule: Comparative Perspectives*, ed. Guillermo O'Donnell, Philippe C. Schmitter, and Laurence Whitehead (Baltimore: Johns Hopkins University Press, 1986), p. 4. In fairness, it should be noted that Whitehead acknowledges that he and his collaborators selected cases of peacetime transitions in noncommunist countries in which the "international setting provided a mildly supportive (or destructive) background which was often taken for granted and which seldom intruded too conspicuously on an essentially domestic drama."

75. Huntington, *Third Wave*, p. 112.

76. A good recent survey is provided by James A. Caporaso and David Levine, *Theories of Political Economy* (New York: Cambridge University Press, 1992). See also Martin Staniland, *What Is Political Economy? A Study of Social Theory and Underdevelopment* (New Haven: Yale University Press, 1985).

77. Robert A. Packenham, *Liberal America and the Third World: Political Development Ideas in Foreign Aid and Social Science* (Princeton: Princeton University Press, 1973).

78. Huntington notes in *The Third Wave*, p. 21, that "in 1962 ¼ thirteen governments in the world were the products of coups d'état; by 1975, thirty-eight were."

79. Samuel P. Huntington, *Political Order in Changing Societies* (New Haven: Yale University Press, 1968).

80. See Ted Robert Gurr, *Why Men Rebel* (Princeton: Princeton University Press, 1970). For a good overview of this literature, see Joan Nelson, "Participation," in *Understanding Political Development*, eds. Myron Weiner and Samuel P. Huntington (New York: Little, Brown, 1987), pp. 103–59.

81. Samuel Popkin, *The Rational Peasant* (Berkeley: University of California Press, 1979); Robert H. Bates, "Modernization, Ethnic Competition, and the Rationality of Politics in Contemporary Africa," in *State versus Ethnic Claims: African Policy Dilemmas*, ed. Donald Rothchild and V. A. Olorunsola (Boulder, Colo.: Westview, 1983), pp. 152–71.

82. See, for instance, Robert Kaufman, *Transitions to Stable Authoritarian-Corporate Regimes: The Chilean Case* (Beverly Hills, Calif.: Sage, 1976); Juan Linz, *The Breakdown of Democratic Regimes: Crisis, Breakdown and Reequilibration* (Baltimore: Johns Hopkins University Press, 1978).

83. John Londregan and Keith Poole, "Poverty, the Coup Trap and the Seizure of Executive Power," *World Politics* 42 (1990): 151–83; Mark J. Gasiorowski, "Economic Crisis and Political Regime Change: An Event History Analysis," *American Political Science Review* 89 (1995): 882–97.

84. See, for example, Samuel P. Huntington and Joan M. Nelson, *No Easy Choice: Political Participation in Developing Countries* (New York: Cambridge University Press, 1976).

85. Stephan Haggard and Steven B. Webb, eds., "Introduction," in *Voting for Reform: Economic Adjustment in New Democracies* (New York: Oxford University

Press, 1994); Gordon Richards, "Stabilization Crises and the Breakdown of Military Authoritarianism in Latin America," *Comparative Political Studies* 18 (1986): 447–85; and John Markoff and Silvio Duncan Baretta, "Economic Crisis and Regime Change in Brazil: the 1960s and the 1980s," *Comparative Politics* 22 (1990): 421–44.

86. Richard Westebbe, "Structural Adjustment, Rent Seeking and Liberalization in Benin," in *Economic Change and Political Liberalization in Sub-Saharan Africa,* ed. Jennifer A. Widner (Baltimore: Johns Hopkins Press, 1994), pp. 80–100; in the same collection of essays, see Michael Bratton, "Economic Crisis and Political Realignment in Zambia," pp. 101–28.

87. See Claude Ake, "The Unique Case of African Democracy," *International Affairs* 69 (1993): 239–44.

88. *Ibid.*

89. See among others, Henry S. Bienen and Mark Gersovitz, "Consumer Subsidy Cuts, Violence, and Political Stability," *Comparative Politics* 19 (1986): 25–44; Joan M. Nelson, ed., *Economic Crisis and Policy Choice: the Politics of Economic Adjustment in the Third World* (Princeton: Princeton University Press, 1990); Joan M. Nelson, ed., *Fragile Coalitions: The Politics of Economic Adjustment* (Washington, D.C.: Overseas Development Council, 1989); Stephan Haggard and Robert Kaufman, *The Politics of Economic Reform* (Princeton: Princeton University Press, 1992); and John Walton and David Seddon, *Free Markets and Food Riots: The Politics of Global Adjustment* (Oxford: Blackwell, 1994). Ricardo Salvatore has even argued that outbreaks of popular protest in response to elite-driven free-market reforms fit a recurring pattern in Latin American history. See Salvatore, "Market-Oriented Reforms and the Language of Popular Protest: Latin America from Charles III to the IMF," *Social Science History* 17 (1993): 485–523.

90. See Guillermo O'Donnell, *Modernization and Bureaucratic-Authoritarianism.* A critique and discussion of O'Donnell's thesis was provided by David Collier, ed., *The New Authoritarianism in Latin America* (Princeton: Princeton University Press, 1979).

91. John Sheahan, "Market Oriented Policies and Political Repression in Latin America," *Economic Development and Cultural Change* 28 (1980): 267–92.

92. The destabilizing impact of economic adjustment was argued before the current round of democratization by Thomas M. Callaghy in his essay, "Lost Between State and Market: The Politics of Economic Adjustment in Ghana, Zambia and Nigeria," in *Economic Crisis and Policy Choice,* ed. Joan M. Nelson (Princeton: Princeton University Press, 1990). On the more recent period, see Barbara Grosh, "Through the Structural Adjustment Minefield: Politics in an Era of Economic Liberalization," in *Economic Change and Political Liberalization in Sub-Saharan Africa,* ed. Jennifer A. Widner (Baltimore: Johns Hopkins Press, 1994), pp. 29–46; Henry Bienen and Jeffrey Herbst, "The Relationship Between Political and Economic Reform in Africa" (unpublished paper, USAID, 1995); and Ernest Harsch, "Structural Adjustment and Africa's Democracy Movements," *Africa Today* 40 (1993).

93. In a prescient essay, Larry Diamond made such arguments as early as 1988; see Diamond, "Introduction: Roots of Failure, Seeds of Hope," in *Democracy in Developing Countries: Volume Two, Africa,* ed. Larry Diamond, Juan J. Linz, and Seymour Martin Lipset (Boulder, Colo.: Lynne Rienner, 1988), pp. 26–8.

94. Paul M. Lubeck and Michael Watts, "An Alliance of Oil and Maize? The Response of Indigenous and State Capital to Structural Adjustment in Nigeria," in *African Capitalists in African Development,* ed. Bruce Berman and Colin Leys (Boulder, Colo.: Lynne Rienner, 1994), p. 214.

95. Adam Przeworski adds that successful economic reform is inherently a technocratic exercise, which is difficult to sell to the population. Przeworski, *Democracy and the Market.* Both these arguments are developed by the contributors to Peter Gibbon, Yusuf Bangura, and Arve Ofstad, *Authoritarianism and Democracy and Adjustment* (Uppsala, Sweden: Nordiska Afrika Institutet, 1992). In particular, see Bjorn Beckman's essay, "Empowerment or Repression? The World Bank and the Politics of African Adjustment."

96. Donald Share and Scott Mainwaring, "Transitions Through Transaction: Democratization in Brazil and Spain," in *Political Liberalization in Brazil,* ed. Wayne A. Selcher (Boulder, Colo.: Westview, 1986).

97. Huntington, *Third Wave,* p. 69. See also Mancur Olson, "Rapid Growth as a Destabilizing Force," *Journal of Economic History* 23 (1963): 453–72.

98. Max Weber, *The Protestant Ethic and the Spirit of Capitalism* (New York: Scribner's, 1958); also Ronald Inglehart, "The Renaissance of Political Culture," *American Political Science Review* 82 (1988): 1203–30.

99. Lucian W. Pye, *The Mandarin and the Cadre: China's Political Cultures* (Ann Arbor: Center for Chinese Studies, University of Michigan, 1988), pp. 30–5. See also, Pye, *Asian Power and Politics: The Cultural Dimension of Authority* (Cambridge: Belknap, 1985). For example, Pye shows how Maoist doctrines have interacted with older Confucian ideology to produce a distinctive political tradition, which affects all of the country's political institutions. He links the Chinese propensity for hierarchy, the emphasis on socialization, and the deep distrust of pluralism within the present political system to this twin heritage. Tucker presents a similar type of analysis regarding the fusion of old Russian and Stalinist traditions in the modern Soviet Union, in Robert C. Tucker, *Political Culture and Leadership in Soviet Russia* (New York: Norton, 1987); and Timothy J. Colton and Robert C. Tucker, *Patterns of Post-Soviet Leadership* (Boulder, Colo.: Westview, 1995).

100. Robert D. Putnam, *Making Democracy Work: Civic Traditions in Modern Italy* (Princeton: Princeton University Press, 1992). To explain why regional governments in northern Italy are more effective than their southern counterpart, Putnam points to norms and networks of civic engagement that were first fostered in the medieval city-states of Northern Italy and discouraged by the Norman regime in the highly centralized kingdom of Sicily.

101. *Ibid.,* p. 180. At least some work on democratization has suggested that such deep-seated traditions can affect the dynamics and outcome of transition. Huntington hypothesizes that the expansion of Christianity promotes democratization by emphasizing individual dignity and separation between church and state. He explains the predominance of Catholic countries among the democratizers of the Third Wave as the result of changes within the Catholic Church since the Second Vatican Council of the early 1960s. Huntington, *Third Wave,* pp. 82–5.

102. Naomi Chazan, "Between Liberalism and Statism: African Political Cultures and Democracy," in *Political Cultures and Democracy in Developing Countries,* ed.

Larry Diamond (Boulder, Colo.: Lynne Rienner, 1993), pp. 67–108. The quotation is from page 68.

103. Michael Schatzberg, "Power, Legitimacy and 'Democratization' in Africa," *Africa* 63 (1993): 445–61.

104. Bayart, *L'Etat en Afrique.*

105. In addition to Bayart's work, see Achille Mbembe, "Power and Obscenity in the Post-Colonial Period," in *Rethinking Third World Politics,* ed. James Manor (London: Longman, 1991), pp. 166–82; Comi Toulabor, "Jeu de Mots, Jeux de Vilains: Lexique de la Derision Politique au Togo," *Politique Africaine* (September 1981): 55–71; Michael Schatzberg, "Power, Legitimacy and 'Democratization' in Africa," *Africa* 63 (1993): 445–61; and Stephen Ellis, "Power and Rumour in Togo," *Africa* 63 (1993): 462–77.

106. See, for instance, T. Fernyhough, "Human Rights and Precolonial Africa," in *Human Rights and Governance in Africa,* ed. Robin Cohen et al. (Gainesville: University of Florida Press, 1993), pp. 39–73; D. Maxwell Owusu, "Democracy and Africa: A View from the Village," *Journal of Modern African Studies* 30 (1992): 369–96.

107. See, for instance, Claude Ake, "The Unique Case of African Democracy," 239–44; and Wamba-Dia-Wamba, "Beyond Elite Politics of Democracy in Africa," *Quest* 6 (June 1992): 28–41.

108. Michael Crowder, "Botswana and the Survival of Liberal Democracy in Botswana," in *Decolonization and African Independence: The Transfers of Power, 1960–1980,* ed. Prosser Gifford and William Roger Louis (New Haven: Yale University Press, 1988); and Patrick Molutsi and John Holm, "Developing Democracy When Civil Society is Weak," *African Affairs* 89 (1990): 323–40.

109. Fabien Eboussi-Boulaga, *Les Conférences Nationales en Afrique Noire: Une Affaire à Suivre* (Paris: Karthala, 1993).

110. Two excellent sets of contributions to this debate can be found in Walter O. Oyugi, ed., *Democratic Theory and Practice in Africa* (London: James Currey, 1988); and Patrick Chabal, ed., *Political Domination in Africa: Reflections on the Limits of Power* (Cambridge: Cambridge University Press, 1986).

111. Crawford Young, *The African Colonial State in Comparative Perspective* (New Haven: Yale University Press, 1994), p. 283. In the same section, Young also refers to the influence of "subliminal codes of operation" and "a mystique of power" coming from the colonial predecessor.

112. In Chabal, ed., *Political Domination (1986),* in particular the essay by John Lonsdale, "Political Accountability in African History," pp. 126–58.

113. Stephen Ellis, "Democracy in Africa: Achievements and Prospects," in *Action in Africa: The Experience of People in Government, Business and Aid,* ed. Douglas Rimmer (London: James Currey, 1994). Such approaches allow one to reinterpret economic arguments, within a political economy framework. Thus, the reliance of many African states on donor support for their revenues can in part be viewed as motivated by the low capacity of fiscal extraction, itself a product of a desire to avoid public accountability. The absence of a need to tax their populations has allowed African governments to continue the colonial state's status as essentially unconnected to the citizenry. Jane Guyer has assessed the impact of this at the local level in her fine essay on "Representation Without Taxation: An Essay on Democracy in Rural Nigeria," *African Studies Review* 35 (1992): 4–80.

114. Ruth Collier, *Regimes in Tropical Africa* (Berkeley: University of California Press, 1982); Jennifer A. Widner, "Political Reform in Anglophone and Francophone African Countries," in *Economic Change and Political Liberalization,* ed. Widner (Baltimore: Johns Hopkins University Press, 1994), pp. 49–79.

115. Juan J. Linz, "Totalitarian and Authoritarian Regimes," in *Handbook of Political Science,* vol. 3, ed. Fred Greenstein and Nelson Polsby (Reading, Mass.: Addison-Wesley, 1975), 191–357.

116. Robert A. Dahl, *Polyarchy: Participation and Opposition* (New Haven: Yale University Press, 1971), in particular, Ch. 1.

117. *Ibid.,* p. 4.

118. Huntington, *Third Wave,* 41–7, 588 and passim.

119. Alain Rouiquié, "Demilitarization and Institutionalization of Military-Dominated Polities in Latin America," in *Transitions from Authoritarian Rule: Comparative Perspectives,* ed. Guillermo O'Donnell, Philippe C. Schmitter, and Laurence Whitehead (Baltimore: Johns Hopkins University Press, 1986), pp. 108–36.

120. Karen L. Remmer, "Exclusionary Democracy," *Studies in Comparative International Development* 20 (1986): 64–85.

121. The definition is derived from Douglas North and is cited by James A. Caporaso and David Levine, *Theories of Political Economy* (Cambridge: Cambridge University Press, 1992), p. 149.

122. Maurice Duverger, *Political Parties: Their Organization and Activity* (New York: Wiley, 1963); Douglas Rae, *The Political Consequences of Electoral Laws* (New Haven: Yale University Press, 1967); and Arend Lijphart, "The Political Consequences of Electoral Laws, 1945–1985," *American Political Science Review* 84 (1990): 481–96.

123. See the essays in Peter A. Hall, ed., *The Political Power of Economic Ideas* (Princeton: Princeton University Press, 1989); and Margaret Weir and Theda Skocpol, "State Structures and the Possibilities of Keynsian Responses to the Great Depression in Sweden, Britain and the United States," in *Bringing the State Back In,* ed. Peter Evans et al. (Cambridge: Cambridge University Press, 1985), pp. 107–67.

124. See Peter Katzenstein, ed., *Between Power and Plenty* (Madison: University of Wisconsin Press, 1978); and Peter Gourevitch, *Politics in Hard Times: Comparative Responses to International Economic Crises* (New York: Oxford University Press, 1986).

125. See, for instance, Michael Bratton, "Beyond the State: Civil Society and Associational Life in Africa," *World Politics* 41 (1989): 407–30.

126. Douglass C. North, *Institutions, Institutional Change, and Economic Performance* (New York: Cambridge University Press, 1990), p. vii.

127. Terry Lynn Karl, "Dilemmas of Democratization in Latin America," *Comparative Politics* 22 (1990): 7.

128. Kathleen Thelen and Sven Steinmo, "Historical Institutionalism in Comparative Politics," in *Structuring Politics: Historical Institutionalism in Comparative Analysis,* ed. Steinmo, Thelen, and Frank Longstreth (Cambridge, Cambridge University Press, 1992), pp. 1–32. See also Peter Hall, *Governing the Economy: The Politics of State Intervention in Britain and France* (Oxford: Oxford University Press, 1986); and G. John Ikenberry, David A. Lake, and Michael Mastan-

duno, eds., *The State and American Foreign Policy* (Ithaca: Cornell University Press, 1988).

129. Thelen and Steinmo (1992) *Ibid.*, p. 3.
130. *Ibid.*, p. 7 (emphasis in original).
131. *Ibid.*, p. 12.
132. As Adam Przeworski says, "Reforms are precisely those modifications [to rules] of the organization of conflicts that alter the prior probabilities of realizing group interests given their resources." See "Some Problems in the Study of Transition to Democracy," in *Transitions from Authoritarian Rule: Comparative Perspectives*, eds. Guillermo O'Donnell, Philippe Schmitter, and Lawrence Whitehead (Baltimore: Johns Hopkins University Press, 1986), p. 58.
133. Thelen and Steinmo (1992), p. 10.
134. In Thelen and Steinmo's words, it is "less useful to subsume macro (systems level) structures into the definition of institutions than it is to maintain a narrower focus and examine how these forces are mediated by ... intermediate-level institutions." For example, "the salience of class to actual political behavior depends on the extent to which it is reinforced and reified through state and societal institutions – party competition, union structures, and the like" (11). They also argue that "Another of the strengths of historical institutionalism is that it has carved out an important theoretical niche at the middle range that can help us integrate an understanding of general patterns of political history with an explanation of the contingent nature of political and economic development" (27–8).
135. *Ibid.*, p. 2.
136. The debate was sparked by Juan J. Linz in "Excursus on Presidential and Parliamentary Democracy," in *The Breakdown of Democratic Regimes,* ed. Linz and Alfred Stepan (Baltimore: Johns Hopkins University Press, 1978). See also Linz, "On the Perils of Presidentialism," *Journal of Democracy* 1 (1990): 51–72; Donald L. Horowitz, "Comparing Democratic Systems," *Journal of Democracy* 1 (1990): 73–83; Scott Mainwaring, *Presidentialism, Multiparty Systems and Democracy: The Difficult Equation,* Kellogg Institute Working Paper, no. 144 (Notre Dame: University of Notre Dame, September 1990); and Alfred Stepan and Cindy Skach, *World Politics* 46 (1993): 1–22. Juan Linz and Arturo Valenzuela present an overview of these debates in *The Failure of Presidential Democracy: Comparative Perspectives* (Baltimore: Johns Hopkins University Press, 1995). For dissenting views that draw attention to varieties and strengths of presidential systems, see Matthew S. Shugart and John M. Carey, *Presidents and Assemblies: Constitutional Design and Electoral Dynamics* (Cambridge: Cambridge University Press, 1992); and Mark P. Jones, *Electoral Laws and the Survival of Presidential Democracies* (Notre Dame: University of Notre Dame Press, 1995).
137. Aristide Zolberg, "The Structure of Political Conflict in the New States of Tropical Africa," *American Political Science Review* 62 (1968): 70.
138. Thelen and Steinmo, *Historical Institutionalism,* p. 2.
139. For general theoretical discussions of this and related issues, see Anthony Giddens, *The Constitution of Society: An Outline of the Theory of Structuration* (Cambridge, Mass.: Polity Press, 1984); and Michael Taylor, "Structure, Culture and Action in the Explanation of Social Change," *Politics and Society* 17 (1989): 115–62.

140. Young, *African Colonial State,* p. 41.
141. Krasner, "Approaches to the State," 225.
142. Reuschemeyer, *Capitalist Development and Democracy,* p. 7.
143. Krasner, "Approaches to the State," 225.
144. *Ibid.*
145. Catherine Boone, *Merchant Capital and the Roots of State Power in Sénégal, 1930-1985* (Cambridge: Cambridge University Press, 1992), p. 4.
146. See Joel Migdal, *Strong Societies and Weak States: State-Society Relations and State Capabilities in the Third World* (Princeton: Princeton University Press, 1988).
147. Malloy and Seligson, *Authoritarians and Democrats: Regime Transition in Latin America* (Pittsburgh: University of Pittsburgh Press, 1987) p. 239.

2

NEOPATRIMONIAL RULE
IN AFRICA

Throughout this book we ask whether regime transitions in sub-Saharan Africa resemble democratization in other parts of the world. The nature of political authority and its embodiment in political institutions differ in Africa in several significant respects from other world regions that have undergone fundamental change in recent years. We contend that these differences critically affect the dynamics and outcomes of distinctive democratization processes in the sub-Saharan region. This chapter introduces this thesis by briefly reviewing the nature of formal and informal political institutions in postcolonial Africa. We then develop several hypotheses linking these institutions to specific traits of regime transitions in Africa in the early 1990s. We cast the argument comparatively in order to highlight differences among political regimes, both between Africa and the rest of the world but also among African countries themselves.

NEOPATRIMONIAL RULE

The institutional hallmark of politics in the *ancien régimes* of postcolonial Africa was neopatrimonialism. The term is derived from the concept of patrimonial authority, which Max Weber used to designate the principle of authority in the smallest and most traditional polities.[1] In patrimonial political systems, an individual rules by dint of personal prestige and power; ordinary folk are treated as extensions of the "big man's" household, with no rights or privileges other than those bestowed by the ruler. Authority is entirely personalized, shaped by the ruler's preferences rather than any codified system of laws. The ruler ensures the political stability of the regime and personal political survival by providing a zone of security in an uncertain environment and by selectively distributing favors and material benefits to loyal followers who are not citizens of the polity so much as the ruler's clients.

Weber distinguished patrimonial authority from rational-legal authority, in which the public sphere is carefully distinguished from the private sphere; written laws and bureaucratic institutions routinize the exercise of authority and protect individuals and their property from the whims of capricious leaders. His definition of patrimonialism may provide an accurate description of the political systems of small, isolated communities with rudimentary economies, including African chiefdoms in the precolonial era, and the practices of patrimonialism may persist at the local level in a number of different settings.[2] But it does not adequately characterize any of the national political systems existing in our times, the smallest and poorest of which possess bureaucratic institutions and written laws. Yet, it is clear that some nations in the developing world, most notably in sub-Saharan Africa, retain in modified form many of the characteristics of patrimonial rule. As a result, political scientists have found it useful to characterize as *neopatrimonial* those hybrid political systems in which the customs and patterns of patrimonialism co-exist with, and suffuse, rational-legal institutions.[3]

As with classic patrimonialism, the right to rule in neopatrimonial regimes is ascribed to a person rather than to an office, despite the official existence of a written constitution. One individual (the strongman, "big man," or "supremo"), often a president for life, dominates the state apparatus and stands above its laws. Relationships of loyalty and dependence pervade a formal political and administrative system, and officials occupy bureaucratic positions less to perform public service, their ostensible purpose, than to acquire personal wealth and status. Although state functionaries receive an official salary, they also enjoy access to various forms of illicit rents, prebends, and petty corruption, which constitute a sometimes important entitlement of office. The chief executive and his inner circle undermine the effectiveness of the nominally modern state administration by using it for systematic patronage and clientelist practices in order to maintain political order. Moreover, parallel and unofficial structures may well hold more power and authority than the formal administration. To summarize, the characteristic feature of neopatrimonialism is the incorporation of patrimonial logic into bureaucratic institutions.

Insofar as personalized exchanges, clientelism, and political corruption are common in all regimes, theorists have suggested that neopatrimonialism is a master concept for comparative politics, at least in the developing world. Robin Theobold argues that "some of the new states are, properly speaking, not states at all; rather, they are virtually the private instruments of those powerful enough to rule."[4] Christopher Clapham claims that neopatrimonialism is "the most salient type [of authority]" in the Third World because it "corresponds to the normal forms of social organization in precolonial societies."[5] We make a finer distinction – namely, that although neopatrimonial practices can be found in all polities, it is the *core* feature of politics in Africa and in a small number of other states, including Haiti, and perhaps Indonesia and the Philippines.[6] Whereas personal relationships occur on the margins of all bureaucratic systems, they constitute the foundation and superstructure of political institutions in Africa. As a result, scholars of African politics have embraced the neopatrimonial model,[7] or they have analyzed the same general phenomena under related theoretical labels, including "personal rule," "prebendalism," and the "politics of the belly."[8]

Does it make sense to speak of neopatrimonial institutions? Can the practices we have described be viewed as defining rules and norms that shape individual behavior and structure societal relationships? Jackson and Rosberg answer "no," stating that in Africa, "the rulers and other leaders take precedence over the formal rules of the political game ... the rules do not effectively regulate political behavior."[9] Neopatrimonialism *does* undermine formal rules and institutions, and it may be true that in the despotic tyrannies of a small number of leaders like Idi Amin or Macias Nguema, politics becomes almost entirely arbitrary and unpredictable. Nonetheless, we argue that when patrimonial logic is internalized in the formal institutions of neopatrimonial regimes, it provides essential operating codes for politics that are valued, recurring, and reproduced over time.[10] In Africa, these same practices exist across more than 40 countries and have persisted after the death or retirement of the first generation of national leaders. The broad routinization of an established set of behavioral norms and procedures is testimony that neopatrimonial practices are more than the idiosyncratic expressions of individual leaders. In particular, it is possible to discern at least three – albeit informal – political institutions that have been typically stable, predictable, and valued in Africa's neopatrimonial regimes.

PRESIDENTIALISM

The first such institution we call *presidentialism*. Presidentialism implies the systematic concentration of political power in the hands of one individual, who resists delegating all but the most trivial decision-making tasks. In Africa, personal dictators emerged from either the army or a dominant political party, but they consolidated power by asserting total personal control over formal political structures.[11] As a result on consolidation, presidentialism contributed to the weakening of already frail structures within the military, the judiciary, and the civil service. Ironically, the disempowerment of formal institutions vis-à-vis the presidency was accompanied by the multiplication of public offices and the increasing size of governments in postcolonial Africa. It was not unusual for cabinets to include some 35 to 50 offices; yet ministers were virtually powerless, because all significant decisions were made in the president's office or through personal emissaries. As Hastings Banda put it in 1972, "Nothing is not my business in this country: everything is my business, everything. The state of education, the state of our economy, the state of our agriculture, the state of our transport, everything is my business."[12]

Although presidentialism promoted some formal institutions – notice the predilection for presidential constitutions – we are referring to the informal dimensions of the term. Across Africa, power was deeply personalized. Political life was structured around dyadic exchanges between strongmen and their acolytes, which together comprised clientelist pyramids and factional networks. Strongmen also exerted considerable discretion over national patterns of domination. Over time, rulers like Kenneth Kaunda in Zambia, Sekou Touré in Guinea, and Felix Houphouët-Boigny in Côte d'Ivoire left a deep personal imprint on national politics, molding their countries' political rules and rhetoric. The personalization of power was both cause and consequence of the political longevity of neopatrimonial rulers. They were more likely to remain in power than leaders in other regime types; regular coups d'état and the appearance of political instability notwithstanding, the average African leader from independence to 1987 still retained power considerably longer than counterparts in postcolonial Latin America or Asia.[13]

Neopatrimonial rulers were also likely to promote a cult of personality. They dominated the national media, which described their every public action with gushing enthusiasm; their likenesses graced the currency, their portraits hung in every public building, and the national printing press periodically published collections of their speeches and writings. As Ellis writes, "The cultivation of religious and cultural symbols ... [was] calculated to demonstrate to the Togolese that Eyadéma was semi-divine and that his government was endowed with supernatural authority."[14] After a time, the style and symbolism of national politics came to reflect the personalities of the leader. Under the guise of his policy of *authenticité* for example, Mobutu convinced Zairians to abandon their Christian first names, adopt *abacos* (the special collarless jackets he liked to wear), and address each other as *citoyen*.[15]

Moreover, like a traditional monarch, the neopatrimonial leader often cultivated the image of the pater familias, who was directly responsible for the people's welfare and was willing to entertain and redress individual grievances personally, without the intermediation of the state apparatus. Paternalistic rhetoric was used to legitimate nondemocratic authority. As Schatzberg has argued, "The imagery and language of father and family are widespread in Africa because they strike a resonant and deeply embedded cultural chord."[16] This paternalism was present in official discourse, which often encouraged a view of the ruler as that of a stern but fair father figure.

In addition, supreme leaders openly encouraged public expressions of personal beneficence. Houphouët-Boigny, for example, engaged in regular "dialogues" with groups of citizens in a practice clearly meant to evoke the palaver of the traditional chieftaincies.[17] In tours around the country, he would meet local elites, listen to their grievances, and promise redress. The systematic recourse to clientelism that was the hallmark of these regimes ritualized face-to-face contact between the ruler and his subjects. This paternalism cut both ways, for the state's coercive tendencies were also highly personalized, from the widely accepted rumors in Togo that Eyadéma practiced black magic against his political enemies, to the perhaps apocryphal stories that Ahidjo personally approved all exit visas for Cameroonians wishing to leave the country, or that Nguema Macias of Equatorial Guinea personally participated in the physical torture of his political enemies.[18] Here too, rumor and exaggeration were encouraged by rulers eager to cultivate a larger-than-life image.

As a result of presidentialism, African political regimes were distinctly non-bureaucratic, despite the fact that they possessed a large state apparatus with all the outward trappings of a formal-legal order. Nor could they be viewed as corporatist, a label that is sometimes given to the authoritarian regimes of Latin America or Asia. Leaders of postcolonial African countries may have pursued a corporatist strategy to the extent that they attempted to direct political mobilization along controlled channels. But African leaders rarely used bureaucratic formulas to construct authoritative institutions and seldom granted subsidiary spheres of influence to occupational interest groups within civil society. African regimes did not display the formal governing coalitions between organized state and social interests or the collective bargaining over core public policies that characterize corporatism. At best, African efforts to install corporatist regimes constituted a policy output of an ambitious political elite rather than a reflection of strong class interests within domestic society.

Moreover, power was absolute. Personal rulers dominated their political systems to a much larger extent than is the case in bureaucratic polities. Power was not restrained by legal niceties or systems of checks and balances. That does not mean that these rulers were omnipotent; typically the weak and ineffectual state apparatus responded to their orders fitfully, and the rulers were often constrained by the need to maintain balance across complex ethnic or clan divisions. Yet it does mean that rulers and their closest cronies were not bound by the dictates of the law and tried to emasculate or eliminate formal institutional checks on the executive. The independence of the legislative and judicial branches was severely limited, and neopatrimonial rulers were typically deeply suspicious of any form of institutional pluralism. As a result, neopatrimonial regimes were typically highly exclusionary and the strongman tended to rule by decree; institutions of participation existed in name only and could not check the absolute powers of the chief executive. The strongman may even have preempted his own removal from office by declaring himself president-for-life. As we shall see later, there was, nonetheless, a wide and significant variation in the degree to which plural and participatory institutions managed to endure in these regimes.

In sum, neopatrimonial leaders consciously promoted an image of omnipotence, which exaggerated the already considerable degree to which they dominated national politics. Both the reality and the myths of presidentialism suggest that the personal interaction between the "big man" and his extended retinue *defined* African politics, from the highest reaches of the presidential palace to the humblest village assembly.

CLIENTELISM

A second informal institution of neopatrimonialism was *systematic clientelism*. Neopatrimonial strongmen all relied on the award of personal favors. Within the state, these favors typically took the form of public sector jobs; within society, the distribution of public resources through licenses, contracts, and projects. In return for material rewards, clients mobilized political support and referred all decisions upward in a mark of loyalty to patrons.[19] This happened at every level; at the top, the ruler's faithful political aristocracy was rewarded with prebendal control of public offices, monopoly rents, and the possibility of creating its own clientelist networks. These positions as a result demonstrated a seemingly inexorable increase over time. In Côte d'Ivoire, Tessy Bakary notes, the number of departments, sub-prefectures, and communes went from 4, 19, and 17 at independence to 36, 137, and 135, respectively, by 1987. Similarly, the average size of cabinets increased by a factor of 2.5 during the same period, the Economic and Social Council went from 25 to 120 members, and the single party's political bureau increased from 15 to 302. This inventory does not include positions in the diplomatic service or the parastatal sector, also in rapid expansion during this period.[20] Typically, these positions came with various perks such as official house and car, staff, and pension. Nor were patronage and clientelist benefits limited to the political aristocracy; Bates and Collier report that Kenneth Kaunda controlled 40,000 patronage positions in Lusaka alone during the 1980s, through the United National Independence Party (UNIP), which he dominated.[21]

Systematic clientelism led neopatrimonial rulers to promote state intervention in the economy. The fact that political authority rested on the selective allocation of state resources to individuals created a powerful incentive for extensive regulation of economic activity, through which the incumbent elite gained control over a wide range of monopolies and economic rents. In sum, public resources were privatized to the benefit of the coterie of presidential loyalists. To a certain extent, these dynamics describe all types of political regimes, but African neopatrimonial regimes were distinctive in the extent to which systematic clientelism was generalized. A fiscal study of Cameroon estimated that various exemptions granted by the government and tax fraud resulted in a revenue shortfall equivalent to 18 to 22 percent of gross domestic product (GDP).[22] A study of tax administration in the Gambia estimated the losses associated with tax evasion at 70 percent of total public revenue, noting that only a fifth of all registered companies filed income tax returns.[23] In other words, by setting high rates of taxation, governments created various economic rents that could be used to dispense political favors. In other countries, it was not unusual for one third of all imports to benefit from a special political exemption from import duty. Indeed, in neopatrimonial regimes, virtually all economic policy was motivated at least in part by the economic rents provided to the state elite.

STATE RESOURCES

A third informal institution was the *use of state resources* for political legitimation, and it was closely linked to the reliance on clientelism. Neopatrimonial leaders made little distinction between the public and private coffers, routinely and extensively dipping into the state treasury for their own political needs. President Ahidjo of Cameroon kept a large proportion of his country's oil revenues in a personal offshore bank account, to be spent during the course of the year as he saw fit. Houphouët-Boigny regularly pocketed a tenth of his country's cocoa exports, spending it on grandiose prestige projects that flattered his image as the country's founding father.[24] Mobutu amassed a huge personal fortune, widely assumed to be roughly equivalent to Zaire's national debt, largely by extracting a cut from the country's diamond and copper exports.[25] When state coffers ran dry by 1992, however, Mobutu returned the favor by using this "rainy day fund" to meet the army's wage bill, suggesting that the purloined spoils had never been meant to serve as personal enrichment for its own sake.

As a consequence of both clientelism and the use of state resources, neopatrimonial regimes demonstrated very little developmental capacity. Lacking political legitimacy, rulers survived through coercion and clientelism but often failed to exercise complete control over the polity. The large state apparatus they had created as much for patronage as anything else was costly as well as inept, undisciplined, and unresponsive to their orders. Public investment was inadequate because a disproportionate share of public monies went to pay a bloated salary bill for the large number of offices reserved for the political class. In sum, there was a contradiction between the regime's redistributive practices and long-term accumulation.[26] Typically, public infrastructure was poorly maintained and state agents lacked operating funds; office equipment was old and run down, the few state cars that were functioning were privately appropriated by top officials, and gas coupons were sold for profit or not budgeted for. As a result, the state was barely proficient at even basic functions and was further undermined in the 1980s by the growing fiscal crisis, which resulted in sharply reduced real salaries. In effect, the neopatrimonial state exercised only limited effective sovereignty over the national territory; outlying regions were not fully policed and the state could neither enforce its own laws and regulations nor prevent fraud along its borders.

Moreover, the constant redistribution of state resources for political purposes led to endemic fiscal crisis and diminished prospects for sustained economic growth.[27] The dynamics of neopatrimonial rule ensured that African states routinely outspent their revenues by a large margin. Pervasive rent-seeking and political manipulation of economic policy resulted in a state apparatus that was both too large relative to the economy and too weak to effectively collect revenues.[28] The high-level corruption in Nigeria during the early 1990s led to the disappearance of oil revenues for the state that were worth as much as a tenth of GDP each year.[29] Indeed, the recent history of Africa was characterized by a decline in state revenues as a proportion of the economy, particularly as the continent's economic crisis worsened during the 1980s. By 1980, central government revenues amounted to 18.3 percent of gross national product in the 23 African countries for which there were data, compared to an average of 30.5 percent in OECD countries.[30] Because of this low extractive capacity, most African states came to rely increasingly on foreign aid to pay for basic functions. In Zambia, for instance, aid was equivalent to 32.7 percent of GNP by 1993, whereas government revenues amounted to 11.9 percent of GDP in 1991, down from some 27 percent in 1980.[31]

Concomitantly, neopatrimonialism created an economic climate of uncertainty and risk that scared away investors or directed them toward short-term speculation. The viability of existing enterprises was undermined by the exactions of state agents, as well as by the doldrums in the economy. As a result, African economies suffered from a shortage of long-term private investment, which further condemned them to slow economic growth. The state's need for revenues, coupled with an inability to confront the politically powerful, led it to tax excessively a narrow range of economic agents. For most of Africa's postcolonial history, that meant the taxation of the cash-crop–producing peasantry, which responded by decreasing its output or smuggling agricultural products to neighboring countries.[32] The case of Ghana was egregious: In the world's largest producer of cocoa at independence, with a peak of 560,000 tons in 1965, cocoa production declined to 249,000 tons by 1979, largely because state taxation undermined producer incentives. By 1970, the government passed on less than 37 percent of total cocoa export receipts to the producers themselves, down from 72 percent in 1960.[33]

INSTITUTIONAL VARIATIONS IN AFRICAN REGIMES

That virtually all African regimes could be viewed as neopatrimonial should not obscure the significant variation in political institutions that evolved across the different states in the region. Typologies of sub-Saharan political regimes have been advanced in the African politics literature to capture such institutional differences.[34] Following Dahl's classic formulation, we find it useful to distinguish among neopatrimonial regimes according to the extent of political competition (or contestation) and the degree of political participation (or inclusion).[35]

POLITICAL COMPETITION

First, Africa's neopatrimonial regimes varied in the extent to which at least some members of the political system were allowed to compete over elected positions or public policy. Even when state elites worked to eliminate, control, or coopt opposition parties, they sometimes tolerated pluralism within the single party or in the lobbying activities of nonstate associations. At one extreme, opposition parties were formed and even allowed into the legislature in a small number of countries. At the other extreme, some governments banned any and all questioning of the policies formulated by an inner group of politicians. In between, islands of contestation were tolerated, either independently of the state or formally under the authority of the ruling party.

A cursory examination of electoral competition since African independence confirms this variation. Elections in Africa are generally depicted as empty and largely symbolic exercises designed to legitimate officeholders. And, indeed, following a lone competitive election at independence, that is apparently what many African elections became. Between independence and 1989, 106 presidential and 185 direct parliamentary elections were held in the 47 countries of sub-Saharan Africa (Table 1). In the presidential elections, the winning candidate on average reportedly received 92 percent of the vote; moreover, in 64 of those elections, the winner officially received above 95 percent of the votes, whereas the opposition candidate won at least a quarter of the vote in only 10 cases. Thus, for instance, Houphouët-Boigny won all six of the presidential elections held in Côte d'Ivoire between 1960 and 1989, with a reported average of 99.7 percent of the vote. A bit more competition was tolerated in parliamentary elections, perhaps because they threatened less the power of the ruler, but even here the winning party won an average of 83 percent of the votes and 88 percent of the seats. In 29 countries, opposition parties were never allowed to win a single seat over the course of 150 separate elections. Since these averages include the relatively open elections held right at independence, they really do suggest that, at least in terms of political competition, elections were largely empty rituals.

Indeed, in many of the countries of the region, rulers could not countenance electoral challenge and used elections in an entirely self-serving manner. As Chazan noted, "The essential purpose of the ballot in this type of election is to provide the existing government a semblance of popular approval."[36] In fact, governments in these countries were quick to discontinue elections when they threatened to lead to the expression of discontent. But elections were not necessarily completely meaningless in political terms. They provided opportunities for the strongman to tour the country, dispense favors, hone the regime's ideological rhetoric, and, as we show in the next chapter, mobilize a measure of political participation through the ruling party. But generally they did not include meaningful political competition.

Nonetheless, one can distinguish at least three forms of limited electoral competition in postcolonial Africa. First, a small number of regimes consistently sustained multiparty politics from independence onward. Botswana, the Gambia, Mauritius, Sénégal (at least since 1980), and Zimbabwe all provide examples of stable, functioning multiparty rule, in which reasonably free and fair elections were held on a regular basis. It is easy to see flaws in these democracies; with the exception of Mauritius, the stability of democratic rule was facilitated by the presence of a dominant party, which was never seriously challenged; thus, the majority party in Botswana, the Gambia, and Sénégal won an average of 85.8 percent, 81.7 percent, and 86.8 percent, respectively, of seats contested in multiparty elections. In all cases, the opposition was harassed, and patterns of electoral abuse witnessed elsewhere on the continent were not entirely absent. Nonetheless, these states had begun to institutionalize multiparty electoral competition before 1989.

Second, some countries experienced brief interludes of democratic rule between longer periods of authoritarianism. Excluding the five countries just discussed, we found 19 elections in 12 countries since 1970 in which an opposition party won at least one seat. These elections typically occurred in countries charac-

Table 1. *Elections in Sub-Saharan Africa, Independence to 1989*

Country	Presidential Elections	Winner's Share (mean % votes)	Legislative Elections	Winner's Share (mean % seats)
Angola	0	—	0	—
Bénin	3	84.2	5	100.0
Botswana	0	—	5	85.8
Burkina Faso	2	77.3	3	57.0
Burundi	1	99.6	2	81.8
Cameroon	6	97.6	8	90.9
Cape Verde	0	—	2	100.0
Central African Republic	3	80.5	3	95.3
Chad	2	96.2	2	100.0
Comoros	2	99.7	3	73.7
Congo	2	100.0	5	100.0
Côte d'Ivoire	6	99.7	6	100.0
Djibouti	2	87.3	2	100.0
Eq. Guinea	2	97.9	2	100.0
Ethiopia	0	—	6	100.0
Gabon	5	99.6	7	95.1
Gambia	2	65.7	5	81.7
Ghana	2	75.5	4	76.1
Guinea	5	99.7	4	100.0
Guinea–Bissau	0	—	0	—
Kenya	0	—	6	99.1
Lesotho	0	—	1	38.3
Liberia	6	82.6	6	89.8
Madagascar	5	86.8	7	74.2
Malawi	0	—	4	100.0
Mali	2	99.9	5	100.0
Mauritania	4	97.7	4	100.0
Mauritius	0	—	4	57.3
Mozambique	0	—	0	—
Namibia	0	—	1	—
Niger	3	99.8	3	100.0
Nigeria	2	40.6	3	56.5
Rwanda	5	97.3	5	100.0
São Tomé	0	—	0	—
Sénégal	6	87.7	7	93.4
Seychelles	3	95.6	3	100.0
Sierra Leone	2	97.6	6	62.5
Somalia	1	99.9	4	78.7
South Africa	0	—	8	71.8
Sudan	3	98.2	8	70.6
Swaziland	0	—	1	87.5
Tanzania	6	94.9	5	100.0
Togo	5	98.3	4	100.0
Uganda	0	—	4	68.4
Zaire	3	99.1	5	92.8
Zambia	5	83.4	6	89.9
Zimbabwe	0	—	1	80.0
Total/Average	106	92.0	185	88.0

terized by political instability and fragmentation in which a succession of military and civilian rulers failed to overcome the complex ethnoregional divisions that undermined regime legitimacy. These elections were often tainted by accusations of fraud, and their deficiencies contributed to the delegitimation of the democratic order, but they did include real political competition. Nigeria's Second Republic, for example, held multiparty elections in 1979 and 1983. In each, there was considerable malpractice both before and during the polling, and the September 1983 elections were marred by extensive violence and increased ethnic tensions. The December 31, 1983, coup that ended the Second Republic actually singled out these electoral problems as justification for military intervention.[37]

Third, and more ambiguously, some of Africa's single-party regimes institutionalized limited but real competition within the ruling party. The party presented more than one candidate for each parliamentary district or held competitive primaries before legislative elections. In these cases, the electorate had a chance to vote an incumbent representative out of power. Detailed analysis of these elections was beyond the scope of our study, but we identified 14 countries with at least one intraparty competitive election (including Cameroon and Togo in the 1980s) and a smaller number of countries (notably Kenya, Tanzania, Zambia in the 1970s, and Côte d'Ivoire after 1980) in which rules of intraparty competition were in place for several elections. The impact on the political class was occasionally quite marked; for example, in the 1985 Ivoirian parliamentary elections, only 64 members of the outgoing parliament were reelected in a field of 546 candidates for 175 seats. Similarly, in the 1985 Togolese elections, only 20 out of 66 deputies were reelected. In the 1988 Zambian elections, two sitting senior ministers were defeated.

Granted, such competition was always controlled. Neopatrimonial rulers used emerging electoral institutions to assert presidential prerogatives over the single party and to discipline the political class.[38] Even when the strongman did not intervene in the selection of candidates, the electoral turnover of legislators clearly weakened party notables relative to the president. The attractiveness of intraparty competition may well have derived from the fact that it facilitated the circulation of elites and introduced fresh blood into the system, yet never shook the legitimacy of the regime or of the ruler himself.[39] And because a member of parliament could expect a generous salary and allowances, it also enabled the patron to redistribute desirable patronage positions. Indeed, the size of legislatures was expanded to accommodate the demand for paid posts; the average African legislature grew from 89.5 seats to 140 seats between the first parliamentary postindependence election and the end of 1989. This inflation was very clear in Côte d'Ivoire, for instance, where the parliament grew from 70 to 175 seats between 1960 and 1989, and in Zambia, where it grew from 75 to 136.

The extent to which controlled intraparty competition actually added to the competitiveness of the regime was uncertain, but it was potentially significant. It allowed a measure of parliamentary accountability to voter concerns as incumbents and challengers struggled to demonstrate an ability to bring home the bacon. Barkan captures well these dynamics in the Kenya of the 1970s when he writes that elections amounted to "local referenda on the ability of individual incumbents to secure state resources for their home areas.... Because elections were truly competitive, incumbents were held accountable for their activities and forced to be attentive to the concerns of their constituents."[40]

Elections provided one indicator of the degree of competition, but there were others as well. In particular, it was possible to notice key differences among African regimes in the degree of institutional pluralism that survived in civil and political society through the 1970s and 1980s. Most African regimes tried to eliminate, weaken, or take over any nongovernmental institution that might contest their legitimacy and authority. These included opposition political parties, which were illegal in 32 states as late as 1989. Also included were a wide variety of nongovernmental organizations, such as farmer associations and producer cooperatives, trade unions, professional groups, and business associations, as well as media organizations. As a result of state-directed repression and cooptation, civil society was generally weak and less developed in Africa than elsewhere in the developing world.

Nonetheless, the available data on associational life suggests striking contrasts within Africa. In 1989, four countries in the sub-Saharan subcontinent did not have a single registered trade union, and only one officially sanctioned union was tolerated in an additional total of 18 countries. At the other extreme, 16 African countries could claim at least five legally registered trade unions. Similarly with business associations: The 16 countries with only one or fewer such groups could be contrasted with the nine countries in which at least 10 business bodies were officially registered. Such examples could be multiplied – for example, with reference to churches and the press. They suggest that, in associational life as in the conduct of national elections, the degree of institutionalized political competition in Africa was far from constant across African regimes.

POLITICAL PARTICIPATION

African regimes also varied in the degree of political participation allowed. Because of limited institutional pluralism, decision making in public affairs was typically restricted to elites with a narrow social base. Only rarely was the population at large consulted about public policies, and then through a single party or approved membership associations. Kasfir has argued that most African regimes tried to circumscribe political participation, by "shrinking" the public arena in the years after independence.[41] Relative to the heady days of the independence struggle that may well be true. Nonetheless, most regimes continued to allow some participation and were much more likely to clamp down on competition.

Here, too, significant differences are apparent from a survey of the countries in Africa. We tabulated the number and frequency of elections, and recorded the officially reported voter turnout rates. To repeat, between independence and the end of 1989, there were 106 presidential and 185 direct parliamentary elections in the 47 countries of the sub-Saharan region, for an average of 2.30 and 4.02 elections, respectively (see Table 1). These averages mask sharp differences; thus, 16 countries never held a single presidential election, but 12 held four or more. Parliamentary elections were more evenly distributed; 13 countries held two elections or fewer, and 20 held five or more. We should not forget that the very choice not to hold direct elections was a way of limiting participation in some countries.

Some sense of the extent of political participation can be obtained with reference to voter turnout rates: first, the proportion of registered voters that was said to have turned out; and second, the proportion of the total population that reportedly voted.[42] Here, too there was surprising variation. The range across all countries for which we have data are an average 85.2 percent and 39.3 percent, respectively, for presidential elections and an average 77.8 percent and 33.5 percent for parliamentary elections. But these voter turnout rates are difficult to interpret; officially proclaimed, they were clearly manipulated in many instances. Nonetheless, the data did not suggest the kinds of obstacles to widespread participation that scholars have reported for Latin America.[43] In fact, there were virtually no de jure limits on the franchise in postcolonial Africa. In contrast to the historical record in Europe or Latin America, African states never instituted literacy, gender, property, or income requirements for the right to vote.

If anything, reported participation rates were suspiciously high and suggest considerable fraud, at least in some countries. What are we to make of the official results for elections in Côte d'Ivoire and Cameroon, for example, according to which well over 90 percent of registered voters – or roughly two thirds of the adult population – voted six times in less than three decades in noncompetitive contests? Even allowing for fraud, however, participation rates did vary, particularly the percentage of the adult population voting. For instance, in the 1988 presidential election in Sénégal, 59 percent of all registered voters cast a ballot, but this amounted to little more than roughly a third of the total population. Less than half of the adult population voted, on average, in 10 countries holding at least one election, according to official numbers. Low turnout may well have been a way for voters to show their dissatisfaction with available candidate choices, or it may have reflected more mundane apathy, reinforced by the practical difficulties of registering and casting a ballot.[44] In any event, and except in the racial oligarchies of South Africa and Namibia, low turnout did not necessarily imply governmental attempts to limit the franchise, as in other parts of the world.

How can we explain these differences in degrees of political competition and participation across countries? A full explanation is well beyond the scope of this study, but some national patterns are evident. First, variation can be traced to the political dynamics of the immediate postindependence years; the circumstances in which different leaders consolidated power partly determined the degree of pluralism that came to characterize the existing regime.[45] When a dominant party emerged early during the period of competitive party politics at indepen-

Table 2. *Elections in Which Winning Party Failed to Gain a Majority of Seats*

Country	Election	Seats/ Total	Winning Party	Outcome in Parliament
Sudan	1958	63/173	UMMA	dissolved 1958
Nigeria	1979	168/449	NPN	dissolved 1983
Lesotho	1970	23/60	BNP	dissolved 1970[a]
Sudan	1986	100/260	UMMA	dissolved 1989
Sudan	1965	75/173	UMMA	dissolved 1968
Uganda	1963	37/82	UPC	dissolved 1969
Sierra Leone	1963	28/62	SLPP	—
Sudan	1968	101/218	UDP	dissolved 1968
Sierra Leone	1967	32/66	APC	military coup[b]
Mauritius	1976	34/70	MMM	—
Burkina Faso	1978	28/57	UDV–RDA	dissolved 1980

[a]Electoral results are invalidated and election is suspended by sitting prime minister.
[b]Military coup is reversed following junior officer countercoup, which restores Siaka Stevens's All People's Congress government to power in April 1968.

dence, that party was typically able to integrate, coopt, or eliminate other political parties and to install stable civilian single-party rule, at least until the first leader retired. This was the pattern in countries like Tanzania, Côte d'Ivoire, and Zambia. In the absence of a dominant party from the independence struggle, ensuing regimes were characterized by considerable instability and a greater reliance on coercion, notably through military intervention.[46]

A closer look at electoral data confirms that close elections that did not decisively promote one political party over the others were associated with political instability in postcolonial Africa. Table 2 lists all elections held in sub-Saharan Africa between independence and 1989 in which the incumbent party did not win a majority of seats. In each case, except following elections in Sierra Leone in 1962 and Mauritius in 1976, the parliament was dissolved extralegally within the next couple of years. It is difficult to separate cause and effect. Minority governments were more likely to be contested, particularly in ethnically divided countries, and to result in party fragmentation. Intense partisanship and infighting, fueled by the zero-sum struggle for state resources, often mobilized ethnic identities and led to societal polarization. On the other hand, in countries like Tanzania, ethnic fragmentation did not lead to political conflict, for the ruling party was able to garner support throughout the country.

Partly overlapping this first set of factors, distinct variants of neopatrimonial regimes emerged as a result of specific historical attempts to overcome tensions created by ethnic, linguistic, and regional heterogeneity, which varied markedly across states. Very few regimes in Africa adopted a discourse of exclusivity, preferring to expend resources to promote cultural assimilation and a sense of nationhood.[47] Participatory rituals were considered useful precisely because they provided rulers with carefully controlled opportunities to demonstrate broad-based legitimacy.

Rulers used a variety of mechanisms to attempt to maintain national cohesion and their own popularity. Within a number of countries, for instance, great efforts were made to equilibrate public expenditures across regions. Rothchild notes for Kenya and Nigeria during the late 1970s and early 1980s that public expenditures were patterned on a "proportionality principle" to achieve fairness among provinces, and his survey of the senior staff of the Ghana civil service in 1972 showed "remarkably close parallels between the ethnic proportions in the civil service and the society at large."[48] Sometimes rulers agreed informally to rough ethnic, communal, or regional quotas for official positions. Even more commonly, leaders extended material inducements to a smaller set of social elites in order to promote various kinds of accommodation within the political class, arrangements that resulted in relatively high levels of elite participation and competition.[49] In these regimes, rulers promoted intermediaries who represented specific subnational constituencies at the top of the government.[50] These served as the rulers' emissaries and ensured that constituencies received fair shares of state benefits. The ruler might devolve this role to traditional chiefs in recognition of their authority, or he might designate members of the political class, notably through appointments to cabinet-level positions. If the latter, cabinet reshuffles were interpreted in terms of an elaborate ethnic calculus in which each group was assumed to be entitled to a recognized ratio of seats.

The ethnic calculus led to constant pressure to increase the number of important offices, so that the demands of diverse groups could be met. Even as it expanded competition within the political elite, the proliferation of positions complicated the supremo's ability to manage the regime. Could the members of the political aristocracy be trusted? Would they eventually wrest away the clientelist networks and rents on which rule was founded? Neopatrimonial leaders responded to such fears by systematically promoting the turnover of officeholders: No minister, backbencher, parastatal manager, governor, or prefect could ever be allowed to forget that a position was owed to the strongman, who could and would take it away sooner or later. Particularly vulnerable were men and women who had committed *lèse majesté* by developing independent networks of influence and power.

This dynamic helps to explain why so many rulers were willing to introduce competition within the single party; the introduction of such reforms in Cameroon, Togo, and Côte d'Ivoire during the 1980s signaled in each case a clear executive attempt to weaken the political class. More generally it explains one of the striking characteristics of these regimes: the rapid turnover of personnel. Thus, during Ahidjo's 24 years in power, he had 8 different ministers of finance, 11 ministers of agriculture, 12 ministers of the national economy, and 9 ministers of foreign affairs.[51]

Managing the political class by the circulation of officeholders strengthened the hand of the supremo but had the inbuilt disadvantage of generating an entire class of discontented elites. Leaders could always bring purged barons back to defuse emerging problems; a case in point is Mobutu's on-again, off-again relationships with Nguza Karl-I-Bond and Etienne Tshisekedi, in which the two men were repeatedly brought back from disgrace and even prison to occupy high-level positions in Mobutu's cabinet. Nonetheless, over time, the ranks of the discontented swelled, particularly after the economic and fiscal crisis erupted in the 1980s and began to necessitate the state's retrenchment and its acceptance of a freer civil society. As Heilbrunn notes, "Disaffected elites resented their exclusion from the patronage networks of authoritarian regimes and hence established independent bases of power in voluntary associations beyond the immediate reach of the state."[52]

These practices did increase political participation and competition in some states. All African neopatrimonial regimes, it should be emphasized, however, promoted social stratification and inequality. In some cases, the intermediate barons served their communities well and promoted significant reallocation of state resources across the territory. Nonetheless, their interest in representing a constituency was often essentially fictitious, and the effective redistribution that took place was limited to a relatively small elite. As Schatzberg writes, using neopatrimonial metaphors, "A major social and political divide thus occurs between those who can 'eat' and those who cannot; between those who command the forces of the night and those who are its victims.... In most cases, the 'winners' ... are usually inside the state, while the losers are usually on the outside looking in."[53]

Other regimes pursued approaches that relied more extensively on a mixture of ideology and coercion to maintain national unity and political stability. As a result, they were less likely to tolerate participation and competition. This was often the case for military regimes. Military coups were more likely in countries that had failed to emerge from independence with a stable government, often because of factional disputes within the political class.[54] Once the military intervened a first time, it suppressed formal institutions of competition and participation, which it argued had caused the instability and which it probably viewed as a threat to its own hold on power. Newly installed military regimes invariably outlawed political parties and independent associations, closed parliaments, and circumscribed the jurisdiction of civilian tribunals.

Yet military leaders soon found it difficult to rule without recourse to civilian institutions. Almost immediately, they were forced to call on civil servants to provide the technical expertise necessary to keep the government running. Over time, they began to adopt many of the institutional practices they had initially derided. Following Mobutu's lead, such rulers distanced themselves from the military and sought to civilianize their regimes, including by perfecting neopatrimony. Nonetheless, countries that had lived through military rule for any length of time were likely to have lower levels of political competition and political participation. Some military regimes, notably radical regimes such as that of Ethiopia under Mengistu or of Burkina Faso under Sankara, continued to rely less on material inducements or more strictly limited their beneficiaries through-out their tenure.[55] Even as these regimes proved willing to increase levels of participation somewhat, notably by creating single parties or by convening sham elections, they continued to eschew virtually any form of significant competition.

FIVE MODAL REGIMES

It is now possible to identify modal variants of African political regimes that embody distinct combinations of political participation and political competition. These regimes are distinguished by whether the population was broadly or narrowly mobilized (participation) and by the plurality of political associations (competition). Figure 5 identifies five modal regime variants that together collectively exhaust the range of political arrangements predominant in postcolonial Africa. It places them in a property space defined, following Dahl, by the extent of participation (x axis) and competition (y axis). The figure also shows where African regimes stood in relation to Remmer's four ideal regime categories: exclusionary and inclusionary authoritarianism, and exclusionary and inclusionary democracy.[56]

For the most part, African postcolonial regimes were variants on a neopatrimonial theme. At least three modal forms – military oligarchy, plebiscitary one-party system, and competitive one-party system – featured "big man" rule. Between them, these three types (n = 40) accounted for most of sub-Saharan Africa's political regimes in 1989 (see Table 3). Even Africa's multiparty systems (n = 5), in which chief political executives were checked to a degree by opposition parties and competitive elections, showed tendencies toward personal rule. Only the settler oligarchies of South Africa and Namibia (n = 2) clearly departed from Africa's neopatrimonial norm; with their stronger, centralized state and military apparatus and their closer adherence to legal-rational administrative procedures, they more closely resembled the bureaucratic-authoritarian regimes that had been common a decade earlier in Latin America and Southern Europe.

We do not offer these modal regimes as immutable categories. Actual African regimes reflected their own peculiar postcolonial histories that encompassed shifts from one regime variant to another. For example, Zaire transited from military oligarchy to plebiscitary one-party system after Mobutu created in 1966 the Popular Revolutionary Movement (MPR) as the country's sole political party; Cameroon transited from a plebiscitary to a competitive one-party system in 1985 when Biya introduced multiple candidate lists for municipal and legislative elections; and Zimbabwe transited from a settler oligarchy to a formal multiparty system with independence in 1980. In part as a result of such changes, actual regimes displayed characteristics of more than one type, combining features of each at one time or another. In fact, this possibility is inherent in the logic of our framework, which proposes neopatrimonial rule as a master concept that embraces a variety of subsidiary regime types. We now describe each of these variants.

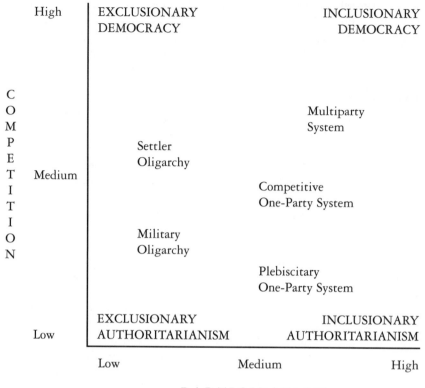

Figure 5   Modal Regimes in Sub-Saharan Africa, Independence to 1989

THE PLEBISCITARY ONE-PARTY SYSTEM

This form of neopatrimonial regime allowed extremely limited competition but encouraged a high degree of political participation. Mass participation was orchestrated from above and channeled through symbolic rituals of endorsement for the personal ruler, his officeholders, and his policies. Voters were simultaneously mobilized and controlled through one-party "plebiscites," which included elections and officially sponsored rallies and demonstrations.[57] Electoral turnout rates and affirmative votes for the president typically exceeded 90 percent, results that suggested genuine participation, even if electoral competition was highly restricted by the government. Between elections, the regime employed a party machine to distribute patronage to a fairly wide array of economic and regional interests. Despite these participatory rituals, the plebiscitary one-party system was decidedly undem-

Table 3. *Modal Regimes by Country, Sub-Saharan Africa, 1989*

Plebiscitary One-Party Systems (n = 16)	Military Oligarchies (n = 11)	Competitive One-Party Systems (n = 13)	Settler Oligarchies (n = 2)	Multiparty Systems (n = 5)
Angola	Burkina Faso	Cameroon	Namibia	Botswana
Bénin	Burundi	Central African	South Africa	Gambia
Cape Verde	Chad	Republic		Mauritius
Comoros	Ghana	Côte d'Ivoire		Sénégal
Congo	Guinea	Madagascar		Zimbabwe
Djibouti	Lesotho	Mali		
Equatorial Guinea	Liberia	Malawi		
Ethiopia	Mauritania	Rwanda		
Gabon	Nigeria	São Tomé		
Guinea–Bissau	Sudan	Seychelles		
Kenya	Uganda	Sierra Leone		
Mozambique		Tanzania		
Niger		Togo		
Somalia		Zambia		
Swaziland				
Zaire				

ocratic because it precluded genuine political competition. Opposition political parties were proscribed, and only one candidate from the official party appeared on the ballot.

The one-party plebiscitary regime in Africa was characteristically headed by a first-generation leader, either civilian or military. If civilian, the leader was usually the grand old man of nationalist politics who had won independence in the early 1960s; if military, he commonly had come to power in the first round of coups in the late 1960s or early 1970s. This latter group of leaders typically tried to civilianize and legitimize the regime by abandoning military rank and uniform and attempting to construct mass-mobilizing political parties. Examples included Mobutu in Zaire and Kérékou in Benin. As a result, by 1989 the plebiscitary one-party system had become the most common type of neopatrimonial regime in Africa.

THE MILITARY OLIGARCHY

By contrast, the military oligarchy was an exclusionary form of neopatrimonial rule. Elections were few or entirely suspended; all decisions were made by a narrow elite behind closed doors. There was a visible personal leader, but power was not completely concentrated in the hands of one man; decisions were made somewhat more collectively by a junta, committee, or cabinet that often included civilian advisers and technocrats alongside military officers. There was a degree of competitive debate within the elite, and objective criteria were brought to bear in assessing policy options. Implementation occurred through a relatively professional civil or military hierarchy, and executive institutions were maintained in at least a token state of readiness and effectiveness.[58]

The military oligarchy tended to be led by a younger generation of junior military officers who had come to power in a second, third, or later round of coups during the late 1970s and 1980s. The military retained a much larger role in the polity than was the case in plebiscitary regimes, even when the latter were headed by leaders who had emerged out of the military. Political participation was severely circumscribed, not only because elections were eliminated in the early years of military rule but also because existing political parties and most civic associations were banned. In radical regimes such as those in Burkina Faso or Congo, the military filled this political space with so-called people's committees to disseminate its message.[59] Although military oligarchs sometimes espoused a populist ideology, their methods of rule did not include genuine participation, at least until such time as these leaders began to make good on promises to return to civilian rule.[60] This reflected the military's deep distrust of politics and politicians.[61] The military oligarchy variant of neopatrimonial regimes was exemplified, among others, by the governments of Jerry Rawlings in Ghana (1981–92) and Ibrahim Babangida in Nigeria (1985–93).

THE COMPETITIVE ONE-PARTY SYSTEM

This less common variant of the one-party system was as inclusive as the plebiscitary variant, but (as the label suggests) it was somewhat more competitive. It was distinguished from the military oligarchy in its toleration of limited political competition at the mass as well as elite levels. Elections in these neopatrimonial systems allowed for two or more candidates in party primaries or parliamentary elections. Voters possessed a restricted electoral choice among candidates from a single official party with an established policy platform. To be sure, candidates who enjoyed the support of the ruling strongman stood at an advantage in elections, but this did not always reliably protect them against defeat at the hands of voters. Even though personal rulers attempted to depoliticize society and manipulated electoral rules, voters seemed sufficiently attracted by the available choices to sustain genuine turnout figures at relatively high, though declining, levels.[62] Such regimes were also relatively stable, resisting military intervention.

As an aspect of institutional longevity, the competitive one-party regime was characteristically headed by a nationalist founding father like Kaunda of Zambia or Houphouët-Boigny of Côte d'Ivoire.[63] Sometimes the original ruler engineered a smooth but nondemocratic leadership transition to a handpicked successor (as to Moi in Kenya or Mwinyi in Tanzania).[64] In these regimes, long-serving leaders had consolidated and institutionalized support in ruling parties and were, or considered themselves to be, politically secure.[65] A degree of pluralism was tolerated, so that significant opposition to the government was allowed on the fringes of the single party and in the press and among civic associations, which were strong by African standards.

THE SETTLER OLIGARCHY

As we have mentioned, the settler form of rule did not share the core features of Africa's neopatrimonial regimes. Instead, it resembled the bureaucratic-authoritarian regimes constructed by Europeans in those parts of the colonial world where settlers gained *de facto* control of the state.[66] Settler oligarchies approximate exclusionary democracy. The dominant racial group used the instruments of law to deny political rights to ethnic majorities, usually through a restrictive franchise and emergency regulations backed by hierarchically organized coercion. At the same time, however, settlers reproduced functioning democracies within their own microcosmic enclaves, with features like elections, leadership turnover, loyal opposition, independent courts, and some press freedoms, all reserved exclusively for whites. Thus, at the same time that they permitted quite far-reaching measures of political competition, these regimes proscribed access to the political process by limiting participation. The classic case is of course South Africa, which with Namibia was the only remaining settler oligarchy in Africa by 1989, though half a dozen other African countries in the eastern and southern subcontinent shared a settler colonial heritage. Because of their peculiar institutional origins, one would expect settler oligarchies to display distinct transition dynamics, discussion of which is reserved for Chapter 5.

THE MULTIPARTY SYSTEM

Multiparty regimes display relatively high levels of both participation and competition. Because they have met the minimal requirements for the installation of a democratic order, we do not include them in the following discussions of the dynamics of recent regime transitions. In these regimes, voters enjoy guarantees of universal franchise and equality before the law that are largely enforceable, and a plurality of political parties is free to contest elections that are largely open. The shortcomings of African multiparty systems, which are discussed more fully elsewhere (see Chapter 7), include weak opposition parties, intimidation of opposition supporters by incumbent governments, and an absence of leadership turnover. The multiparty systems of Botswana, Sénégal, and Zimbabwe are all imperfectly democratic in these respects, and when unchecked, their leaders show marked tendencies to lapse into neopatrimonial habits. African multiparty systems can be thought of as hybrid regimes in which the formal rules of electoral democracy vie with informal personal ties of "big men" to define and shape the actual practice of politics.

TRANSITIONS FROM NEOPATRIMONIAL RULE

We are now ready to assess the extent to which the neopatrimonial nature of regimes in Africa affects the process of democratization. On the one hand, one would expect transitions from neopatrimonial rule to have shared characteristics – for example, centering on struggles over the legitimacy of dominant, personalistic leaders. On the other hand, one would also expect the dynamics of political change to be highly variable, reflecting the different institutional regimes devised by strongmen. Hence the need to emphasize both the commonalities *and* variations in transition dynamics and outcomes.

Bearing this in mind, let us now turn to our central questions:

How does neopatrimonialism influence whether transitions ever begin?
How do they subsequently unfold?
How do they eventually turn out?

We pursue a twin track of comparative analysis. In this chapter, we compare political transitions in Africa with those in other regions of the world where political authority is not neopatrimonial. In the following chapters, we ask whether the differences in the degree of political competition and participation present among African states since independence can help to explain differences in transition dynamics and outcomes.

The recent literature on democratization in Europe and Latin America converges on a common account of regime transition.[67] According to this scenario, transition begins when a moderate faction within the state elite recognizes that social peace and economic development cannot adequately legitimate an authoritarian regime. These softliners promote a political opening by providing improved guarantees of civil and political rights and later conceding the convocation of free and fair elections. The greatest hazard to democratic transition comes from a backlash by elements of a hardline faction within the political elite, manifest in threats by the military to execute a reactionary coup. To forestall hardliners, government and opposition leaders meet behind the scenes to forge a compromise pact to guarantee the vital interests of major elite players, thereby smoothing the way to democracy.

We propose that political transitions from neopatrimonial regimes depart from this model scenario in the following major respects.

Transitions from Neopatrimonial Regimes Originate in Political Protest

As argued earlier, neopatrimonial practices cause chronic fiscal crises and inhibit economic growth. In addition, however much leaders strive for ethnic balance, neopatrimonial rule tends toward particularistic networks of personal loyalty that grant undue favor to selected kinship or subnational groupings. Taken together, shrinking economic opportunities and exclusionary rewards are a volatile recipe for social unrest. Mass popular protest is likely to break out, usually over the issue of declining living standards, and to escalate into calls to remove incumbent leaders. Unlike corporatist rulers, personal rulers cannot point to a record of stability and prosperity to legitimate their rule.

Endemic fiscal crisis also undercuts the capacity of rulers to manage the process of political change. A critical moment arrives when public resources dwindle to the point at which the government can no longer pay civil servants and the latter join antiregime protesters in the streets.[68] Shorn of the ability to maintain political stability through the distribution of material rewards, neopatrimonial leaders resort erratically to coercion, which in turn further undermines the regime's legitimacy. The final showdown arrives when the government is unable to pay the military.

As a result of twin political and economic crises, regime transitions are more likely to originate in society than in the corridors of elite power. The existing literature is inconsistent on this point. O'Donnell and Schmitter assert that "there is no transition whose beginning is not the consequence – direct or indirect – of important divisions within the authoritarian regime itself."[69] Yet the same authors note that authoritarian rulers usually miss opportunities to open up when the regime is riding a wave of economic success, instead, "attempt[ing] liberalization only when they are already going through some serious crisis."[70] We read this to mean that political liberalization is as much an elite *response* as an elite initiative. It also begs the question of how leaders apprehend the existence of a "crisis"; presumably, elites are awakened to the necessity of reform by an outpouring of protest. Indeed, O'Donnell and Schmitter elsewhere concede that ordinary citizens commonly take a leading role in transitions: Whereas "political democracies are usually brought down by conspiracies involving a few actors ... the democratization of authoritarian regimes ... involves ... a crucial component of the mobilization and organization of large numbers of individuals."[71]

The well-known distinctions between top-down, bottom-up, and negotiated transitions are helpful here.[72] One might be tempted to predict that, since personal rulers centralize so much decision-making power in their own hands, neopatrimonial regimes would undergo elite-initiated transitions.[73] But the evidence presented in the next chapter indicates that transitions in Africa seem to be occurring more commonly from below. In general, neopatrimonial rulers are driven by calculations of personal political survival: They resist political openings for as long as possible and seek to manage the process of transition only after it has been forced on them.

The structure of political incentives in neopatrimonial regimes helps to explain why political actors from civil society rather than state elites initiate transitions. When rule is built on personal loyalty, supreme leaders often lose touch with popular perceptions of regime legitimacy. They lack institutional ties to corporate groups in society through which to receive signals about the strength of their popular support. Instead, they surround themselves with sycophantic lieutenants who, to protect their own positions, tell the leader what he wants to hear and shield him from dissonant facts. Thus, even skillful personalistic leaders lack a flow of reliable information that would enable them to soundly judge the need for, and timing of, political liberalization. Instead, they react to popular discontent by falling back on tried and true methods of selective reward and political repression. To be heard, ordinary citizens have little choice but to persist with protest and raise the volume of their demands in order to penetrate the conspiracy of silence surrounding the supremo. In sum, personal rulers are unlikely to initiate political liberalization or relinquish power without a struggle; they have to be forced out.[74]

We have argued that personalistic rulers who are overly sensitive to threats to their authority set about weakening all independent centers of power beyond their control. Transitions from neopatrimonial rule are therefore conditioned by the weaknesses of state and civic institutions. In the absence of formal institutional mechanisms for political competition, the protagonists find difficulty in reaching a compromise formula to end the regime. Because it provides few institutional channels for negotiation over rules and power sharing, personalistic rule instead gives rise to all-or-nothing power struggles.

Ironically, because neopatrimonial rule also undercuts civil society, it also weakens the foundation for antisystem change. Thus, when political protest does burst out against neopatrimonial regimes, it is usually spontaneous, sporadic, disorganized, and unsustained. True, opposition parties, human rights organizations, and trade unions mushroom as soon as the regime's repressive capabilities weaken, but they are fragmented, impoverished, and themselves lacking traditions of participatory politics. In this context, the emergence of the church as a primary actor in the transitions of several African countries reflects, as much as its own prestige and power, the absence of credible secular candidates to lead the opposition.[75] Because civil society is underdeveloped, the completion of the transition and the consolidation of any subsequent democratic regime become problematic.

In Neopatrimonial Regimes, the Transition's Outcome Hinges on the Fate of the Dictator

The presidentialism of neopatrimonial regimes has major implications for the dynamics of the transition. Power is so concentrated that the disposition of the regime is synonymous with the personal fate of the supreme ruler. Opposition leaders understand that real political change is unlikely to occur as long as the big man remains, since he has set all the rules and could manipulate any new ones to limit their impact. As a result, his overthrow or flight becomes the primary objective of the opposition throughout the transition. The fate of longstanding authoritarian leaders can be a major bone of contention in other regimes, as witnessed for instance in the transition from bureaucratic authoritarianism in Chile in 1989; but in neopatrimonial regimes, it typically is the single issue that unifies and motivates the opposition. Ideological and organizational cohesion are likely to be strictly ancillary concerns.

For his part, the strongman identifies the sustainability of the regime with his own political survival and is likely to make major efforts to ride the wave of protest. This confusion between self- and national interest is not unique to personal dictatorships, but it has more serious implications there. Leaders in other regimes might believe themselves to be essential, but they are rudely reminded of the need to compromise by other institutions – for example, when the military and judiciary refuse to repress protest. Because personal dictators can deploy public revenues (however limited these may be) in support of personal survival, they can avoid accountability to the state's own institutions.[76]

The willingness of leaders to step down instead often depends on whether they fear prosecution for having abused state powers and privileges. Unchecked personal dictators are most likely to have committed egregious abuses, leading them to cling most desperately to power. Even when friendly powers promise protection from extradition demands as an inducement to accept retirement, leaders with a poor human rights record and a history of state violence may hesitate to give up the protection of office without amnesty. They fear the opposition's promises to prosecute them, and recalling the ignominious exile of the Marcoses of the Philippines or the Shah of Iran, worry that they will never be safe.

As a result, the demise of personal dictators is usually protracted and painful, with incumbents tenaciously clinging to power. At worst, the most stubborn incumbents may even allow the destruction of their nation's economic and political structures as a cost of personal political survival.[77] Over time, the ruler's authority over persons and territory and the very existence of the state as an organized body may become a fiction. The leader shrinks to little more than a local warlord who survives by controlling some resources and retaining the loyalty of a segment of the old coercive apparatus.

Neopatrimonial Elites Fracture over Access to Patronage

The ruler's systematic reliance on clientelism, another key informal institution of neopatrimonial regimes, also conditions transition dynamics. At face value, one would expect elite cohesion to be particularly problematic in governing coalitions built on the quicksand of clientelism. By arguing that African transitions were initiated by political protest, we do not wish to claim that factionalism among rulers is unimportant. But we side with the view that "political struggle ... begins as the result of the emergence of a new elite that arouses a depressed and previously leaderless social group into concerted action,"[78] rather than with "a move by some group within the ruling bloc to obtain support from forces external to it."[79] At issue is whether the leadership of the reform coalition comes from inside or outside the incumbent group.

Favoring the latter interpretation, we argue that the dimensions of elite factionalism are distinctive in personalistic regimes.[80] The conventional distinction between hardliners and softliners does not capture the essential fault line within a neopatrimonial elite.[81] Instead of fracturing ideologically over whether or not to liberalize, neopatrimonial elites are more likely to take sides pragmatically in struggles over spoils. Their political positions come to be defined according to whether they are *insiders* or *outsiders* in relation to the patronage system.

Elite fragmentation occurs as follows. Neopatrimonial regimes are characterized by rapid turnover of political personnel. To regulate and control rent-seeking, to prevent rivals from developing their own bases, and to demonstrate power, rulers regularly rotate officeholders.[82] Rulers typically expel potential opponents from government jobs, from approved institutions like ruling parties, or even from the country itself. Even if dissenters can sometimes expect to be later forgiven and brought back into the fold, such practices establish a nonaccommodative pattern of politics. Whereas insiders enjoy preferential access to state offices and associated spoils, outsiders are left to languish in the wilderness. The more complete their exclusion from economic opportunity, the more strongly outsiders are motivated to oppose the incumbent regime. Outsiders take refuge from official institutions in civil society, the parallel economy, or international exile. From these locations, they grasp for control of popular protest movements, usually by promoting symbols (such as multiparty democracy) that can convert economic grievances into demands for regime change.

Meanwhile, the insiders in a patrimonial ruling coalition are unlikely to promote political reform. Stultified by years of obeisance to the official party line, they have exhausted their own capacity for original or innovative thinking. Recruited and sustained with material inducements, lacking an independent political base, and thoroughly compromised in the regime's corruption, they are dependent on the survival of the incumbent. Insiders typically have risen through the ranks of political service and, apart from top leaders who may have invested in private capital holdings, derive livelihood principally from state or party offices. Because they face the prospect of losing all visible means of support in a political transition, they have little option but to cling to the regime, to sink or swim with it.

Even if the state elite does begin to fragment over the pace of political reform, such splits are governed more by considerations of self-interest than ideology. At some point during the transition, waverers may calculate that their access to rents and prebends is best served by crossing over to the opposition. As patronage resources dwindle, incumbent leaders try to tighten their grip on revenues (especially export returns and foreign aid) in order to reward the loyalty of remaining insiders and to attempt to buy back the outsiders.[83] In sum, the operations of neopatrimonialism tend to simultaneously create a defensively cohesive state elite and a potential pool of alternative leaders outside of the state.

Elite Political Pacts Are Unlikely in Neopatrimonial Regimes

Pacts are "more or less enduring compromises ... [in which] no social or political group is sufficiently dominant to impose its ideal project, and what typically emerges is a second-best solution."[84] They have featured prominently in the literature because of their role in democratic transitions in Spain, Brazil, and Venezuela.[85]

Some of the conditions conducive of pact-making are present in the late stages of neopatrimonial rule, such as the interdependence of competing players and the inability of anyone to impose a preferred outcome. But other conditions are absent. First, incumbent and opposition leaders are usually so polarized from winner-take-all power struggles that there is slim possibility that moderate factions from either side can negotiate an agreement. Instead, transitions unfold along a path of escalating confrontations until one side or other loses decisively. To the extent that transitions occur without setting a precedent for compromise, the chances are reduced that any resultant democratic regime can be sustained and consolidated.

In addition, the likelihood of pacts is a function of the degree of formal political institutionalization in a regime. In corporatist regimes, the parties to a political pact are the acknowledged leaders of major interest blocs within state and society and, by carrying their supporters along, can make agreements stick. In neopatrimonial regimes, political leaders may represent no more than a tiny coterie of clients and may be unable to build a political consensus around any intra-elite agreement. The emerging political parties and civic groups typically lack organizational traditions, experience, and funds and find it difficult to escape factionalism. As a result, contending opposition leaders within a pluralistic social movement do not usually have the authenticity and legitimacy to strike a deal on behalf of dissident factions.

Under neopatrimonialism, the prospect of compromise depends more on the personality, management skills, and governing institutions of the incumbent ruler. A leader who has attempted to legitimate a personalistic regime with populistic rhetoric – for example, of "peoples'" democracy or "African" socialism – is more likely to respond positively to demands for political liberalization than a leader who has ruled on the basis of claims of traditional paternalism or revolutionary purity. A leader who has allowed political rivals to live freely within the country is more likely to strike a deal on the rules of transition than a leader who has systematically eliminated or exiled opponents. As we show in the next chapter, a number of such deals were struck during Africa's transitions of the early 1990s. We contend, however, that neopatrimonial practices generally reduce the possibility of a grand compromise of power sharing. Rather, as argued earlier, the strongman and his entourage have to go.

In Neopatrimonial Regimes, Transitions Are Struggles to Establish Legal Rules

As struggles over the rules of the political game, regime transitions determine the future constellation of winners and losers in the socioeconomic realm.

Here, too, the institutional features of the previous regime shape the status of rules and the nature of rule-making conflicts. Corporatist regimes elsewhere in the world may have been installed by extraconstitutional means and may have involved the suspension of constitutional rights. But to the extent that this form of authoritarian rule was bureaucratic, it was rule-governed, and its participants were acculturated in important respects to a rule of law.

Because personalistic leaders enjoyed sweeping discretion to make public decisions, transitions from neopatrimonial regimes are concerned fundamentally with whether rules even matter.[86] The opposition, which commonly includes lawyers within its leadership ranks, calls for the rule of law.[87] Indeed, in its different national and international manifestations, the law is one of the more potent weapons the opposition has at its disposal. In an effort to establish the primacy of legal rules, it challenges the regime to end human rights violations, lift emergency regulations, allow registration of opposition parties, hold a sovereign national conference, limit the constitutional powers of the executive, or hold competitive elections. At some moment in the struggle, the content of the constitution and the electoral laws become points of contention. In other words, the opposition attempts to reintroduce rule-governed behavior after a prolonged period in which such niceties have never existed or have been suspended.

Part of the opposition's objective in establishing legal rules is to gain access to resources monopolized by the ruling clique. In the context of a democratic transition, the opposition is most immediately interested in the regime's control of the media and other electoral campaign assets. In the longer run, business interests in the opposition may be keen to permanently alter the rules about government intervention in the economy. At this point, internal conflicts may emerge within the opposition over the extent of regime transition, with old-guard politicians often seeking to limit rule changes to ensure that they can benefit from state patronage or business opportunities once they capture state power. Thus, the struggle over political rules is often a pretext for or a prelude to even more fundamental economic struggles that are laid bare in efforts to strip neopatrimonial rulers of their political monopolies.

During Transitions from Neopatrimonial Regimes, Middle-Class Elements Align with the Opposition

Struggles over the status of property rights reveal the deeper structure of a regime's social base. The relationship between state and capital in Latin America and Southern Europe is very different from that of African countries. Corporatist regimes promote accumulation through "triple alliances" with foreign and national private capital, and draw domestic political support from the expanding entrepreneurial middle classes.[88] This structure of political support has maintained or deepened great inequalities of wealth and income, which in turn limit the options for transition. Under capitalism, democracies can be installed only gradually without disrupting the distribution of assets, or by a popular upsurge, a rapid transition, and the introduction of redistributive policies, which risk provoking right-wing forces to intervene to reverse the transition. Some analysts argue that to achieve a stable democracy the right wing must therefore do well in a founding election and that the left must accept the inviolability of the bourgeoisie's property rights.[89]

Because neopatrimonial regimes are embedded in precapitalist societies, one would expect different transition trajectories. The pervasiveness of clientelism means that the state has actively undermined capitalist forms of accumulation. Property rights are imperfectly respected, and there are powerful disincentives against private entrepreneurship and long-term productive investments. Unlike in Latin America, governing alliances between military rulers and a national bourgeoisie are uncommon. Instead, the weak national bourgeoisie of Africa is frustrated by state ownership, overregulation, and official corruption. Rather than regarding the incumbent regime as the protector of property rights, private capital opposes the use of the state machinery by a bureaucratic bourgeoisie to appropriate property for itself. Thus, instead of demanding that property rights be ruled out of bounds, the national bourgeoisie in transitions from neopatrimonialism wants to include them in the new rules of the political game.

This explains the tendency of emergent middle classes in Africa to side with the democratic opposition rather than to uphold the incumbent government. Businessmen and professionals often take on political leadership roles in the opposition, drawing in other middle-class factions, like public servants, whose downward economic mobility is a powerful impetus to protest. These elements are unlikely to pose a threat to the acceptance of a new government established by a founding election, because any new government is likely to be more economically liberal than its predecessor, but also because bourgeois elements are unlikely to turn to military officers in a quest to reverse democratization. In transitions from neopatrimonial rule, the threat of backlash comes mainly from the military acting alone, with the emergent middle classes being the strongest and most articulate advocates of civilian politics.

To conclude, political transitions from neopatrimonial rule display distinctive features that can be gleaned from comparisons with transitions elsewhere in the world. And we have argued that, even if regime transitions are characterized by considerable uncertainty and some serendipity, the outcome of political struggles depends critically on the way that power was exercised by the rulers of previous regimes. We turn – after presenting a summary of transition features – to test this politico-institutional argument against empirical data from Africa.

ENDNOTES

1. See Max Weber, *Economy and Society* (New York: Bedminster Press, 1968); and Robin Theobold, "Patrimonialism," *World Politics* 34 (1982): 548–59.
2. For diverse examples and theoretical discussions from different perspectives, see S. Schmidt, James Scott, J. Guasti, and C. Lande, eds., *Friends, Followers and Factions* (Berkeley: University of California Press, 1976).

3. A good introduction to these issues is provided by Samuel N. Eisenstadt, *Traditional Patrimonialism and Modern Neopatrimonialism* (London: Sage, 1972); see also Christopher Clapham, *Third World Politics: An Introduction* (Madison: University of Wisconsin Press, 1985).
4. Theobold, "Patrimonialism," 549.
5. Clapham, *Third World Politics,* p. 49. See also Guenther Roth, "Personal Rulership, Patrimonialism, and Empire-Building in the New States," *World Politics* 20 (1968): 194–206.
6. See, for example, Harold Crouch, "Patrimonialism and Military Rule in Indonesia," *World Politics* 31, (1979); and Paul D. Hutchcroft, "Oligarchs and Cronies in the Philippine State: The Politics of Patrimonial Plunder," *World Politics* 44 (1992): 414–50.
7. Key early works in an increasingly rich and varied literature include Jean-Claude Willame, *Patrimonialism and Political Change in the Congo* (Stanford: Stanford University Press, 1972); Victor T. Levine, "African Patrimonial Regimes in Comparative Perspective," *Journal of Modern African Studies* 18 (1980): 657–73; Thomas M. Callaghy, *The State–Society Struggle: Zaire in Comparative Perspective* (New York: Columbia University Press, 1984); Richard Sandbrook, *The Politics of African Economic Stagnation* (Cambridge: Cambridge University Press, 1986); Jean François Médard, "The Underdeveloped State in Africa: Political Clientelism or Neo-patrimonialism?" in *Private Patronage and Public Power: Political Clientelism in the Modern State,* ed. Christopher Clapham (London: Frances Pinter, 1982); and John Waterbury, "Endemic and Planned Corruption in a Monarchical Regime," *World Politics* 25 (1973): 533–55.
8. See, respectively, Robert H. Jackson and Carl G. Rosberg, *Personal Rule in Black Africa* (Berkeley: University of California Press, 1982); Richard Joseph, *Democracy and Prebendal Politics in Nigeria: The Rise and Fall of the Second Republic* (Cambridge: Cambridge University Press, 1987); and Jean-François Bayart, *l'Etat en Afrique* (Paris: Fayard, 1989). Jean-François Médard has reviewed and compared these different terms and argues the theoretical differences are trivial or mostly semantic. Médard,"l'Etat Néo-patrimonial en Afrique Noire," in *Etats d'Afrique Noire: Formation, Mécanismes et Crises,* ed. Jean François Médard (Paris: Karthala, 1994), pp. 323–53.
9. Jackson and Rosberg, *Personal Rule,* p. 10.
10. See Irving L. Markovitz, introduction to *Studies in Power and Class in Africa* (Oxford: Oxford University Press, 1987), p. 5 for a parallel critique of Jackson and Rosberg.
11. Writing about Mobutu's consolidation of power, Callaghy speaks of the systematic "dismantlement of inherited structures, especially departicipation and depoliticization," including the emasculation of parliament, the elimination of the position of prime minister, the banning of all parties and youth organizations, and the centralization of state power away from the provinces to Kinshasa. Callaghy, *State-Society Struggle,* p. 171.
12. Quoted in Jackson and Rosberg, *Personal Rule,* p. 165. The authors go on to note that at one time or another, Banda personally held ministerial portfolios for agriculture, foreign affairs, works and supplies, natural resources, and justice, as well as holding ownership of agricultural estates and private companies.
13. Henry S. Bienen and Nicolas van de Walle found that a third of all African leaders are still in power after eight years in office, compared to 5 percent and 18 per-

cent of all Latin American and Asian leaders, respectively. See their essay "A Proportional Hazard Model of Leadership Duration," *Journal of Politics* 54 (1992): 693.

14. Stephen Ellis, "Rumour and Power in Togo," *Africa* 63 (1993): 465.
15. Crawford Young and Thomas Turner, *The Rise and Decline of the Zairian State* (Madison: University of Wisconsin Press, 1985); Michael Schatzberg, *The Dialectics of Oppression in Zaire* (Bloomington: Indiana University Press, 1988), especially Ch. 5.
16. Michael Schatzberg, "Power, Legitimacy and 'Democratization' in Africa," *Africa* 63 (1993): 451.
17. Jean François Médard, "la Régulation Socio-Politique," in *Etat et Bourgeoisie en Côte d'Ivoire*, ed. Yves A. Fauré and Jean-François Médard (Paris: Karthala, 1982).
18. Ellis, "Rumour and Power in Togo"; Jean-François Bayart, *l'Etat au Cameroun*, 2nd ed. (Paris: Presses de la Fondation Nationale de Sciences Politiques, 1985), pp. 141–57, for analysis of the centralization of power under Ahidjo.
19. On this point see Joseph, *Democracy and Prebendal Politics in Nigeria*, in particular Ch. 5. On the recent evolution of these phenomena, see the excellent analysis in René Lemarchand, "The State, the Parallel Economy, and the Changing Structure of Patronage Systems," in *The Precarious Balance: State and Society in Africa*, ed. Donald Rothchild and Naomi Chazan (Boulder, Colo.: Westview, 1988), pp. 149–71.
20. Tessy Bakary, "Côte d'Ivoire: l'Etatisation de l'Etat," in *Etats d'Afrique Noire: Formation, Mécanismes et Crises*, ed. Jean François Médard (Paris: Karthala, 1994), 72–3.
21. Robert H. Bates and Paul Collier, "The Politics and Economics of Policy Reform in Zambia," in *Political and Economic Interactions in Economic Policy Reform*, ed. Robert H. Bates and Anne O. Krugger (Oxford: Blackwell, 1993), p. 391.
22. Quoted in Nicolas van de Walle, "Neopatrimonialism and Democracy in Africa, with an Illustration from Cameroon," in *Economic Change and Political Liberalization in Sub-Saharan Africa*, ed. Jennifer A. Widner (Baltimore: Johns Hopkins Press, 1994), p. 137.
23. Cited in Mamadou Dia, *A Governance Approach to Civil Service Reform in Sub-Saharan Africa*, World Bank Technical Paper, no. 225 (Washington, D.C.: The World Bank, 1993), p. 21.
24. Jean-Louis Gombeaud, Corinne Moutout, and Stephen Smith, *La Guerre du Cacao: Histoire Secrète d'un Embargo* (Paris: Calmann-Lévy, 1990).
25. Steve Askin, "Mobutu's Wealth: How He Got It, How He Spends It" (paper presented to the annual meeting of the African Studies Association, Baltimore, MD, November 1–4, 1990).
26. Médard, "L'Etat Néo-Patrimonial," pp. 347–9.
27. Within a large literature that makes this point, see Sandbrook, *Politics of African Economic Stagnation;* Thomas M. Callaghy, "The State and the Development of Capitalism in Africa: Theoretical, Historical and Comparative Reflections," in *The Precarious Balance: State and Society in Africa*, ed. Rothchild and Chazan (Boulder, Colo.: Westview, 1988), pp. 67–99; and Nicolas van de Walle, "Neopatrimonialism and Democracy in Africa."
28. The World Bank estimated that in the early 1980s, government consumption constituted 17 percent of GDP in sub-Saharan Africa, 50 percent higher than

in a sample of other developing countries. *Adjustment in Africa: Reforms, Results and the Road Ahead* (Washington, D.C.: The World Bank, 1993), pp. 23–4.

29. Cited from *The Economist* in Larry Diamond, "Nigeria: The Uncivil Society: The Descent into Praetorianism," *Politics in Developing Countries: Comparing Experiences with Democracy,* 2nd Ed., ed. Larry Diamond, Juan Linz, and Seymour Martin Lipset (Boulder: Lynne Rienner, 1995), 417–91.

30. Estimated from Table 12 of The World Bank, *World Development Report, 1993* (Washington, D.C.: Oxford University Press, 1993), 260–1. Admittedly, such aggregate numbers disguise quite a large variation within both categories of countries and are based on data of often suspect quality. On the decline of Africa's fiscal base and on the difficulties of raising central government revenues in Africa, see Dennis Anderson, *The Public Revenue and Economic Policy in African Countries,* World Bank Discussion Paper, no. 19 (Washington: World Bank, 1987); and Karim Nashashibi et al., *The Fiscal Dimensions of Adjustment in Low-Income Countries,* Occasional Paper Number 95. (Washington, D.C.: International Monetary Fund, April 1992).

31. The aid numbers are cited in the Organization for Economic Cooperation and Development (OECD), *Development Assistance Committee Report, 1994* (Paris: OECD, 1995), H8; the revenue data are cited in the World Bank, *World Development Report* (Washington, D.C.: World Bank, 1984 and 1993).

32. The seminal examination of these issues remains Robert H. Bates, *Markets and States in Tropical Africa: The Political Basis of Agricultural Policies* (Berkeley: University of California Press, 1981).

33. Cited in D. K. Fieldhouse, *Black Africa 1945–1980: Economic Decolonization and Arrested Development* (London: Allen and Unwin, 1986), p. 145.

34. Seven distinct regime types, based loosely on seven criteria, are proposed in Naomi Chazan, Robert Mortimer, John Ravenhill, and Donald Rothchild, *Politics and Society in Contemporary Africa* (Boulder, Colo.: Lynne Rienner, 1988). Ruth Berins Collier, *Regimes in Tropical Africa* (Berkeley: University of California Press, 1982) proposes five regime types. See also Roger Charlton, "Dehomogenizing the Study of African Politics: The Case of Interstate Influence on Regime Formation and Change," *Plural Societies* 14 (1983): 32–48; Crawford Young, *Ideology and Development in Africa* (New Haven: Yale University Press, 1982); and Dirk Berg-Schlosser, "African Political Systems: Typology and Performance," *Comparative Political Studies* 17 (1984): 121–51.

35. Robert Dahl, *Polyarchy: Participation and Opposition* (New Haven: Yale University Press, 1971).

36. Naomi Chazan, "African Voters at the Polls: a Re-examination of the Role of Elections in African Politics," *Journal of Commonwealth and Comparative Politics* 17 (1979): 136–58, quoted from p. 137.

37. Diamond, "Nigeria: The Uncivil Society," p. 440.

38. For example Tessy Bakary, "Côte d'Ivoire: Une Décentralisation Politique Centralisé," *Géopolitique Africaine* 2 (June 1986).

39. Chazan develops this argument in "African Voters at the Polls," 137–9.

40. Quoted on page 172 in Joel D. Barkan, "The Rise and Fall of a Governance Realm in Kenya," in *Governance and Politics in Africa,* ed. Goran Hyden and Michael Bratton (Boulder, Colo.: Lynne Rienner, 1991), pp. 167–92. See pages

182–3 for a description of the different strategies Moi used to undermine the competitiveness of these elections.

41. Nelson Kasfir, *The Shrinking Political Arena: Participation and Ethnicity in African Politics with a Case Study of Uganda* (Berkeley: University of California Press, 1976).

42. These two measures are highly correlated: Pearson's r = 0.672, P = 0.000.

43. Karen L. Remmer, "Exclusionary Democracy," *Studies in Comparative International Development* 20 (1986): 64–85.

44. This is argued by Chazan, "African Voters at the Polls," 149–50.

45. Collier, *Regimes in Tropical Africa.*

46. Numerous studies have chronicled and analyzed this process. The *locus classicus* remains Aristide Zolberg, "The Structure of Political Conflict in the New States of Tropical Africa," *American Political Science Review* 62 (1969): 70–87; see also Zolberg, *Creating Political Order: The Party States of West Africa* (Chicago: University of Chicago Press, 1966); Henry S. Bienen, *Tanzania: Party Transformation and Economic Development* (Princeton: Princeton University Press, 1967); William Foltz, "Political Opposition in Single-Party States of Tropical Africa," in *Regimes and Opposition,* ed. Robert A. Dahl (New Haven: Yale University Press, 1973); and Samuel Decalo, *Coups and Army Rule In Africa* (New Haven: Yale University Press, 1976).

47. The exceptions include South Africa before 1994, of course, but also arguably present-day Sudan and Mauritania where Arab/Islamic regimes are increasingly excluding non-Arab/non-Muslim segments of the population. Donald Rothchild and V. A. Olorunsola, eds., *State versus Ethnic Claims: African Policy Dilemmas* (Boulder, Colo.: Westview, 1982).

48. Donald Rothchild, *Pressures and Incentives for Cooperation: The Management of Ethnic and Regional Conflicts in Africa* (United States Institute of Peace, 1996), Ch. 3, p. 7.

49. Rothchild and Olorunsola, *State Versus Ethnic Claims;* and Bayart, *L'Etat en Afrique.*

50. Rothchild, *Pressures and Incentives for Cooperation,* Ch. 2–3.

51. These numbers are cited in Pierre Flambeau Ngayap's fascinating description of Cameroon's political class, *Qui Gouverne le Cameroun?* (Paris: l'Harmattan, 1983).

52. John Heilbrunn, "Social Origins of National Conferences in Bénin and Togo," *Journal of Modern African Studies* 31 (1993): 277.

53. Schatzberg, "Power, Legitimacy and 'Democratization,'" 450.

54. For example, J. Craig Jenkins and Augustine J. Kposowa, "The Political Origins of African Military Coups: Ethnic Competition, Military Centrality, and the Struggle over the Postcolonial State," *International Studies Quarterly* 36 (1992): 271–91.

55. On Ethiopia, see Christopher Clapham, "State, Society and Political Institutions in Revolutionary Ethiopia," in *Rethinking Third World Politics,* ed. James Manor (New York: Longman, 1991), especially pp. 248–52; on Burkina Faso, see René Otayek, "The Revolutionary Process in Burkina Faso," in *Military Marxist Regimes in Africa,* ed. John Markakis and Michael Waller (London: Frank Cass, 1986), pp. 95–6.

56. We adopt the terminology used by Remmer, "Exclusionary Democracy," 64–8.

57. See Collier, *Regimes in Tropical Africa,* 104–8 for a discussion.

58. Henry S. Bienen, *Armies and Parties in Africa* (New York: Africana Publishing, 1979); Samuel Decalo, *Coups and Army Rule in Africa*, pp. 231–54.

59. Even then, Samuel Decalo notes the military sought to limit the power and autonomy of the party, despite Leninist principles regarding the supremacy of the party over all other political institutions. Decalo, "The Morphology of Military Rule in Africa," in *Military Marxist Regimes in Africa*, ed. John Markakis and Michael Waller (London: Frank Cass, 1986), pp. 134–5.

60. Henry S. Bienen suggests that, even when they may have liked to, military elites lacked the organizational capabilities to develop grassroots support. Bienen, "Military Rule and Political Processes: Nigerian Examples," *Comparative Politics* 10 (1978): 205–25.

61. Back in 1968, Samuel P. Huntington wrote, "The problem is military opposition to politics. Military leaders can easily envision themselves in a guardian role; they can also picture themselves as the farseeing impartial promoters of social and economic reform in their societies. But with rare exceptions, they shrink from assuming the role of political organizer. In particular, they condemn political parties." Huntington, *Political Order in Changing Societies* (New Haven: Yale University Press, 1968), p. 243.

62. The trend of depoliticization, involving both a demobilization of formerly active participants and the cooptation or elimination of opposition power centers, is well covered in Kasfir's *Shrinking Political Arena*. On the characteristics of single-party elections in Africa, see Fred M. Hayward, *Elections in Independent Africa* (Boulder: Colo.: Westview, 1987); Chazan, "African Voters at the Polls"; and D. G. Lavroff, ed., *Aux Urnes l'Afrique! Elections et Pouvoirs en Afrique Noire* (Paris: Pedone, 1978). On elections in Tanzania and Kenya, two regimes that fit this category well, see Jan Kees Van Donge and Athumani Liviga, "The 1985 Tanzanian Parliamentary Elections: A Conservative Election," *African Affairs* 88 (1989): 47–62; and Goran Hyden and Colin Leys, "Elections and Politics in Single-Party Systems: The Case of Kenya and Tanzania," *British Journal of Political Science* 2 (1972): 389-420.

63. Côte d'Ivoire moved progressively to competitive primaries within the single party after 1980. Bakary, "Une Décentralisation Politique Centralisé"; Yves A. Fauré, "Nouvelle Donne en Côte d'Ivoire," *Politique Africaine* 20 (December 1985).

64. Kenya was a classic example of a competitive one-party regime until 1986 when Moi abolished the secret ballot in favor of "queue voting" in full public view, effectively eliminating voter choice (see Table 2).

65. Henry S. Bienen and Nicolas van de Walle, "Of Time and Power in Africa," *American Political Science Review* 83 (March 1989): 19–34.

66. Michael Bratton, "Patterns of Development and Underdevelopment: Toward a Comparison," *International Studies Quarterly* 26 (1982): 333–72; Kenneth Good, "Settler Colonialism: Economic Development and Class Formation," *Journal of Modern African Studies* 14 (1975): 597–620.

67. In addition to the works already cited, see Enrique A. Baloyra, ed., *Comparing New Democracies:Transitions and Consolidation in Mediterranean Europe and the Southern Cone* (Boulder, Colo.: Westview, 1987); James M. Malloy and Mitchell A. Seligson, eds., *Authoritarians and Democrats: Regime Transitions in Latin America* (Pittsburgh: University of Pittsburgh Press, 1987); Karen L. Remmer, "New

Wine or Old Bottlenecks? The Study of Latin American Democracy," *Comparative Politics* 23 (1991): 479–98; Robert A. Pastor, ed., *Democracy in the Americas: Stopping the Pendulum* (New York: Holmes and Meier, 1989).

68. Thus, Chris Allen argues that "in failing to pay salaries [the Kérékou regime in Bénin] ... signed the death warrant it had drafted by its own gross corruption, for it led to the actions of 1989 that in turn caused the regime's collapse." Allen, "Restructuring an Authoritarian State: Democratic Renewal in Bénin," *Review of African Political Economy* 54 (1992): 46.

69. Guillermo O'Donnell and Philippe Schmitter, *Transitions from Authoritarian Rule: Tentative Conclusions About Uncertain Democracies* (Baltimore: Johns Hopkins University Press, 1986), p. 19.

70. *Ibid.,* p. 17.

71. *Ibid.,* p. 18.

72. Juan J. Linz, "Crisis, Breakdown and Reequilibration," in *The Breakdown of Democratic Regimes,* ed. Linz and Alfred Stepan (Baltimore: Johns Hopkins University Press, 1978); Samuel P. Huntington, "How Countries Democratize," *Political Science Quarterly* 106 (1992): 579–616; René Lemarchand, "Africa's Troubled Transitions," *Journal of Democracy* 3 (1992): 98–109.

73. Huntington finds only six cases of transitions by "replacement," that is, from below. Huntington, *Third Wave,* p. 113.

74. A similar argument is made in Richard Snyder, "Explaining Transitions from Neopatrimonial Dictatorships," *Comparative Politics* 24 (1992): 379–400.

75. Paul John Marc Tedga, *Ouverture Démocratique en Afrique Noire?* (Paris: L'Harmattan, 1991), p. 84.

76. News reports in mid-1992 indicated that Zaire's national currency, printed in Germany, was being flown directly to Mobutu's luxury yacht on the Zaire river for use as he saw fit (*Africa News,* 24 May 1992); amidst a crumbling economy, and although the average civil servant had not been paid in months, Mobutu was still personally ensuring the support of key followers, including elements of the armed forces charged with protecting him. "Mobutu's Monetary Mutiny," *Africa Confidential* 5 February 1993; and "Zaire, a Country Sliding into Chaos," *Guardian Weekly* (Manchester), 8 August 1993.

77. See René Lemarchand's well-informed essay, "Mobutu and the National Conference: The Arts of Political Survival" (Gainesville: University of Florida, unpublished manuscript, 1992).

78. Dankwart A. Rustow, "Transitions to Democracy: Towards a Dynamic Model," *Comparative Politics* 2 (1970): 352.

79. Przeworski, "Some Problems in the Study of the Transition to Democracy," in O'Donnell et. al., *Transitions from Authoritarian Rule* (1986), p. 56.

80. A large literature analyzes factional conflict within the African state elite; see Richard Sandbrook, "Patrons, Clients, and Factions: New Dimensions of Conflict Analysis in Africa," *Canadian Journal of Political Science* 5 (1972): 397–432; and Bayart, *L'Etat en Afrique,* especially pp. 261–77.

81. For Huntington, the success of democratization largely hinges on the ability of "liberal reformers" within the government to outmaneuver the "standpatters."

82. Waterbury argues with respect to the monarchy in Morocco, "The king's degree of political control varies directly with the level of fragmentation and factionalization within the system.... The king must always maintain the initiative

through the systematic inculcation of an atmosphere of unpredictability and pro-visionality among all elites and the maximization of their vulnerability relative to his mastery." Waterbury, "Endemic and Planned Corruption."

83. van de Walle, "Neopatrimonialism and Democracy in Africa."

84. O'Donnell and Schmitter, *Transitions from Authoritarian Rule,* p. 38.

85. See, respectively, Raymond Carr and Juan Pablo Fusi Aizpurua, *Spain: Dictator-ship to Democracy* (London: Allen and Unwin, 1979); Frances Hagopian, "Democ-racy by Undemocratic Means? Elites, Political Pacts and Regime Transition in Brazil," *Comparative Political Studies* 23 (1990): 147–70; and Terry Lynn Karl, *Pe-troleum and Political Pacts: The Transition to Democracy in Venezuela,* Latin America Program Working Paper 107 (Washington, D.C., The Wilson Center, 1981).

86. Confronted by a journalist on national television with evidence that the govern-ment had disregarded its own laws in the manipulation of voter lists on the eve of the legislative elections of March 1992, the Cameroonian minister of territo-rial administration explained that "laws are made by men, and are no more than reference points." Cited in Célestin Monga, "La Recomposition du Marché Poli-tique au Cameroun (1991–1992)" (Yaounde, Cameroon: GERDDES (le Groupe d'études recherches sur la démocratie et le développement économique et social), 1992, unpublished paper), p. 10.

87. The National Bar Associations played leading opposition roles in Cameroon, Mali, the Central African Republic, and Togo. See Tedga, *Ouverture Démocratique en Afrique Noire,* pp. 64–72.

88. Peter Evans, *Dependent Development: The Alliance of Multinational, State and Local Capital in Brazil* (Princeton: Princeton University Press, 1979); and David Col-lier, ed., *The New Authoritarianism in Latin America* (Princeton: Princeton Uni-versity Press, 1979).

89. O'Donnell and Schmitter, *Transitions from Authoritarian Rule,* pp. 62, 69. See also Daniel H. Levine, "Paradigm Lost: Dependence to Democracy," *World Politics* 45 (1988): 377–94.

3

AFRICA'S DIVERGENT
TRANSITIONS, 1990–94

Commentaries on sub-Saharan regime transitions run the gamut from giddy Afrophilia to gloomy Afropessimism. First assessments were hopeful, seeing the peaceful electoral displacement of authoritarian regimes in countries like Bénin and Zambia as harbingers of "political renewal" and "second liberation."[1] A critical backlash soon followed in the wake of a series of disputed elections in places like Angola and Kenya. At best analysts pondered thoughtfully about the sustainability of multiparty competition under conditions of ethnic fragmentation and elite corruption[2] or at worst lapsed into apocalyptic warnings of impending civil disorder in the wake of the "stalling ... winds of change."[3]

In our view, analysts should not rush to judgment but instead adopt a detached and broadly comparative view of what is essentially a mixed situation of democratization in Africa. As Peterson suggests, "Democratic development will not be a uniform, linear process."[4] Even in democratizing countries, transitions unfold with occasional steps back for every step forward. As some countries advance, others regress into authoritarian rule. And some years are better for democratization than others, making long-term predictions from short-term trends risky at best; for example, although there was a preponderance of democratic transitions in Africa in 1991 and 1994, there was a flurry of flawed elections in 1992 and 1993.[5] At any given time, optimists can discover reasons for celebration in some countries, and skeptics will find their worst fears confirmed in others.

By the end of 1994, the closing date for this study, the diversity of transition outcomes in Africa was compellingly illustrated by the contrasting fates of Nigeria and South Africa. Political developments in these regional giants have always influenced events in surrounding countries and helped to characterize the politics of the continent as a whole. Against the odds, South Africa made a harmonious transition to multiracial power-sharing under a government of national unity by means of democratic elections in April 1994. At the other end of the continent, Nigerians ended a carefully calibrated program of local, regional, and parliamentary elections by voting for presidential candidates in June 1993, in a poll that was atypically free of irregularities. In this case, however, the military government stepped in to abort the announcement of election results and to suspend all democratic institutions. From the army emerged a new dictator who, by imprisoning prodemocracy activists and crushing an oil workers' strike, tightened the old regime's grip on power.

It is therefore inappropriate to announce either the triumph or the exhaustion of the democratic impulse in Africa. Rather than seeking simple cross-continental generalizations, we must recognize that African countries are embarked on divergent and circuitous paths. In this regard, we find much to recommend Michael Chege's nuanced analysis about the "mixed record" of the African regimes that have charted political courses "between Africa's extremes."[6] And we endorse Achille Mbembe's observation that "Africa, in effect, is heading in several directions simultaneously; at present we do not possess adequate tools to analyze this kind of movement in its complexity."[7]

This book proposes some tools. The present chapter provides a summary description of the extent, dynamics, and outcomes of regime transitions in sub-Saharan Africa between 1990 and 1994. Although the following chapters try to explain the causes of these events and their outcomes, our first objective is less to explain than to catalogue, with as much precision as possible, what actually happened and how. In so doing, we discern that transition events unfolded according to a rough sequence of "phases." We use the term "phases" advisedly, without intending to imply that transition processes were teleological, always progressing toward a preordained goal, such as democracy. Indeed, the chapter shows that transitions did not unfold smoothly, being characteristically interrupted by blockages, deviations, or setbacks. And it demonstrates that African regimes have been launched on highly *divergent* political paths. Alongside democratic outcomes can be found precluded, blocked, and flawed transitions.

But there were enough commonalities in the dynamics of political struggle and accommodation for us to tease out some dominant themes and sequences. Transitions in Africa usually began with spontaneous popular protests against a political-economic crisis, evolved through struggles over the rules and resources of political liberalization, and ended with the installation of some kind of new regime. The experience of each African country was a singular variation on this theme. Important departures and exceptions are noted and summarized where they occur. Significantly, some of the new regimes resulting from the transitions of the early 1990s were democracies, but the majority were not.

PHASES OF REGIME TRANSITION

A CRISIS OF POLITICAL LEGITIMACY

By the 1980s, authoritarian rulers in Africa's patrimonial regimes typically faced a crisis of political legitimacy. This crisis was manifest in a loss of faith among

African citizens that state elites were capable of solving basic problems of socioeconomic and political development. Leaders had damaged their own claim to rule by engaging in nepotism and corruption, which led to popular perceptions that those with access to political office were living high on the hog while ordinary people suffered. The erosion of political legitimacy built to crisis proportions because authoritarian regimes did not provide procedures for citizens to peacefully express such grievances and, especially, to turn unpopular leaders out of office.

In traditional African societies, chiefs or village heads were expected to guarantee the livelihood of the community, typically by entreating the spiritual powers to provide adequate rainfall and bountiful harvests. Leaders who persistently failed to satisfy community needs could be removed from office.[8] A similar sort of performance-based political compact was struck at the time of independence. African nationalist leaders staked a claim to political authority not only on a pledge to break the political shackles of foreign domination but also on promises to deliver the material advantages that ordinary people had observed but never enjoyed under colonial rule. Realistically or not, Africans expected that independence would bring both political freedoms and higher standards of living.

In practice, they obtained neither. Once in office, African political elites set about consolidating their hold on power by centralizing control over public life. Rulers weakened parliamentary prerogatives, granted themselves extended terms in office, and introduced single-party constitutions. They imprisoned or intimidated opponents, enclosing mass political activity within state-sanctioned associations. When political challengers made legitimate bids to displace the holders of power, they were usually foiled by arbitrary changes to the rules of political competition that enabled incumbents to retain office virtually indefinitely.

Leaders also established economic monopolies. The first two decades of African independence saw extensive state intervention as the government took control of production and distribution in a wide range of sectors. The proliferation of public enterprises and the ever-increasing size of the civil service provided political elites with opportunities to shore up political support by distributing jobs and rents to followers. Not unexpectedly, these economic institutions performed better as conduits for the distribution of political spoils and the creation of personal fortunes than as instruments of increased output and national economic growth.[9]

By the early 1980s, the contradictions of neopatrimonial politics came home to roost. Many African rulers had succeeded in their single-minded drive to consolidate power; leaders such as Houphouët-Boigny in Côte d'Ivoire and Hastings Banda in Malawi were among the longest-serving heads of state in the world.[10] Yet, two decades after independence, their policies and political practices had led more than half the nations of sub-Saharan Africa to bankruptcy, and most of the remaining states required regular transfusions of Western public capital. The diversion of public surpluses into private consumption led to a prolonged economic downturn, chronic government budget deficits, and slumping mass living standards. Ever larger numbers of citizens, including even previously privileged public sector employees and other segments of Africa's nascent middle classes, experienced the trickling up of poverty.

Perversely, the economic crisis undercut the material foundations of neopatrimonial rule: With ever fewer resources to distribute, political elites faced a growing problem of how to maintain control of clientelist networks. As Gavin Williams puts it "the contraction of resources at their disposal led those in power to appropriate ever larger shares. This narrowed their capacity to co-opt elites and maintain a measure of popular acceptance."[11] This problem was exacerbated when, during the 1980s, international donors and lenders demanded structural adjustment reforms to restrict the number of jobs in the public sector and curb the free availability of public services. The penetrative capacity of central government, always limited and often contested, was further undercut as key public services – especially in education, health, and public security – deteriorated or collapsed. Shorn of distributive resources, incumbent leaders tended to resort increasingly to coercion, at least insofar as they were able to retain the loyalty of the best-armed factions within the military. By the end of the 1980s, many incumbent African leaders found themselves politically isolated.

Given the coincidence of economic hardship and immovable leaders, it was only a matter of time before the problem of declining living standards took on political overtones as people began to attribute their material hardships to the mismanagement of public functions by incompetent and unresponsive leaders. In Claude Ake's apt words, "The foundation upon which Africa's democracy movement is based is the bitter disappointment of independence and post-independence plans – the development project being a prime example. Poor leadership and structural constraints have turned the high expectations of independence into painful disappointment."[12] He concludes that "ordinary people ... are calling for a second independence having concluded that the politics of the present leadership, far from offering any prospect of relief from underdevelopment, has deepened it immensely."[13]

Analysts are divided on whether a crisis of political legitimacy leads to the breakdown of authoritarian regimes. Adam Pzeworski has argued that systems of domination can survive without cultivating supportive beliefs among citizens: "One may believe that the regime is totally illegitimate and yet behave in an acquiescing manner."[14] Instead, what is required for transition is the emergence of an alternative leadership. Other scholars such as Samuel Huntington emphasize "the deepening legitimacy problems of authoritarian systems in a world where democratic values were widely accepted [and] the dependence of those regimes on performance legitimacy."[15] We accept that a loss of legitimacy does not always bring down strong leaders; nonetheless we note the presence of what can reasonably be viewed as a profound legitimacy crisis in every case of a disintegrating authoritarian regime in Africa by the middle 1980s. The African evidence certainly suggests that a loss of legitimacy is a necessary, if not a sufficient condition of transition from authoritarian rule and that the breakdown of authoritarian regimes can begin even in the absence of a cohesive opposition movement under an alternative leadership.

THE BIRTH OF ECONOMIC PROTESTS

Africa's regime transitions in the early 1990s usually began with popular protests. Pinpointing the genesis of these events is difficult because there is no logical place to start a chronology. In postcolonial Africa, populations rarely remained passive in the face of political abuses or worsening life conditions: students, workers, civil servants, and professionals regularly voiced their opinions in protests, boycotts, demonstrations, strikes, and riots.[16] For example, within two years of independence in the Congo, a strike by 35,000 workers in Brazzaville in August 1963 led to the displacement of the first government. University student protests were common in other francophone countries such as Mali, Côte d'Ivoire, or Sénégal throughout the 1970s, as well as in anglophone Kenya, Zambia, and South Africa.[17] In Sudan, in March 1985, protests against subsidy cuts on basic consumer goods escalated into calls for the resignation of President Nimiery and his subsequent ouster.

In most African countries before 1990, sporadic outbreaks of popular protest were not directed at explicit political goals, let alone at regime change. More commonly, protests were driven by the economic concerns of urban groups over particular policy measures that directly affected their material interests. Demonstrations were calculated to bring immediate relief from economic hardships rather than systemic political changes. Incumbent rulers routinely managed such outbursts by briefly closing institutions (usually the national university or a dissident trade union), expelling protest ringleaders, and coopting others to ensure future quiescence.

Toward the end of the 1980s, popular protests became less easy to contain.[18] Because these outbursts appeared to follow familiar patterns, leaders at first may have underestimated their importance. Typically, as in Bénin, unrest originated among university students demonstrating against cutbacks in government scholarships or allowances, or over campus grievances. In Gabon, in January 1990, students took strike action over shortages of instructors and poor study facilities; in Niger they mobilized against educational policy reforms in February 1990; and in Côte d'Ivoire in the same month, several inopportune electricity cuts immediately before midterm exams sparked the first significant protests.

The protests became progressively politicized. In the first place, more established stakeholders began to speak up. For example, in Zambia from 1985 onward, administrative and parastatal employees, later joined by doctors and nurses, embarked on a wave of wildcat strikes in the public sector. In Guinea in early 1990, teachers struck over complaints of inadequate pay and working conditions, and in Mali violent demonstrations broke out in response to the government's eviction of street traders from the city center in Bamako. In these instances, protesters were responding to austerity measures such as subsidy cuts, salary reductions, or price increases introduced as part of economic adjustment programs.

Civil unrest gathered momentum when diverse urban groups joined forces in loose protest coalitions. The most common galvanizing issue was the loss of purchasing power in an environment of increasing economic uncertainty. In Côte d'Ivoire in February 1990, university faculty and public employees joined students and workers in a strike against cuts in public sector pay and new taxes on private income. In April of the following year, in Gabon, students took to the streets of Libreville to support the demands of teachers for salary increases. In countries where labor movements enjoyed a measure of organization and independence, the preferred weapon of protest became the general strike. Led by a national confederation of trade unions, workers in the industrial, clerical, and transport sectors engaged in coordinated work stoppages in a succession of countries: in Congo in September 1990, in Niger in November 1990, in Gabon and Guinea in May 1991, and in Cameroon and Mauritania in June 1991.[19] These had serious economic consequences – for example, paralyzing transport and commerce in cities across West Africa as absent workers turned them into *villes mortes*.[20]

In exceptional cases, the confrontation with the government focused on political issues from the outset, as when protesters exposed abuses of power committed by incumbent leaders. In Burkina Faso in October 1987, for example, students boycotted classes to protest the military coup that had led to the death of the populist leader Thomas Sankara. In Kenya, campus troubles broke out in February 1990 over the alleged involvement of government security forces in the murder of Foreign Minister Robert Ouko, who was widely perceived as a potential political rival to President Moi. In the same month, an unofficial opposition grouping organized demonstrations in Kinshasa and three other towns in Zaire to commemorate the anniversary of the murder of the country's first prime minister Patrice Lumumba. Although student leadership of political protests may have reflected the heedlessness of youth, it also probably represented young people's lack of attachment to the political values of the nationalist generation. Young urban males were the shock troops of most early protests, though in the Mauritanian capital of Nouakchott, open opposition to the Taya government began with demonstrations by groups of women demanding information on relatives who had "disappeared."

The social composition of early opposition movements was almost exclusively urban. It is true that the 1980s witnessed the rise of peasant organizations in countries like Mali and Madagascar, as well as a wider array of village associations to defend the economic interests of rural populations.[21] Nonetheless, we found little evidence of rural unrest in the first protest phase of regime transition in any African country. Except where armed insurgencies were afoot, the countryside remained politically placid, fulfilling its usual role of following social trends originating in towns and also perhaps reflecting the relative benefits that economic adjustment reforms had brought to farmers. Because early popular protests raised economic grievances, they tended to occur in those urban areas where economic activities were concentrated, even if these were not administrative capitals. Hence, the protest movement began on the Copperbelt in Zambia, the heart of the country's extractive mineral enterprises, and in Douala, Cameroon's economic hub.

Who were the protest leaders? At this stage, protests occurred spontaneously without careful planning, or they were initiated by elements – like students – who were unable to induce other social groups to follow them over the long haul. Trade union officials played a significant role in organizing general strikes but, with the exception of Frederick Chiluba in Zambia, were unable to seize leadership of emerging opposition coalitions. Instead, early economic protests signified the existence of a pool of disgruntled urbanites who had been alienated by government policies and performance but who lacked leadership, organization, or a clear political agenda. This mass constituency was ripe for appropriation by ambitious leaders who could articulate an appealing message of political change.

INITIAL GOVERNMENT RESPONSES

Governments reacted to these early protests with familiar formulas of threat, repression, and selective compromise. Incumbent responses were shaped both by the nature of the protesters' demands and by the availability of public resources. Where protests were directed at bread-and-butter issues and where the government could draw upon patronage rewards, national leaders tried to placate protesters with piecemeal economic concessions. In Côte d'Ivoire, President Houphouët-Boigny reduced student boarding fees and delayed, before eventually renouncing, cuts in civil service pay. In Gabon, President Bongo announced an improved public sector salary scale as well as health benefits and social security reforms. In Guinea, after stalling for many months, the Conté government eventually responded to a recurrent teachers' strike by doubling civil servant salaries and halving the pay of government ministers.

Governments were more likely to employ armed repression in places where the early manifestations of protest were explicitly political. Take the examples cited in the previous section: In Burkina Faso, the Campaoré government purged Sankara loyalists and forced them into exile, even executing those who remained within the army; in Zaire, the police violently dispersed Lumumba sympathizers, arresting protest leaders; and Moi of Kenya ordered paramilitary units to open fire on mourners at the Ouku funeral and imposed bans on public demonstrations and "rumor-mongering." At this stage, incumbents who were confident of their control over the means of coercion regularly used the security apparatus of the state to foil the emergence of challengers. In Cameroon, President Biya had lawyer Yondo Black and eighteen other dissidents arrested and tried for subversion. In Gabon, Joseph Renjambé, secretary general of the leading opposition party, was assassinated; protesters immediately charged that incumbent President Bongo had ordered the killing.

At least in the short run, economic concessions were a more politically effective response than coercion. Although salary awards were insufficient to avert subsequent general strikes in Gabon and Guinea, both Bongo and Conté were able to retain political power. Repression, on the other hand, was likely to arouse the unhappiness of the international community and threaten the flow of aid, on which some governments were extremely dependent. It was also counterproductive, begetting escalating rounds of protest and providing a political rationale around which opponents could organize and combine. For example, the most violent riots since independence in Kenya in July 1990, in which 20 people were killed and more than 1,000 arrested, were a direct popular reaction to the Moi government's decision to detain the emergent leaders of a nascent opposition alliance. And the February 1991 street protests in Niger were prompted by delays over the investigation of student deaths in earlier unrest.

Some political leaders ran out of political options early in the transition process. In countries where the national treasury had been depleted by prolonged economic mismanagement, governments could no longer afford the luxury of buying off opponents by distributing patronage. Moreover, the international donors who were financing economic austerity programs would not countenance slippage in economic policy reform. Nor, for any number of reasons, was the alternative available of calling out the security forces: Either the leader did not have the stomach for repression, or the army would refuse to fire on civilians. A critical consideration was whether the leader could retain support from loyal military units, which in turn was conditional on whether the government could continue to pay them.

By 1990, leaders like Kérékou of Bénin and Kaunda of Zambia discovered that they had exhausted the resources needed to buy off or crush a spreading protest movement. Indeed, the government of Bénin had become a net debtor to the domestic banking system and had begun to delay salary payments as early as 1986.[22] After about mid-1987, President Kérékou lacked the necessary backing within the military to order the armed dispersion of student demonstrators. In Zambia, Kenneth Kaunda retained enough support from army and paramilitary units to put down a coup attempt by a rogue officer in June 1990. But in the same month, he was unable to fully restore subsidy cuts when urbanites rioted over increases in the price of staple foods despite having revoked such increases in response to protests twice before, in 1976 and 1986. By June 1990, his government had become so dependent on international economic assistance that he no longer enjoyed the political flexibility to make popular economic concessions.

THE POLITICIZATION OF DEMANDS

In previous years, rewards and repression had served to quell unrest. Not so in the 1990s. Spurred by deepening economic distress and reacting against heavy-handed government tactics, protesters began to insist on political change. For the first time, narrow economic interests were superseded by widespread calls for the ejection of national leaders and the reintroduction of plural politics.

Protesters began by linking their economic grievances to official corruption and mismanagement, which they blamed for worsening economic conditions. It was no accident that protests turned political in the context of revelations of financial scandals involving top political leaders. In Bénin, public realization that Kérékou's cronies had plundered the state banking and credit system "helped shape political consciousness ... [and gave] rise to the local phrase *'laxisme-béninisme'* to describe the regime's true ideology."[23] In Côte d'Ivoire, a target of protests was the Basilica of Yamoussoukro, the gilded replica of St. Peter's of Rome built at a reported cost of some $145 million, in the home village of the President Houphouët-Boigny. And in Zaire, President Mobutu Sese Seko found himself confronted with frank criticism from civic groups about his ill-gotten personal fortune amassed in Swiss bank accounts. Striking civil servants openly displayed the slogan *"Mobutu, voleur!"*

The political demands of the protesters were at first highly personalized, aimed simply at the removal of top leaders who had lost public confidence. In Togo in April 1991, for example, campus protesters demanded Eyadéma's resignation but did not indicate what they hoped would follow. And in Nigeria in May 1992, a protest against increases in transport fares escalated into calls for the departure of Babangida.

Although propelled mainly by a rage of antiincumbency, the political demands of protesters in some African countries gradually took on a prodemocracy cast. The injection of elements of political liberalism into opposition ideology was closely linked to the emergence of leaders who were able to give voice to the inchoate yearnings of citizens. Rustow has argued that the political struggle of democratization is catalyzed "as the result of the emergence of a new elite that arouses a depressed and previously leaderless social group into concerted action."[24] In sub-Saharan Africa, mass opposition had already been aroused, but it lacked clear direction and a sense of political alternatives. Part of this deficit was addressed when leadership of African protest movements passed from students and workers to political elites. Some of these elites – drawn from the churches, business, and the professions – were new to the national political arena, while others – notably former politicians expelled from the old regime – were hardened from long years of experience in public life.

Under authoritarian regimes in Africa, open opposition to the political order had always been a quixotic and dangerous undertaking. The fall of the Berlin Wall in November 1989, which symbolized the collapse of one-party communist regimes in Eastern Europe, emboldened dissidents. A flurry of brazen political statements was issued in early 1990 that centered on a criticism of one-party rule and raised the banner of multiparty competition for the first time in a generation. On New Year's Day in Nairobi, Kenya, the Reverend Timothy Njoya of the Presbyterian Church of East Africa attacked monopolistic political arrangements in Africa, likening them to failed and crumbling communist regimes.[25] Just a day earlier, Frederick Chiluba, chairman of the Zambia Congress of Trade Unions, had asked publicly at a labor rally, "If the owners of socialism have withdrawn from the one-party system, who are the Africans to continue with it?"[26] Meanwhile, in Cameroon, the February 1990 arrest of Yondo Black for attempting to form an opposition political party led his successor at the head of the national bar association, Bernard Muna, to call openly for multiparty elections. These kinds of statements and the resulting political events in one country were assiduously followed in neighboring countries, where they may have inspired subsequent protests.

Following these initiatives, the multiparty cause spread to the streets. Crowds in Nairobi flashed a two-fingered sign indicating support for political pluralism and for the release of two former cabinet ministers imprisoned for attempting to hold a multiparty rally. In Lusaka, the crowds chanted multiparty slogans as they set ablaze a shrine commemorating President Kaunda's role in the nationalist struggle. In many countries, general strikes were politicized to the point that they became mass movements for multiparty politics. In Gabon, riots in Port Gentil turned into open support for the opposition *Parti Gabonais du Progrès,* and in Congo, the labor confederation hammered home demands for free union elections and registration of new political parties. In Madagascar, scattered protests by a loose coalition of *forces vives* (active forces) by mid-1991 escalated into a general strike that demanded the installation of a provisional government that would include opposition leaders.

Thus, within months of the onset of political transitions, the character of mass protest in Africa had changed. Sporadic outbursts over economic grievances gave way to social movements with political agendas. As the movements became politicized, protesters directed their wrath to symbols of the corruption and mismanagement, such as public monuments and state-owned shops. Within each country, the movement spread outward from the capital to multiple urban centers. As one commentator noted for Bénin, "Demonstration[s] extended far beyond Cotonou; reportedly almost every person and vehicle up to the Togo border carried a branch of leaves in solidarity with those protesting the regime."[27] And for the first time, stirrings of political mobilization became evident in the countryside – for example, as farmers in Mali convened a national meeting in December 1991 to demand land rights, local taxation powers, and the right to independently unionize.[28]

Yet Africa's mass protest movements displayed key weaknesses. First, the emergence of opposition leaders did not always guarantee impressive levels of political organization. At this stage, entrenched governments continued to proscribe unofficial political organizations, forcing adversaries to improvise strategies of confrontation from underground. Denied access to state resources, they fell back on meager pickings from the underdeveloped private sector and the cash-strapped informal sector. Coordinated prodemocracy campaigns emerged only in places like Nigeria, South Africa, and Zambia during later phases of political transition, after governments lifted restrictions on party and civic organizing and after business interests stepped forward with financing. Until then, protest actions remained largely spontaneous; opposition "leaders" rode the wave of unrest rather than directing it.

Second, the social composition of the protest movements was an uneasy amalgam of diverse social elements ranging from workers to businessmen, from students to professionals, from human rights activists and church leaders to regional elites, out-of power politicians, and former military officers.[29] Each of these groups represented distinctive, even conflicting interests that were temporarily papered over in a popular crusade to eject unpopular autocrats. Notably, the loose alliance of business and labor interests – which was central to the coordinated opposition movements that emerged in Nigeria, South Africa, and Zambia – seemed destined to fall apart over conflicting economic interests once immediate political objectives were obtained.

Third, the democratic credentials of Africa's protest movements were questionable. To be sure, the idea of competitive elections caught on quickly as a popular rallying cry, but it was not clear whether incumbent and would-be leaders would conduct elections fairly and accept the verdict of the voters. A few new leaders (from the professional and human rights communities) were probably genuinely committed to universal norms of liberal democracy, but others (especially businessmen and former politicians) more likely planned to use elections to gain political office and access to public resources. Indeed, many protest participants seemed to view democracy instrumentally: Rather than being an end in itself, it was a political means to bring about improvements in livelihood and well-being.

In sum, the diverse groups that spearheaded the political protest movements in Africa came together to expel entrenched autocrats but not necessarily to change political regimes. Support for political rights and institutional pluralism was sparked mainly insofar as these were the antithesis of a discredited system. When protesters began to call for competitive elections, they articulated few systematic plans to permanently change the rules of the political game. It was unclear whether they would simply accept a more benign dictator, or whether they wished to increase political participation and change the procedures with which the people would henceforth regularly choose their own leaders.

Under these circumstances, an observation made about postcolonial Africa's first effort at protest-led change, in the Congo in 1963, was apropos for the 1990s: "The powerful revolutionary movement had no real political strategy of transformation ... no real organized political alternative. People wanted a new regime, a better regime – that was all; [but] they had no clear political conditions or directives."[30] A more recent news analysis pointed in similar terms to the shallowness of the early democratic commitment, which signaled little more than a general discontent with the political status quo: "Many Africans are now so poor they are prepared to back virtually any demand as long as it implies change. More political parties? Fine, as long as something changes."[31]

THE ONSET OF POLITICAL REFORMS

Wherever multiparty sentiment raised its head, the first reaction of incumbent rulers was to mount a defense of the status quo. In Sierra Leone, President

Momoh rejected the multiparty idea with promises instead to encourage "broadly-based participation" within the one-party state.[32] The rhetoric of rattled leaders, often betraying a panicky overreaction, revived old arguments about the supposed advantages of unipartism. Kaunda of Zambia warned darkly that party competition would constitute a return to "stone age politics" of ethnic conflict and electoral violence. Mugabe of Zimbabwe joined Moi of Kenya in vilifying Western support for multipartism as unwarranted interference in the sovereign rights of African states.[33] Implicit in all such arguments was the notion, bluntly expressed by General Kolingba of the Central African Republic, that Africa was "not ready for multiparty democracy."[34] Ironically, this was precisely the argument used by colonial officials to delay granting political independence to Africans three decades earlier.

Nonetheless, after protest demands had turned political, most African heads of state embarked on a course of political liberalization. It is important in this context to note the common conceptual distinction between liberalization and democratization.[35] These processes of political change are complementary and may occur sequentially or simultaneously, but they are ultimately autonomous, both analytically and in practice. Whereas liberalization refers to the political process of reforming authoritarian rule, democratization refers to the construction of the institutions of divided power. In this study, we define political liberalization as the relaxation of government controls on the political activities of citizens, with particular reference to civil liberties.[36]

In referring to political changes in the Soviet Union, Valerie Bunce prefers the term "political liberalization" to "democratization" because the former does not assume an end result of stable democracy. While there is merit to Bunce's concerns, we prefer not to unduly stretch the concept of liberalization to embrace the core democratic institution of competitive elections; we wish to be able to distinguish authoritarian regimes that have merely liberalized from regimes that have been installed as a consequence of competitive election.[37]

The liberalization reforms undertaken by incumbent rulers in Africa in the early 1990s displayed common features. First, incumbents seemed to believe that limited reform would palliate the need for real democratization. By conceding political reforms, African strongmen beat a tactical retreat, grasping the reform nettle in a bid to direct the inexorable change process to their own advantage. Others liberalized more reluctantly, because they had no other choice. Either way, the sudden introduction of long-denied civil liberties did not signify that leaders had undergone overnight conversion, emerging as born-again democrats. Instead, liberalization was an effort by embattled incumbents to belatedly legitimate their rule without tightening controls over lax administration, endangering economic privileges, or surrendering political power. As Huntington writes, leaders used political openings "as a way of defusing opposition to their regime without fully democratizing.... liberalizers did not, however, wish to introduce fully participatory competitive elections that could cause current leaders to lose power."[38]

Furthermore, against a background of growing acknowledgement of human rights norms – symbolized by the ratification of the African Charter of Human and Peoples' Rights by 40 African states by 1990 – autocrats found greater difficulty in committing and hiding violations. Typically, political reform started when rulers loosened restrictions on opponents through (first a selective, later a blanket) amnesty for detainees imprisoned for coup attempts or antigovernment protests. In cases in which harsh political repression had forced opponents to flee abroad – as from Angola, Equatorial Guinea, and Seychelles – political exiles were invited home with promises that they would not be arrested. Sometimes, prominent returning exiles – such as Gilchrist Olympio in Togo and Trovoada and da Graça in São Tomé – went on to lead opposition groups under the newly liberalized dispensation. The most dramatic rehabilitation of a national political leader took place in February 1990 under the glare of worldwide television coverage when Nelson Mandela was released after three decades of detention. At the same time, South African president F. W. de Klerk lifted the ban on political groupings and announced negotiations for a multiracial constitution. Released prisoners of conscience subsequently reentered the political arena in Bénin, Cameroon, Congo, Togo, and Zaire, among other countries.

Incumbents also loosened restrictions on freedom of expression – for instance, by lifting government media monopolies. The government of Tanzania, for instance, eased curbs on press freedom and allowed its own newspapers to carry relatively unfettered debates on the merits of single-party rule. Taking immediate advantage of political openings, African journalists launched literally scores of newspapers and newsmagazines across the continent, almost all speaking with critical voices. Half a dozen lively independent weekly newsmagazines in Swahili and English emerged in Tanzania that bemoaned the government's slow march toward multiparty elections. Even in Chad, the *Ndjamena Hebdo* defied the government, not only by its very appearance but by advocating reform. Political opinions that government censors had previously outlawed as subversive entered mainstream discourse and contributed to flourishing counterhegemonic critiques. The letters-to-the-editor sections of news publications were flooded with an outpouring of political argument. Even within government-controlled media, journalists sought the expression of alternative viewpoints as a counterweight to discredited official propaganda.[39]

African governments were less amenable to extending freedoms of political association, perhaps because this aspect of liberalization implied momentum toward the relegalization of political parties. Already, the number of independent voluntary organizations was growing within civil society, and these groups were adopting increasingly political functions – for example, human rights monitoring and worker or voter education.

As a way of forestalling these trends, leaders embarked on self-directed reforms of the core political institutions – especially ruling parties – over which they were confident of control. For example, in March 1990 President Traoré of Mali initiated a series of conferences on the "exercise of democracy" within the framework of the ruling Democratic Union of Malian People (UDPM). Similarly, President Moi, although seeming to respond to a long-standing request from church leaders for a forum on "The Kenya We Want," packed a 1990 party Review Commission with party stalwarts and tried to rule out discussion of constitutional issues (the Kenya African National Union was then the sole official party). And in mid-1991, King Mswati III of Swaziland established a commission to conduct public forums concerning the reform of the "traditional" institutions of indirect representation through a hierarchy of chiefs. In all cases, however, officials lost control over these gatherings as citizens took advantage of narrow official openings to vent an uninhibited range of political viewpoints.

ONE STEP FORWARD, TWO STEPS BACK

As well as being partial, top-down reforms were halting and episodic. Some leaders granted minor political concessions with one hand while cracking down with the other. Mobutu of Zaire unleashed his presidential guard in a massacre of students at the University of Lubumbashi just two weeks after announcing a return to political pluralism. Ratsiraka of Madagascar, having just ordered the abolition of press censorship, ordered the violent dispersal of a peaceful protest march on the presidential palace, which left 100 dead.

Nor were liberalization reforms irreversible. Cosmetic political openings were easily closed. For example, in Equatorial Guinea, Obiang Nguema reneged on a promise to grant amnesty to political exiles returning from Europe by arresting them as they arrived home. In Malawi, Hastings Banda found it expedient to release long-time detainee Vera Chirwa after the death in custody of her husband in October 1991, but reversed himself by December 1992, slapping former exile Chakufwa Chihana behind bars on sedition charges. The most cynical strongmen may intentionally have announced reforms that they had no intention of implementing. In other cases, promises made by one leader were derailed by a successor. In Sierra Leone, for example, Momoh's gradual political opening was abruptly interrupted by a military coup whose leaders imposed a state of emergency and media censorship.

A liberalized political climate proved hard to sustain. In countries like Chad and Uganda, soldiers continued to engage in acts of intimidation, torture, and extrajudicial execution in civil war zones.[40] In Nigeria and Kenya among other places, governments reverted after brief openings to the use of public security legislation to arrest journalists, to limit access to official "secrets," and to ban publications.[41] Elsewhere, notably in Cameroon and Zambia, incumbent leaders made the most of police powers to deny permission for opposition groups to hold meetings or marches, thereby restricting newly won freedoms of association and assembly.

Instead, the onset of liberalization reforms marked an intensification of political struggle. Incumbent presidents had reacted to opposition challenges as they arose without really comprehending the breadth and intensity of popular dissatisfaction; their tentative openings often were improvised attempts to pre-empt more serious change. Halfhearted concessions did not satisfy mass demands for political pluralism, signaling instead that the incumbent had been political-ly wounded. Consequently, popular protests often escalated following the first concessions. The largest rallies in Bénin occurred after Kérékou abandoned Marx-ism–Leninism, a gesture that citizens dismissed as a palliative in a context of de-mands for immediate salary payments and fundamental political changes. In Madagascar, the increasing tempo of mass marches, some involving hundreds of thousands of participants, proclaimed that incumbent efforts to mix concession with crackdown were not working.

On balance, however, there were more advances than setbacks in the liberal-ization phase of African regime transitions. In most African countries, basic free-doms were more readily available by the end of 1992 than in the 1980s (see In-troduction, Figure 2). As the vulnerabilities of repressive regimes were revealed, ordinary citizens became less fearful of state power and were less inclined to re-main silent and passive when civil liberties were trampled. Independent institu-tions in civil society – like news publications and watchdog groups – began to erect checks and balances, however fragile, against the discretionary excesses of dictators. If not yet fully empowered, Africans were at least emboldened. This awakening of independent political activity was the most profound innovation of Africa's interlude of liberalization.

CONSTITUTIONAL REFORM

Confronted with dogged resistance, many rulers began to recognize the need to renew political legitimacy. Citizens began to entertain the possibility, unthink-able earlier, that single-party regimes might be forced to expose themselves to multiparty elections of indeterminate outcome.

A major breakthrough occurred with the advent of national conferences.[42] As an emergency measure, certain African rulers conceded that elites from civil society could gather in an open national forum to propose solutions for the coun-try's politicoeconomic crisis. National conferences were ad hoc assemblies repre-senting a wide range of individual and corporate interests that lasted from a few days to several months, contained several hundred to several thousand delegates, and were often chaired by a nominally neutral church leader. The Bénin meeting attracted some 500 participants, but subsequent conferences were larger, with 1,200 participants at the Congo sessions and as many as 4,000 delegates in Zaire. Occurring in 11 African countries between 1990 and 1993, national conferences were a largely francophone phenomenon (occurring in Bénin, Chad, Comoros, Congo, Gabon, Mali, Niger, Togo, and Zaire) though deliberative assemblies were also convened by Ethiopia's interim government in July 1991 and at the Conference for a Democratic South Africa (CODESA) in December 1991.[43] As an original form of political association, national conferences amounted to an in-digenously generated African contribution to political institution building and regime transition.[44] Their large size and broadly representative character have been variously interpreted as an updated version of government by traditional village assembly,[45] an African adaptation of the French revolutionary heritage of the Estates General,[46] or as an essentially antidemocratic exercise in which elites from a highly fragmented civil society spoke mainly for themselves.[47] Tessy Bakary has gone so far as to label several of the national conferences as in effect a "civilian Putsch."[48]

On a formal level, some national conferences were astonishingly successful at rewriting constitutions. In a common sequence of events, the conferees seized the function of law-giving by declaring themselves sovereign. Using these newly claimed powers, they typically went on to abrogate the existing constitution, dissolve the sitting legislature, and establish a transitional government. Even if the president was not supplanted as head of state, he was required to work with an interim prime minister selected by the conference and to surrender powers over finance, defense, and foreign affairs. The conference then proceeded to draft a new constitution, or established an independent commission to do so, submitting this document to a national referendum. On an even more ambitious level, the national conferences set out to review the informal ground rules of politics that lay beneath written laws. Their success was much more limited in this latter objective. Although the conferees inveighed against official corruption and discussed indictments against particular rulers and specific cronies, there was little attempt to come to grips with the sociological causes of corruption. One searches in vain for the equivalent of the night of August 4, 1789, when the French Estates General, having turned itself into the National Assembly, voted to abolish all feudal privileges.

Moreover, incumbent rulers fought back. Some – like Paul Biya in Cameroon and André Kolingba in the Central African Republic – refused to countenance a national conference at all, turning this issue into the central demand of the reform coalition. Other leaders tried to twist the process to their advantage; Bongo in Gabon caught the opposition off guard when he convened a national conference without warning and then manipulated the proceedings.[49] Yet others remonstrated and dissembled. For example, Eyadéma pulled his government delegation out of the Togo conference when it declared itself sovereign, and he suspended it when the conferees attempted to remove his powers over the armed forces. In South Africa, the opposition walked out of CODESA in June 1992, interrupting proceedings for several months in favor of a strategy of "rolling protests."[50] In all these cases the process of constitutional reform was derailed while power struggles played themselves out.

Governments that did not hold national conferences fashioned alternate routes toward constitutional reform. In some cases, the supreme leader convinced a top organ of the ruling party to require a sitting legislature to amend key clauses in an existing constitution. In other cases, incumbent rulers found it necessary to charter a nominally nonpartisan commission whose membership included at least a token opposition presence.[51] Opposition forces were rarely satisfied with either the procedures or the results of such official plans. President Mwinyi's constitutional commission in Tanzania, which was charged to ascertain national opinion on multipartism, drew its entire membership from the ruling Chama Cha Mapinduzi (CCM). In Ghana, Jerry Rawlings packed the constitutional commission with his own supporters, stretched out the constitutional drafting deadline, and inserted clauses into the final document favorable to his Peoples' National Defense Council (PNDC). In Zambia, the government's revisions to the constitution proved unacceptable to the opposition, which threatened to boycott promised elections unless further changes were made.

In almost all African countries, a similar set of constitutional reforms was introduced in quick succession. First, political parties were relegalized, often accomplished by the simple expedient of repealing the clause in the national constitution that endowed a single party with monopoly status. In Côte d'Ivoire, Kenya, and Seychelles, rubber-stamp legislatures took the requisite action after the top leader signaled that he would no longer resist. Military strongmen convinced ruling military councils to make constitutional concessions in Burkina Faso and Burundi. The new rules of competitive politics commonly encouraged a proliferation of small parties. Whereas in 1975, the number of registered political parties in sub-Saharan African countries averaged 1.9, by 1993 this figure had risen to 15.9, in a range from two registered parties in Nigeria to 62 in Burkina Faso.[52]

Second, reformers sought to establish the constitutional separation of powers. Implicit in the relegalization of political associations was the severance of linkages between official parties and the state and the repeal of constitutional provisions for party supremacy in political decision making. In Angola, not only was the party separated from the state, but the army was separated from the party. Moreover, the new constitutions strengthened legislative bodies vis à vis the executive branch – for example, introducing powers to confirm presidential appointees and investigate the financial performance of government agencies. Constitution-makers also adopted limits on the number of terms in office that national presidents could serve, usually requiring them to step down after two five-year terms. Of the 37 African constitutions that were in force by 1994, all but four contained provisions for term limits.[53] The introduction of term limits went to the heart of regime transitions in Africa, driven as they were by a mass consensus that old-guard leaders had outstayed their welcome.

Third, most African governments announced dates for multiparty presidential and parliamentary elections. Wherever incumbents retained real power, they manipulated the electoral timetable. If they judged their chances of winning to be good, the timetable was usually brisk; if they feared defeat, it was more likely to be protracted and uncertain. When time was short, reformers were unable to undertake extensive revisions of electoral codes and had to enter election campaigns under old sets of rules that favored incumbents. Because transitional constitutions were at best imperfect compromise documents, opposition leaders – for example, in Cape Verde and Zambia – promised further legal reform if they won power. Once a polling date was announced, however, attention turned to the election campaign.

FOUNDING ELECTIONS

Campaigns for Africa's founding elections were boisterous affairs that released pent-up political energy and repeatedly threatened to spin out of control. Despite the dire straits of most African economies, though perhaps unsurprisingly after three decades of one-man rule, campaigns centered more on personalities than policies. To the extent that substantive matters were discussed at all, opposition leaders charged that the holders of power were corrupt and incompetent, all the while adopting a calculated vagueness concerning plans to restore future economic growth and social welfare. With few socioeconomic achievements of their own to point to, incumbents tended to run on claims about their stature as internationally recognized leaders or on platforms of peace and stability, painting gloomy scenarios of interethnic chaos should they lose the election. All sides let loose with vitriolic personal attacks on their rivals, heightening an atmosphere of wild rumor that often centered on speculations about the shifting political allegiances of the military.

Because liberalization reforms were incomplete or ongoing, electoral campaigns were suffused with continuing struggles over political rules. At the heart of these struggles was opposition concern over the close coupling of ruling party and state, an institutional linkage that was held to be inappropriate in a new era of multiparty competition, not to mention a source of undue incumbent advantage. Predictably, officeholders used state power to tilt the rules of political competition in their own favor – for example, by ignoring or amending constitutional and electoral rules. In Cameroon, Biya rushed to a presidential election in October 1992 in apparent violation of a constitutional provision requiring the resignation of the president prior to an unscheduled early election.[54] In Kenya, Moi pushed through a constitutional amendment shortly before the December 1992 election, requiring the winner to obtain 25 percent of the votes in five out of the country's eight provinces, a move widely seen as a benefit to a national incumbent against regionally based opponents.[55] In Zambia, Kaunda retained the power to supersede the constitution by maintaining a state of emergency in effect throughout the election campaign. Throughout francophone Africa, incumbents worked through the ministry of the interior or its equivalent to maintain direct control over the appointment of electoral personnel and the implementation of campaign and polling procedures. Elsewhere, they refused to reopen outdated or inaccurate voter registers, with the common effect of disenfranchising young, mobile people whose political affiliations tended toward the opposition.

The occupants of state office also deployed public resources for partisan electoral purposes. The election campaigns of incumbent leaders were funded from the national treasury, sometimes – as in Kenya, Zambia, Ghana, and Malawi – with an observably negative impact on the government's budget deficit. These campaigns involved more or less explicit attempts at vote-buying, ranging from promises of future development projects through the distribution of campaign paraphernalia (T-shirts were especially popular items among the ill-clothed), to outright cash payments to individual voters. While ruling party officials were ferried to campaign rallies in government vehicles (with the party's top candidate often arriving in the presidential helicopter), opposition parties made do by piecing together private resources. While incumbents established their own preferred campaign schedule, opposition parties commonly discovered that police permits for campaign rallies were unavailable or canceled at the last minute.

With a few exceptions – like Angola, where armed clashes occurred between supporters of MPLA and UNITA in the final weeks of the campaign, and Kenya, where government agents provoked ethnic pogroms in the politically contested Rift Valley area – Africa's election campaigns were generally peaceful. Scattered incidents of political violence occasionally broke out only as polling day approached. Nor was electoral fraud inordinately common during polling and vote-counting. If there was interference in the conduct of African transition elections, it tended to take the form of intimidation or inducements well before the polls (see Chapter 6).

Although outspent and outmaneuvered, opposition forces enjoyed certain strengths of their own. They could offer appealing political messages of antiincumbency and prodemocracy that captured the giddy aspirations of the moment; opposition visions of a brighter future, however ill-formed or impractical, generated larger and more animated crowds than the thin and sullen ranks that were dutifully rounded up for official campaign rallies. For the first time, opposition parties could disseminate their messages through independent newspapers that were quickly snapped up by eager readers; occasional grudging access – though hardly equal time – was even occasionally obtained on state-controlled radio and television. Significantly, the opposition's political base penetrated the apparatus of the state, with schoolteachers and other public employees openly allowing their partisan preferences to be known. Although the old regimes tried to prohibit civil servants from political activity, in practice these "dissidents within" quietly reallocated public resources toward opposition causes. In defining moments in selected countries, judicial and police officials chose to reassert their professionalism and neutrality – for example, by refusing to implement orders to quash opposition rallies or by ruling against the state in legal cases concerning campaign fairness.

The effectiveness of the opposition in electioneering, however, depended greatly on the strength of its fledgling political organizations and whether they could unify into a coherent coalition. In most cases, the new crop of political "parties" constituted little more than an ambitious politician, a handful of acolytes, and a nonexistent base of members and finances. The new atmosphere of associational freedom encouraged the unchecked proliferation of weak organizations, internecine bickering, and the fragmentation of opposition movements. Even the most effective opposition movements were hamstrung by shaky finances. The new political parties therefore commonly turned to wealthy business patrons who, in return for supplying ready campaign cash, claimed top party leadership posts or promises of future political favors. Widespread animosity toward the strongman combined with financial needs to create odd coalitions of business, labor, and intellectuals that were inherently unstable but could be briefly effective as electoral vehicles.

In the struggle over rules and resources, opposition forces once in a while obtained at least part of what they wanted. Sometimes they won changes in voting rules, as when the MMD pressured the Zambian government to agree that party agents could accompany ballot boxes from polling sites to counting centers. At other times, they gained access to campaign resources, as when the Cameroon communication ministry conceded that all political parties should have free and equal TV and radio air time in the two weeks preceding the elections. The opposition movements' most successful electoral demand was for election monitoring by independent groups of international and domestic observers. Incumbent leaders had to be pushed to accede to this demand, which many saw as a risky abdication of sovereign authority. They ultimately agreed, however, perhaps calculating that, in the event that they won the elections, a neutral certification of electoral fairness would help to legitimize their own victories. When observers were able to announce that elections had been "free and fair," a foundation was created for a new political regime based on the rule that top political leaders were chosen by the people.

DIVERGENT TRANSITION PATHS

The existence of continent-wide political trends did not mean that every African was destined to march in lockstep. Far from it. African countries embarked on distinctive and divergent paths of political change; most importantly, some arrived at a democratic regime while others failed to do so. We identify the major forks in the branching tree of regime transitions by posing the following questions:

Did protest occur?
Was there political liberalization?
Did the country complete a democratic election?

Figure 6 represents diagramatically the various paths charted by African countries during the period of regime transition. The numbers in parentheses signify the number of countries that did (Yes) or did not (No) experience protest, liberalization, and free elections. Notice that a reduced sample size is used here and in the rest of this study; instead of the full population of all 47 sub-Saharan African countries, we now focus on the 42 countries that had authoritarian regimes in 1989. In other words, the five countries with existing multiparty regimes at that time – Botswana, Gambia, Mauritius, Sénégal, and Zimbabwe – were held aside because they had previously undergone a regime transition through competitive elections. We restore this set of cases to analysis in Chapter 7 when we assess the longer-term performance – and limitations – of actual democracies in Africa.

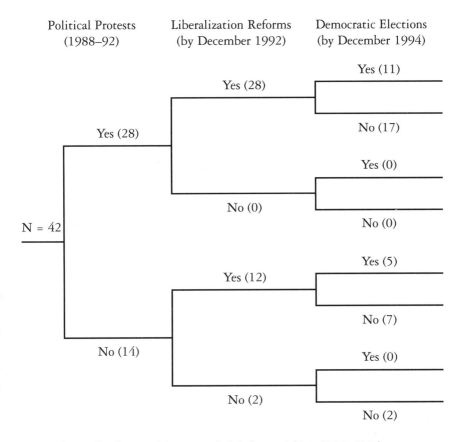

Political Protests (1988–92) — Liberalization Reforms (by December 1992) — Democratic Elections (by December 1994)

Figure 6   Paths of Regime Transition, Sub-Saharan Africa, 1988–1994

For now, we explore each fork in the transitions diagram, beginning with protest. We would not have identified protests as a general catalyst of political change in Africa unless these events had been widespread. According to data collected for the period 1988 to 1992, street demonstrations calling for political reform occurred in a majority of the countries under review (28 out of 42). The tendency for African transitions to be sparked by protest should not deflect attention, however, from the 14 African countries that experienced no mass disturbances during this period. If a country was consumed by internal war, opposition to the incumbent regime was sidetracked from peaceful political demonstration into armed struggle (Angola, Ethiopia, Liberia, Mozambique, and Somalia). Even where relatively stable governments managed to restrict armed insurrections to up-country regions, civilian opposition activity was risky in the context of the regime's security controls (Djibouti, Rwanda before 1994, Sudan, and Uganda). In countries without armed opposition groups, opposition elements were poorly organized and easily outmaneuvered by incumbent state elites (Burundi, Cape Verde, Lesotho, São Tomé, and Seychelles). Thus, although political protest was widespread, it was not universal.

The second branch in the transitions tree distinguishes the incidence of liberalization reforms. Notably, almost all African regimes opened up to some degree by the end of 1992. Only two African countries entirely avoided meaningful political reforms. In Liberia, the repeated failure of three warring factions to abide by externally brokered peace agreements impeded progress toward the establishment of a timetable for general elections.[56] And in Sudan, the military government of Muhammed al-Bashir ceded power behind the scenes to the National Islamic Front but by December 1994 had failed to follow through on a pledge to "return to democratic rule."[57] As noted before, promising early openings during political transitions were sometimes sealed again later. Deliberalization occurred even in some of Africa's long-standing multiparty regimes – for example, when President Abdou Diouf of Sénégal briefly placed his principal political opponent in administrative detention following violence after the legislative elections of May 1993.[58]

Notably, the absence of political protest did not preclude movement down a path of transition. In the war-torn countries, political liberalization came about as the product of the terms of an internationally supervised peace agreement (Angola and Mozambique) or an outright guerrilla victory (Ethiopia). More commonly – in 11 of the 14 countries that did not experience protest – incumbent rulers took the lead by introducing political openings at their own initiative. They did so either as part of a planned power transfer from military to civilian rule (for example, Burundi, Lesotho, Somalia, and Uganda), or as one-party leaders of small states that were strapped for donor development resources (for example, Djibouti, Cape Verde, and Seychelles). It is therefore noteworthy that, although transition processes in Africa were usually driven from below by mass protest, they were sometimes initiated from the top down at the behest of incumbent rulers. Not only does this observed variance in the onset of transition beg explanation, but as an explanatory variable in its own right, it suggests subsequent divergences in transition trajectories.

Finally, on the outermost branchlets of the transition tree, political paths parted according to whether African countries convened a democratic election (see Figure 6, last column). Sixteen sub-Saharan countries met this minimal procedural test for a transition to democracy by the end of 1994. In these cases, new governments were installed following competitive elections that were freely and fairly conducted, in which the losers accepted the verdict of the voters. Given the critical precedent of Bénin, and the global wave of democratization in the late twentieth century, one might be tempted to assume democratic outcomes throughout Africa.[59] But this would be unwarranted. Alongside the 16 governments that convened democratic elections by the end of 1994, 26 governments either failed to hold elections (13) or in their elections fell short of basic standards of free and fair conduct (13).

At this stage, we simply wish to catalogue the diversity of transition paths traced by African countries. With reference to Figure 6, we discerned five basic paths of regime transition in Africa in the period ending in 1994 (see last column, nonzero branches). In this chapter, we simply note these paths, reserving analysis of interesting relationships among their elements – for example, between protest and liberalization reforms, or between liberalization and democratic elections – until later.

First, democratization occurred most frequently in countries that *liberalized following political protests.* Eleven African countries completed this general path.[60] This modal route to democracy led from protest, through liberalization, to free and fair elections (see Figure 6, top branch).

Second, the most common path of regime transition was *liberalization without democratization.* More countries (17) followed this path than the previous one, making it the *most* common transition path of all. In these countries, the old regime experienced political openings following popular protests but failed to consummate a democratic transition via free and fair elections.

Third, democratization was possible *without protest.* Five countries held democratic elections under circumstances in which the initiative to liberalize had been taken by political elites in the absence of political pressure from below.[61]

Fourth, when elites took the lead on liberalization, the more common outcome was a *failure to democratize,* a path traced by seven countries.

Finally, transition was entirely precluded in the two countries (Liberia and Sudan) that experienced neither protest nor liberalization.

How can the outcomes of these transition trajectories be categorized? The distribution of African countries by transition outcomes is reported in Table 4. We assumed that, by definition, a *precluded* transition would lead to a dead end. We then combined countries that experienced democratic elections, regardless of whether initiated by protesters or elites, into a single category of *democratic* transition outcomes (n = 16). And we distinguished among nondemocratic outcomes, not so much in terms of the pathways that led to them but by the more important criteria of whether elections were convened and conducted fairly. Where incumbent elites avoided elections, we deemed the transition *blocked* (n = 12); where incumbents accepted an electoral test but manipulated its conduct or results, we discerned a *flawed* transition outcome (n = 12).

We conclude this chapter by describing each of these outcomes and the forms of political regime they spawned.

In the two cases where transitions were *precluded,* political conditions were unconducive to the construction of any kind of functioning form of governance. Most notably, endemic civil war made the internal security situation so uncertain that civil society was cowed or destroyed, political elites were preoccupied with military conflicts, and efforts at political reform could not get underway. Protagonists were unable to agree on the boundaries of the political community, let

Table 4. *Transition Outcomes, Sub-Saharan Africa, 1994*[a]

Precluded Transitions	Blocked Transitions	Flawed Transitions	Democratic Transitions
(2)	(12)	(12)	(16)
Liberia	Angola	Burkina Faso	Bénin
Sudan	Burundi	Cameroon	Cape Verde
	Chad	Comoros	Central African Republic
	Ethiopia	Côte d'Ivoire	Congo
	Guinea	Djibouti	Guinea-Bissau
	Nigeria	Equatorial Guinea	Lesotho
	Rwanda	Gabon	Madagascar
	Sierra Leone	Ghana	Malawi
	Somalia	Kenya	Mali
	Tanzania	Mauritania	Mozambique
	Uganda	Swaziland	Namibia
	Zaire	Togo	Niger
			São Tomé
			Seychelles
			South Africa
			Zambia

[a] As of December 31, 1994.

alone the rules for selecting political leaders and making public policy. In Liberia, regime transition was precluded by the collapse of the apparatus of the central state, and with it the authority of the incumbent regime.[62] In Sudan, where the center held, regime transition was precluded by the intransigence of the incumbent rulers, who used popular armed resistance in the south of the country as an excuse to harden the regime.

In a larger number of countries (12), transitions were *blocked*. Political reforms were launched but never fully realized. Most commonly – as in Zaire and Rwanda – rulers made insincere and tactical concessions aimed at buying time to shore up collapsing authority, with no apparent intention of implementing elections or surrendering power. Alternatively – as in Nigeria and Togo – a powerful corporate group such as the military became threatened by the pace and direction of reform and intervened to nip it in the bud. Sometimes – as in Tanzania and Uganda – the timetable for reform set by state elites was so protracted that, by the end of 1994, it still had not run its course. Whatever the reason, in blocked transitions an initially promising process bogged down.

In the same number of countries (12), incumbent strongmen could not halt opposition demands for political reform. Instead, they allowed the reform process to unfold to a considerable extent, often actually losing control over the process. For example, and often explicitly against their better judgment, incumbent rulers acquiesced to competitive elections. At the same time, however, they exploited the powers of incumbency to dictate the rules of the political game by manipulating electoral laws, monopolizing campaign resources, or interfering with the polls. The results – as in Cameroon, Gabon, Ghana, and Kenya – were dubious elections that usually returned the incumbent. Such transitions were *flawed*.

Democratic regimes emerged only through valid electoral transitions. If we add the countries (16) that experienced democratic transitions between 1990 and 1994 to the five preexisting African multiparty regimes, then 45 percent of African countries can be said to have obtained the minimal attributes of democracy by the end of 1994 – 21 "democracies" out of 47 sub-Saharan countries. Conspicuously, however, democracy in Africa was an attribute of small states. Out of 21 extant democratic regimes, nine had 1989 populations of fewer than 2 million and four had populations of fewer than 1 million. Hence, the proportion of Africans living under democratic regimes was a mere 25 percent of the total population of the continent.[63]

And how meaningful were democratic political innovations? Changes to the formal architecture of political regimes did not necessarily break the mold of African politics or prevent the endurance of deeply ingrained habits of rule. As has been documented, postcolonial African politics was forged in the crucible of neopatrimonialism (see Chapter 2). Even after 1990, political leaders continued to struggle for the prize of state office, not merely in an altruistic bid to serve the public but also as a means to personal economic gain and in order to accumulate resources with which to build a political following. A view of public office as the object of political contestation is entirely consistent with a notion of indirect democracy based on the election of political representatives. Indeed, multiparty elections encouraged a scramble for high positions in which an expanded array of contenders used proven tactics of promising future material benefits to loyal voters. Under the surface of dramatic regime change flowed deep currents of political continuity.

Moreover, Africa's democratic transitions often led to the installation of extremely fragile regimes. One such regime collapsed even before the period of transition had wound down: The government of Melchior Ndadaye, elected in Burundi in June 1993, succumbed almost immediately to a military coup. In Niger, a military coup would similarly overthrow the regime of President Mahamane Ousmane in January 1996; it had never managed to establish a working majority in parliament during its two and a half years in power.[64] In other places – like Mali, Guinea, and Lesotho – the tentative acceptance of democratic rules was soon marred when ethnic blocs, students, or the military reignited violence as a means to press political demands. Some elected governments – like Congo and Zambia – fell back temporarily on state of emergency decrees to contain perceived dissent, evoking Latin American models of *"democradura"* (hard democracy). By 1995, the remaining new democracies entered a second round of elections that would help to determine whether competitive politics would become institutionalized. These challenges of consolidating democratic regimes are discussed in Chapter 7.

All other political transitions in Africa resulted in nondemocratic regimes. Especially following flawed transitions (and during transitions temporarily blocked by an elongated timetable), the resultant regime was a liberalized form of autocracy in which new political freedoms (for example, to criticize the government) coexisted uneasily alongside practices of governance inherited from the past. Liberalized authoritarianism – called *dictablanda* in the Latin American context – is an unstable form of regime. Its political openings were easily and summarily shut as strongmen placed ever heavier reliance on a shrinking circle of military loyalists. In the worst-case scenarios, blocked or precluded transitions led to an intensification of political conflict, to anarchy (a regime without rules of any kind), and to the implosion of the authority of the state.

Africa's incipient democracies thus emerged amidst the persistence and mutation of various forms of personalistic authoritarian regimes. Explaining the dizzying variation in the onset, dynamics, and outcomes of Africa's regime transitions is the object of the following chapters.

ENDNOTES

1. Richard Joseph, "Africa: The Rebirth of Political Freedom," *Journal of Democracy* 2 (1992): 11–25; Dag Hammarskjold Foundation, *The State in Crisis in Africa: In Search of a Second Liberation* (Uppsala, Sweden: Dag Hammarskjold Foundation, 1992); Goran Hyden and Michael Bratton, "Preface," in *Governance and Politics in Africa,* ed. Hyden and Bratton (Boulder, Colo.: Lynne Rienner, 1992); George Ayittey, *Africa Betrayed* (New York: St. Martin's Press, 1992).
2. The editors of *Africa Demos* conceded that "as the new year [1993] begins, we are no longer so optimistic. The struggle for democracy has been forced onto a new and disadvantageous plane," 3 (1993): 14. See also René Lemarchand, "Africa's Troubled Transitions," *Journal of Democracy* 3 (1993): 98–109.
3. Marguerite Michaels, "Retreat from Africa," *Foreign Affairs* 72 (1993): 93. In the gothic vein, see also Robert D. Kaplan, "The Coming Anarchy: How Scarcity, Crime, Overpopulation, Tribalism, and Disease Are Rapidly Destroying the Social Fabric of Our Planet," *Atlantic Monthly* 273 (1994): 44–65.
4. David Peterson, "Africa's Rocky Ascent," *Freedom Review* 24 (1993): 17.
5. For the data on which these statements are based, see Chapter 6, Table 7.
6. Michael Chege, "Between Africa's Extremes," *Journal of Democracy* 6 (1995): 44–51.
7. Achille Mbembe, "Complex Transformations in Late 20th-Century Africa," *Africa Demos* 3 (1995): 28.

8. For perceptive accounts of practices of political accountability in African societies, see John Lonsdale, "Political Accountability in African History," and Donal Cruise O'Brien, "Wails and Whispers: The People's Voice in West African Muslim Politics," both in *Political Domination in Africa*, ed. Patrick Chabal (Cambridge: Cambridge University Press, 1986), pp. 126–57, 71–83.

9. Many authors have endeavored to explain why the African state has performed poorly as an instrument of capitalist development. Among the most persuasive are Goran Hyden, *No Shortcuts to Progress: African Development Management in Comparative Perspective* (Berkeley: University of California Press, 1983); Richard Sandbrook, *The Politics of Africa's Economic Stagnation* (Cambridge: Cambridge University Press, 1985); Thomas Callaghy, "The State as Lame Leviathan: The Patrimonial Administrative State in Africa," in *The African State in Transition*, ed. Zakis Ergas (New York: St. Martin's Press, 1987); and Catherine Boone, *Merchant Capital and the Roots of State Power in Sénégal, 1930–1985* (Cambridge: Cambridge University Press, 1992). These issues are further explored in Chapter 3.

10. At the end of 1987, 17 of the African rulers in office had been in power 10 years or more. See "Appendix," in Henry S. Bienen and Nicolas van de Walle, *Of Time and Power: Leadership Duration in the Modern World*. (Stanford, Calif.: Stanford University Press, 1991).

11. Williams, "Africa in Retrospect and Prospect," *Africa South of the Sahara, 1994* (London: Europa Publications, 1995), p. 6.

12. Claude Ake, "The Unique Case of African Democracy," *International Affairs* 69 (1993): 239.

13. *Ibid.,* 240.

14. Adam Pzeworski, "Problems in the Study of Transition to Democracy," in *Transitions from Authoritarian Rule: Comparative Perspectives,* vol. 3, ed. Guillermo O'Donnell, Philippe C. Schmitter, and Laurence Whitehead (Baltimore: Johns Hopkins University Press, 1986), p. 53.

15. Samuel P. Huntington, *The Third Wave: Democratization in the Late Twentieth Century* (Norman: University of Oklahoma Press, 1991), p. 45.

16. For example, John A. Wiseman, "Urban Riots in West Africa, 1977–1985," *Journal of Modern African Studies* 24 (1986): 509–18; Robert H. Bates, *Markets and States in Tropical Africa: The Political Basis of Agricultural Policies* (Berkeley: University of California Press, 1981), pp. 31–2; Peter Anyang' Nyong'o, *Popular Struggles for Democracy in Africa* (London: Zed Books, 1987); and Achille Mbembe, *Afriques Indociles* (Paris: Karthala, 1988).

17. On the francophone countries, see Achille Mbembe, *Les Jeunes et L'Ordre Politique en Afrique Noire* (Paris: l'Harmattan, 1985). For an even broader comparative view that includes North African cases, consult Mahmood Mamdani and Ernest Wamba-dia-Wamba, eds., *African Studies in Social Movements and Democracy* (Dakar, Sénégal: Council for the Development of Social Science Research (CODESRIA), 1995).

18. These political protests are described and analyzed in Albert Bourgi and Christian Castern, *Le Printemps de l'Afrique* (Hachette: Paris, 1992); and Paul John Marc Tedga, *Ouverture Démocratique en Afrique Noire?* (Paris: l'Harmattan, 1991). See also Samuel Decalo, "The Process, Prospects and Constraints of Democratization in Africa," *African Affairs* 91 (1992): 7–35; and Célestin Monga, *Anthropologie de la Colère: Société Civile et Démocratie en Afrique Noire* (Paris: l'Harmattan, 1994).

19. In Mauritania, where the labor movement was divided, the strike was observed only in selected sectors and some members of the workers' confederation denounced it as illegal.

20. In the best-known example of this phenomenon, a coalition of opposition groups in Cameroon initiated "Operation Ghost Town" in May 1991 to shut down commerce from Monday to Friday every week until the government would agree to accept a national conference to discuss democratization. Although failing to have much impact in the capital city of Yaoundé, the shutdown seriously undercut public transport and market and other retail activity in Douala. The strike, which was always most effective in the western part of the country, gradually faltered as workers and traders found they could not afford to sustain it. Kenneth B. Noble, "Strike Aims to Bleed Cameroon's Economy to Force President's Fall," *New York Times*, 5 August 1991; and "Cameroon: Crisis or Compromise," *Africa Confidential*, 25 October 1991. For a broader overview of this period, see also Luc Sindjoun, "Cameroun: Le Système Politique Face aux Enjeux de la Transition Démocratique, 1990–93," in *l'Afrique Politique, 1994: Vue sur la Démocratisationa Marée Basse*, ed. Patrick Quantin (Paris: Karthala, 1994), pp. 143–66; and the sometimes useful albeit very biased Zacharie Ngniman, *Cameroun: la Démocratie Emballée* (Yaoundé, Cameroon: Editions Clé, 1994).

21. For a survey of these issues in francophone Africa, see Dominique Gentil and Marie Rose Mercoiret, "Y a-t-il un Mouvement Paysan en Afrique Noire?", *Revue Tiers Monde* 32 (1991): 867–86.

22. Richard Westebbe, "Structural Adjustment, Rent Seeking, and Liberalization in Benin," in *Economic Change and Political Liberalization in Sub-Saharan Africa*, ed. Jennifer A. Widner (Baltimore: Johns Hopkins University Press, 1994), pp. 87, 88. He notes that in all of francophone Africa, salaries as a proportion of revenues were highest in Bénin.

23. Chris Allen, " 'Goodbye to All That': The Short and Sad Story of Socialism in Bénin," *Journal of Communist Studies* 8 (1992): 68.

24. Dankwart A. Rustow, "Transitions to Democracy: Toward a Dynamic Model," *Comparative Politics* 2 (1970): 352.

25. *Weekly Review* (Nairobi), 5 January 1990.

26. *Times of Zambia*, 31 December 1989.

27. Westebbe, "Structural Adjustment," p. 95.

28. R. James Bingen, "Agricultural Development Policy and Grassroots Democracy in Mali: The Emergence of Mali's Farmer Movement," *African Rural and Urban Studies* 1 (1994): 57–72.

29. See Ake, "Unique Case," 239.

30. Ernest Wamba-dia-Wamba, "The Experience of Struggle in the People's Republic of Congo," in *Popular Struggles for Democracy in Africa*, p. 103.

31. *Africa Confidential*, 27 July 1990.

32. *Africa South of the Sahara, 1994*, p. 758.

33. At the time, Mugabe was swimming against the tide by advocating an end to multiparty competition. He was eventually forced to recant his commitment to create a one-party state when a vote in the ruling party's Politburo revealed him to be almost totally isolated on the issue. *Africa Confidential* 31 (June 1990).

34. *Marchés Tropicaux et Méditerranéens*, 18 May 1990.

35. Guillermo O'Donnell and Philipe C. Schmitter, *Transitions from Authoritarian Rule: Tentative Conclusions about Uncertain Democracies,* vol. 4 (Baltimore: Johns Hopkins University Press, 1986), p. 7. See also Doh Chull Shin, "On the Third Wave of Democratization: A Synthesis and Evaluation of Recent Theory and Research," *World Politics* 47 (1994): 142; and William Tordoff, "Political Liberalization and Economic Reform in Africa," *Democratization,* 1 (1994): 100–15.

36. Defined this way, *political* liberalization is an analogue of *economic* liberalization. It reduces government intervention in the political marketplace, breaks up public monopolies of political authority, and allows greater pluralism of opinions and associations.

37. Bunce, "The Struggle for Liberal Democracy in Eastern Europe," *World Policy Journal* 7 (1990): 395–430.

38. Huntington, *Third Wave,* p. 129.

39. In a major victory for Africa's independent press, the 1991 Windhoek Declaration committed the United Nations Educational, Social and Cultural Organization (UNESCO) to move away from supporting state-run news institutions in favor of a plurality of nongovernmental media initiatives. For an overview of liberalization in the African media see G. I. Faringer, *Press Freedom in Africa* (New York: Praeger, 1991) and John C. Merrill, ed., *Global Journalism: Survey of International Communication* (New York: Longman, 1995), pp. 209–68.

40. Amnesty International, *Amnesty International Report* (London: Amnesty International, 1992).

41. Leonard Sussman, "New Seeds of Press Freedom," *Freedom Review* 24 (1993): 65–7.

42. The best summary account in English is provided by Célestin Monga, "National Conferences in Francophone Africa: An Assessment," (paper presented to the annual conference of the School for Advanced International Studies [SAIS] African Studies Program, Washington, D.C., April 15, 1994). See also Pearl Robinson, "The National Conference Phenomenon in Francophone Africa," *Comparative Studies in Society and History* 36 (1994): 575–610; and F. Eboussi Boulaga, *Les Conférences Nationales en Afrique Noire* (Paris: Editions Karthala, 1993).

43. The Ethiopian national conference was carefully stage-managed by the Ethiopian Peoples' Revolutionary Democratic Front, which prepared the agenda and created several of the groups that attended. J. Stephen Morrison, "Ethiopia Charts a New Course," *Journal of Democracy* 3 (1992): 127. The heavy hand of the incumbent also shaped the proceedings of the national conferences in Gabon and Zaire. In Burkina Faso, Blaise Campaoré convened a sham conference of his own design *after* elections that was suspended within two weeks as a result of disagreements over broadcasting the proceedings.

44. "Viewed as an institution, [the] national conference has ... been instrumental ... in the transition towards democracy ... [enabling] political reforms that might make it possible for certain leaders to hand over power in an orderly transition." Momar Coumba Diop and Mamadou Diouf, "Statutory Political Successions: An Afterword," *CODESRIA Bulletin* (Dakar: Center for the Development of Social Science Research in Africa) 3 (1991): 8. This is also the central argument of Boulaga's *Les Conferences Nationales* (1993).

45. Boulaga, *Les Conferences Nationales,* 147–62.

46. Robinson, "The National Conference Phenomenon," 590–6.
47. Nicolas van de Walle, "Neopatrimonialism and Democracy in Africa, with an Illustration from Cameroon," in *Economic Change and Political Liberalization in Sub-Saharan Africa,* ed. Jennifer A. Widner (Baltimore: Johns Hopkins University Press, 1994), p. 140.
48. Bakary, "Une Autre Forme de Putsch: La Conférence Nationale Souveraine," *Géopolitique Africaine* 15 (1992).
49. C. Mba, "La Conférence Nationale Gabonaise: Des Congrès Constitutif du Rassemblement Social Démocrate Gabonais aux Assises pour la Démocratie Pluraliste," in *Afrique 2000,* 7 (1991): 75–90.
50. Andrew Reynolds, ed., *Election '94: South Africa: The Campaign, Results and Future Prospects* (New York: St. Martin's Press, 1994), pp. 9–11.
51. As in Cameroon, Ghana, Guinea, Rwanda, Sierra Leone (under Momoh), Somalia (under Siad Barre), Uganda, and Zambia.
52. *Africa South of the Sahara, 1976* and *Africa South of the Sahara, 1994.*
53. Gisbert H. Flanz, *Constitutions of the Countries of the World* (Dobbs Ferry, N.Y.: Oceana Publications, 1995). In 1994, constitutions were suspended in Gambia, Nigeria, and Sudan and were being redrafted in Ethiopia, South Africa, and Uganda. Countries whose presidential constitutions made no mention of term limits were Angola, Central African Republic, Guinea Bissau, and Mauritania.
54. National Democratic Institute for International Affairs, *An Assessment of the October 11, 1992 Election in Cameroon* (Washington, D.C.: NDI, 1993), p. 22.
55. International Republican Institute, *Kenya: The December 29, 1992 Elections* (Washington, D.C.: IRI, 1993), p. 22.
56. At the time of writing, general elections in Liberia were scheduled for October 1995, with the installation of an elected government to follow in January 1996. Yet the warring factions had not fully disarmed.
57. *Africa South of the Sahara, 1995,* p. 884. During the period when the rest of Africa was liberalizing, Sudan alienated Western aid donors over reports by human rights monitoring groups of disappearances and massacres in Juba and the Nuba mountains.
58. On these events, see "Sénégal: Damaged Credentials," *Africa Confidential* 35 (15 April 1994). On the broader issues of the crisis of Senegalese democracy, see Babacar Kante, "Sénégal's Empty Elections," *Journal of Democracy* 5 (1994): 96–107.
59. In one further respect, Bénin blazed a trail. In the current round of elections in Africa, five African countries held competitive polls before Bénin's March 1991 contest (see Table 7). But in no case was a sitting head of government ejected. In Namibia, the country was effectively governed by a South African administrator-general who obviously was not a contestant in the country's independence elections. In Comoros, the incumbent president Ahmed Abdallah was assassinated in a short-lived, mercenary-led military coup just four months before the March 1990 election. In Cape Verde and São Tomé and Príncipe, incumbent presidents Pereira and da Costa respectively retired from politics rather than contest their nation's first competitive races. In Côte d'Ivoire, incumbents ran and won. Thus Bénin distinguished itself by alternating leaders in an election.
60. Benin, Central African Republic, Congo, Guinea–Bissau, Madagascar, Malawi, Mali, Namibia, Niger, South Africa, and Zambia.

61. Cape Verde, Lesotho, Mozambique, São Tomé, and Seychelles.

62. See William Zartman, ed., *Collapsed States: The Disintegration and Restoration of Legitimate Authority* (Boulder, Colo.: Lynne Rienner, 1995), especially the chapter by Martin Lowenkopf, "Liberia: Putting the State Back Together," pp. 91–108.

63. This observation complements the classic insights of Robert Dahl and Edward Tufte in *Size and Democracy* (Stanford: Stanford University Press, 1973) and, more recently, Axel Hadenius, *Democracy and Development* (Cambridge: Cambridge University Press, 1992) , pp. 123–7.

64. P. M. Decoudras, "Niger: Démocratisation Reussie, Avenir en Suspens," in *l'Afrique Politique, 1994: Vue sur la Démocratisation a Marée Basse,* ed. Patrick Quantin (Paris: Karthala, 1994), pp. 45–57.

4

EXPLAINING POLITICAL PROTEST

Regime transitions are complex processes with multiple phases. Because their intricacies are difficult to capture as a whole, they must be disaggregated for purposes of analysis. This study breaks the concept of regime transition into three parts: we seek to explain first political *protest,* then political *liberalization,* and finally *democratization.* These elements constitute the core aspects of regime transitions – namely, how transitions start, unfold, and end. They are consistent with the phases of regime transition outlined in the previous chapter.

We do not mean to imply that regime transitions invariably start with political protest, always dynamically lead to political liberalization, or inevitably result in democratic outcomes. Each of these elements is a *variable.* The extent to which there are protests, liberalization, and democratization – indeed, whether there is a transition at all and what form it takes – can be expected to alter from country to country. In the next three chapters, we treat each element of transition as a separate problem to be explained. In this chapter, the dependent variable is political protest.

The outbreak of political protest signals to incumbent leaders that the regime faces a crisis of legitimacy. By taking to the streets to express political concerns, citizens demonstrate that they lack confidence that existing governmental institutions are capable of responding to popular demands. By withdrawing consent to be governed, political protesters proclaim that, although the state may remain dominant, it has lost hegemony. The persistence of political protest, even in the face of state repression, indicates that the old regime has begun to break down. And if unrest prompts incumbent leaders to make concessions, then protests have sparked the onset of a political transition.

In this study, we define political protest as the frequency of mass actions directed at political goals. Qualifying for inclusion are street demonstrations, boycotts, strikes, and riots. A mass action has a political purpose when protesters make explicit demands for changes in political rights or rulership. Political protests are thereby distinguished from mass actions driven exclusively by economic grievances. Using *Africa South of the Sahara* as a consistent source, we measured the frequency of political protest by the number of these events occurring in each African country during the 10-year period between 1985 and 1994 (for further details, see the Appendix).

In this chapter, we seek to explain why political protest broke out more frequently in some African countries than in others. We tackle the explanatory task in an explicitly theoretical manner by subjecting contending explanatory frameworks to empirical tests. Following the logic of Chapter 1, we ask first whether economic and international explanations can carry the burden of explaining patterns of protest in Africa. Showing that they have limited utility, we then test a politico-institutional approach and find it more compelling. We conclude by proposing a multivariate model of political protest that draws on all approaches.

TESTING ECONOMIC EXPLANATIONS

Do political protests originate in underlying economic conditions? Such conditions can potentially influence the onset of regime transitions in several distinct ways: as a function of the structure of the economy, through changes in economic performance, or as a response to economic policy reforms.

ECONOMIC STRUCTURE

As mentioned earlier, structural theorists have firmly established that wealthy countries are most likely to obtain political democracy.[1] This might lead one to propose that African countries with the highest levels of gross national product per capita would experience the most frequent prodemocracy protests. Certainly, the richest economy on mainland Africa – oil-exporting Gabon, with a GNP per capita of $2,960 in 1989 – was the site of frequent and violent anti-government demonstrations in the early 1990s, which disrupted and jeopardized the performance of the petroleum sector. South Africa, by any measure one of the most economically advanced countries on the continent, was repeatedly wracked by a sustained succession of major protests emanating from urban townships and mine compounds. At the other end of the ladder of economic development, the self-provisioning, low-income peasant populations of agrarian Rwanda, Mozambique, and Uganda did not experience peaceful prodemocracy marches in the capital city.

Perhaps more plausibly, one could hypothesize that entrenched poverty and deprivation engender antisystemic political action, leading to the expectation that popular protest would break out in the poorest African countries.[2] Country cases can also be found to support this countervailing view. The political transition in Bénin occurred in an economy producing less than $400 per person per year and was driven at first by the economic grievances of urban protesters. Protest-led political resistance was also the order of the day in nearby Niger and Mali (with a 1989 GNP per capita of $290 and $270, respectively), each of which was poorer still than Bénin. At the other end of the continuum, the island nation of Seychelles, which with a 1989 GNP per capita of $4,230 was richer even than Gabon, appeared to be innoculated against political protest in the late 1980s, in part perhaps because of the material well-being of its citizens.

The evidence from the country cases is therefore contradictory, suggesting the absence of a systematic relationship between these economic and political variables. In a test using all eligible sub-Saharan countries (n = 42), we confirmed that the level of economic development and the frequency of political protest were essentially unrelated.[3] Prodemocracy demonstrations occurred frequently in both very low-income African countries as well as in the richest, middle-income countries. Nor was there a curvilinear relationship by which *both* propositions found some support, with protest being a function of *either* relative wealth *or* extreme poverty. Rather, protests occurred in African countries with middling incomes (for example, Guinea, $430; Mauritania, $500) about as frequently as in all African countries.

Nor did the introduction of statistical controls for potentially confounding variables – such as the geographic size of the country, the extent of urbanization, or the growth rate of the economy – reveal a greater correlation between political protest and national wealth. Moreover, the frequency of political protest bore no statistical relationship to the structure of the economy as measured by either the proportion of gross domestic product (GDP) derived from manufacturing or the proportion of the labor force engaged in agriculture. And, surprisingly, given that urban-based economic interest groups were at the forefront of popular mobilization in Africa, the frequency of protest was also unrelated to the percentage of the population living in towns.

Instead, urbanization apparently helped to ensure that, in places where protest occurred, its onset was accelerated. In other words, the *first* protests broke out in the urbanized countries of Africa.[4] The clearest example is South Africa, where six out of ten persons lived in towns and where politically motivated protest stretched back several decades through the Soweto uprising of 1976 to the Sharpeville massacre of 1960.[5] Urbanized Bénin, Gabon, and Zambia were also prominent among the countries in which the widespread phenomenon of politicized uprising first began in the mid- to late 1980s.[6] By contrast, populations in largely rural countries that were employed mainly in agricultural occupations were late to jump on the protest bandwagon. Protests in Malawi, for example, did not break out until March 1992, later than in any other African country.

Except for the fact that protests started early in urbanized economies, the economic structure of African countries had little bearing on the onset of protest, at least as discerned through sometimes very weak national data. Popular resistance to authoritarian rule in Africa was apparently no more likely to occur in relatively prosperous, diversified economies than in low-income, agrarian ones.

ECONOMIC CHANGE

Perhaps, instead, political transitions were related to *changes* in the economy over time. Again, the literature suggests a brace of alternative hypotheses. As discussed in Chapter 1, political instability could be theorized to result from either rapid economic growth or economic decline, although the latter hypothesis seems more plausible for Africa. Again, we could not reject the null hypotheses. We found no systematic relationship between the rate of economic growth and the extent of political protest.[7] Protesters not only took to the streets in countries with negative rates of economic growth like Zaire (average annual GNP per capita change, 1980 to 1989 = −2 percent) but also in countries with respectable growth rates like Cameroon (+3.2 percent). At the same time, citizens remained silent across other countries that experienced a similarly broad range of economic conditions. Interestingly, there was a complete absence of political protests both in Lesotho, the fastest-growing African country in the sample (average annual GNP per capita growth rate = +5 percent) and in Mozambique, whose economy was shrinking the fastest (−8.2 percent).[8] If anything, protest tended to occur in stagnant economies − that is, in 17 out of the 21 countries with average growth rates between −1.5 and 1.5 per annum.

What if economic growth was relevant to mass political mobilization only at particular levels of economic development? Perhaps, for example, negative growth had politically explosive effects mainly for middle-income African countries. One might expect that economic crisis would be most severely felt in countries whose citizens had earlier tasted the good life but later came to experience straitened circumstances. The fact that political protest occurred frequently in the two African countries that slipped from middle-income to low-income status between the 1960s and 1980s (Nigeria and Zambia) suggests a possible relationship here. In Nigeria, for example, economic growth slowed after 1981 in response to the decline in world petroleum prices. Plummeting foreign exchange earnings led to import shortages, with manufacturing enterprises struggling to operate without essential raw materials and spare parts. A sharp fall in industrial activity was exacerbated by a series of poor harvests, an overvalued currency, and a widening public budget deficit. Of course, the protests of the late 1980s were often motivated by noneconomic concerns, such as differences over religious practices between Muslims and Christians in the north and ethnic disputes over the creation of new states and relocation of capital cities. But it could be argued that the country's dismal economic performance fueled these disputes.[9]

Robert Bates has argued that the unimpressive performance of African governments in the economic realm was particularly susceptible to political ramifications because economic management had been so politicized for so long.[10] Because governments had used interventionist economic policies in neopatrimonial fashion to maintain political stability, the breakdown in performance was bound to occasion a political crisis. Although there was important intercountry variation, the entire African continent could be argued to be traversing a generalized economic crisis that would put its political institutions under stress.

Nonetheless, cross-national analysis suggests that the likelihood of political protest in African countries in the late 1980s and early 1990s is inexplicable in terms of the severity of the economic crisis they faced. The "riches-to-rags" proposition that political protest was a response to sharp economic decline did not withstand a general test. When statistically controlled for level of development, economic performance continued to bear no meaningful relationship to the incidence of protest.[11] Nor did the alarm bells of economic crisis – like runaway currency inflation or large fiscal deficits – signal the onset of protest.[12] To be sure, countries like Zaire and Zambia that experienced inflation rates in excess of 100 percent during 1989 were likely to encounter frequent protests in subsequent years. But by the same token, frequent protest was also experienced in many countries in the African Financial Community (CFA) Franc Zone – including Bénin, Cameroon, and Central African Republic, among others – whose inflation rates were held in check by a fixed exchange rate pegged to the French franc.

Fully comparable data on the size of central government fiscal deficits was unavailable for the full sample of countries; nonetheless, here too the impression from partial data is that there is little or no relationship between the size of fiscal deficits and the emergence of protest.[13] Protests emerged in high-deficit countries like Côte d'Ivoire (with a fiscal deficit of 17.8 percent of GDP in 1989, excluding external grants) but not in Mozambique (24.1%); whereas low-deficit countries like Cameroon (5.3%) or Togo (6.2%) also suffered through major protest. In sum, under existing policy conditions and with the available data, we could discover no clear linkage between economic crisis and the outbreak of political unrest in Africa.

We do not mean to suggest that the worsening of economic performance across the countries in our sample was irrelevant to the emergence of political protests. Politics across Africa in the late 1980s took place against a background of ubiquitous economic crisis. But the data clearly suggest that the severity of the economic crisis cannot explain the extent, timing, or outcome of the protests, which were therefore apparently always mediated by other factors.

ECONOMIC REFORM

Economic crises trigger a need for policy *reform*. The most important development in economic policy in Africa in the 1970s and 1980s was the widespread adoption by African governments of orthodox structural adjustment programs. The reforms aimed initially at emergency measures to stabilize the economy by eliminating deficits on the public budget and external trading accounts and later at a long-term program to instill economic growth by reducing government controls and interventions in favor of market prices and institutions.[14]

Did economic policy reform lead to political protest? Thirty-eight African governments signed some 244 stabilization or adjustment loans with the World Bank and the International Monetary Fund between 1980 and

1989.[15] Importantly, this indicator was positively and significantly related to the incidence of political protest between 1985 and 1994.[16] Governments that adopted a large number of adjustment programs – as in Côte d'Ivoire (12 loans), Togo (12), Madagascar (11), and Central African Republic (10) – tended to face frequent political protests. By contrast, those governments that took fewer economic reform initiatives – like Ethiopia (1), Lesotho (1), and São Tomé (3) – commonly avoided mass civil unrest in the streets of the capital city.

Interpreting this finding is complicated. To be sure, particular political protests often began as mass reactions against donor-mandated austerity measures, but there was little solid evidence of a methodical linkage between the actual implementation of structural adjustment programs and subsequent street demonstrations.[17] The number of adjustment programs that governments entered into with the international financial institutions (IFIs) was a poor indicator of their ability or willingness actually to undertake policy reform; the effective rate of implementation of these programs was quite low.[18] Also, the extent of austerity, the ostensible catalyst of protest, was a function as much of the severity of a country's economic crisis as of a donor's momentary policy prescription. And because agreements with the IFIs brought additional aid, they eased the need for austerity, so that *ceteris paribus* one would expect fewer protests, not more.

Why, then, was the number of adjustment loans so strongly and positively correlated with popular protest? We believe that constant policy dialogue and donor conditionality, no matter how toothless, served over time to erode governments' legitimacy and to increase popular perceptions that leaders were not in full control of policy making. Even unimplemented, adjustment programs were blamed by affected populations, who rarely made the distinction between hardships caused by the economic crisis and those brought on by the reform program. Resorting to donor assistance to overcome economic crisis undermined the popular legitimacy of governments, making them seem weak defenders of national sovereignty and beholden to foreign interests.

The role of economic factors in the emergence of political protest in 1989 can be illustrated with reference to Togo. By regional standards, Togo's economic performance was about average, with a rate of GDP growth of 1.4 percent from 1980 to 1989. It enjoyed extremely low inflation, thanks to its membership in the Franc Zone. Togo had been one of the first African countries to turn to the IFIs for help with a structural adjustment program, when its phosphate exports began to sag in the late 1970s, and it had signed 12 different adjustment loans during the 1980s. Implementation of these adjustment programs was slow and uneven: The Eyadéma regime was too neopatrimonial to accept true liberalization of the economy but increasingly came to rely on infusion of donor finance to meet its obligations.[19] But enough reform had been undertaken to gain a grade of "fair" from the World Bank for the macroeconomic policy stance in 1990 to 1991.[20] Indeed, by the late 1980s, when political protest began, there were tentative signs that economic growth was rebounding, after several years of decline.[21] Unlike neighboring Bénin, for example, the government had not accumulated arrears on civil service wages.

Clearly, the economic performance of the Eyadéma government was less than scintillating; years of stagnation and stop–start reform with the IFIs had exacted a significant cost on the country's middle classes and eroded the regime's legitimacy. The perception that cuts in stipends for university students – mandated by the World Bank – had been manipulated to favor northerners had caused some restiveness on campuses. Nonetheless, the protests of 1989 and 1990 had their immediate origins in the actions of the Commission of Human Rights and the Bar Association and Eyadéma's clumsy attempts to contain them. The protests were overtly political and did not focus on specific economic demands.[22] Indeed, for all African countries, the relationship between economic adjustment and mass protest was mediated by the political factor of regime legitimacy; protest was most likely where incumbent governments were seen as excessively dependent, needlessly repressive, or both.

TESTING INTERNATIONAL EXPLANATIONS

Do international political factors provide any more leverage than economic ones in explaining political protest? If so, precisely which international forces were at work, and how? Were African protesters emboldened by citizens in other countries who rose up against their own governments? Or were incumbent African leaders weakened by the ouster of Soviet bloc dictators, the collapse of one-party regimes abroad, and the imposition of political reform conditions for development aid? It is most likely that all these factors were present and reinforcing.

Quite clearly, the timing of the wave of African democracy experiments in the early 1990s derived importantly from the end of the Cold War. The radical shift in the international environment marked by the demise of the superpower rivalry appears to have been a major stimulus to domestic political changes within African countries. After all, innovations in African governance were far more frequent after 1989 than before. The end of the Cold War – operationalized as the fall of the Berlin Wall on November 11, 1989 – was highly correlated with the occurrence of political protest, liberalization reforms, and multiparty legislative elections in African countries.[23] At face value, therefore, external influences appear to be an important theme of the story of democratization in Africa.

Yet the changing international context was a common condition for the continent as a whole. On its own, it cannot explain variations in the extent of protest and reform across different African countries. To test for international effects, we therefore turned attention to the assorted ways in which African countries were incorporated into global state and market systems through mechanisms like development aid and loans. We asked: Was the propensity for protest a function of the relationships between African countries and the Western donor community?

DONOR PRESSURE

The rivalry between the United States and the Soviet Union during the Cold War (1945–89) contributed to the construction and maintenance of authoritarian regimes in Africa. The global contest for geostrategic spheres of influence led both superpowers into alliances with African strongmen, who became skilled at winning external support by declaring ideological affinity with an international patron or threatening to cross over to a rival camp. The Soviet Union allied itself with some of the poorest countries on the continent – like Ethiopia and Mozambique – which could not pay for arms shipments to put down internal resistance or demonstrate the viability of a socialist one-party state developmental model.[24] For its part, the United States became entangled with some of Africa's most egregiously despotic regimes – including those in Zaire, Somalia, and Sudan that were top U.S. aid recipients – and with nondemocratic insurgency movements like Jonas Savimbi's Union for the Total Independence of Angola (UNITA).[25]

By the mid-1980s, however, under the reformist influence of Mikhail Gorbachev's "new thinking," Soviet foreign policy came to stress reestablishment of good relations with the West.[26] Accordingly, military assistance to client states and movements was reduced significantly by the close of the 1980s as the superpowers agreed to settle nettlesome regional conflicts in Southern Africa and the Horn. For example, on December 22, 1988 – a date that symbolizes the end of the Cold War in Africa – the Americans and Soviets brokered a tripartite agreement between Angola, Cuba, and South Africa to permit the independence of Namibia in return for the extraction of Cuban troops from Angola.

The end of the Cold War had significant implications for the foreign policies of Western powers. Once the Soviet threat faded, the United States "lost the urge to intervene in African conflicts," standing aside during the armed overthrow of governments in Liberia and Chad and entering cautiously with relief missions in Somalia and Rwanda only after massive humanitarian crises could no longer be ignored.[27] The end of the Cold War also enabled Americans to assert moral preferences through international diplomacy by embarking on one of their periodic crusades to promote democracy.[28] While cutting back on overall aid commitments to Africa, the U.S. government began to concentrate resources in countries that not only undertook market reforms but also promised to respect civil and political liberties.[29] European governments introduced modest political conditions of their own, symbolized by French President Mitterrand's declaration at a Franco-African summit at La Baule in June 1990 that "from now on ... France will link its aid to the efforts of those heading toward more freedom."[30] In practice, however, the Europeans continued to grant priority to political stability and to commercial ties with former colonies in Africa, thus insisting less vociferously than the Americans on democratic and governance reforms.[31]

By the 1990s, however, African political leaders discovered that they could no longer court external support simply by professing Marxism–Leninism or anticommunism. In order to obtain development assistance, they henceforth had to

show willingness to observe human rights, practice efficient and honest governance, and hold genuinely competitive elections. Thus, the end of the Cold War
found most African governments more vulnerable to Western pressures and thus
more likely to respond to protest with political reform. This logic certainly provides a plausible explanation for the emergence of political protest in the late
1980s. But does it explain the variation in protest across African countries?

We speculated that the more economically dependent a country, the more its
population would perceive that its government was politically vulnerable. According to this line of reasoning, high levels of international indebtedness and aid
dependence should predict popular uprisings. Measures of debt and aid flows for
African countries in 1989, however, were generally unrelated to the frequency of
political protest.[32] As an alternative, we created a variable for political conditionality that recorded instances in which donors publicly announced that particular loans or grants would be conditional on progress on human rights or democratic governance.[33] Again we found that the imposition by donors of explicit
political conditions was largely unrelated to domestic protests. In the next chapter we discuss the role donors played in subsequently shaping the transition.
Here, we simply conclude that donor pressures for democratization apparently
did not inspire mass uprisings.

POLITICAL DIFFUSION

Alternatively, African protest movements may have been directly inspired by the
example of protests in other countries, first the mass street demonstrations that
swept Eastern Europe in the spring of 1989, and then the democracy movements
elsewhere in Africa. Information about these ground-shaking events was broadcast throughout Africa by international media outlets like Cable News Network
(CNN), the British Broadcasting Corporation (BBC), and Radio France International (RFI). Because the African audience for these global news outlets was concentrated among educated elements in towns, the collapse of Leninist regimes in
the Soviet bloc mostly affected urban elites. The fall of strongmen in Eastern Europe – especially Ceausesçu in Romania and Honneker in East Germany – revealed that personal rulers had a very narrow base of political support. From this
perspective, Mobutu's announcement of liberalization reforms in April 1990 and
Kaunda's turnabout on the admissibility of multiparty elections in September
1990 can be read as a response as much to the unseemly demise of international
allies as to the insistent demands of domestic demonstrators. Similarly, opposition elites in African churches, labor unions, and universities drew inspiration
from European leaders like Pope John Paul II, Lech Walesa, and Vaclav Havel
and may even have borrowed from them tactics of civil disobedience.

Ordinary citizens – especially if they lived outside towns, spoke local lan-
guages, and relied for information on government-controlled newspapers and
radio programs – were less well informed about political resistance half a world
away. In any event, political developments closer to home seemed more relevant

to Africans than distant events in Europe. The Algerian experience was formative in which riots in October 1988 led to the legalization of opposition parties and the defeat of the ruling National Liberation Front (FLN) in local elections in 1990. The Algerian precedent generated popular interest mainly in the Islamic and francophone parts of Africa, but its spread was limited by sparse coverage in official news outlets. Nonetheless, it did reveal to citizens that African one-party regimes were more fragile than their leaders might like to portray. The release of Nelson Mandela from a South African jail in February 1990 received much wider attention across the continent and was celebrated by official media as the final nail in the coffin of colonialism in Africa. Among the unintended effects of publicity about Mandela's long walk to freedom, however, was the implication that even the strongest authoritarian regimes in Africa could be forced into political compromises by sustained campaigns of mass agitation.

Did political protest spread systematically within Africa from one country to another? To be convincing, a diffusion theory must first show that the internal affairs of a given country are open to international political influences. We tested the frequency of political protest against indicators of the number of contiguous neighboring countries, a measure of international openness used elsewhere in the literature.[34] This measure assumes that the more international borders a country had, the more its population was susceptible to political demonstration effects. Admittedly, this measure has limitations. It portrays diffusion effects from immediate neighbors only, not from more distant African countries, Eastern Europe, or elsewhere. The latter are better captured by a measure of the number of television sets per capita. This measure, as we show later in this chapter, was positively correlated with protest.[35] As predicted, protest was found to be statistically more frequent in countries with a larger number of contiguous neighbors.[36] We also found that political protest tended to occur differentially across broad geographic regions, with countries in West Africa experiencing protest more frequently than countries in East Africa.[37]

Others have noted that colonial affiliations fostered interpersonal and institutional linkages across territories and facilitated the spread of one-party states and military regimes.[38] Such ties, even if decaying over time and more salient to elites than masses, plausibly formed a conduit for political learning about strategies for democratization among opposition movements. Thus, one would expect the diffusion of prodemocracy sentiment across international borders to be strongest among countries previously ruled by the same colonizing power. The African data supported this proposition. We found a positive association between the frequency of political protests and the number of neighbors colonized by the same European power as the host country.[39] Substantively, this finding drew attention to the concentration of protest events in the early 1990s in the contiguous states of former French west and central Africa, countries linked by close past and present relations with France, shared francophone communications media, and the pull of Parisian cultural and intellectual life. As the recent round of regime transitions got underway, frequent political protests were recorded in countries like Mali (with 6 former French colonial neighbors), Central African Republic (5), and Congo (4).

The openness of African countries to international influences, however, did not lead automatically to a contagious epidemic of protest. Analysis of all sub-Saharan African cases revealed that political protest occurred no more frequently in countries that bordered on regimes that had already embarked on political transition than in countries insulated from such precedents. Transiting regimes were considered to be any country that had experienced either political protest or liberalization reforms. Any general trend toward externally driven protest was canceled out by a contrary inclination to internally generated resistance. For every country that followed a neighbor down the route of popular protest, another country forged its own path.

Consider some examples. Only five countries in Africa were rocked by frequent political protests in the aftermath of transition events in two or more neighboring states: Central African Republic, Gabon, Malawi, Mali, and Togo. In Mali, for example, prodemocracy demonstrations organized by the National Committee for Democratic Initiative (CNID) and the Alliance for Democracy in Mali (ADEMA) were apparently modeled on precedents of a year earlier in Côte d'Ivoire.[40] The popular upsurge in Togo seemed to be a direct result of events in Bénin, the proceedings of whose national conference were broadcast live on national radio and avidly followed in neighboring countries. At the other end of the continent, Malawian exiles built support for a protest movement in their own country from a base in Zambia by means of an externally directed campaign of "anonymous samizdat faxes" that "played a critical role in demonstrating ... that the emperor had no clothes."[41]

The presence of transiting neighbors also helped to explain the *timing* of political events. The starting date of protest and reform was very strongly correlated with the proportion of neighboring countries that had previously experienced the onset of regime transition.[42] We take these results to confirm that, at least for countries that started late, regime transitions partly followed a neighbor's lead. The onset of transition was delayed in several African countries – Angola, Djibouti, Equatorial Guinea, Ghana, and Lesotho – until they were entirely surrounded by transiting neighbors. Again, however, elites appeared to be more strongly affected than masses by international demonstration effects: In all these countries, the reform process was closely managed by incumbent political elites and was accompanied by popular protest in only two cases (Equatorial Guinea and Ghana). These protests occurred late in the day – for example, in downtown Malabo not until 100 demonstrators risked a tentative rally against Obiang Nguema in December 1992. Thus, for a subset of "follower" countries, regime transitions were prodded forward by demonstration effects in the neighborhood. And for Africa as a whole, such demonstration effects became increasingly important over time.

By the same token, other African protest movements were *sui generis*. Domestic protesters took go-it-alone initiatives in six countries, including several large or symbolic ones: Bénin, Comoros, Côte d'Ivoire, Madagascar, South Africa, and Zambia. Protests in these countries were innovative in the sense that they did not imitate any precedent set in a neighboring country. Notably, Comoros and Madagascar – French-speaking islands in the Southern African region – were geographically isolated not only from the mainland but from the west and central African francophone bloc. In both countries, protests ignited for internal reasons. In Comoros, demonstrators violently objected to a constitutional amendment, approved in a rigged referendum, that granted president Ahmed Abdallah a third six-year term as President. In Madagascar, political protest was first manifest in a street celebration responding to the seizure of a government radio station by rebel soldiers and their announcement that President Ratsiraka had been overthrown. As might be expected, protests started early among innovator countries, essentially before the end of 1989.

The limits of political diffusion as an explanation for protest were also demonstrated by another group of countries – namely, those that were virtually surrounded by regimes undergoing political transition but that themselves managed doggedly to avoid outbreaks of political protest at home. This group included Uganda (4 neighbors in transition), Angola (3), Mozambique (2), and Burundi (2). Internal conditions such as civil war or military prohibitions on civilian politics, or both, made it difficult and dangerous for opposition movements to organize protests against incumbent governments. Moreover, in Uganda, President Yoweri Museveni avoided protest by skillfully managing internal dissent: Armed rebels were repeatedly offered amnesty, political parties were suspended but not banned, and alternate channels of controlled local participation were set up through a hierarchy of elected resistance committees.[43] In all these cases, internal political conditions outweighed demonstration effects from the immediate international environment.

We therefore conclude that international and economic factors played supportive but essentially secondary roles in explaining political protest in Africa. Our analysis reveals that the number of structural adjustment programs and the number of bordering countries of the same colonial heritage help to explain political protest. But other aspects of Africa's crisis of economic production and post–Cold War environment were not systematically linked to the onset of protest-led regime transition in the 1990s. Such broad international and economic trends provided an omnipresent backdrop against which regime transitions began but were not themselves primary determinants of where, when, and how political protest would break out. The weight of explaining protest must rest elsewhere.

THE EFFECTS OF POLITICAL INSTITUTIONS

This book posits that regime transitions are shaped by the institutional legacy of preceding political regimes. Earlier, we introduced Dahl's classic observation that regimes are distinguishable along two key politico-institutional dimensions: the extent of political participation and the degree of political competition. This section begins to put the institutional legacy thesis to an empirical test. It measures how much political participation and political competition were actually allowed by regimes in postcolonial Africa up to 1989, and it explores whether these institutional attributes help to explain the onset of regime transitions through protest.

POLITICAL PARTICIPATION

Does the level of political participation under previous regimes have any bearing on whether and how political transitions start? To capture political participation, we began by measuring the electoral behavior of African citizens as represented by voter turnout figures. As detailed in Chapter 2, our data set contains an original set of official voter turnout figures (as percentages of registered voters and total population) for each presidential and parliamentary election from independence to 1994. As before, we acknowledge profound reservations about the reliability of African electoral data prior to 1990. Because some official voter turnout figures are concocted, it would be difficult to interpret correlations with indicators of transition trajectory. It is perhaps all to the good, therefore, that we found no such relationships. However we measured voter turnout – as official counts of percentage of registered voters in the last election before 1989, as percentage of total population in the last election before 1989, as mean percentage of registered voters for all elections from independence to 1989, or as mean percentage of total population for all such elections – it was never significantly associated with any transition characteristic, including the frequency of political protest.

How, then, to measure participation? A simple alternative indicator was constructed by counting the number of direct national elections held in independent African countries before the end of 1989 (see Table 1). We considered that the incidence of elections stood as an adequate proxy for the extent to which citizens played a part in national political life. Moreover, reporting of election frequency was hardly vulnerable to deliberate official misrepresentation. We derived three versions of this variable: the number of presidential elections, the number of legislative elections, and the total number of elections. Indirect elections, in which citizens were permitted to vote for local representatives only, who in turn chose higher levels of leadership on a restricted franchise, were excluded. The variation across African countries was considerable, with the total number of elections ranging from a low of zero (in the former Portuguese colonies[44]) to a high of 14 (for Cameroon) over the 30-year postcolonial period. Because the total number of elections discriminated against parliamentary systems – which, constitutionally, did not hold presidential elections – we confirmed results against the number of legislative elections.

The total number of elections under postcolonial regimes was positively, strongly, and significantly related to the incidence of political protest in the present era.[45] So was the number of legislative elections.[46] But how secure were these links? Could they be spurious, an artifact of some other influence, such as the duration of political independence?[47] After all, one would expect countries that were decolonized earlier to have held more elections by 1989. A statistical control for the length of independence slightly weakened the correlations but, importantly, the relationships remained positive and significant.[48]

Country cases pointed consistently in the same direction. At one end of the continuum, one-party participatory regimes with long-standing electoral traditions consistently experienced high levels of political protest. Between independence and 1989, the governments of Cameroon, Côte d'Ivoire, Gabon, Madagascar, Kenya, and Zambia each faced voters in five or more legislative elections that were usually held regularly according to a constitutionally established schedule. Yet political protest occurred with high frequency in all these countries.[49] At the other pole, the governments of the former Portuguese colonies of Angola, Guinea–Bissau, Mozambique, and São Tomé never faced voters in direct elections. They assumed power as militarized liberation movements and instituted hierarchies of indirect political representation, with party officials at each level electing loyal cadres to successive tiers of so-called people's assemblies. These indirect elections were regularly postponed, and leadership changes often occurred or were attempted through internal plots and coups. In part because the old regimes in these countries failed to establish an institutional tradition of mass participation, they experienced virtually no political protest.[50]

We interpret these findings to mean that, where elections were a regular feature of African political regimes, elites and masses became socialized to accept participatory political roles. Both groups internalized the rule that elections had to be convened on a regular cycle and that citizens would turn out *en masse* to endorse the ruling party's candidates. The role of elections in institutionalizing political participation has been noted in the literature on African politics. Naomi Chazan observes that "elections are taking on a new meaning within the African political context (and) may eventually provide the key to establishing an African-derived formula for constructive political participation."[51] Dennis Cohen depicts elections as a means of regulating conflict in which "demands for participation from the masses and for departicipation from the ruling class alternate in strength."[52]

These arguments call for a reinterpretation of the shibboleth about departicipation in postcolonial African politics.[53] First, popular participation surely declined when compared to the nationalist fervor that propelled political independence. But the more relevant comparison is not with this unusual interlude of heightened mobilization but with the period of more normal politics that preceded it. By any standard – including the breadth of the franchise, the number of elections, and the number of practicing voters – political participation was higher in civilian political regimes after political independence than in the colonial regimes that came before. Second, although the political arena surely shrank in the postcolonial era, it did so more through "decompetition" than "departicipation." Incumbent political leaders were likely to hamstring their opponents by closing or coopting independent power centers rather than by eliminating opportunities for controlled mass mobilization. They expended more political resources on shutting down opposition parties or dissident trade unions than they did on canceling or postponing elections or abandoning other rituals of symbolic political participation.

Under plebiscitary political regimes, political participation actually expanded. Some populist leaders wove a web of rhetoric about "peoples' participation" and "one-party participatory democracy" which raised expectations that citizens had a right to be consulted. Almost all leaders sponsored rallies to celebrate national holidays and attempted to associate the supreme leader with national symbols. In some cases, they organized protest marches to pillory "enemies" of the regime. Indeed, rather than steering mass grievances into a substantive debate about alternative policies, one-party regimes consciously promoted carefully orchestrated mass demonstrations as a means of allowing citizens to let off steam. It was not uncommon, for example, for the youth or women's wing of the ruling party to gather support for official policies or to denounce dissenters through demonstrations outside the gates of the presidential palace.

Most important, leaders of African civilian one-party regimes institutionalized a regular cycle of elections from which they rarely deviated. Those military leaders who chose to stay in power also found it necessary to loosen bans on political activity, to create official political parties, and to jump on the electoral bandwagon by introducing plebiscitary polls. Reflecting these trends, the frequency of national elections across Africa actually increased somewhat from 90 during the 1970s to 106 during the 1980s. Even when the slightly larger number of independent countries in the latter decade is taken into account, the trend was toward a gradual increase in the number of elections per country over time.[54]

To be sure, political participation was difficult to sustain in the absence of political competition. Official reports of voter turnout in these elections were plausible for some countries (especially those with competitive one-party regimes), averaging 50 percent of registered voters in Kenya and 61 and 73 percent in Zambia and Madagascar, respectively. With some fluctuations, voter turnout tended to gradually fall over time in these regimes. Declining turnout was surely attributable in part to increasing citizen frustration with the limited choice of approved candidates offered by the ruling party. We surmise that, desiring greater political competition, former voters and nonvoters therefore sought alternative channels of participation outside of elections. One such manifestation was protest action.

At minimum, however, the rules of the political game in African one-party regimes allowed for voting. The experience of African voters in regular elections became embedded in their expectations about citizenship and in recurrent patterns of mass political behavior. That most elections in postcolonial Africa were partly or completely noncompetitive apparently was less germane. Even if a choice of candidates was limited or absent and even if reported election results did not faithfully reflect the expressed will of the electorate, elections still encouraged people to play a part in politics. In spite of the limitations of African elections – or perhaps because of them – African voters were poised by the end of the 1980s to exercise the familiar urge to participate. Only this time, they did so through nonelectoral outlets such as strikes, riots, and demonstrations. By the end of the 1980s, when African citizens were primed to rebel, ruling parties lost their grip on such events. Instead, the mass demonstration – itself an emergent institution of plebiscitary politics – was taken up with a vengeance by regime opponents.

POLITICAL COMPETITION

The Party System

Does the level of political competition under previous regimes have a bearing on whether and how political transitions start? We examined these questions in terms of political competition among institutions at different levels of the polity: among political parties in the national legislature and among voluntary associations and the mass media in civil society. In all instances, we took a plurality of institutions to indicate the presence of political competition.

Electoral data again provided a starting point for measuring competition among political parties. For each African election from independence to 1994, our data set included information on the total number of legislative seats available for contestation, the number of parties winning seats in the legislature, and the number of seats that each party won.[55] Such figures, which are relatively immune from official misreporting, are useful indicators of the competitiveness of political regimes. They directly reflect the presence of rules designed to manage political pluralism. For example, when a military regime promulgated rules to close a sitting parliament, zero seats were available; alternatively, when a single-party regime outlawed party competition, the ruling party captured 100 percent of the available seats. If the prevailing political rules permitted interparty competition, however, its extent was reflected in the relative shares of seats won by each party.

We found a connection between the extent of political competition between parties under the previous regime and the occurrence of popular protest. A positive relationship was discerned between the number of parties in the legislature in 1989 and the frequency of mass demonstrations.[56] By 1989, authoritarian leaders in Africa had either suspended legislatures (n = 10) or had permitted only one ruling party to hold legislative seats (n = 28). Strikingly, regimes without active political parties never experienced frequent protest; if protest occurred at all in no-party regimes, it did so only infrequently. By contrast, three out of the four authoritarian regimes that permitted more than one party in a sitting legislature (Madagascar, Namibia, South Africa) experienced frequent political protest.[57] At minimum, this finding implied that a competitive party system provided an institutional context for organizing open political dissent.

But how far can we push this inference? The measure of political competition was further refined by recording the winning party's share of seats in sitting legislatures in 1989. By itself, this variable had limited power to predict protest in a bivariate test. We reasoned, however, that the effects of political competition might be masked by economic and international factors already known to be related to the incidence of protest, notably the number of structural adjustment programs and the number of neighboring countries with a shared colonial heritage (see previous sections of this chapter). Once we controlled statistically for these variables, a link between political competition and popular protest became visible. Other things being equal, the winning party's share of legislative seats in 1989 was positively related to the frequency of protest.[58]

Although it was not straightforward, the relationship was interesting. Political protest was least likely in military regimes; it was somewhat more likely in multiparty systems; but it was most likely in one-party systems. These scenarios made sense once each was interpreted in terms of key country cases.

Political protest rarely occurred in Africa's military regimes because the state elite's control of the apparatus of coercion and the absence of available party channels for political expression made it too risky. In Burundi, for example, a military committee of national salvation composed of 31 army officers headed by Pierre Buyoya had suspended the 1981 civilian constitution and dissolved the former ruling party, the Union for National Progress (UPRONA). Following entrenched precedents set by previous regimes, Buyoya ruled through minority Tutsi domination of key political institutions, notably the army, civil service, and judiciary. The party representing the majority Hutu population had been forced into exile, and its followers had learned from the deaths of hundreds of thousands of kinsmen in ethnic massacres in 1972 and 1988 that open political competition could be costly in the extreme. As in Burundi, regime transitions under no-party military regimes rarely began with protest.

Protests occurred more regularly in regimes that allowed other parties to exist. In these regimes, leaders had already conceded that the interchange of competing political ideas was a legitimate part of the political process. By the mid-1980s in Namibia, for example, South Africa's quest for an "internal settlement" unsupervised by the United Nations had led to the establishment of an unelected national assembly representing most political parties except the South West African Peoples' Organization (SWAPO). Significantly, in 1986, the South African courts issued a ruling permitting SWAPO to hold public meetings inside the country. By 1988, trade unionists joined schoolchildren and students in a national boycott in favor of SWAPO's demands for the release of political detainees and the withdrawal of South African troops from Namibia. The existence of multiple parties – even, in this case, under the constrained conditions of foreign occupation – provided channels through which protest could be expressed.

Protest was most likely to occur, however – and to escalate into a standoff between incumbents and opposition – under one-party regimes. Less heavy-handed than military oligarchies, these regimes possessed representative political institutions in the form of a ruling national party and an elected legislature. But because in practice single-party monopolies blocked or restricted the expression of popular preferences, citizens had little choice but to experiment with informal, even extralegal, modes of participation outside of official party or legislative channels.

For example, the Democratic Party of Côte d'Ivoire (PDCI) achieved a virtual monopoly over political life by the time of political independence in 1960 and enjoyed the privileged status of sole legal party in the country until 1990. By the mid 1980s, it tolerated limited contestation within its ranks, which President Houphouët-Boigny deftly managed, with the help of state resources.[59] During this extended period of single-party rule, Houphouët attempted to defuse periodic political unrest through national "dialogues" that allowed grievances to be aired but that prevented the formation of independent representative organs. Strikes over deteriorating economic conditions in the early 1980s led to the closure of educational institutions and the suspension of teachers' and students' unions. By 1988, Houphouët had seized control of the secondary school teachers' union – the only independent syndicate in the country – and detained its leaders. These actions not only failed to prevent, but probably helped to prompt, unprecedented outbreaks of mass protest at salary cuts and new taxes announced in March 1990. Unlike his military counterparts in neighboring Guinea, Mali, and Togo, however, Houphouët never deployed troops to suppress dissent.[60] Especially in civilian one-party regimes where they judged that incumbent political elites would not or could not resort to repression, citizens were more willing to risk protest. The political cost of repressing dissent – notably vis à vis the donors – was also higher for these regimes.

What about changes in the level of political competition over time? We constructed an index of political competition for each African country to depict the changing institutional structure of the political party system during the postcolonial era. Specifically, we calculated the number of years after independence spent under multiparty, one-party, and no-party rule. This variable, unlike earlier indicators of political competition, took account of prior historical experience with plural party politics.[61] Interestingly, the competitiveness index was related to the timing of political protest: The longer a country's institutional experience with competitive party systems, the sooner that prodemocracy protest was likely to break out.[62]

For example, South Africa, which consistently operated a multiparty political system after independence (at least for its white minority), found itself confronted with early outbreaks of protest from the black majority. Madagascar, which retained a multiparty regime for 14 years after independence (longer than any other African country that subsequently abandoned multipartism), also experienced earlier-than-normal outbreaks of protest. By contrast, the multiparty experiment under a constitutional monarchy launched at the independence of Swaziland soon collapsed when King Sobhuza seized absolute power in 1973. As a no-party regime from that time onward, Swaziland was one of the last African countries to experience political protests. What are the reasons for this observed relationship between an institutional history of political competition and the accelerated emergence of protest movements? Perhaps previous experience with competitive politics helped to pluralize opposition movements, to establish institutional channels for expression of political diversity, and to prime incumbent regimes to expect dissent. Whatever the reasons, the finding was reinforced by the observation that the more recently a country had undergone a competitive election, then the earlier the onset of protest-led transition.[63]

To summarize, political competition stood in a complex relationship to the advent of political protest after 1989. Mass demonstrations were most likely to break out if the institutional structure of the old regime in 1989 was a single-party monopoly. But if, during some earlier interval(s) of postcolonial history, a regime had allowed competition among political parties, political protests erupted more rapidly. This raises the possibility that the institutional heritage of political competition can live on, albeit latently. Leonardo Morlino contends that a previous experience with party organization "freezes" allegiances and alignments in such a way that they "hibernate" during an authoritarian interlude, only to reeemerge when democratic elections are restored.[64] Mass demands for political rights were most likely to arise in countries where political rights had been enjoyed in an earlier era but had subsequently been denied. It seems plausible that, once exposed to rights of free speech and association, citizens would not abandon them but hold them in abeyance until such time as it was safe to compete again.

Indeed, previous organizational experience provided former opposition parties with latent resources to be remobilized, even if in disguised or modified forms. Leaders of banned opposition parties quickly reemerged from the woodwork once it became possible to contest openly for political office. In countries that had suffered under particularly repressive authoritarian regimes – like, say, Burundi, Equatorial Guinea, or Malawi – the "prodemocracy" opposition tended to accrete around political factions and parties that had fled into exile. In countries where the *ancien régime* had been somewhat more benign and out-of power politicians had been able to stay at home, the resurrection of party structures took place internally. In Zambia, for example, the Movement for Multiparty Democracy (MMD) built partly on the organizational foundations of former parties like the African National Congress (ANC) in the south, the United Party (UP) in the west, and the United Progressive Party (UPP) in the north. Similarly, the Union for Democracy and Social Progress (UDPS), which emerged as the leading opposition force in Zaire in the 1990s, was a revival of the second party that Etienne Tshisekedi had tried to launch in 1982. In Ghana, the military regime of Jerry Rawlings forbade emergent political associations from using the names or slogans of political parties that had been banned in 1981; nevertheless, new parties still clustered around the organized traditions and "ancestral voices" of Danquah and Nkrumah.[65]

The institutional restoration of former opposition parties had contradictory effects on the onset of regime transitions. On one hand, it helped to speed political change by reducing the time needed by regime opponents to construct an apparatus for mass mobilization. On the other hand, institutional precedents also impeded change. To the extent that old policy programs were given a new lease on life – including discredited efforts to restore traditional leaders or to promote ethnic subnationalism – the prodemocracy forces were weakened from within. This dynamic was particularly clear in a country like Cameroon. There, opposition to the Biya government soon splintered along all-too-familiar lines: Northern elites reformed the independence-era northern party of ex-president Ahidjo under the banner of the National Union for Democracy and Progress (NUDP), while several largely discredited southern politicians claimed the banner of the Union of Cameroonian Populations (UPC), the now-mythical party that had been violently repressed by the French in the early 1960s. For their part, the anglophone elites of the northwest rallied around a largely new party called the Social Democratic Front (SDF).[66]

To the extent that former political organizations served as vehicles to resurrect the personal careers of failed, old-guard politicians, opposition politics threatened to lapse into familiar patterns of neopatrimonialism. Despite these contradictory effects, however, one institutional continuity was clear: protests broke out frequently in and were more likely to be sustained in single-party regimes that had outlawed the political organizations of their opponents. Party traditions probably facilitated the channeling, mobilization, and perhaps even the financing to continue what had begun as largely spontaneous protest.

Civil Society

There is more to political competition, however, than rivalry among political parties. The openness of a regime to contestation among political forces also depends on its tolerance toward institutions in civil society. To what extent did postcolonial leaders in Africa permit ideas and organizations that were independent of state control? Apart from political parties, did citizens form other, nonstate organizations to represent felt identities and articulate group interests? Was there lively public discourse on political and policy issues?

A plural civil society contains a high density of voluntary associations and a wide diversity of communications media.[67] Our data set includes summary indicators of these institutions for sub-Saharan African countries.[68] As mentioned in Chapter 2, the data revealed considerable variation in the numbers of legally registered organizations that lay beyond the ambit of the state. At one extreme were more pluralistic civil societies, such as Nigeria, which in 1989 had large numbers of trade unions (66), business associations (53), and church-based development institutions (730).[69] At the other extreme were one-dimensional societies like Guinea, Mauritania, Somalia, Djibouti, and Comoros in which associations either did not exist at all or, where they did, were monopolized by the state. Countries with a dense population of citizen groups in one sector of society also tended to display civic activism in other sectors. And vice versa: If associational life and public discourse were stunted in one corner of society, they tended to be impoverished throughout. In sum, civil society did not thrive to the same extent cross-nationally; it was a variable, not a constant.

What bearing does political competition in civil society have upon the likelihood of democratization? One would expect that a competitive civil society with a plurality of independent political tendencies could prompt mass efforts to install democracy from below. Indeed, voluntary groups and independent media might have been vehicles through which popular demands were organized and disseminated.

These expected statistical relationships generally held. Especially the number of trade unions – but also the number of business associations and press publications – were positively and very strongly correlated with the frequency of protest.[70] The results were equally clear with respect to the timing of protests. Early protest events were strongly associated with countries with a higher number of business associations and trade unions.[71] Just as strikingly, a higher number of daily newspapers, periodicals, and publishers, as well as televisions per capita, portended earlier protest.[72]

These positive results warrant discussion. Given the prominence of strikes and other industrial actions in prodemocracy movements in Africa, trade unions were obvious institutional channels for the expression of political protest. In countries with pluralistic labor movements like South Africa, Niger, and Zambia, industrial action was at the center of mass uprisings, and the trade unions helped to provide an organizational infrastructure for opposition movements. Indeed, unions that resisted incorporation into authoritarian regimes often served as guardians of political competition during periods when political parties had been banned.[73] In addition, by the close of the 1980s, splits also began to appear in official labor movements, with dissident factions defecting to the opposition. Thus, governments that had successfully subordinated the labor movement in the past – as in Gabon, Bénin, Congo, and Zaire – encountered increasing difficulty in maintaining discipline as workers chose individually and in groups to join protesters in the streets. In short, the positive effect of labor mobilization on political protest was probably even stronger and more significant than our data on the extent of labor union organization (based, after all, on official government statistics) could fully reveal.

Similarly, our expectation was confirmed that an active business community played a leading part in the onset of regime transitions. The often miniscule business class in African countries commonly contained individuals who, by virtue of ownership of resources outside the state, had an independent base from which to articulate political dissent. Private entrepreneurs, sometimes speaking on behalf of chambers of commerce, were among the earliest critics of statist economic policy and economic mismanagement by state elites. They also figured prominently among those outsiders ejected, or who defected, from incumbent ruling coalitions, later making themselves available for opposition leadership roles. Typically, an emergent opposition leader was an independently wealthy former cabinet minister who used private funds to bankroll forums in which liberal views could be expressed. While these middle-class leaders harbored ambiguous feelings about the unpredictable and potentially destabilizing effects of mass demonstrations, they probably nevertheless recognized that regime change could not begin without pressure from below. In some places – notably Zambia, Kenya, and South Africa – temporary alliances between select elements of business and labor helped to modulate and target the application of mass protest.[74]

As for the media, we confirmed statistically that a free press played a critical role in launching regime transitions in Africa. For example, Nigeria and South Africa – whose media sectors were the most sophisticated, diverse, and independent in Africa – experienced high levels of protest. Independent dailies in these countries disseminated information about public opinion, including protest letters to the editor and popularity polls on incumbent leaders. Contrast the role of open communication in these cases with Cape Verde and São Tomé, neither of which had a daily newspaper in 1989 and experienced no protest through 1994. The common situation where a single daily newspaper was owned by the government or ruling party – as, for example, in Malawi, Niger, and Sierra Leone – was usually associated with intermediate levels of protest. A major innovation in the run-up to transitions was the emergence of periodical publications, especially weekly newsmagazines, ranging from the thoughtful to the rabid. Even minor political factions could issue small-circulation weeklies or monthlies which, as potent sources of antiregime critiques, helped to create a climate and constituency for protest. And the importance of television as a medium of political communication reconfirmed the location of protest in urban areas and the influence of images of "people power" from revolutions abroad.

TOWARD A MULTIVARIATE MODEL

In this chapter, we have reported indicative evidence that the institutional legacy of postcolonial African regimes was systematically linked to the onset of regime transitions, as marked by political protest.

The first important institutional precedent was a heritage of political participation. We found that regular elections and mass electoral turnout became institutionalized as rituals of governance for civilian regimes in Africa. Even leaders who seized power by military coup found it necessary to secure electoral legitimacy for themselves or hand it back to civilians via elections. More important, citizens were able to turn rituals of plebiscitary participation to their own advantage. We discovered a strong relationship between the frequency of elections under previous postcolonial regimes and the frequency of political protests during the watershed years around 1990.

The second relevant institutional consideration was political competition. We found that one-party regimes that had outlawed opposition organizations at some time in the past were likely to confront mass protests. These protests were often mobilized around the institutional outlines of banned or exiled parties. Furthermore, we found that political protest was highly likely to emanate from civil societies that were relatively plural and competitive. Where independent labor unions and business associations were well organized and where a free press flourished, entrenched regimes were much more likely to face demands for their ouster.

For the most part, economic conditions and international relations had less direct effects on the onset of regime transition. The recent round of political protests in Africa were driven primarily by domestic political concerns. But there were two important exceptions to this generalization. First, governments that responded to economic crisis by accepting policy reform agreements with the IFIs (measured by the number of structural adjustment programs) and countries that were open to political communication from abroad (measured as the number of bordering countries with the same colonizer) were likely to encounter protest. Moreover, the positive relationship between television ownership and the early and frequent outbreaks of urban political protest can be read not only as a sign of a nascent civil society but also as evidence of the international diffusion of political ideas. At very least, these economic and international effects deserved to be included in any overall explanation.

To this end, we constructed a multivariate model of political protest using this pool of variables. Exactly how much explanatory power did each factor have? Could these factors be whittled down to a few strong contenders? To what extent could protest thereby be explained? And could our politico-institutional account withstand a multivariate test?

We estimated several simple ordinary least squares (OLS) regression equations to apply these questions to the frequency of political protest (see Table 5).

Our best fitting equation, Model A, contained four variables previously demonstrated to be related to protest.[75] Even when controlled for one another, all factors continued to have demonstrable impact, each within generally accepted levels of statistical significance.[76] Together they accounted for over half the variance in the frequency of political protest in African countries, from 1985 to 1994. *Political competition* in civil society (measured as the number of trade unions allowed by the previous regime) emerged as the most important explanatory factor.[77] Our model estimated that each trade union increased the incidence of protest by 0.25. The extent of *political participation* (measured as the number of elections under all previous postcolonial regimes) was the second weightiest factor,[78] again with a significant positive effect on protest. Each election increased the incidence of protest by about 0.57. We contend that these findings constitute suggestive evidence of the power of politico-institutional factors in explaining protest-led transitions. Simply put, our model suggests that protest was more likely to break out where there was some semblance of institutional tradition of competition and participation.

Nonetheless, complete explanations of social phenomena are usually multivariate. Our estimated model also shows that a politico-institutional analysis is strengthened if placed in international and economic contexts. Model A incorporates the fact that political protest in Africa took place in a context of multiple open borders and sundry structural adjustment agreements. In particular, the estimated coefficients suggest that protest was significantly more likely in coun-

Table 5. *Multiple Regression Estimates of Political Protest, 1985–1994*

Variable	Estimates		Signif- icance	Explained Variance
	(B)	(Standard- ized B)	(p- value)	
Model A				
Number of Trade Unions	0.250	0.475	0.000	
Number of Elections	0.567	0.290	0.022	
Number of Bordering Countries, Same Colonizer	0.816	0.219	0.073	
Number of Structural Adjustment Programs	0.364	0.202	0.091	
			Multiple R	0.749
			R Square	0.561
			Adj. R Square	0.514
			Standard Error	5.272
			F	11.830
			Sig. F	0.0000

(n=42)

tries with a large number of bordering countries having had the same colonizer, confirming our earlier bivariate result, and highlighting the weight of the fran- cophone states of French west Africa in the sample. We also confirm the politi- cally destabilizing effect of donor-driven economic reform loans on African coun- tries. Notably, however, neither factor was statistically significant beyond a relaxed threshhold.[79] We interpret this model to mean that the onset of African regime transitions was driven principally from within but against a background of political and economic influences from abroad. In the chapters that follow, we continue to probe the relative explanatory power of these competing theoretical frameworks in relation to later aspects of transition – namely, political liberal- ization (in Chapter 5) and democratization (in Chapter 6).

ENDNOTES

1. See sources cited in Chapter 1, especially Seymour Martin Lipset, *Political Man: The Social Basis of Politics* (New York: Doubleday, 1960), and Larry Diamond, "Economic Development and Democracy Reconsidered," *American Behavioral Scientist,* 35 (1992): 450–99.

2. Robert H. Bates, "The Impulse for Reform in Africa," in *Economic Change and Political Liberalization in Africa,* ed. Jennifer A. Widner (Baltimore: Johns Hopkins University Press, 1994), p. 23: "All else being equal ... the less attractive the prevailing conditions, the greater the willingness to gamble on reform ... we would expect to see reformist political gambles being taken in countries subject to economic stagnation and poverty."

3. Pearson's r = 0.008, P = 0.960. The level of economic development was measured as GNP per capita in 1989.

4. Pearson's r = −0.423, P = 0.025.

5. The South African population was 58.9 percent urban in 1989, the highest rate of urbanization in Africa with the exception of desertified Djibouti.

6. Proportions of those countries' populations living in towns were 37.2 percent, 44.9 percent, and 49.0 percent, respectively.

7. Pearson's r = 0.034, P = 0.834. Growth was measured as the average annual rate of increase in GNP per capita between 1965 and 1989. See World Bank, *World Development Report* (Washington, D.C.: World Bank, 1991). African countries generally performed dismally on this indicator, with 17 out of the 40 available cases registering an average negative growth rate for the period.

8. The sample of African countries undergoing transition (n = 42) did not include Botswana, a long-standing multiparty regime whose economic growth rate for the 1980s averaged +8.5 percent.

9. Jeffrey Herbst and Adebayo Olukoshi, "Nigeria: Economic and Political Reforms at Cross Purposes," in *Voting for Reform: Democracy, Political Liberalization and Economic Adjustment,* ed. Stephan Haggard and Steven Webb (New York: Oxford University Press, 1994); and Peter Lewis, "Economic Statism, Private Capital and the Dilemmas of Accumulation in Nigeria," *World Development* 22 (1994): 437–51.

10. Robert H. Bates, "The Impulse to Reform," in *Economic Change and Political Liberalization in Sub-Saharan Africa,* pp. 13–28.

11. The independent variable is GNP growth rate from 1980 to 1989, controlled for GNP per capita, 1989. The data reveal a positive correlation between the level of economic development and economic growth rates (Pearson's r = 0.432, P = 0.003), indicating that richer African countries have tended to grow faster than poor ones.

12. Inflation was measured variously, both as the percentage rate of currency inflation in 1989 and as the average annual such rate from 1980 to 1989.

13. See the data in Lawrence Bouton, Christine Jones, and Miguel Kiguel, *Macroeconomic Reform and Growth in Africa,* World Bank Policy Research Working Paper, no. 1394 (Washington, D.C.: World Bank, December 1994), Table B2, which cover roughly half of the countries in sub-Saharan Africa.

14. For a recent accounting of progress (or lack thereof), see World Bank, *Adjustment in Africa: Reforms, Results, and the Road Ahead* (New York: Oxford University Press, 1994).

15. The data were adapted from Eva Jesperson, "External Shocks, Adjustment Policies, and Economic and Social Performance," in *Africa's Recovery in the 1990s: From Stagnation and Adjustment to Human Development,* eds. Giovanni Cornia, Rolph van der Hoeven, and Thandika Mkandawire (New York: St. Martin's Press, 1992), p. 12.

16. Pearson's r = 0.422 , P = 0.005.
17. For data and discussions of the issues, see Henry S. Bienen and Mark Gersovitz, "Economic Stabilization, Conditionality and Political Stability," *International Organization* 39 (1985): 729-54; Stephan Haggard and Robert Kaufman, *The Politics of Economic Reform* (Princeton: Princeton University Press, 1992).
18. For example, Paul Mosley, Jane Harrigan, and John Toye, *Aid and Power: The World Bank and Policy-Based Lending in the 1980s* (London: Routledge, 1991). Governments sign agreements with creditors in order to secure international finance but often do not implement many of the reforms to which they commit themselves. Indeed, some states have undertaken repeated adjustment programs, precisely because they have continued to miss targets on the promised policy reforms. Thus, for example, in its latest assessment of adjustment progress in Africa, the World Bank argues that macroeconomic policies worsened between 1981 and 1991 in Côte d'Ivoire and Togo, which each received 12 different adjustment loans from the Bank and Fund.
19. The best account of the Eyadéma system of rule is probably provided by Comi Toulabor, *Le Togo sous Eyadéma* (Paris: Karthala, 1986).
20. World Bank, *Adjustment in Africa*, p. 58.
21. *The Economist Intelligence Country Reports,* various issues.
22. We acknowledge the useful information provided to us by John Heilbrunn regarding the Togo case.
23. For protest, t = −4.78, sig. (two-tailed) = 0.001. For liberalization, t = −7.72, sig. (two-tailed) = 0.000. For elections, t = −2.67, sig. (two-tailed) = 0.028.
24. Elizabeth Valkenier, *The USSR and the Third World: An Economic Bind* (New York: Praeger, 1983); and Jerry Hough, *The Struggle for the Third World* (Washington, D.C.: The Brookings Institution, 1986).
25. Peter J. Schraeder, *United States Policy Toward Africa: Incrementalism, Crisis and Change* (New York: Cambridge University Press, 1994); Larry Diamond, "Promoting Democracy in Africa: U.S. and International Policies in Transition," unpublished paper, 1994.
26. Eric Herring, "The Collapse of the Soviet Union: The Implications for World Politics," in *Dilemmas of World Politics: International Issues in a Changing World,* ed. John Baylis and N. J. Rengger (Oxford: Clarendon Press, 1992). Also Margot Light, "Moscow's Retreat from Africa," *Journal of Communist Studies* 8 (1992): 21–40.
27. Michael Clough, *Free At Last? U.S. Policy Toward Africa and the End of the Cold War* (New York: Council on Foreign Relations, 1992), p. 12.
28. Joel Barkan notes that "promoting democracy as a U.S. foreign policy objective is not new," with current Africa policies being "replications or partial replications of earlier efforts in selected countries (e.g., Germany and Japan after World War II, in Vietnam and Latin America in the 1960s)." Barkan, "Can Established Democracies Nurture Democracy Abroad? Lessons from Africa" (paper presented at a Nobel Symposium on Democracy's Victory and Crisis, Uppsala University, Uppsala, Sweden, August 27–30, 1994). See also Robert Packenham, *Liberal America and the Third World: Political Development Ideas in Foreign Aid and Social Science* (Princeton: Princeton University Press, 1973).
29. United States Agency for International Development (USAID), *The Democracy Initiative* (Washington, D.C.: USAID, 1990). For skeptical commentaries on this

shift in foreign policy, see Joel Barkan, "Can Established Democracies Nurture Democracies?"; and Todd J. Moss, "U.S. Policy and Democratization in Africa: The Limits of Liberal Universalism," *Journal of Modern African Studies* 33 (1995): 189–209.

30. J. Coleman Kitchen and Jean-Paul Paddack, "The 1990 Franco-African Summit," *CSIS Africa Notes* (Washington, D.C.: Center for Strategic and International Studies), no. 115 (30 August 1990).

31. The ambiguities of French government attitudes are explored in Jean François Bayart, "Réflexions sur la Politique Africaine de la France," *Politique Africaine* 58 (1995): 41–50; Tony Chafer, "French African Policy: Towards Change," *African Affairs* 91 (1992): 37–51; Comi Toulabor, "Paristroika et Revendication Démocratique," in *Etats et Sociétés en Afrique Francophone,* ed. Daniel C. Bach and Anthony A. Kirk-Greene (Paris: Economica, 1993), pp. 119–38.

32. Total external debt as a percentage of GNP, 1989. Pearson's r = −0.077, P = 0.640. Overseas development assistance as a percentage of GNP, 1989; Pearson's r = −0.330, P = 0.070.

33. 0 = no political conditions, 1 = general donor pressure for political reform, 2 = explicit political conditions for loans or aid.

34. J. Lutz, "The Diffusion of Political Phenomena in Sub-Saharan Africa," *Journal of Political and Military Sociology* 17 (1989): 99, 104.

35. Pearson's r = 0.377, P = 0.018.

36. Pearson's r = 0.344, P = 0.026.

37. Phi = 0.459, sig. = 0.031. Countries were coded according to whether they fell in west, east, central, or southern Africa (U.S. Dept. of State map, 1985). The following patterns emerged: Whereas 12 out of 14 (86 percent) of the countries in west Africa experienced protest, only 4 out of 12 (33 percent) in east Africa did so; the rates for central Africa (77 percent) and southern Africa (71 percent) lay in the middle ground. The significance of regional differences was highlighted by contrasting the outlier region (in this case east Africa) with all other regions (phi = 0.447, sig. =0.004).

38. Lutz, "Diffusion of Political Phenomena," 93, 94, 100, 108. He notes that political elites in francophone Africa served together in colonial territorial councils and party groupings and that British military units in east and central Africa were formed on a cross-territorial basis. These ties "led to the politicians and officers in the new nations looking upon their counterparts in either the former French or British territories respectively as appropriate reference groups." On balance, however, such identities were probably stronger in francophone than anglophone Africa. And colonial affiliation was probably more important to the diffusion of the single-party model than to the contagion of military coups, in which geographic proximity was preeminent.

39. Pearson's r = 0.426, P = 0.005.

40. Pierre Englebert, "Mali: Recent History," *Africa South of the Sahara, 1995* (London: Europa Publications, 1995), p. 82.

41. Daniel N. Posner, "Malawi's New Dawn," *Journal of Democracy* 6 (1995): 139–40.

42. For the date of first political protest, Pearson's r = 0.667, P = 0.000. Caution in interpretation is warranted for the small subsample of countries with protest (n = 28). For the beginning date of liberalization, Pearson's r =0.583, P = 0.000 (n = 40).

43. Nelson Kasfir, "The Tension Between Progressive Populism and Democratization in Uganda" (paper presented at the 1989 annual meeting of the American Political Science Association, September 3, 1989); E.A. Brett, "Neutralising the Use of Force in Uganda: the Role of the Military in Politics," *Journal of Modern African Studies* 33 (1995): 129–52; and Holger Bernt Hansen and Michael Twaddle, eds., *Changing Uganda: The Dilemmas of Structural Adjustment and Revolutionary Change* (London: James Currey, 1991).

44. These countries instituted indirect voting procedures. Such procedures also reduced scores for the number of elections in Swaziland (1), Cape Verde (2), and Uganda (3).

45. Pearson's r = 0.436, P =0.004.

46. Pearson's r = 0.429, sig. = 0.005.

47. In order to avoid outlying cases that would skew results, we set the maximum length of independence from 1956, the date that Sudan was decolonized. Thus, countries that had been independent for longer periods (such as Ethiopia, Liberia, and South Africa) were scored (like Sudan) as having 34 years of independence (i.e., 1956 to 1989 inclusive).

48. For total number of elections, Pearson's r = 0.324, P = 0.039.

49. On average 17 instances of protest over the 10-year period from 1985 to 1994, a figure in the 70th percentile of the range.

50. On average 1.25 instances of protest, a figure in the 5th percentile of the range.

51. Naomi Chazan, "African Voters at the Polls: A Re-Examination of the Role of Elections in African Politics," *Journal of Commonwealth and Comparative Politics* 17 (1979): 137.

52. Dennis Cohen, "Elections and Election Studies in Africa," in *Political Science in Africa: A Critical Review,* ed. Yolamu Barongo (London: Zed Press, 1983), p. 87.

53. Nelson Kasfir, *The Shrinking Political Arena* (Berkeley: University of California Press, 1976); Fred M. Hayward, "Political Participation and Its Role in Development: Some Observations from the African Context," *Journal of the Developing Areas* 7 (1973): 591–612. See also Joan Nelson, "Political Participation," in *Understanding Political Development,* ed. Samuel Huntington and Myron Weiner (Boston: Little, Brown, 1987), 103–59.

54. There were 43 independent countries in Africa in 1975 and 46 by 1985. On average there were therefore 2.09 elections per country in the 1970s and 2.30 during the 1980s.

55. From these data we calculated the following: the percentage of seats captured by the winning party in each election; the average winner's share of seats over all available elections before 1990; the number of competitive elections in which more than one party had been permitted to hold seats in the legislature; and the number of years since a competitive election had been held in each country.

56. Spearman's r = 0.323, sig. = 0.037. Institutional indicators of political competition among parties were related to political protest *only* when the latter variable was measured in ordinal categorical form. There were no relationships with the interval level measure of absolute numbers of protests. Hence, we can report only the results of nonparametric statistical tests and urge the reader to treat the findings as tentative. Indeed, as subsequent multivariate analysis reveals, other measures of political competition — notably among institutions in civil society – do a better job of predicting protest.

57. The one exception was Liberia, which experienced guerrilla insurgency instead of peaceful political protest. Long-standing multiparty systems are excluded form this calculation.

58. Pearson's r = 0.458, P = 0.009.

59. Tessy Bakary, "Côte d'Ivoire: Une Décentralisation Politique Centralisé," *Géopolitique Africaine* 2 (June 1986). The best introduction to the regime remains Yves Fauré and Jean François Médard, *Etat et Bourgeoisie en Côte d'Ivoire* (Paris: Karthala, 1982).

60. Yves A. Fauré, "L'Economie Politique d'une Démocratisation: Eléments d'Analyse à Propos de l'Experience Récente de la Côte d'Ivoire," *Politique Africaine* 43 (1991): 31–49.

61. We scored each party system (P) according to the number of parties allowed: accordingly, a no-party system = 0, a one-party system = 1, and a multi-party system = 2. We then counted the number of years (Y) that each country had spent between 1956 and 1989 under each kind of party system (*Africa South of the Sahara, 1990*). The competitiveness score (C) was derived as follows: $C = PY_1 + PY_2 \ldots + PY_3$. This index scored South Africa, which consistently maintained a multiparty regime, at the top (C = 66); at the bottom was Equatorial Guinea (C = 4), which had maintained a personalistic dictatorship over many years. (South Africa = 34 years × multiparty system (2) = 66; Equatorial Guinea = {1 year × multiparty polyarchy(1)} + {18years × no-party system (0)} + {2 years × one-party system (1)} = 4). Burkina Faso (C = 23) and Togo (C = 25), each of which had mixed regime histories with numerous changes of party system, approximated the median competitiveness score.

62. Pearson's r = −0.463, P = 0.013.

63. Pearson's r = 0.426, P = 0.024.

64. Morlino, "Democratic Establishments: A Dimensional Analysis," in *Comparing New Democracies,* ed. Enrique A. Baloyra (Boulder, Colo.: Westview, 1987), 66–7. See also Seymour Martin Lipset and Stein Rokkan, "Cleavage Structures, Party Structures and Voter Alignments," in *Party Systems and Voter Alignments: CrossNational Perspectives,* ed. Lipset and Rokkan (New York: Free Press, 1967).

65. To quote the felicitous phrase of Richard Jeffries and Clare Thomas, "The Ghanaian Elections of 1992," *African Affairs* 92 (1993): 343.

66. See Milton Krieger, "Cameroon Democratic Crossroads, 1990–1994," *Journal of Modern African Studies* 32 (1994): 605–28; and Luc Sindjoun "Cameroun: le Système Politique Face aux Enjeux de la Transition Démocratique, 1990–1993," in *l'Afrique Politique: Vue sur la Démocratisation à Marée Basse,* ed. Patrick Quantin (Paris: Karthala, 1994).

67. For theoretically informed work on civil society, see Michael Walzer, "The Idea of Civil Society," *Dissent* (1991): 293–304; Jean L. Cohen and Andrew Arato, *Civil Society and Political Theory* (Cambridge: Massachusetts Institute of Technology Press, 1993); and Ernest Gellner, *The Conditions of Liberty: Civil Society and Its Rivals* (London: Penguin, 1994). For a virtuoso account of the positive effects on democratic governance of popular "civic engagement" through voluntary associations see Robert D. Putnam, with Robert Leonardo and Raffaelle Y. Nanetti, *Making Democracy Work: Civic Traditions in Modern Italy* (Princeton: Princeton University Press, 1993). On the application of the civil society concept to Africa, see Michael Bratton, "Beyond the State: Civil

Society and Associational Life in Africa," *World Politics* 41 (1989): 407–30; Larry Diamond, "Introduction," in *Democracy in Developing Countries: Africa*, ed. Diamond, Juan J. Linz, and Seymour Martin Lipset (Boulder, Colo.: Lynne Rienner, 1988), pp. 23–4; and John Harbeson, Donald Rothchild, and Naomi Chazan, eds., *Civil Society and the State in Africa* (Boulder, Colo.: Lynne Rienner, 1994).

68. Although it is not easy to measure the degree of pluralism or competition within civil society in Africa, it is not impossible. We located sources that enabled us to systematically record for most African countries the numbers of business associations, trade unions, daily newspapers, periodicals, and publishers in 1989 (*Africa South of the Sahara, 1990*) and the numbers of church-sponsored schools and medical facilities in 1973 (*World Christian Encyclopaedia: A Comparative Study of Churches and Religions in the Modern World, A.D. 1900–2000*, Oxford: Oxford University Press, 1982).

69. On Nigeria's increasingly active civil society and its relations with the state, see Adebayo Olukushi, ed., *The Politics of Structural Adjustment in Nigeria* (Portsmouth, N.H.: Heinemann, 1993).

70. For the number of trade unions in 1989, Pearson's r = 0.539, sig. = 0.000. For business associations, Pearson's r = 0.452, P = 0.003. For periodical publications, Pearson's r = 0.423, sig. = 0.005. Countries with large numbers of voluntary associations, notably Nigeria and South Africa, were outliers in these analyses. Diagnostic tests indicated that these cases did not unduly influence results. For example, the bivariate relationship between the number of trade unions and the frequency of protest remained significant when these cases were dropped (n = 40); and the significance and strength of the relationship between the number of business associations and the frequency of protest actually rose.

71. For business associations, Pearson's r = −0.505, P = 0.006. For trade unions, Pearson's r = −0.404, P = 0.028.

72. Pearson's r = −0.463, −0.390, −0.457, and −0.512; P = 0.013, 0.040, 0.014, and 0.008, respectively.

73. On Zambia, see Lise Rakner, *Trade Unions in Processes of Democratization: A Study of Party Labour Relations in Zambia* (Bergen, Norway: Christian Michelsen Institute: 1992).

74. A cursory review of the biographies of Africa's new leaders suggests that a business background has become a main channel of political recruitment in Africa's new democracies. Businesspersons occupy cabinet positions, notably in economic ministries. The last chapter of this book indicates that personal wealth has become a prerequisite for access to political office and discusses the consequences of such a trend for economic policy and egalitarian democracy.

75. Encompassing and diagnostic tests were used to assess the statistical validity of this model. R-square, F-test, and standard error measures were used to compare competing models, but no significant differences were found. White and Breusch-Pagan tests failed to detect a heteroskedastic disturbance. Durbin-Watson tests to detect the presence of first order autocorrelations were inconclusive. Normal probability plots of the standardized residual were used to determine if nonlinear relationships between independent and dependent variables were hidden in the analysis; none were observed.

76. P = < 0.10.

77. See standardized B scores; institutional precedents of political competition account for over 40 percent of the variance in protest.
78. In both cases, P = < 0.05.
79. Probabilities < 0.010 can be acceptable for multiple regression. Recalculated using a one-tailed test, the international and economic variables become significant at this level.

5

EXPLAINING POLITICAL LIBERALIZATION

Political liberalization entails the reform of authoritarian regimes. It comes to pass when public authorities relax controls on the political activities of citizens. Often described as a political opening, political liberalization involves official recognition of basic civil liberties. In such openings, governments restore previously repudiated freedoms of movement, speech, and association to individuals and groups in society. Examples of political liberalization include the release of political prisoners, the lifting of government censorship, and the relegalization of banned political parties. As an analogue of economic liberalization, political liberalization reduces government intervention in the political market, breaking up monopolies of political authority and allowing a plurality of opinions and organizations. In short, political liberalization broadens political competition.

When do political openings occur? The prevailing view in the literature is that political liberalization launches regime transition – that is, an incumbent elite, driven by divisions within its own ranks, initiates concessions to its opponents. We have argued, however, that the impetus for political reform originated within the ruling elite in only a minority of African cases; more commonly, African regime transitions began with popular protest. With such impetus, political liberalization is best viewed as a government *response* to pressures emanating from domestic (and sometimes international) political arenas. Liberalization is thus an intermediate phase of transition that occurs *between* the onset of protest and the emergence of a new regime equilibrium.

As an interim aspect of protest-led transitions, political liberalization has two other key features. First, because it involves the relaxation of rules about who has access to politics and the state, liberalization reform is an object of political struggle between incumbents and their opponents. Incumbents generally try to maintain the status quo, adhering as closely as possible to a tailor-made set of closed political rules that have served them well in the past, countenancing change only to the extent that they believe it improves their chances of holding on to power. Opponents, for their part, continually seek to precipitate ever wider political openings in an effort to reduce the disadvantages they face under the prevailing rule order. In this sense, struggles over the rules of the political game are at the heart of liberalization dynamics.

Second, political liberalization does not ensue once and for all; it is an ongoing process that happens in a series of incremental steps. Political elites rarely grant all their concessions in one fell swoop, preferring instead to surrender minimum advantage at any one time. As leaders observe responses to their first reforms, they learn whether the liberalization process must be advanced and deepened or whether they can stand pat. Occasionally, they may even calculate that, without penalty, they can reverse direction by retracting concessions made earlier. Thus, liberalization is a step-by-step process of gradual advancement toward a more open political regime, but the process does not preclude temporary setbacks or permanent reversals along the way.

In this study, political liberalization is measured as the change in the civil liberties score assigned to each African country by *The Comparative Survey of Freedom* between 1988, the last year in which all African countries were unambiguously governed by *ancien régimes,* and 1992, the year in which the trend of political openings peaked across the continent (for further details and discussion see the Appendix). This indicator, which accurately captures our definition of political liberalization, is based on a conception of civil liberties as "the freedoms to develop views, institutions and personal autonomy apart from the state."[1] The *Survey's* 13-point checklist of civil liberties includes such questions as:

Are there free and independent media?
Is there freedom of assembly and demonstration?
It there freedom of political organization?
Are citizens protected from unjustified political terror, imprisonment, exile, and torture?
Is there equality under the law?

By this index, a clear majority of African regimes – 33 out of 42 – made overall improvements in civil liberties between 1988 and 1992 (see Appendix, Table 12).[2] The greatest gains in political liberalization were made by governments that started from a very low base of rights observance and that abandoned an ideological commitment to Marxism–Leninism (e.g., Bénin, Cape Verde, Congo, Ethiopia, Mozambique, and Angola). In these countries, the national constitutions were rewritten to include individual rights for the first time, or governments sharply improved their observance of those rights. The extent of political opening may have been less far-reaching elsewhere, but it was certainly widespread, with more than two dozen additional African countries making gains in political liberalization between 1988 and 1992. In these cases, governments introduced measures to lift emergency regulations or placed stronger powers of enforcement behind existing constitutional guarantees.

As always, prevailing trends in African politics were offset by contrary cases in which some countries charted divergent paths. During the same period, five African governments failed to improve their performance in respecting civil liberties (Djibouti, Malawi, Mauritania, Nigeria, and Somalia), and in four countries, governments actually cracked down by further restricting rights (Liberia, Sierra Leone, Sudan, and Uganda). By 1994, Malawi had opened up, and Mauritania and Nigeria had slid back.

This chapter addresses three questions, each in a section that follows:

Why did incumbents and opponents act as they did in struggles over liberalization?
Can patterns be discerned in these struggles?
What explains the extent of political reforms provided in African countries?

STRUGGLES OVER LIBERALIZATION

Earlier we described the processes of political liberalization as they unfolded in Africa. Here we begin to explain these dynamics and outcomes. We start by asking:

What were the major rule disputes?
What strategies and resources did protagonists employ?

RULES

Struggles over liberalization concerned the fundamental rules by which the game of politics would be played. At stake were several regime-defining issues. The first concerned the extent to which African regimes would be governments of laws or governments of men. On this issue, neopatrimonial leaders sought to retain arbitrary latitude over rule-making, whereas the opposition, egged on by the lawyers in their midst, sought to introduce formal and legal constraints on the powers of political executives. A second issue concerned the locus of state sovereignty and the source of political legitimacy. Whereas incumbents appealed to their status as father figures of a symbolic nation, opposition forces convened national conferences to stake a claim to popular sovereignty. Third, at the heart of struggles over liberalization was the issue of political competition. Military and one-party leaders obviously preferred monopolistic political arrangements expressed through singular political institutions controlled from the top. Opponents sought a much less restrictive framework, demanding that a plurality of political forces be allowed to contend for power in a more open and liberal political atmosphere.

Given the sweep of these issues, the political struggles of the liberalization phase centered on constitutional reform. Thoughtful reform advocates saw a rare opportunity to get the rules right, from which many good things would supposedly follow. By freeing up the interplay of competing forces in the polity, they hoped to obtain the governmental accountability and responsiveness that had so far eluded Africans. The content of constitutional reforms proposed by opposition movements was similar in most countries (see Chapter 3): a bill of universal human rights, repeal of clauses restricting the number of political parties, term limits on the executive presidency, and measures to enhance the independent powers of the legislative and judicial branches of government. The liberalization phase often came to consist of the proceedings of some sort of constitutional assembly or commission, the drafting or amendment of a founding charter, and its ratification through a referendum or enactment by parliament. Only when opposition movements considered that thereby the playing field had been roughly leveled, did they agree to contest elections. This is not to say that rule disputes ended after the promulgation of a liberalized constitution; indeed, the protagonists continued to tussle over electoral rules (see Chapter 6) and the application of the constitution (see Chapter 7). These controversies, however, were essentially secondary to the establishment of a foundation of rules for the political game writ large.

The principal constitutional objective of the opposition was to uncouple the apparatus of the state from the institutions of a ruling military or party. The blurring of institutional boundaries was particularly pronounced in single-party regimes where the central committee of the ruling party had been the main forum for policy-making and where the state-run media had fostered the impression that the party and government were one and the same thing. Such institutional fusion had profound material consequences because the ruling party could always make use of privileged access to public resources to build its own organization and reward its own supporters. The material advantages of incumbency became a sore point as transitions moved from liberalization to electoral phases. The opposition soon realized that the incumbent leader would not hesitate to use state funding to underwrite his own electoral campaign and to exercise his command over the state media to gag electoral candidates who held nonofficial viewpoints. To the extent that the struggle over rules masked an underlying struggle to control material resources, the stakes were high. Indeed, in the context of neopatrimonialism, one has to question whether the opposition's concern for rule changes was mainly a means for outsiders to gain inside access to public wealth.

This section once again draws attention to the issue of formal-legal rules in transitions from neopatrimonial systems. Do such rules really matter? One interpretation of the flurry of constitution-making in the early 1990s is that it reflected the gradual emergence of a rule of law. Yet a contrary view is that rapid liberalization during this period only drew attention to the shallowness and malleability of basic political rules in Africa. The constitutions that emerged during transitions continued to reflect both the preferences of neopatrimonial strongmen and their powers to revise rules almost at will. For example, President André Kolingba of the Central African Republic dissembled throughout the entire transition, ruling by decree even after conceding the appointment of a prime minister, selecting the members of the opposition with whom he would engage in what he called a "national debate," and suspending the announcement of results for the country's first presidential elections.

This example, by no means exceptional, raises major concerns. Is it enough to get the formal rules right? In part, elements within the opposition naively placed too much faith in constitutional reform, overlooking the fact that dominant leaders had always flouted laws in Africa. Indeed, the arbitrary manipulation of rules was a defining characteristic of neopatrimonial regimes and transitions and even of their aftermath. Accordingly, if at least some opposition leaders regarded rule changes instrumentally as a means to securing their own access to public resources, how would they behave once in office? As we shall see, leaders of cohesive opposition movements were willing to proceed to elections even under imperfect constitutional rules, promising to attend later to remaining issues of political reform. Whether in fact they lived up to commitments to provide further political openings is an empirical question addressed in Chapter 7. For the moment, suffice it to say that the new cohort of leaders learned, both from the practices of their neopatrimonial predecessors and from their own involvement in transition struggles, that the rules of the political game in Africa were highly pliable. This did not augur well for the institutionalization of a rule of law in Africa's experimental democracies.

STRATEGIES

We have argued that during the liberalization phase incumbents and oppositions vied to define the political rules of a new regime yet to be born. In pursuit of this goal, opposition tactics ran the gamut from joint public statements, threats to boycott elections, and lobbying of the donors to the organization of mass marches and national strikes, all designed to mobilize public opinion against the government. Tactics varied as a function of the nature of the prodemocracy coalition that emerged. When organized labor defected from the government or when university students were mobilized, mass marches and strikes were more likely to feature prominently. When these groups held back, however, prodemocracy forces found it difficult to sustain organized shows of strength, and popular protest became episodic and more easily dismissed.

For their part, incumbent rulers selected strategies to limit the extent of the power they would have to surrender to the emergent opposition. At one extreme, these included various attempts to physically repress the opposition and, at the other, attempts to placate it by conceding a part of the protesters' list of demands. In between, rulers pursued various combinations of intimidation, temporization, manipulation, and accommodation.

The opposition's goals initially emphasized the restoration of political and civil rights, including freedom of the press and the release of political prisoners, all demands that governments could meet unilaterally by passing a decree or revoking a long-standing ban or state of emergency. In addition, to allow it to function openly and without restriction, the opposition sought the legalization of multiple political parties.

Here, transitions separated along two broad axes. In some countries, authorizing the opposition was handled administratively or as a single amendment to the constitution. In Gabon, Cape Verde, and Côte d'Ivoire, for instance, opposition parties were quickly legalized, paving the way for multiparty legislative elections.[3] Incumbents often deliberately forced the pace by calling subsequent snap elections in the hope of catching an ill-organized opposition off guard. In other countries, the dynamics of the transition were more protracted, with elections delayed until after a broader constitutional struggle had been settled. Here, each side sought constitutional reform for their own strategic reasons. Quite commonly, the opposition viewed immediate elections as political suicide until changes in the political rules had leveled the playing field. The opposition demanded constitutional reform to take away at least some of the advantages the regime would enjoy in an electoral contest. In Zambia, for instance, significant constitutional reform was almost certainly necessary to separate the single party from the state, so completely had the old order enshrined their coupling. Not only was UNIP's Central Committee the government's main policy-making forum, but the party's partisan activities were bolstered by state budgetary resources, the active complicity of the administration, and the support of a controlled press.[4] As a result, the opposition demanded constitutional reforms to weaken the executive and its emergency powers before moving to elections.

Incumbents sought to retain their constitutional advantages. The protests and increasing donor pressures had forced them to recognize that some change was necessary, but they tried to contain liberalization to a minimum that would protect their hold on power. They sought to divide the opposition, gain donor support, and grant concessions only in piecemeal fashion, retaining the political rules that would give them advantage in a more open system. An initial response to the protests was to promote internal reform of the single party, both as an effort to forestall multiparty competition and to prepare for it. Such preemptive reforms took place in Gabon, Kenya, Togo, Cameroon, Madagascar, Sierra Leone, Burkina Faso, and Congo.

When reform proved to be too little too late, rulers were put once again on the defensive and forced to consider the issue of relegalizing political parties. Most of them ultimately conceded an open-party system, but others retained restrictions on party formation. Senghor's 1974 precedent in Sénégal, in which he had authorized only three "official" political parties, one to the left and one to the right of his own dominant faction, was influential. Under this sort of quasiliberalization, the ruling party "retained control of political patronage, the electoral machinery and security services, thus tolerating opposition while retaining power."[5] Perhaps the retention of some measure of power and patronage was what General Babangida of Nigeria had in mind when in 1989 he banned multiple emergent political groupings led by old-guard politicians and chartered two official parties in their place. And both Museveni of Uganda and Mswati of Swaziland chose to experiment with no-party systems in which supposedly competitive elections were held on a nonpartisan basis. Another common remaining restriction was that parties could not form on ethnic or regional lines. In Angola, political parties had to have support in at least 14 of 18 provinces in order to obtain registration; in Tanzania, all new political organizations had to demonstrate support in both Zanzibar and the mainland. In this sense, liberalization reforms were often tentative and incomplete.

Although recognizing that some fundamental change was inexorable, rulers still believed a formal constitutional review process might be a useful instrument of delay and prevarication. In Zambia and Tanzania respectively, Kaunda and Mwinyi each proposed the establishment of a constitutional commission, believing in all likelihood that its work could be controlled. Malawi's ruler proposed a referendum on multiparty politics in late 1992, evidently still convinced he would win it. In Bénin, establishing a much noticed precedent, it was Kérékou himself, and not the opposition, who suggested convening a national conference on "democratic renewal" in February 1990. Bongo of Gabon followed suit in March, albeit with very different results. National conferences would eventually be held in Congo (it opened February 25, 1991 and lasted 3 months), Togo (July 8, 1991; 1 month), Mali (July 19, 1991; 15 days), Niger (July 29, 1991; 40 days), Zaire (August 7, 1991; over a year, with interruptions), South Africa (December 1991, two years, also with interruptions),[6] and Chad (January 15, 1993; 11 weeks). National conferences are assessed in greater detail later; here, suffice it to note that although most francophone countries in West Africa would eventually convene such assemblies, those in East Africa did not (as in Burundi, Djibouti, Madagascar, Rwanda, and Seychelles). These institutions in the making were critical in this phase of struggle over political rules. Their nominal purpose was constitutional change, and they would lead to popular referenda on new constitutions in all these countries except for Zaire and Chad.

Indeed, national conferences marked the climax of struggles over political rules in these transitions. The delegates to some national conferences declared themselves sovereign – as in Bénin, Congo, and Niger – and went on to publicly accuse the old ruler of crimes and to replace him with an interim government headed by a technocrat, in preparation for multiparty elections. Other incumbent rulers anticipated this outcome and acted to forestall the conference's seizure of power; in the most extreme cases – notably Togo and Zaire – rulers manipulated the conference proceedings and defied the right of the conferees to appoint an interim prime minister, thereby creating an unstable dyarchy of contending governments. At the heart of these stalled attempts at liberalization were struggles over public resources as embodied in control of the national treasury and armed forces.

In the thrust and parry of the transition, one side's actions directly prompted reactions from the other. The extent to which governments resorted to repression and manipulation was evaluated and coded for each of the countries in the sample.[7] These variables reflected tentative value judgments and should be treated with care, but they did provide compelling evidence of the dialectical nature of transition dynamics. Thus, the best predictor of whether the government would repress the opposition was the incidence of political protest.[8] Repression was thus best understood as a response by incumbents to the initiatives of opponents. Long accustomed to a monopoly over public affairs, governments found difficulty in accepting what they viewed as a challenge to their hegemony. In Cameroon, Togo, and Zaire, the army was called in to shoot on protesters, a show of strength that resulted in numerous victims. In Gabon, Kenya, Togo, Nigeria, and Zaire, the regime was widely believed to be behind the murders of prominent prodemocracy leaders. In other countries, newspapers were closed and journalists arrested, and opposition leaders were subjected to harassment, house arrest, or incarceration.

Interestingly, however, manipulation of official rules was also positively and strongly related to protest.[9] Incumbent leaders appeared to respond to protest with a combination of *both* repressive measures *and* various ruses, deceptions, and false promises. Indeed, governments appeared to view manipulation and repression as complementary and mutually reinforcing strategies rather than as substitutes.

The master of this was surely Mobutu in Zaire, who officially declared his commitment to in-depth political reform as early as April 1990, but then immediately proceeded to undermine it with a combination of brutal crackdown and calculated evasions that soon left observers little doubt as to his real intentions. Mobutu first announced that he would give up membership in the single party, the Popular Movement for Renewal (MPR), to "place himself above all parties," but he clearly continued to use the party to his advantage and resumed its presidency a year later. He continued his time-worn strategy of combining stick and carrot in relationships with opponents. On the one hand, he exacted reprisals on opposition politicians, including by permitting the pillage by soldiers of their businesses.[10] On the other, he provided various material incentives for opponents to rejoin the presidential majority, and would name three of them prime minister in succession during the transition: Etienne Tshisekedi (July 1991), Nguza Karl-I-Bond (November 1991), and Faustin Birindwa (March 1993).[11] In Kinshasa, his commitment to multiparty politics was soon derided as little more than "multi-mobutism."

Mobutu's manipulative strategy was particularly clear with regard to the national conference. After promising one in mid-1990, he postponed it five times before finally convening it in August 1991. A government-run preparatory commission approved some 2,850 individuals nominally representing some 159 political parties, the public, and state institutions but a large proportion of whom Mobutu believed to be loyal to him. During the conference, which would stretch out for over 18 months, he would try to influence its outcome by alternatively ignoring the meeting and its deliberations, bribing its participants, threatening them, and (in February 1992) having his prime minister suspend it. Mobutu eventually ignored the Haut Conseil de la République (HCR), the legislative body which had been elected by the national conference and which claimed full sovereignty, recognizing instead a "Government of Broad National Union and Public Salvation." By mid-1993, amidst growing chaos and economic meltdown, the country was blessed with two governments, two legislatures, and even two worthless currencies. From his presidential hideaway in Gbadolité, 1,000 kilometers from Kinshasa, Mobutu continued to profess his attachment to democratic reform.[12]

RESOURCES

What determined actors' choices of strategy in this phase of the transition? To answer this question, we need to focus on the relative strength of the protagonists and the resources they could bring to bear on their own behalf. Opposition forces typically struggled to overcome two important resource deficits. First, in most countries, opposition organizations were underfinanced and could not compete with the relative fiscal might of the state. In the early stages of transition, propelled by the press and by mostly spontaneous protests in the major cities, finances did not pose a significant constraint; they became much more important as the transition wore on and national elections approached. Even the biggest opposition parties that emerged were ragtag affairs compared to single parties that enjoyed the full complicity of the state apparatus. Two sources of funding were available to opposition groups: citizens living abroad and prominent businessmen at home. The courting of the latter, in particular, became a significant feature of several transitions. Individual businessmen played a key role in the prodemocracy movements of countries like Cameroon, Ghana, Kenya, Nigeria, Malawi, and Zambia, and venture capital made its way to parties in other countries as well.

Many businessmen were motivated to support the democracy movement because they were dissatisfied with the share of state resources they could obtain under the old regime. In Cameroon, for example, opting for the opposition came naturally to many Bamileke businessmen, whom Biya had purposely excluded from profitable rent-seeking opportunities. Much the same could be said for Ashanti backing for Adu Boahen in Ghana's presidential elections in 1992. Business support of the democracy movement was usually best understood as an investment decision: Businessmen wanted to pick the right horse. For this reason, they were sometimes wary of openly opposing the incumbent until his demise seemed assured. In Niger, some Hausa trading families hedged their bets by providing discreet support to each of the candidates in the presidential elections of February 1993.[13]

Second, opposition forces were weakened by their fragmentation. Typically, prodemocracy forces included as many as two dozen different organizations, often with quite distinct preoccupations and agendas. Consolidating these disparate forces, or at least maintaining their unity and coordinating their actions, became a top priority of the opposition. Tenuous unity might be achieved through an umbrella organization: In Cameroon, the best the opposition could muster was a National Coordinating Committee, which tried to mold a common agenda from some 25 organizations but which was contested even within the opposition. In Zaire, some 130 parties sought a modicum of coordination by forming the Sacred Front (Front Sacré). Political parties that would compete in elections, like the Forces Vives in Madagascar, which included more than 15 organizations, or the Alliance for Democracy in Mali (ADEMA) in Mali, with some five parties, were little more than loose coalitions.

Incumbent rulers used several tactics to exacerbate the opposition's lack of cohesion. For instance, Presidents Bongo, Biya, and Mobutu encouraged party fragmentation by extending enticing provisions for state financing of registered political parties. In other countries, individual leaders of the opposition were offered various material inducements to cross over to the government side. In a curious but by no means uncommon turn of events, Dakole Diassala, a prominent Kirdi politician from Northern Cameroon, who had long been a political prisoner for his opposition to the Biya regime, was released shortly before the March 1992 legislative elections after a deal with Paul Biya. Diassala would eventually join the presidential majority in parliament and receive the lucrative cabinet position of minister of posts and telecommunications.[14]

Government strategies were also constrained by the various resources available to them. Rulers had long relied on the patronage, rent-seeking, and corruption possibilities afforded by the state apparatus to retain political support. They now turned to the state once again but with varying results. Leaders like Houphouët-Boigny retained enough administrative control to fully exploit these resources and limit defections from his own camp. On the other hand, in Bénin, Kérékou found the state apparatus no longer responded to his commands. These differences were in part linked to the country's fiscal situation. The Béninois government was completely bankrupt and Kérékou's promises to reward loyalty rang hollow, since he had not been able to meet his government's payroll for months.

Relatedly, the continuing support of the Western donors was another critical variable dictating government strategy. Donor support provided a critical flow of resources on which certain governments were totally dependent. On the other hand, the courting of donor support was not compatible with a strategy that favored repression, and governments that actively sought to maintain full donor support were more likely to push through strategies of manipulation to deal with the demands of the protesters. In Togo, pressures from the American, German, and in particular the French embassies, led Eyadéma to accept the convening of a national conference in the summer of 1991 and to publicly urge restraint on his soldiers. In the following months, however, once reassured of renewed French government support, Eyadéma took advantage of the excesses of the opposition and the turbulence of the transition to step up the repression of the prodemocracy movement and take back concessions previously agreed to.[15]

An important factor was the ability of a government to repress the prodemocracy movement, and that depended largely on the extent to which it could count on the support of the military. In Togo, to continue the example, the mostly Kabré army was totally loyal to Eyadéma and willing to fight to retain its privileges.[16] In Cameroon, Biya found the army's leadership more than willing to direct the repression of the democratic movement in the provinces. On the other hand, the military in several countries made it clear to the ruler that it would not intervene against protesters or enforce a state of emergency, effectively removing repression as a viable choice for the government. The announcement by Niger's army in March 1991 that it was withdrawing from the single party and would no longer intervene on behalf of the government against the protesters forced President Saibou to the negotiating table of the national conference. Fuller analysis of the role of the military during liberalization and later phases of transition is offered in Chapter 6.

THE STRUCTURE OF TRANSITION PROCESSES

So far, we have argued that the relative financial and organizational strength of oppositions and governments varied across countries, conditioning the political strategies of each side. The issue is whether these strategies are best characterized as purely contingent, the result of providence or the actions of individual agents, or whether they adhere to underlying patterns. Is there a structure to transition dynamics? And can any such patterns be attributed to institutional precedents?

We argue that a complete explanation of dynamic transition processes must take into account the political legacies of previous regimes. There is no denying that the importance of contingent factors increased as the transition proceeded. Personal idiosyncracies, the rivalries between individual leaders, and the miscalculations of agents acting in a very uncertain environment all played a role in directing the transition. In highly personalized regimes with weak formal institutions, the opinions and character traits of incumbents were bound to have a critical influence on, for example, decisions to resort to brutal repression or devious political manipulation.

Nonetheless, we think that key regularities can be discerned below a surface of apparent chaos. We have shown how political protest at the outset of transitions was shaped by the nature of inherited political institutions; now we argue that individual agency *during* transitions was similarly structured by legacies bestowed from the past.

We attempt to demonstrate the validity of our politico–institutional approach by proposing four modal paths of African transitions, which we link to the nature of preexisting political institutions. First, we examine the relatively small number of *managed transitions* and show why they were more likely to occur in the regimes we defined as military oligarchies; second, we focus on the transitions achieved through *national conferences* and demonstrate why they were more likely to take place in plebiscitary one-party regimes; third, we discuss the transitions that moved to *rapid elections* quickly after the onset of protest and link them to a competitive one-party legacy. Finally, in contrast to these paths leading from neopatrimonial regimes, we note the distinctive trajectory of *pacted transitions* that occurred in countries with an institutional heritage of settler oligarchy. In each case, we hypothesize that transition dynamics derive from the combinations of political competition and participation that existed in pretransition regimes.

MANAGED TRANSITIONS

All African governments tried to manage the process of political reform, in the sense that they endeavored to master the evolving situation in order to minimize the concessions made to the opposition. We define managed transitions, however, as those in which governments went beyond such maneuvers, seeking to actively oversee a process of political reform by initiating the process, establishing its timetable, or setting its ultimate parameters. Either the government agreed to return the country to multiparty democracy in response to the emergence of protest, or it did so even before protests had erupted, albeit often as a response to the advent of prodemocracy unrest elsewhere in the region. Nigeria's Babangida government had promised a return to civilian rule as early as 1986, for instance, first to be achieved by 1990, then by October 1992, and eventually by August 1993.[17] Flight Lieutenant Jerry Rawlings had first outlined a process of democratization for Ghana as early as 1987 but had achieved little progress until donor pressures and popular discontent compelled the regime to speed up its lapsed timetable.[18]

Strikingly, military regimes always sought tight management of any regime transition. Managed transitions occurred most commonly in military oligarchies – that is, regimes in which the ruler governed directly through the armed forces, having severely circumscribed institutions of competition and participation, notably through the suspension of parliament, the outlawing of political parties, and the emasculation of the civilian judiciary. Burkina Faso, Burundi, Guinea, Ghana, Lesotho, Nigeria, Mauritania, and Uganda all embarked on managed transitions in the early 1990s, albeit with divergent outcomes.[19]

We consider that managed transitions were most likely in military oligarchies because of their institutional characteristics. Military oligarchs came to power by force and governed with force. Thus, the degree of military penetration of polity and society was likely to be a key factor in determining the dynamics and outcome of the regime transition.[20] Where the military was not immersed in governmental affairs, they could more easily adopt a hands-off attitude; but where they composed, led, or participated in the governing coalition, they necessarily played a more directive role. The latter was particularly true of military oligarchies in which small networks of officers dominated decision making with a shallow stratum of senior civil servants, and participatory politics was severely limited. In contrast to Latin America, however, African military rulers were more reticent about handing power back to civilians and initiated managed transitions either without great sincerity or in response to popular protests and pressures.[21] In this sense – as well as in the practices of "big man" politics by army generals – transitions from military oligarchies remained typical of the general neopatrimonial pattern.

By the late 1980s, African military regimes were typically facing a crisis of legitimacy. Their inability to deliver the economic growth they had promised during the takeover, the population's democratic aspirations, and the military's own promises of an eventual return to civilian rule all conspired in this direction. The military remained highly ambivalent about giving up power and its privileges. Indeed, the events in Nigeria up to and following the June 1993 elections, the results of which General Babangida refused to accept, suggest quite dramatically that at least some of these promises to hand back power were less than genuine.[22] Nonetheless, because the eventuality of a political transition was inherent to the logic of most military regimes, military oligarchs found it possible to respond to the crisis by renewing promises of a managed transition and agreeing to a more precise and perhaps shorter timetable.

A managed transition appealed to the military for several reasons. Primarily, it flattered the military's idealized view of itself as a rational, orderly, and organized force trying to impose order on an inherently disorderly civilian political arena. For military oligarchs, the biggest challenge was how to gradually allow political participation. The efforts of Babangida, Rawlings, and Museveni to engineer the transition process, specifying rules about the formation of voluntary associations, political parties, and the phasing of elections, were revealing in this respect. Babangida's micromanagement of reform included naming the members of a national election commission, convening a constituent assembly, banning and unbanning individual politicians, and the stunning announcement in October 1989 to limit the number of political parties to two, which he actually named the Social Democratic Front and the National Republican Convention, the first to be "a little to the left" and the second "a little to the right."[23]

Furthermore, the military's near monopoly on the means of coercion afforded military rulers significantly enhanced control over transition dynamics and outcomes. Maintaining popular support and legitimacy during the transition was less crucial for military governments, which could choose to rely on repression more systematically than could civilian regimes.[24] Moreover, because the military oligarchy had quashed participatory politics, the transition unfolded with little or no organized opposition powerful enough to contest the regime's timetable. For example, the regime had typically imposed a ban on party activity. In more inclusive systems, political leaders may have wanted to manage the transition unilaterally, but their plans were usually overtaken and pushed aside by civic organizations capable of acting upon their disagreements with the government. In countries with military regimes, on the other hand, the weakness of these organizations compelled them to accept the government's plans. Moreover, whatever defects the managed transition may have had, it did have the advantage of reducing uncertainty and imposing a kind of accountability on the state that weak social actors may have found advantageous.[25]

For their part, military governments found the reduction in political uncertainty appealing; it could promote political compromises that brought outsiders back in, protect the position of the military as an institution, limit the possibilities of getting punished for its role in various abuses of power, and slow down or halt the transition if it began to evolve in an unfavorable direction. In addition to the aborted transition in Nigeria, these dynamics were evident in Ghana. Rawlings had first created a National Commission for Democracy (NCD) in July 1990, which had sponsored public seminars to discuss a future constitution, but he reiterated his preference for a no-party system. As the widespread support for multiparty politics became clear, however, Rawlings surprised even his own followers by unexpectedly announcing a two-year timetable to release political detainees, promulgate a multiparty constitution, and hold competitive elections.[26] The proposed process seemed eminently reasonable, yet was carefully designed to maximize every advantage for the incumbent. For example, he stacked the constitutional reform commission with PNDC stalwarts and redrafted its report to include clauses providing amnesty to officers from the military regime. He also waited until May 1992, only six months before the elections, to lift the ban on parties; and he separated presidential and parliamentary elections by a month to help dissociate himself from the less popular PNDC.[27] The opposition had little choice but to accept Rawlings's dictates lest their complaints provide the government with an excuse to discontinue the reform process.

NATIONAL CONFERENCES

National conferences were a major organizational innovation of African regime transitions. Patterned on both traditional village assemblies and the Estates General of the French Revolution, they brought together the national elites to address the country's political problems and attempt to formulate new constitutional rules. National conferences resulted in governmental changes in Bénin, Congo, and Niger and the exertion of intense political pressure on incumbent rulers, as in Zaire and Togo.

Why did countries hold national conferences? Because most of them were held in West Africa and in francophone countries, it is tempting to explain them as resulting from international diffusion dynamics. There is evidence, for example, that Bénin's national conference was followed carefully in neighboring Togo and that one of the key organizers of the Bénin meeting subsequently offered advice to the prodemocracy forces there.[28] There is similarly much reason to think that the Central African Republic and Cameroonian governments resisted convening a national conference after learning of its dangers from neighboring countries.

Similarly, national conferences can be explained in contingent political terms as a convenient way out of a stalemate between incumbent and prodemocracy protesters. Thus, the convocation of a national conference was highly correlated with prior protest and prior government repression of the protest.[29] After efforts at repression failed to quell the first political demonstrations, incumbents commonly responded to ongoing protest by conceding that a national conference could be held. In Congo, for example, President Sassou-Nguesso agreed to the opposition's demand for a conference only after the army chief of staff declared the army neutral and unwilling to continue repressing strike activity.[30] The national conferences turned into forums in which opposition forces struggled to push liberalization reforms further forward and incumbents sought to hold them back.

Thus, the specific form and discourse of the national conference can be at least partially explained with recourse to arguments about international political diffusion and contingent political dynamics. But we still need to ask why such meetings fulfilled the needs they did. What was their attraction to the protagonists of the transition? Why did conferences emerge in some countries and not in others? A politico-institutional approach can help to answer these questions and provide key insights about transition dynamics in the process.

First, it is interesting that 10 of the 11 countries that held national conferences were plebiscitary regimes in 1989 or had past plebiscitary experience.[31] Earlier, we defined plebiscitary one-party regimes as civilian (or civilianized military) one-party regimes in which there was little or no competition within the single party but which exhibited all the trappings of participatory electoral politics such as mass rallies, regular elections, and referenda. The 10 plebiscitary regimes that convened national conferences had been ruled for an average 15 years by a single party that outlawed competition both in civil society and within its own ranks. Of these countries, only two had had any previous experience with competitive one-party rule: Mali and Togo. Strictly speaking, Mali should be considered separately, since its conference was convened after the coup that toppled the old regime. In any event, in both cases the experience with political competition was extremely shallow: for just two years prior to 1989 in Mali and for only five years in Togo. In both cases, incumbent leaders had introduced internal party competition mainly as a maneuver to preserve control over the political class.

Our interpretation is that the characteristics of the plebiscitary one-party regime made the national conference appealing to both opposition and ruling elite. The tradition of ritualistic participation combined with the absence of effective political competition provided a measure of political voice in a context of declining legitimacy.[32] The plebiscitary tradition created enough political space for the emergence through protest of a nascent opposition to whom the national conference appealed for several reasons. First, the existing rules of the political game provided considerable inbuilt advantages to the regime, and the opposition quickly understood that their reform was a prerequisite for political change. The opposition conceived of the national conference as an impartial public forum in which to refashion more advantageous ground rules that for the first time would include provisions for genuine political competition. Thus, a national conference was more likely in countries that had not had competitive elections recently.[33] After years of stifled competition and empty electoral rituals, the only legitimate forum was one that brought together all tendencies and parties to change the ground rules of competition in preparation for meaningful elections.

Plebiscitary regimes had typically convened elections as often as had competitive one-party regimes. Unlike in the latter, however, competitive elections could not be inaugurated until the protagonists agreed on rules for political competition. The opposition was strong enough that the regime could not completely disregard or repress its calls for a national palaver. At the same time, the opposition was too divided and inexperienced to contest elections successfully, particularly if the elections were to be carried out by the administration under prevailing rules. The opposition was composed typically of several dozen parties, few of which had a national appeal or program and which were poorly organized outside of a few urban areas. Opposition leaders knew they were likely to lose an electoral contest in which the regime held all the cards. The national conference therefore appealed to the opposition for strategic reasons as a forum that would help to conceal its weaknesses.

For its part, the regime was attached to its characteristic plebiscitary protocols, which it believed to be politically useful. For example, Kérékou at first apparently believed that the national conference could be used to vindicate his regime and restore its stability. When the crisis of legitimacy erupted, rulers were predisposed to the holding of a national conference, which they viewed as harkening back to familiar forms of direct democracy that posed little real threat to the regime. Such a forum would allow the incumbent to make minimal concessions, permit opponents to let off steam, and perhaps even end up with a show of support. Rulers acted as if they initially believed that they could turn such events to their advantage, just as they always had done.[34]

Leaders and oppositions thus proceeded toward a national conference with very different understandings of what it would achieve. The former saw it as another harmless participatory ceremony that would provide the regime with a much needed boost, whereas the latter saw it as the first step in a democratic takeover. Such a misunderstanding could not last long, and the critical point came when the national conference demanded full sovereign power. The regime resisted, recognizing that real political competition would pose grave dangers to its hold on power. The ultimate outcome varied then, determined by the relative strengths of the parties. Strong leaders like Biya or Eyadéma were able to avoid the conference or limit its impact; more desperate leaders like Kérékou and Sassou Nguesso gave in, convincing themselves it had become the best alternative. Indeed, for both of them, the national conference turned into a useful forum for negotiating what had become an inevitable loss of power. Thanks to their participation, each assured his peaceful retirement and the absolution from guilt for human rights and corruption abuses.[35]

Although the national conference was a logical extension of the institutional configuration of the plebiscitary regime, it is important to note that international and contingent forces did influence whether or not it occurred. In particular, specific leaders learned from the transition experiences in neighboring countries. Initially, leaders in Bénin and Congo quickly agreed to national conferences whose implications were still not certain. After these conferences had turned into devastating public inquisitions into the regimes' patrimonial malfeasance and incompetence and had ultimately stripped the leaders of executive powers, other leaders understood that they had little to gain from agreeing to a conference and steadfastly resisted opposition demands. Plebiscitary forms continued to appeal to these leaders but were now sought elsewhere – for example, through organized mass marches on behalf of the regime or through sham conferences of one form or another.

With the exception of South Africa, all national conferences resulted, not in compromise, but in a zero-sum victory for one side or another and the defeat of the losing side. Thus, in Bénin, Congo, and Niger the incumbents collapsed at the conference itself; in Zaire and Togo, the opposition achieved Pyrrhic victories at the conference but made mistakes that would eventually play into the incumbent's hands and ensure his survival.[36] The fact that winners took all in African national conferences augured badly for democratic consolidation, because it suggested that transiting countries still lacked a political process for arriving at negotiated solutions, and a balance of power that would ensure that transition agreements had broad support, and therefore could be enforced.

RAPID ELECTIONS

It is striking that other civilian one-party regimes in Africa shunned the national conference route. In this group were Cameroon, Central African Republic, Côte d'Ivoire, Kenya, Madagascar, Malawi, Rwanda, São Tomé, Seychelles, Sierra Leone, Tanzania, and Zambia. They typically embarked on a path directly to competitive elections without pausing to convene a national forum to draw up new rules for the political game.

The reasons for which these countries avoided national conferences were varied. In countries with relatively well-established institutional traditions of competitive one-party rule, opposition demands for a national conference were either weak (e.g., Kenya) or nonexistent (e.g., Tanzania, Zambia), and the opposition campaign made immediate multiparty elections the core demand of its campaign. In the countries that switched to internal party competition during the 1980s, citizens demanded national conferences, but skillful and resourceful incumbent leaders either called early elections (e.g., Côte d'Ivoire, Gabon, and São Tomé) or resisted conceding to demands for a conference (e.g., Central African Republic and Cameroon).

As a whole, this group of countries averaged 11 years as competitive one-party regimes, a reasonably lengthy institutional heritage by postcolonial African standards. Eight out of 14 of these countries actually retained competitive one-party status in 1989, and two more – Kenya and Madagascar – had substantial earlier experience with this form of rule. Compared to other African autocracies, these regimes embodied significantly more political competition, most notably within the single party but also within civil society.

In 11 out of 13 extant competitive one-party regimes, multiparty elections were eventually held.[37] In general, these states moved directly to elections without convening national conferences because there was sufficient consensus among political elites that, with relatively minor adjustments to guarantee genuine competition, elections could be held without a major overhaul of the rules of the political game. How can this be explained? Again, there is evidence to suggest that institutional legacies from the old regimes help to explain why these states transited directly.

Competitive one-party regimes had been vulnerable to collapse when economic crisis and programs of donor-mandated economic policy reform cut down on the resources available to the ruler to manage the political game. The rotation of the political personnel became more chaotic, with the ranks of outsiders swelling and security declining for insiders, paving the way for discontent and recriminations. Often, these conflicts took on a generational dimension, with younger members of the political class finding the doors of rapid promotion within the single party increasingly closed to them. In Côte d'Ivoire, for instance, the majority of politicians who defected from the ruling PDCI to lead the opposition during the transition were the third and fourth generations of party elites, men and women who had entered political life in the 1970s and 1980s, respectively, and had seen their ambitions frustrated by elders within the party, particularly once the economic crisis struck and the rent-seeking pie contracted.[38]

The political transition was sparked by an upsurge of popular sentiment against the regime, that then exacerbated these stresses in the elite coalition. The first casualty of political crisis tended to be the sustainability of the integrative formulas that had cemented national unity and ensured political stability. The pluralistic mechanisms that had promoted elite accommodation and compromise now hastened the transition, and at the same time channeled it.

Although the rules of the political game favored the governing party, the opposition was confident enough to move directly to an election without first convening a national conference. They wanted to avoid the time-consuming processes of debating and ratifying a new constitution for fear that incumbents might take advantage of delays to recant or recoup. They further calculated that, by channeling protest sentiment into antiincumbent votes, they could win a multiparty election under existing institutional arrangements. They demanded only relatively minor adjustments to rules of participation and competition to ensure that any elections, which were the opposition's principal objective, were freely and fairly conducted.[39]

Incumbent responses to these demands depended on whether they were first- or second-generation leaders. Old-guard nationalists like Houphouët or Kaunda calculated that they still enjoyed personal political legitimacy and that their parties had the organizational strength to win a competitive election. These regimes had held elections on a regular basis, and rulers saw them as mechanisms for retaining power. As a result, they were willing to accept the opposition's call for elections; indeed, they often called snap contests in an effort to catch their inexperienced rivals off guard. Confident not only that they retained substantial personal popularity, strongmen thought that official control over the press and the electoral machinery, plus the availability of public funds to finance the ruling party, would ensure a comfortable victory. In the case of the Côte d'Ivoire, at least, this calculation proved to be a sound one. As Fauré suggests, the PDCI's success in the November 1990 legislative elections was due to the fact that "the government, thanks to its effective and very loyal territorial administration, and to the PDCI apparatus, present all over the country down to the most isolated hamlet, controlled electoral operations throughout ... and all official information sources."[40]

The situation was more troubling for second-generation civilian leaders who lacked the historical legitimacy of their predecessors. Without a well-established personal political base, they were less willing to take the risk of multiparty elections; instead, they prevaricated and delayed. Mwinyi stretched out the transition in Tanzania over half a decade, then himself handed over control to a hand-picked successor. When by 1992 Moi could no longer avoid elections, he amended the electoral code to take advantage of the fact that at the time he was the only candidate who could win votes in a majority of the country's regions.[41] The likelihood of ethnic tensions increased sharply in these regimes if and when the transition did not proceed smoothly. Leaders who lacked confidence about their popular base attempted to develop one through ethnic demagoguery once the old integrative formulas no longer appeared capable of assuring political stability. Thus, anti-northern rhetoric began appearing less and less subtly in the discourse of the PDCI, particularly under Konan Bedie, Houphouët-Boigny's successor, and the Moi government appeared to be largely responsible for the sharp and ominous rise of ethnic conflict in Kenya's Rift Valley.[42]

PACTED TRANSITIONS

Regime transitions in Africa's neopatrimonial regimes did not generally follow a *reforma,* or "transformation," route to democracy in which incumbent elites gradually ceded power to their opponents and shared power after the transition.[43] Instead, they tended to occur abruptly via *ruptura,* or "replacement," as incumbent dictators were rudely swept away in elections, or through "reaction" and "repression" as upstart social movements were crushed or collapsed. Weak political institutions did not provide a context in which the agents of state or civil society could convincingly negotiate a democratic bargain to share power. Instead, regime transitions in Africa were zero-sum processes in which the strongest side tended to win conclusively.

As we argued in Chapter 2, the transition dynamics described in the literature on democratization, in which moderate factions in the government and opposition seek common ground through negotiations, simply does not fit most African cases. We find little evidence in Africa of elite pacts in which incumbent and opposition leaders meet behind the scenes to provide mutual assurances that each would respect the vital interests of the other in a future democratic dispensation.

The main exception was transitions from settler oligarchies. There the protagonists were deeply divided along racial and class lines into airtight corporate blocs. Each side could mobilize significant resources, with the opposition holding a clear political advantage but with settlers continuing to control the economy. Faced with a stalemate in which neither side could govern alone, settlers and Africans were forced into compromise agreement that fully suited neither. Transitions from settler oligarchies were often violent and protracted, but they typically ended through negotiation. The contenders for power struck a series of political, military, and economic agreements that divided power (at least for an interim period) and protected minority interests.

Take the case of South Africa.[44] By the late 1980s, the South African government and the African National Congress had arrived at an impasse, with neither able to exclusively obtain its preferred political goals.[45] Each side had been weakened by international developments – the government by political isolation and economic sanctions and the ANC by the withdrawal of Eastern bloc military support – that created new incentives to negotiate a settlement.[46] The route to a transitional government of national unity in 1994 was paved with major concessions on both sides: The ruling whites conceded ANC's core demand of free elections under a universal franchise in a unitary state, and the principal black opposition group accepted rules of proportional representation for elections, job security for white civil servants, and an amnesty for security forces that admitted to crimes under the old regime. Given these precedents of moderation, the country's April 1994 election "was marked by a quite extraordinary atmosphere of goodwill...blacks and whites voted together without conflict."[47]

Trace elements of pacts can be found in transitions elsewhere in southern Africa. Even though occurring a decade earlier, Zimbabwe's independence resulted from a negotiated constitutional accord that traded political power for the black majority for legal and financial guarantees against the nationalization of white-owned land, investments, and pensions. More recent regime transitions in Namibia, Angola, and Mozambique were arbitrated among war-weary combatants in a context in which the superpowers were seeking to exit from regional conflicts. As in South Africa, all these transitions required that the victors in elections accommodate minority groups, commonly by appointing their representatives to cabinet and other positions in governments of national unity. By the end of 1994, every country in southern Africa (except Swaziland) had opened up to multiparty competition, and most of them subsequently proceeded to democratic elections.

Were pacted transitions in southern Africa aided by the region's institutional heritage of settler oligarchy? We propose a possible connection. For all their fatal flaws, settler oligarchies (at least in South Africa, South West Africa, and Rhodesia) had the virtue of institutionalizing political competition. Recall that this chapter began by defining political liberalization as a process of broadening such competition. The process of liberalization would seem to be relatively easier in regimes where competition is tolerated; the main challenge is then the simpler one of expanding the franchise to allow political participation. Liberalization – and hence, democratization – is considerably more difficult where the principles of pluralism have never been built into the institutions of the polity. Where cultural and organizational contexts are unsupportive, the introduction of political contestation can lead to division, polarization, and instability. If this logic is correct, then the prospects for gradual, negotiated political opening are generally better in bureaucratic-authoritarian regimes, provided they display some heritage of political competition, than in neopatrimonial ones.

TESTING COMPETING EXPLANATIONS

Let us now turn from the process of liberalization to its outcomes, at the same time testing our institutional explanation against its main alternatives. Why did national political leaders supply political reforms?

ECONOMIC FACTORS

It seems plausible that authoritarian rulers who failed to obtain economic development were impelled to find alternative ways to legitimize their rule. In order to relieve popular pressures rooted in economic discontent, they may have had few options but to resort to political openings. By relaxing restrictions on civil liberties, it could be argued, leaders calculated that they could distract citizens, at least for a while, from long-standing material hardships, at the same time buying time to address pressing crises. Political liberalization might also have served the useful purpose of currying favor with the international donors and lenders who provided the finance necessary for economic recovery.

Cross-national statistical analysis of the African data revealed, however, that economic factors were largely unrelated to political liberalization. However we measured economic structure, economic change, or economic crisis – using the full range of indicators employed in the previous chapter – they had no discernible effects on the extent of political liberalization. Clearly, an economic crisis provided the context in which struggles over liberalization took place in almost all African countries. However, we found no evidence that the degree of liberalization could be explained in terms of variation in national economic characteristics, at least within Africa.

As before, the only exception was the number of structural adjustment agreements entered into by African governments. In this instance, however, we discovered an inverse relationship between economic and political reform, as indicated by the negative sign on the bivariate correlation coefficient.[48] Governments that had signed numerous adjustment agreements during the 1980s were less likely to move ahead aggressively on political liberalization; and vice versa. Again, interpretation of this finding was complicated; perhaps governments that had demonstrated a capacity to obtain multilateral donor support throughout the 1980s felt confident enough of the continuation of that support, despite the new international concern for good governance. The African data suggest that, at least at the level of stated intentions, leaders did not make tandem commitments to both political and economic reforms. Perhaps they regarded different sorts of reform programs as partially interchangeable, to be tactically shuffled and cross-substituted.

In countries where governments embarked on relatively extensive economic reform programs during the 1980s, leaders enjoyed a wider range of political options in the 1990s, including the ability to limit political liberalization. Notably in Ghana and Uganda, where governments made early and sustained commitments to restore free markets, with extensive multilateral donor support, leaders were later able to get away with minimal political openings. In part this was due to a measure of political satisfaction among citizens who gave incumbent governments credit for restoring economic normalcy in the form of stable currencies and the availability of consumer goods.[49] But it was also due to the willingness of international donors to reward economic reformers with less onerous demands for reform on the political front.

More commonly, political leaders who had not enjoyed good relations with the donors found themselves with very few political options. Having neglected to convince the donors that they were willing to make necessary economic reforms, leaders in countries like Bénin, Congo, and Zambia faced full-blown fiscal and inflation crises by the turn of the decade, getting little sympathy and less help from abroad. Unwilling to countenance the emergency austerity measures required to obtain the renewal of donor support, leaders like Kérékou, Sassou Nguesso, and Kaunda had no alternative but to risk major political concessions. In short, the most extensive political reforms on the continent were undertaken by the most desperate leaders. Especially in the cases of Bénin and Congo, the propensity to political reform was reinforced by donors who advised governments that they would lose essential flows of concessionary capital unless they opened up politically. Indeed, the rulers of the most economically embattled countries in Africa found themselves in a no-win situation: Either they entered into structural adjustment agreements with international financial institutions, thereby risking the wrath of citizens expressed in protest; or they ignored the imperative for economic reform, only to discover that a deepening economic crisis left them with few options but to liberalize politically.

As for the effects of economic factors on the timing of transition events, only one statistically significant finding again emerged, which tends to reinforce this last point. Among African countries that experienced political protest, incumbent leaders reacted with political reforms somewhat more quickly in poor countries than in richer ones.[50] For example, the governments of six countries (Burkina Faso, Chad, Equatorial Guinea, Guinea–Bissau, Niger, and Nigeria) conceded political reforms immediately, within the same month of the first recorded political protests. All these countries had extremely poor economies that generated annual per capita incomes of $330 or lower. Leaders of essentially indigent governments quickly became strapped for resources and soon had to opt for liberalization measures. By contrast, the time lag between first protests and initial political reforms was much more protracted in high-income countries like South Africa. Resourceful leaders of well-endowed governments had the luxury of choosing among numerous options in dealing with protesters' demands – including attempts to coopt or repress opponents – before having to resort to political liberalization.

INTERNATIONAL FACTORS

In the previous chapter, we argued that opposition movements communicated prodemocracy sentiment across international borders within Africa, thus helping to spark protests. Incumbent rulers also benefited from political learning; this time, however, the lessons concerned political liberalization. Some African leaders adopted ideas about political reform from allies in the outside world. Nyerere's influential speech of February 1990 – in which he pronounced that the African one-party state, of which he had been a major architect, was no longer sacrosanct – was inspired by a visit to Leipzig to terminate relations between Tanzania's Revolutionary Party (CCM) and the East German Communist party. Other leaders introduced liberalization reforms following political openings in the neighboring region. In Zimbabwe, Mugabe lifted emergency regulations and released political prisoners in July 1990, in good part because continued restrictions on civil liberties had become hard to justify in the light of de Klerk's political reform program in South Africa.[51]

Some leaders realized that political liberalization could be advantageous, but others drew the opposite conclusion. Although it is impossible to prove, national leaders in late-liberalizing regimes seemed to learn from the political misfortunes of their colleagues in other countries. For example, Kaunda of Zambia reportedly advised Moi of Kenya to adopt a hard line against opponents and election observers because, in his hard-won experience, gradual political openings led inexorably to the ouster of incumbent leaders. Biya probably refused to countenance a national conference in Cameroon in part because its proceedings had led to the indictment and the downfall of presidential colleagues in Bénin and Congo. As Pearl Robinson comments, "Beseiged autocrats resisted convening the national conference because, in essence, they knew the script."[52]

The spread of ideas about political liberalization among ruling elites within Africa thus had contradictory effects for political reform. We did not expect – and did not find – a one-to-one relationship between indicators of political diffusion and the extent of liberalization across African countries.[53] Instead, we assumed that effective international influence would originate from a different quarter, notably from the political conditions imposed by international donors and lenders. What effects did outside pressure for good governance in the aftermath of the Cold War have upon political reforms in Africa? At first, we found that the imposition by donors of explicit political conditions did not systematically encourage the introduction of liberalization reforms. African leaders undertook political liberalization both when donors imposed explicit political conditions (23 countries) and when they withheld this kind of pressure (17 countries). Notably, several African governments that did not liberalize – Liberia, Mauritania, Somalia, Sudan – were under intense donor pressure, including suspension of aid in the cases of Liberia and Sudan, to do so.

This is not to say that isolated examples of effective donor pressure cannot be found. In well-publicized confrontations, a consortium of Western donors acting through the World Bank–chaired Consultative Group, halted program aid while demanding governance reforms in Kenya in November 1991 and in Malawi in June 1992.[54] Shortly thereafter, both Moi and Banda made major political concessions, agreeing to hold a competitive election and a referendum on multiparty democracy, respectively. In these instances, an ultimatum from international donors clearly contributed to political liberalization. By the same token, however, both these governments had previously been under pressure from domestic forces. The Moi government in Kenya faced a campaign of public criticism from church leaders and lawyers from 1986 onward and a series of mass disturbances in Nairobi and regional towns in July 1990. The Banda government was openly criticized by the country's Catholic bishops, whose intervention sparked labor unrest in April and May 1992, prior to the donor ultimatum.

Thus, even in these key cases, it was difficult to discern which sort of pressure – international or domestic, or some combination – was at work.[55] In only two countries in Africa – Mozambique and Seychelles – did international donor conditions lead to political liberalization in the absence of domestic protests. In all other cases, (n = 23) political conditions on international aid were imposed in a setting where domestic political protests had already occurred. At best, one can infer that political reforms had multiple causes. But, in most cases, domestic initiatives came first. We thus tested whether international political conditions were independently influential across the full range of African cases. A statistical control for political protest revealed that donor conditions did indeed influence the extent of liberalization reforms. Unexpectedly, however, donor influence ran counter to what was intended, as indicated by the negative sign on the partial correlation coefficient.[56] In other words, the greater the degree of political conditionality that donors imposed, the less extensive were liberalization reforms.

Several interpretations are possible. First, a large number of African governments undertook anticipatory reforms, that is, in advance of the imposition of explicit donor conditions. Reading the handwriting on the (Berlin) wall, African leaders correctly interpreted the post–Cold War shift in Western foreign policies to mean that aid would be distributed primarily to countries that appeared to be moving toward democracy. Hence, they sought to position their countries favorably in the international contest for scarce development resources and to avoid potential ruptures of concessionary capital flows that could arise if they waited for donors to impose conditions. Anticipatory political reforms were most evident in former Portuguese colonies that had never drawn resources from a close relationship with a well-endowed colonial power. For example, incumbent rulers in Cape Verde and São Tomé not only took the initiative to liberalize extensively, but they did so in the late 1980s, at a time well before Western donors had fully developed their governance conditions.

Second, donors reserved their most stringent conditions for cracking the toughest nuts. They commonly began by communicating their preferences for good governance behind the scenes; in many cases, quiet diplomacy was enough to help nudge leaders toward anticipatory reforms. Explicit conditions on aid were reserved for governments that demonstrated reluctance to adopt a reform agenda. For example, donors cut off aid to countries like Kenya, Malawi, Sudan, and Zaire only late in the transition game after leaders had already proved immune to persuasion. Similarly, resourceful strongmen continued to drag their feet and dig in their heels even after aid was cut, as illustrated by the stalling tactics of Ratsiraka in Madagascar and Mobutu in Zaire. Mobutu was able to survive diplomatic and aid sanctions imposed in 1991 by Zaire's "big three" donors – Belgium, France, and the United States. Indeed, by 1994 he had enticed the West to restore more normal relations by appointing a technocrat to manage the economy and by providing access for international relief agencies to Rwandan refugees.[57] In this light, political liberalization under donor pressure can be seen as a calculated ruse by incumbent rulers who lacked a basic voluntary commitment to democracy. Usually, as with Moi in Kenya, they conceded the bare minimum that they thought donors would accept, with the resulting tentative openings subject to closure again once international pressure abated.

INSTITUTIONAL FACTORS

Hence, we return to our institutional thesis. Were some types of political regime more likely to open up than others? Did the degree of political participation and competition under previous regimes affect the extent of liberalization?

At first, an African citizenry's experience with political participation seemed unconnected to its government's willingness to undertake political reform. Our standard measure of political participation (the number of elections, independence to 1989) showed no bivariate association with the extent of liberalization between 1988 and 1992. A relationship between these two variables emerged only when statistical controls were introduced for the frequency of political protest and the occurrence of a national conference.[58] Interestingly, institutional precedents of participation now stood in a negative relationship to liberalization, with higher prior levels of citizen involvement apparently leading to narrower political openings.

Why might this be? We understand this finding to mean that, alone, mass participation was insufficient to prompt thoroughgoing political reforms. We have demonstrated that plebiscitary precedents of mass mobilization clearly led to popular protest and even to national conferences. But citizen protesters in Africa did not have a clear program of political reforms. They were well aware of what they were *against* – the political abuses and economic mismanagement of the *anciens régimes*—but they never convincingly defined and expressed what they were *for*. The ideology of the "second liberation" was itself shaped by the neopatrimonial milieu from which protest movements emerged; it focused on demands to sweep away old leaders but never enunciated a specific program to install liberal democratic institutions. The political experiences of African citizens led them to a point at which they could confront the old regime but left them poorly prepared to devise new institutional forms with which to replace it.

The shortcomings of the inherited institutional legacy as a base for generating reform is reinforced when we consider precedents of political competition. In this instance, a clear bivariate linkage was evident between our standard measure of political competition (the percentage of legislative seats controlled by the largest political party in 1989) and the extent of liberalization.[59] As with protest, we found that political liberalization was most extensive when reform began from the institutional foundation of single-party, rather than military or multiparty, regimes. Moreover, the more distantly in its past a country had held a competitive election, the broader were the political openings it experienced after 1988.[60] On the other hand, we were unable to spot any difference in extent of liberalization between competitive and plebiscitary one-party regimes. In large part this was due to the impact of national conferences on pushing liberalization forward in the plebiscitary regimes, a point we return to later.

CONTINGENT FACTORS

We do not reduce our argument to the influence of inherited political structures alone. We also tested empirically the impact of political agency and contingent events – in the form of political protests and national conferences – that had helped to shape transition trajectories in Africa. The reader will immediately notice the new analytic status of political protest and national conferences; they are no longer treated as dependent variables to be explained but as independent variables with explanatory power of their own. In previous sections, these factors were shown to be far from random and to be themselves understandable in terms of the legacy of past political institutions. Nonetheless, they in turn had an independent impact on the transition once it got underway.

Did the actions of mass protesters alter the course of political change? After all, protests were disruptive activities whose occurrence was likely to create ripple effects. We used an ordinal estimate of the frequency of protest, 1988 to 1992, to operationalize the independent variable because we wished to limit observations to the period before 1992 when liberalization peaked, thus avoiding any imputation of causality from protests that occurred after liberalization. We found that mass popular protest was positively associated with the introduction of liberalization reforms.[61] Of the 40 African regimes that opened up politically in the first years of the 1990s, a majority (28) did so in conjunction with mass political protest.[62] Notably, mass political demonstrations were always accompanied by reform; there was no country in Africa in which protest occurred where incumbent elites failed to make at least a token political opening (see Figure 6).

As stated earlier, political liberalization was a process in which political reforms were introduced in gradual, incremental fashion. Sometimes the process led through cumulative advances toward a more liberal polity, but often it was disrupted, even reversed, by later episodes of repression. African regimes began to diverge in terms of performance on political liberalization after 1992. Many continued to advance, but others stood still, and still others encountered setbacks by 1994.[63] Was the tenuous nature of political liberalization in Africa related to the source of the reform initiative? One might argue, for example, that incumbent leaders sustained real political openings only if they were pressured persistently to do so by tenacious opposition-led protest movements. Conversely, one could make the contrary case that reforms introduced by leaders under popular pressure would be insincere, hurried, merely tactical, and subject to reversal as soon as pressure was released.

Oddly enough, *both* these propositions found support in the data. We arrived at this conclusion via the following steps. A positive association emerged between the source of the reform initiative and the subsequent trajectory of liberalization, that is, whether countries were "advancers," "stabilizers," or "backsliders" between 1992 and 1994.[64] When incumbent rulers took the political lead, they were usually able to control the reform process; generally, they opened up only so far as they felt they had to and then they froze the reform process. Nine out of 14 such cases of "stabilized" liberalization resulted from elite initiatives. One can therefore conclude that elite-led transitions stopped short at moderate levels of political liberalization, levels that, at least in the near term, were likely to be consolidated. By contrast, when mass protesters initiated transitions, the subsequent processes of liberalization were widely divergent. Although some governments introduced further political reforms, others slid back by gradually revoking reforms that had been made earlier. Mass protests led to 7 out of the 8 cases of "advancing" liberalization in the African sample, and 13 out of the 18 "backsliding" cases. Hence, the confirmation of seemingly contradictory propositions; mass protest led to *both* advances and setbacks. As might be expected, protest-led reform launched a period of contingent change in which the subsequent fate of liberalization reforms was highly uncertain.

Apart from protests, the other major events that impinged on liberalization were national conferences. One of the strongest bivariate relationships in the study linked national conferences with the extent of political reform.[65] Without exception, all 11 countries that convened national conferences recorded advances in liberalization up to 1992; this includes not only the countries that made significant[66] political openings (e.g., Bénin, Congo, Mali) but also those that barely liberalized (e.g., Chad and Togo[67]). By contrast, none of the four countries that experienced setbacks in liberalization in the period between 1988 and 1992 (Liberia, Sierra Leone, Sudan, and Uganda) held national conferences. National conferences were therefore a force for political liberalization: Wherever protesters were able to wrest an incumbent's concession to convene a conference, it always resulted in at least the partial relaxation of authoritarian political controls.

National conferences had certain institutional characteristics: They were formally organized and run, attended by official representatives of recognized social sectors, and highly valued by participants. To the extent that national conferences reproduced historical models of political assembly or took on similar forms across African countries, they created or reinforced organizational precedents. In short, these gatherings imparted a distinctive pattern to Africa's transitions. National conferences thus amounted to more than contingent events. They can be thought of as protoinstitutions that lent structure to the random flow of transition dynamics and pushed African regimes in calculated directions, not least toward political liberalization. Indeed, they played a critical role in advancing transitions from plebiscitary regimes that suffered from a serious deficit in political competition and would otherwise almost certainly not have managed to achieve as much political liberalization as competitive one-party regimes. As such, they were a perfect illustration of the creative energy of transitions, in which actors could use institutional logics derived from the past to chart new courses for the future.

TOWARD MULTIVARIATE MODELS

To summarize: The domestic institutional heritage of postcolonial African regimes (as measured by levels of political participation and political competition) was systematically linked to political liberalization. Compared with effects on protest, however, participatory precedents now had negative effects. Moreover, when intervening landmark events (like political protests and national conferences) were treated as explanatory factors, they helped to cast light on whether liberalization reforms came to pass. Finally, selected economic and international factors (like adjustment agreements and donor pressure) continued to affect the trajectories of transition, though rarely in ways expected or intended. Notably, international donors remained important players in African transitions, though they were more effective at inducing political liberalization through quiet diplomatic persuasion than through highly publicized suspensions of aid.

As before, we sought to estimate a multivariate equation for political liberalization. We again used OLS regression to order and weigh the correlates of reform. Model B includes the full range of variables with proven bivariate explanatory power (see Table 6). Model B was then restricted to establish a parsimonious model with maximum explanatory power.[68]

Model C reveals that political liberalization was a somewhat more random phenomenon than political protest, requiring five variables to predict less

Table 6. *Multiple Regression Estimates of Political Liberalization, 1988–1992*

Variable	Estimates		Signif-icance	Explained Variance
	(B)	(Standard-ized B)	(p-value)	
Model B				
National Conference	1.239	0.408	0.006	
Frequency of Political				
Protest	0.507	0.315	0.049	
Number of Elections	−0.091	−0.260	0.058	
Political Conditions on				
International Aid	−0.414	−0.243	0.075	
Percentage of Legislative				
Seats	0.007	0.208	0.112	
Number of Structural				
Adjustment Programs	−0.064	−0.198	0.170	
Number of Trade Unions	−0.014	−0.147	0.290	
Years Since Last				
Competitive Election	0.009	0.060	0.693	
			Multiple R	0.747
			R Square	0.559
			Adj. R	
			Square	0.452
			Standard	
			Error	1.001
			F	5.222
			Sig. F	0.0003
Model C				
National Conference	1.320	0.434	0.002	
Political Conditions on				
International Aid	−0.292	−0.351	0.021	
Percentage of Legislative				
Seats	0.010	0.296	0.020	
Number of Elections	−0.092	−0.261	0.053	
Frequency of Political				
Protest	0.336	0.207	0.154	
			Multiple R	0.710
			R Square	0.504
			Adj. R	
			Square	0.436
			Standard	
			Error	1.016
			F	7.334
			Sig. F	0.0001

(n = 42)

than one-half of total variance. Clearly, the role of serendipity and national idiosyncracies loomed larger as transitions progressed.

The occurrence of a *national conference* emerged as the most important predictor. Our model estimated that the convening of a conference increased our measure of liberalization by 1.32, suggesting that liberalization was primarily a contingent leadership response to demands by a popular assembly. To some extent, national conferences can be interpreted as an institutionalized expression of *political protest:* Not only were protests and conferences intercorrelated, but protest surfaced as the most important predictor variable when national conferences were removed from the equation.[69] In this light, we must confirm that the political liberalization in Africa unfolded in good part as a process of *interactive agency,* as embattled leaders struggled to find appropriate responses to escalating opposition demands.

At the same time, political liberalization was more likely in certain kinds of political regimes than others. It was most likely in civilian one-party regimes that by definition excluded interparty *political competition* (as measured by the percentage of legislative seats held by the largest party in 1989). Political openings were unlikely in *either* relatively open multiparty systems that were already partially liberalized or in repressive military oligarchies where civilian political institutions were uniformly emasculated. Instead, reform tended to occur under a twin set of institutional requirements: where rulers had seen fit to try to legitimate themselves by constructing civilian political institutions, and where they had imposed a strict monopoly on such institutions. Regime transitions in Africa were forged in the crucible of one-party rule and were a *reaction against* the incapacity of this set of institutions to provide meaningful opportunities for political competition.

Other limits of the plebiscitary heritage were also revealed. Each election held between independence and 1989 was estimated to reduce the extent of liberalization by 0.092. The ritual dance of enforced *political participation* may have created a mass constituency for political protest, as we saw in the previous chapter, but it failed to create a deep popular commitment to liberal values or institutions. Protest demands were never expanded into a public discourse on the meaning of democratic citizenship, including its full range of rights or responsibilities, or channeled into permanent organizations of political representation. Precedents of political participation evoked protest; but alone they rarely institutionalized a process of political liberalization. Only where mass participation was channeled through a national conference did mass participation reliably foster political reform.

ENDNOTES

1. Joseph E. Ryan, "The Comparative Survey of Freedom, 1992–1993: Survey Methodology," in Freedom House, *Freedom in the World: Annual Survey of Political Rights and Civil Liberties, 1992–93* (New York: Freedom House, 1993), p. 77.

2. The 37 liberalizing countries shown in Table 12 (third column, summary row) include four long-standing multiparty regimes that are excluded from our working sample of 42 African countries. It also differs from the 40 liberalizing countries shown in Figure 6 by taking into account the fact that, before the end of 1992, some countries that introduced political reforms had, by revoking them, begun to slide back.

3. In Gabon, Bongo organized and controlled a "national conference" before legalizing parties and convening legislative elections.

4. See Michael Bratton, "Zambia Starts Over," *Journal of Democracy* 3 (1992): 86–8.

5. Gavin Williams, "Africa in Retrospect and Prospect," *Africa South of the Sahara, 1994* (London: Europa Publications, 1994), p. 6.

6. South Africa's Convention for a Democratic South Africa (CODESA) was coded as a national conference, given its close similarity in function and process to national conferences elsewhere in Africa.

7. Repression was defined as government action against the opposition entailing violence or the threat of violence. Three levels of repression were distinguished: no action (= 0), use of mild or threatened violence (= 1), and systematic or severe use of violence (= 2). Manipulation (= 1) was defined as evidence that the government was insincere in its implementation of reform or that it was pursuing diversionary tactics to thwart reforms to which it had otherwise committed itself.

8. Spearman's r = 0.684, sig. = 0.000.

9. Spearman's r = 0.631, sig. = 0.000.

10. A detailed account of the regime's repression during this period is in Lelo Nzuzi, "Zaire: Quatre Années de 'Transition', Bilan Provisoire," in *l'Afrique Politique: Vue sur la Démocratisation à Marée Basse,* ed. Patrick Quantin (Paris: Karthala, 1994), pp. 253–66. See also "Zaire: Pyramids Collapse," *Africa Confidential* 32 (28 June 1991).

11. True, each had a long history of collaboration with Mobutu before leading the opposition against him. For instance, Tshisekedi had been Mobutu's first minister of the interior in 1964, and was deputy president of the National Assembly from 1970 to 1979, before falling out of favor. "A Chequered Career," *Africa Confidential* 32 (9 August 1991).

12. See "Zaire: Mobutu Manipulates at Home and Abroad," *Africa Confidential* 34 (5 November 1993); and "Dual Control," *Africa Confidential* 34 (16 April 1993).

13. Emmanuel Grégoire, "Démocratie, Etat et Milieux d'Affaires au Niger," *Politique Africaine,* (December 1994): 94–107.

14. See Luc Sindjoun "Cameroun: le Système Politique Face aux Enjeux de la Transition Démocratique, 1990–1993," in *l'Afrique Politique: Vue sur la Démocratisation à Marée Basse,* ed. Patrick Quantin (Paris: Karthala, 1994).

15. See John R. Heilbrunn and C.M. Toulabor, "Une si Petite Démocratisation pour le Togo," *Politique Africaine,* (June 1995): 85–100.

16. See John Heilbrunn, "Political Liberalization In Togo," in *Political Liberalization in Francophone Africa,* ed. John C. Clark and David Gardiniers (Boulder, Colo.: Westview, 1997).

17. See Larry Diamond, "Nigeria: The Uncivic Society and the Descent into Praetorianism," in *Politics in Developing Countries: Comparing Experiences with Democracy,* 2nd ed., ed. Diamond, Juan J. Linz, and Seymour Martin Lipset (Boulder, Colo.: Lynne Rienner, 1995), pp. 417–91.

18. On Ghana, see Richard Jeffries and Clare Thomas, "The Ghanaian Elections of 1992," *African Affairs* 92, no. 368 (July 1993): 331–66.
19. We classify Uganda as a military oligarchy, even though it was not a military regime in the normal sense of the word. Museveni, a civilian politician with no military training, came to lead a military insurgency at the head of the National Resistance Movement. We determined that the role and prominence of the military in the regime justifies this classification. Holger Bernt Hansen and Michael Twaddle, "Uganda," in *Democracy and Political Change in Sub-Saharan Africa,* ed. John Wiseman (London: Routledge, 1995), pp. 137–51.
20. See Christopher Clapham and George Philip, "The Political Dilemmas of Military Regimes," in *The Political Dilemmas of Military Regimes,* ed. Christopher Clapham and George Philip (London: Croom Helm, 1985), pp. 1–27.
21. See Claude E. Welch, "Cincinnatus in Africa: The Possibility of Military Withdrawal from Politics," in *The State of the Nations: Constraints on Development in Independent Africa,* ed. Michael F. Lofchie (Berkeley: University of California Press, 1971), pp. 215–38, for a discussion of this point.
22. On these events, see "Nigerian Military Rulers Annul Election," *The New York Times,* 24 June 1993; and "Nigeria: About Turn!," *Africa Confidential,* 30 July 1993.
23. The military government actually drafted the constitutions and manifestos of the two parties. See Diamond, "Nigeria: Uncivic Society," 452 and passim.
24. Nonetheless, the military coup by junior officers which toppled the Traoré regime in Mali in March 1991 shows that there are limits to the extent to which even a military regime can rely on force to maintain its power.
25. "Africa's Troubled Transitions," *Journal of Democracy,* 3 (1992): 103. As Lemarchand argues,"transitions from above are likely to 'deliver' democracy because they generally feature more specific plans concerning the timing, methods, and overall strategy of transition. Transitions from below, on the other hand, usually involve more uncertainty."
26. See "Ghana: Rawlings Against the World," *Africa Confidential* 31 (24 August 1991) and "Ghana: The Return of the Old Parties," *Africa Confidential* 32 (13 September 1991). Rawlings appears to have agreed to the 1992 presidential elections only after his own intelligence services suggested he would win them handily.
27. See Jeffries and Thomas, "Ghanaian Elections of 1992," 235–8, 241.
28. See Heilbrunn and Toulabor, "Une si Petite Démocratisation."
29. Spearman's r = 0.375, sig. = 0.015; and Spearman's r = 0.328, sig = 0.034, respectively.
30. Patrick Quantin, "Congo: Les Origines Politiques de la Décomposition d'un Processus de Libéralisation (Aout 1992–Décembre 1993)," in *l'Afrique Politique: Vue sur la Démocratisation à Marée Basse,* ed. Patrick Quantin (Paris: Karthala, 1994), pp. 167–90.
31. Bénin, Chad, Comoros, Congo, Ethiopia, Gabon, Mali, Niger, Togo, Zaire, the exception being the Republic of South Africa.
32. See Ruth Collier, *Regimes in Tropical Africa* (Berkeley: University of California Press, 1982): 119–24; and Aristide Zolberg, "The Structure of Political Conflict in the New States of Tropical Africa," *American Political Science Review* 62 (1968): 70–87.

33. Put another way, the longer the period since the last competitive election, the more likely that the path to liberalization would be via a national conference (Spearman's r = 0.389, sig. = 0.011). This relationship survived a control for protest, although at a reduced significance level (Pearson's r = 0.287, P = 0.069).

34. Allen, "Restructuring an Authoritarian State,"p. 48. As Allen argues in relation to the national conference in Bénin, "It was conceived originally by the government as a means of discussing mainly the political and economic problems of the time ... and of co-opting the opposition into a joint solution in which the government would retain the leading role."

35. See Monga, "National Conferences in Francophone Africa."

36. See René Lemarchand, "Mobutu and the National Conference: The Arts of Political Survival" (Gainesville: University of Florida, unpublished manuscript, 1992).

37. The exceptions were Rwanda and Sierra Leone, where military intervention and the breakdown of civil order aborted transitions through the end of 1994, the end date for this study. Sierra Leone eventually held founding elections in March 1996.

38. Jeanne Maddox Toungara, "Generational Tensions in the Parti Démocratique de Côte d'Ivoire," *African Studies Review* 38 (1995): 11–38.

39. Describing the 1991 transition in Zambia as "a struggle over the rules of the political game and the resources by which it is played," Bratton notes that "the ruling party [still] employ[ed] all its strength to tilt the rules of political competition in its own favor." Even so, the opposition successfully forced incumbent President Kaunda to forgo a referendum on multiparty politics and move directly to elections. They also felt confident enough to contest the October 1991 election under a less than perfect voter register and constitution. Bratton, "Zambia Starts Over," 82.

40. See Y. A. Fauré, "L'Economie Politique d'une Démocratisation: Eléments d'-Analyse à Propos de l'Experience Récente de la Côte d'Ivoire," *Politique Africaine* 43 (1991): 37.

41. The Kenyan elections are well described in Joel Barkan, "Kenya: Lessons from a Flawed Election," *Journal of Democracy* 4 (1993); and Bard-Anders Andraeson, Gisela Geisler, and Arne Tostensen, *A Hobbled Democracy: The Kenya General Elections, 1992* (Bergen, Norway: Christian Michelson Institute, 1993).

42. See Coulibaly Tiemoko, "Démocratie et Surenchères Identitaires en Côte d'Ivoire," *Politique Africaine* (1995): 143–50; David Throup, "Elections and Political Legitimacy in Kenya," *Africa* 63 (1993): 391.

43. The terms *reforma* and *ruptura* were coined by Juan Linz and Alfred Stepan, eds., *The Breakdown of Democratic Regimes* (Baltimore: Johns Hopkins University Press, 1978), p. 35; the terms "transformation" and "replacement" are Huntington's more jargonistic synonyms (*The Third Wave: Democratization in the Late Twentieth Century*. Norman: University of Oklahoma Press (1991), p. 114). We prefer the clearer distinction between transitions "from above" and "from below."

44. On South Africa's pacted transition see Timothy Sisk, *Democratization in South Africa: The Elusive Social Contract* (Princeton: Princeton University Press, 1995), and Jeffrey Herbst, "Prospects for Elite-Driven Democracy in South Africa" (paper presented at the annual meeting of the African Studies Association, Toronto, November 1994).

45. See Vincent Maphai, "The Politics of Transition Since 1990: Implications of the Stalemate," in Maphai (ed.) *South Africa: The Challenge of Change* (Harare, Zimbabwe: SAPES [Southern Africa Political Economy Series] Books, 1994), pp. 66–91, and Allister Sparks, *Tomorrow is Another Country* (Sandton, South Africa: Struik Books, 1994).

46. For a debate on this issue, see Adrian Guelke, "The Impact of the End of the Cold War on the South African Transition," and John Daniel, "A Response to Guelke: The Cold War Factor in South Africa's Transition," *Journal of Contemporary African Studies* (Grahamstown, South Africa) 14 (1996): 87–100, 101–4.

47. J. D. Omer-Cooper, "South Africa: Toward Democratic Elections," *Africa South of the Sahara, 1995* (London: Europa Publications, 1995), p. 849. "For all its problems, the election was a resounding political success. It provided a quite extraordinary emotional as well as politically liberating catharsis for the vast majority of South Africans of all races. As the results became known, jubilant crowds poured out into the streets in previously unimaginable scenes of goodwill. Thus the new South Africa was born in a far more joyous atmosphere than even the most optimistic had dared to imagine".

48. In its bivariate form, the relationship between adjustment programs (1980–89) and extent of liberalization (1988–92) was statistically significant only at the relaxed level of $P < 0.10$ (Pearson's $r = -0.274$, $P = 0.062$).

49. Jeffries and Thomas have argued that Rawlings retained extensive popular support for exactly this reason. See "Ghanaian Elections of 1992."

50. Using $n = 28$. Pearson's $r = 0.655$, $P = 0.000$; the dependent variable is the time lag in number of months between the first political protest and the first liberalization reform.

51. With reference to South Africa itself, de Klerk apparently learned from the experience of the embattled and politically short-sighted settler regime in Rhodesia not to wait too long before negotiating. Huntington, *Third Wave* (1991), p. 155.

52. Pearl Robinson, "The National Conference Phenomenon in Francophone Africa," *Comparative Studies in Society and History* 36 (1994): 576.

53. As in Chapter 4, the battery of indicators of political diffusion included number of bordering countries, number of bordering countries with the same colonizer, and number of bordering countries with a prior transition event (either protest or liberalization).

54. For accounts of these confrontations, see Barkan, "Kenya: Lessons from a Flawed Election," 85–99; and Larry Garber and Clark Gibson, *Review of United Nations Electoral Assistance* (New York: United Nations Development Program, 1993).

55. We established in Chapter 4 that donor political conditionality did not itself prompt protest.

56. Pearson's partial $r = -0.345$, $P = 0.027$.

57. See, for example, "What Goes Down Can Come Up After All," *The Economist,* 15 April 1995.

58. Pearson's partial $r = -0.331$, $P = 0.037$.

59. Pearson's $r = 0.396$, $P = 0.006$.

60. Pearson's $r = 0.317$, $P = 0.030$.

61. Phi $= 0.316$, sig. $= 0.040$.

62. One cannot automatically conclude that protest was the *cause* of liberalization. In most of these cases (25 out of 28), protest occurred earlier than reforms did, sug-

gesting that mass political initiatives helped to bring about political openings. But in at least three cases – Gabon, Guinea, and Madagascar – the first political protests took place *after* the head of state had announced an initial easing of restrictions on political activity. For example, the parliament in Madagascar adopted constitutional reforms allowing press freedoms and the formation of multiple parties in December 1989; and yet the general strike and daily round of demonstrations calling for the ouster of Ratsiraka did not get underway until 18 months later. In such cases, delayed protests may have encouraged later rounds of reform (for example, the introduction of a transitional government in Guinea), but they were not the spark that ignited the liberalization process.

63. The peak of the recent liberalization trend in Africa occurred during 1992 when 37 countries had recorded perceptible gains (since 1988) in the observance of basic civil liberties. By the end of 1994, however, the number of African countries with improved civil rights records since 1988 had dropped to 28; moreover, 18 had poorer records than they had had in 1992.

64. Phi = 0.466, sig = 0.011.

65. Spearman's r = 0.511, P = 0.001.

66. Advancing three points or more on the Freedom House seven-point civil liberties scale.

67. Which advanced just one point on the Freedom House seven-point civil liberties scale.

68. Following procedures established in Chapter 4, encompassing and diagnostic tests were used to assess the statistical validity of this model. R-square, F-test, and standard error measures were used to compare competing models, and no significant differences were found. White and Breusch-Pagan tests failed to detect a heteroskedastic disturbance. A Durbin-Watson test to detect the presence of first-order autocorrelations was negative. Normal probability plots of the standardized residual were used to determine if nonlinear relationships between independent and dependent variables were hidden in the analysis; none were observed.

69. Controlling for all other variables in Model C, Pearson's partial r = 0.374, P =0.007.

6

EXPLAINING DEMOCRATIC
TRANSITIONS

Democratization involves the construction of participatory and competitive political institutions. The process of democratization begins with political challenges to authoritarian regimes, advances through the political struggles over liberalization, and requires the installation of a freely elected government. It concludes only when democratic rules become firmly institutionalized as well as valued by political actors at large. Democratization is thus a protracted process which, if it obtains at all, unfolds over several generations. We have reviewed the onset of regime transitions in Chapter 4 and will discuss the prospects for democratic consolidation in Chapter 7.

This chapter probes the endgame of regime transition, specifically asking how transitions conclude and how democratic governments are first installed. The end of the transition is marked by the cessation of overt disputes about the rules of the political game and the establishment of a new procedural equilibrium. A fresh regime is installed following landmark events like a founding election (for democratic regimes) or a military intervention or civilian crackdown (for authoritarian ones). According to the definition used throughout, a transition to democracy can be said to have occurred only when a regime has been installed on the basis of a competitive election, freely and fairly conducted within a matrix of civil liberties, with results accepted by all participants. The acceptance of the validity of founding elections by losing parties is crucial because it marks the first tentative consensus on democratic rules.

In principle, the alternation of top leaders is not a necessary condition for democratic transition. Conceivably, an existing ruler could be returned to office in a fair election and could opt thereafter to govern under new rules for enhanced participation and competition. In practice, however, neopatrimonial traditions of personalized rule in Africa make it difficult to separate the outcome of elections from the fate of the ruler. For opponents of the old regime, the ultimate symbol of political change is the downfall of the dictator. Should the incumbent manipulate the transition, survive a competitive vote, and remain in office, challengers are left with the nagging feeling that somehow the transition was incomplete or less than democratic. Moreover, an autocrat who prevails in an open contest can claim a genuine increment of political legitimacy and may well refrain from making major modifications to the way he rules.

We nevertheless maintain our commitment to a minimal and procedural notion of democratic transition. A transition to democracy is best distinguished according to the mechanisms of regime installation rather than by the added requirement of the alternation of leaders.[1] To establish which countries in Africa underwent a transition to democracy by the end of 1994, we focus primarily on the openness and probity of the electoral process and on the willingness of election losers – whether incumbents or challengers – to abide by the will of the people as expressed through the ballot box. In Africa, the characterization of regimes is simplified by the fact that autocrats were usually displaced by genuine elections. Where strongmen survived, we examine whether they did so by fair means or foul. And special attention is given to the nature of opposition movements (whether cohesive or fragmented) and the orientation of the military (for or against political reform) for their interventions were often decisive in determining whether an election was held and whether a democracy – or some other regime – was ultimately installed.

Apart from the installation of a (usually fragile) democracy, African transitions ended in a range of alternate outcomes (see Chapter 3). These included regimes of anarchy (where transitions were "precluded" by violence), military oligarchy (for example, where transitions were "blocked" by state coercion), and liberalized autocracy (via the route of "flawed" competitive elections). We have shown that calculating autocrats often made minor concessions to allow a measure of political competition, not so much as a prelude to meaningful and lasting institutional reform but rather as a temporary expedient to deflect criticism and to cling to power. Liberalization thus commonly occurred without democratization, but the opposite did not hold. Democratization is theoretically and practically impossible without liberalization because democratic institutions can flourish only in a context of civil liberties. Free and fair elections, for example, are feasible only when guarantees are upheld for freedom of speech and political association. But because liberalization comes first, it is all that is possible to achieve in many real-world situations.

Against this background, we seek to identify the factors that distinguish democratic from other regime transitions in Africa in the period from 1990 to 1994. We isolate and interpret founding elections and military interventions as the key events that brought these transitions to an end and installed new governments.

INTERPRETING FOUNDING ELECTIONS

A founding election occurs when "for the first time after an authoritarian regime, elected positions of national significance are disputed under reasonably competitive conditions."[2] For neopatrimonial regimes we add the specific requirement that the top office of chief political executive must be open to multiple candidates. Thus, in Africa's founding elections the office of head of government was openly contested following a period during which multiparty politics had been denied. Such elections heralded regime transition in the sense that they laid down new procedures of political competition that broke with monopolistic authoritarian antecedents and established the potential for democratic rule. In Africa in the early 1990s, founding elections usually took the form of a contest for the presidency, though legislative elections could qualify if the head of government was chosen by means other than a direct election for president.[3]

By these standards, 29 founding elections were held in Africa during the five-year interval between Namibia's historic legislative contest on November 11, 1989, and December 31, 1994, the closing date for this study. These elections are listed chronologically in Table 7. Of this total, the vast majority (26) were direct, multiparty presidential elections conducted according to either a single-round plurality system or a two-round run-off system, with the latter most common in the parts of Africa with a French legal tradition. Only in Lesotho's parliamentary system was a prime minister drawn from the legislative majority, and only in Namibia and South Africa were presidents elected indirectly by the legislature. In reality, this summary underestimates the total extent of electoral activity because legislative elections in presidential systems were not included. Of the 26 regimes with presidential constitutions that held founding elections in the five years up to 1994, 25 also held multiparty legislative elections during the same period. The only exception was Guinea, where, in December 1992, the military-backed government of Lansana Conté announced the indefinite postponement of legislative elections, later proceeding to a disputed presidential contest in December 1993.

What explains the incidence of founding elections? What distinguishes countries that held competitive electoral contests from those that did not? Interestingly, we found no relation between the incidence of a national conference – a phenomenon crucial to political liberalization – and the subsequent convocation of founding elections.[4] Thus, even though national conferences obtained a widespread institutional presence in African regime transitions, they achieved only a mixed record of success in opening the way to competitive elections. Alongside the many countries like Bénin, where a national conference laid down the ground rules for a founding election (see also Congo, Gabon, Mali, Niger, and South Africa), there were others like Chad and Zaire, where competitive general elections were promised to the conferees but never convened, and Ethiopia, where only constituent assembly elections (rather than legislative or presidential elections) were held by 1994.[5] Moreover, national conferences were not a necessary

Table 7. *Founding Elections in sub-Saharan Africa, 1989–1994*[a]

Country	Date	Free and Fair?	Incumbent Ousted?	Loser Accepts?
Namibia[b]	Nov. 11, 1989	Yes	Yes?[d]	Yes[f]
Côte d'Ivoire	Oct. 28, 1990	Yes?[c]	No	No
Comoros	Mar. 3, 1990	Yes?	No	No
Cape Verde	Feb. 17, 1991	Yes	Yes	Yes[f]
São Tomé	Mar. 3, 1991	Yes?	Yes?	Yes[f]
Bénin	Mar. 24, 1991	Yes	Yes	Yes[f]
Zambia	Oct. 31, 1991	Yes	Yes	Yes[f]
Burkina Faso	Dec. 1, 1991	No	No	Yes?[e]
Mauritania	Jan. 24, 1992	No	No	No
Mali	Apr. 26, 1992	Yes	Yes?	Yes[f]
Congo	Aug. 17, 1992	Yes	Yes	Yes[f]
Angola	Sep. 29, 1992	Yes	No	No
Cameroon	Oct. 11, 1992	No	No	No
Ghana	Nov. 3, 1992	Yes?	No	Yes?
Kenya	Dec. 29, 1992	No	No	Yes?
Madagascar	Feb. 28, 1993	Yes	Yes	Yes[f]
Niger	Mar. 27, 1993	Yes	Yes	Yes[f]
Lesotho[b]	Mar. 28, 1993	Yes	Yes	Yes[f]
Burundi	Jun. 1, 1993	Yes	Yes	No
Nigeria	Jun. 12, 1993	No	No	No
Seychelles	Jul. 23, 1993	Yes	No	Yes[f]
Central African Republic	Aug. 22, 1993	Yes?	Yes	Yes[f]
Togo	Aug. 25, 1993	No	No	No
Gabon	Dec. 5, 1993	No	No	No
Guinea	Dec. 19, 1993	No	No	No
South Africa[b]	Apr. 26, 1994	Yes	Yes	Yes[f]
Malawi	May 17, 1994	Yes	Yes	Yes[f]
Guinea–Bissau	Aug. 7, 1994	Yes?	No	Yes[f]
Mozambique	Oct. 27, 1994	Yes	No	Yes[f]

Summary			Free and Fair?	Incumbent Ousted?	Loser Accepts?
	1989	1	Yes 15	Yes 11	Yes[f] 16
	1990	2			
	1991	5	Yes? 6	Yes? 3	Yes? 3
	1992	7			
	1993	10	No 8	No 15	No 10
	1994	4			

Notes to Table 7

---

n = 29
[a]Founding elections are defined as elections in which the office of head of government is openly contested following a period during which multiparty political competition was denied. The sample (n = 29) includes all such elections held in Africa from the Namibian contest of November 11, 1989 to December 31, 1994. It excludes elections in the five countries that had regularly allowed competitive multiparty elections before 1990 (Botswana, Gambia, Mauritius, Sénégal, and Zimbabwe) – that is, had already undergone a founding election.
[b]Unless otherwise indicated, the data in the table refer to presidential elections. Of the 29 elections listed, 26 were presidential. We did not count the legislative elections that took place in Djibouti and Equatorial Guinea on December 18, 1992, and November 21, 1993, respectively, for these took place in a presidential system. Because neither country held a direct presidential election during the period under review, we concluded that the position of head of government was not open to electoral contestation.
[c]Observers reported major violations in polling and counting in elections in Côte d'Ivoire, Sénégal, and the Central African Republic but judged that they were not so severe as to change the overall result. In Ghana and Comoros "observers agreed that procedures on election day were free and fair despite opposition protests or boycotts" (see Melanie Bixby, "Promoting Democracy in Sub-Saharan Africa: AF Policy, Programs and Challenges," Washington, D.C., Department of State AF/RA, June 1994).
[d]In some countries the incumbent did not run. In São Tomé, incumbent president da Costa retired (temporarily) from politics. In Mali, Moussa Traoré was ousted by military coup and his successor, an interim caretaker, did not run in the presidential elections.
[e]In Burkina Faso, the opposition accepted the results only after the parliamentary elections of May 1992.
[f]Denotes a democratic transition.

precondition for founding elections. As noted in the previous chapter, many countries moved directly to elections without pausing to review constitutional and electoral rules in a formal assembly.[6] Indeed, half of all countries in Africa – including eight from the francophone bloc that otherwise favored national conferences – took this shortcut straight to elections.[7]

OPPOSITION COHESION

Instead of national conferences, a different institutional factor helped to explain the convocation of founding elections: the relative cohesion of opposition political forces. We operationalized this factor as a dichotomous categorical variable that contrasted fragmented opposition movements (with multiple leaders and weak organizations) with relatively cohesive ones (with a dominant leader and relatively strong organization).[8] Our definition encompassed information about party dominance and the existence of party coalitions, as well as judgments about the skills of opposition leaders at rallying broad-based support. It was statistically related to objective measurements of the number of opposition parties.[9] Importantly, though, we allowed that an opposition movement with a dominant party could be cohesive even in a setting of numerous parties, as in Angola, Burkina Faso, and South Africa.[10] Conversely, an opposition could be fragmented even in the absence of a plethora of registered political parties (e.g., Uganda) or the presence of restrictive decrees on the number of parties allowed (e.g., Nigeria).

Transforming loose urban protest movements into dominant political parties that could push effectively for elections and organize nationwide election campaigns was a formidable challenge in all African states. Leaders emerged to meet this challenge in very few instances. The distinction between the convergence and splintering of opposition forces is nicely captured by contrasting Zambia and Zaire. The Movement for Multiparty Democracy (MMD) in Zambia was born as an umbrella committee of interest groups whose principal demand was, as its name suggested, the restoration of competitive politics. To form an opposition front, Frederick Chiluba led the trade union movement into a coalition with business, professional, student, and church groups. As well as bridging class and status divides, the urban-based MMD skillfully used the far-flung teachers' and civil servants' unions to mobilize support in the countryside and, through its own multi-ethnic leadership, drew in followers with diverse tribal, linguistic, and regional identities. The MMD marshaled enough popular support to force the country's founding father, Kenneth Kaunda, to move directly to elections.

In Zaire, however, the opposition never effectively came together. The announcement of the restoration of multiparty competition led to a proliferation of political parties, some 130 in all. While nominally united in an alliance known as the Union Sacrée, the opposition was repeatedly outmaneuvered by Mobutu's divisive tactics. Some opposition leaders were tempted to set up their own organizations by his provision of public financing to cover operating costs for new parties. Others accepted Mobutu's inducements to accept positions in the national government, only to find their authority limited and their decisions countermanded by military forces loyal to the president. At the same time, most major contenders engaged in ethnic demagoguery, mobilizing regional power-bases in their own quests to obtain or retain power. By 1994, Mobutu had succeeded in marginalizing his main rival, Etienne Tshisekedi, by placing a moderate technocrat in the post of prime minister and driving a wedge through the opposition alliance. Under these circumstances, a fragmented opposition movement was unable to force the convocation of promised presidential elections.

Opposition cohesion was positively related to the incidence of founding elections.[11] Of the 16 African countries with cohesive opposition movements, 15 held a founding election. We interpreted this to mean that opposition leaders who forged broad social movements in which dissident factions came to share a political agenda – even if only momentarily – were able to induce incumbent rulers to concede competitive elections. The only exception was Swaziland, where the People's United Democratic Movement (PUDEMO) resurfaced in 1990 as the only effective organization demanding a republican constitution and multiparty elections. Even though it faced no serious opposition contender, PUDEMO was unable to break the royal hegemony of King Mswati III or to obtain meaningful reforms to his "traditional" system of political representation. Elections for an expanded national assembly were conducted in October 1993, but because the head of government and other representatives were appointed by the king rather than directly elected in an open poll, these elections failed to "found" a new regime.

Even where elections were held, fragmented oppositions commonly lost. In Côte d'Ivoire, for example, the opposition movement was riven from the outset with personal, ideological, and regional differences which were manifest in 26 political parties, 17 of which fielded legislative candidates. These factions exerted more energy bickering among themselves than in coordinating action against the incumbent. Only the Popular Ivorian Front (FPI) had any credibility as an opposition organization, though its leader – Laurent Gbagbo, a history professor – had little appeal beyond educated classes in urban areas. As the brief election campaign got underway, it became clear that a fractious and barely organized opposition was no match for a PDCI electoral machine that stood ready to cash in on Felix Houphouët-Boigny's residual popularity as the grand old man of Ivoirian politics. Elsewhere, as in Kenya and Malawi, the opposition foundered on the shoals of personal ambition when the leaders of ethnic or regional factions were unable to agree on a single candidate to run against the incumbent president.

By contrast, cohesive opposition movements commonly went on to win founding elections. The MMD in Zambia formed itself into a political party as soon as parties were relegalized, overwhelmed all other opposition parties (none of which obtained legislative seats), and trounced the ruling party in founding elections. Other cohesive opposition movements had somewhat different origins and fates. In Niger, the Alliance of Forces for Change (AFC) was a loose grouping of six independent parties that rallied behind the presidential candidacy of Mahamane Ousmane. Though no coalition partner won as many seats as the former ruling group, the AFC hung together after the election and was able to deprive the largest party of control of the legislature. Rather than comprising a coalition, the Basotho Congress Party in Lesotho was a reincarnation of a banned nationalist party whose internal factionalism was overcome in 1990 under the leadership of Ntsu Mokhlele. This single opposition party swept the polls, capturing all 65 seats in the new national assembly, and denied legislative representation to the party associated with the outgoing regime.

This is not to say that political oppositions that came together around founding elections were ordained to remain united. Protest movements spawned protest voters: Groups with very different grievances were momentarily joined in the common goal of disciplining unpopular leaders. Once this immediate objective was accomplished, divisions of interest reemerged. By rallying support by charging corruption in the old regime, opposition movements ran the risk of being hoist with their own petard, particularly if they were fortunate enough to win the election and to form a new government; henceforth, citizens would judge them by high standards.

FREE AND FAIR?

As might be expected following a political thaw, Africa's founding elections were highly disputatious. Incumbents and oppositions clashed over campaign and voting procedures, with the latter charging that existing electoral rules were insufficiently evenhanded and transparent. The same controversies tended to recur across African countries.[12] Opposition leaders (e.g., in Cameroon, Gabon, Guinea, and Zambia) claimed that voter registration lists were either outdated, disenfranchising large numbers of eligible citizens (especially younger people who were expected to opt for change), or inflated, opening the way to double voting (e.g., in Ghana and Togo).[13] Administrative arrangements were also held to be biased, expressly where a government agency – like the ministry of the interior in the francophone countries – was assigned a lead role in organizing the elections. The protagonists also struggled over access to communications media, notably radio and television, with incumbents exploiting government controls over news broadcasts to grant extensive favorable coverage to the campaign of the ruling party. Opposition parties obtained equal time on state-run media, if at all, only in the closing weeks of campaigns. The final set of disputes concerned election day procedures, especially guarantees for independent oversight of voting, ballot security, ballot counting, and the communication and announcement of election results.

The credibility of elections commonly came to hinge on whether party agents, nonpartisan domestic monitors, and international election observers were permitted to attend to all aspects of the balloting. African governments initially displayed extreme reluctance to accept this innovation, but usually relented in the end, often in an effort to align themselves with donor preferences.[14] With few exceptions, Africa's founding elections were closely scrutinized.[15] Across the continent, nonpartisan groups of African citizens (like GERDDES–Afrique in West Africa and ecumenical church committees in East Africa) attempted to ensure that the elections were not stolen. The regular presence of international observers (like the Commonwealth Observer Group and U.S.–based National Democratic and International Republican Institutes) helped to set international standards and disseminate information on the conduct of elections. Not only did independent oversight generate a more reliable set of elections data than had previously existed for Africa, but the judgments of observers and monitors were crucial in helping to extend or withhold political legitimacy to official election results.

Considering the immense logistical challenges of mounting elections with limited resources and poor communications, Africa's founding elections ran relatively smoothly. Not unexpectedly, incidents arose in which polling stations opened late, voting paraphernalia were in short supply, and irregularities occurred in the counting of votes. Ironically, in April 1994, South Africa's modern bureaucracy proved inadequate to the task of conducting a truly popular election; faced with last-minute changes in the list of candidates and shortages of ballot papers, the Independent Electoral Commission was forced to extend the voting period to four days to accommodate long lines of would-be voters.[16] Where disruption of polls was widespread at local levels – for example, in Cameroon, Gabon, and Guinea – it was "difficult, if not impossible, to pinpoint the extent to which chaotic conditions ... were deliberate."[17] What does seem likely is that any manipulation of elections generally took place well before polling day, mainly through the intimidation of voters and the buying of votes during the election campaign. To be sure, incumbent leaders who indulged in these practices found it easy to mislead late-arriving international observers and to ignore underfunded domestic monitors. Indeed, unwitting international observers were sometimes led – as in Ghana and Kenya – to prematurely and overgenerously endorse flawed elections. On the other hand – as in the Angolan elections of September 1992 – where defeated opposition movements cried foul, their complaints were not always fully justified.

Just how fair were founding elections? About half of these African electoral contests – 15 out of the 29 elections under study (see Table 7, column 3) – appeared to accurately reflect the will of the voters. The list of countries with free and fair elections includes a major regional power (South Africa), countries that had been ruled both by soldiers (Bénin and Congo) and civilians (Zambia and Malawi), and countries emerging from long-standing civil wars (Angola and Mozambique). Interestingly, 6 of the 15 countries were located in southern Africa, suggesting effects of geographical contiguity and shared institutional history. The volume of credible elections in the 1990s was generally higher than for previous one-party elections in the same African countries.[18] Compared with prior electoral experience on the continent, the recent round of founding elections represented an improved record of fair electoral conduct.

At the same time, however, the tree of political transition had numerous branches, including a major fork concerning the integrity of elections. For every African country that enjoyed a free and fair contest there was a counterexample – 14 out of 29 cases – for which the conduct of the polls was questionable. Of these, eight elections were clearly problematic. In Burkina Faso in December 1991, for example, the incumbent's refusal to convene a national conference led five declared candidates for the presidency to boycott the election, leaving Blaise Campoaré, who had resigned his army commission to run as a civilian, to win virtually unopposed.[19] Following the election in Guinea in December 1993, the supreme court invalidated results from prefectures in which the leading opposition candidate for president had easily won, fueling claims that Lansana Conté had fraudulently retained office. For the remaining six elections, it was unclear whether or not they had been free and fair. In these cases (Côte d'Ivoire, Comoros, São Tomé, Ghana, Central African Republic, and Guinea–Bissau), observers noted irregularities in campaign conduct and polling procedures but judged that they were not so serious as to change the overall election outcome. Thus, although electoral integrity improved in some countries, it remained a nagging problem in others. At minimum, the persistence of election tampering suggested that democratic rules for leadership succession were far from fully accepted throughout Africa.

What distinguishes virtuous from corrupt elections? The standard institutional variables that helped to predict political liberalization contributed here. Free and fair elections occurred most frequently in countries with an institutional heritage of civilian one-party regimes that had previously constrained both political participation and political competition.[20] Moreover, the contingent effects of political agency were clearly perceptible; as might be expected, free and fair elections were most likely during transitions in which incumbent leaders abstained from cracking down with state repression and from manipulating the rules of the political game.[21] Finally, the effects of opposition cohesion remained consistent: Just as a unified prodemocracy movement helped to force the convocation of founding elections, so it helped to guarantee that such elections would be conducted under improved standards of integrity.[22] Of the 15 countries with cohesive oppositions, only one experienced a problematic poll.[23] In all other cases, relatively cohesive opposition movements provided an institutional counterweight to electoral manipulation. They helped to keep elections honest.

ELECTION OUTCOMES

How did elections turn out? As reported in the Introduction, founding elections led to an innovation in African politics: the peaceful alternation of leaders. In the five years up to 1994, sitting heads of government were voted out of office in 11 elections (see Table 7, column 4). In three other cases, incumbents did not run and were replaced by elected leaders (see note *d*, Table 7). These historic events included, in the cases of Kenneth Kaunda of Zambia and Hastings Banda of Malawi, the rejection by voters of nationalist founding fathers. At minimum, transition elections had much more uncertain outcomes than elections conducted previously under single-party regimes in which there was only one candidate for the presidency who, predictably, always won.

But the alternation of top leaders did not occur universally or without hitches. For example, in the Central African Republic, André Kolingba annulled elections in progress in October 1992 when preliminary results indicated that he was running fourth in a field of five candidates, with as little as 2 percent of the vote.[24] It took a second electoral defeat in August 1993 and the suspension of French economic and military assistance to convince him to cede the presidency to Ange Félix Patassé on October 22, 1993.[25] Moreover, as noted earlier, several more incumbents were reelected (15 out of 29) than were ousted in founding elections. This outcome was more likely where sitting leaders and ruling parties remained in office during the election campaign and less likely where the transition involved the temporary installation of a transitional government that represented diverse political tendencies and that oversaw the election.

The ouster of incumbents was also more likely when elections were conducted honestly. The use of free and fair elections as a predictor variable revealed a very strong association with the defeat of sitting rulers.[26] Africa's authoritarian strongmen clearly could not survive truly democratic elections. As Huntington pithily puts it: "Elections are not only the life of democracy; they are also the death of dictatorship."[27]

On the other hand, a very strong relationship also existed between fraudulent elections and incumbent victories. Of the 15 incumbents who retained office, 12 did so in elections that fell short of internationally accepted standards. In all these cases the political survival of the strongman was not meaningfully challenged by international observers funded by foreign donors. Incumbents apparently calculated correctly that the international community was often more interested in political stability than in democracy and sometimes would turn a blind eye to flawed elections. These data also demonstrate that, where electoral irregularities occurred, officeholders and their supporters were the main perpetrators. This is not to say that opposition leaders – who, as outsiders to the state patronage system, were supremely anxious to grasp a rare opportunity to gain political office – were above electoral shenanigans. But compared with incumbents, challengers had fewer opportunities and resources at their disposal.

To be sure, incumbents enjoy electoral advantages under all types of political regimes, but such advantages were particularly marked in Africa's neopatrimonial regimes where the chief executive monopolized power and ruled through prebends. Strongmen who suddenly faced an electoral fight showed little restraint in maximizing existing controls over the material, legal, and coercive instruments of state. Using privileged access to government revenues, incumbents bought votes. In Kenya, for example, Moi's ruling party reportedly spent $100 million on the election campaign and increased the money supply by 35 percent in 1992 to spur growth in the months before general elections in clear violation of adjustment agreements with the IFIs.[28] Exercising personal control over lawmaking, incumbents placed legal obstacles in the path of their opponents: In Zambia, for example, Kaunda insisted on maintaining a state of emergency, which enabled him to impede the movements and campaign meetings of his opponents. And, when all else failed, certain presidents unleashed the security forces. In the period preceding elections in Togo, for example, military forces loyal to Eyadéma gunned down participants in prodemocracy rallies, took hostage the prime minister of the transitional government, and were implicated in an assassination attempt on a key opposition leader.

Given the overwhelming advantages of incumbency in neopatrimonial regimes, it is remarkable that multiparty elections in Africa ever led to unexpected outcomes. Against the odds, 16 African countries fulfilled the minimal requirements for a democratic transition between 1990 and 1994 (see Table 7, column 5, Yes). As will be recalled from the definition with which this book and chapter began, a democratic transition occurs when a new government is installed following a competitive election, freely and fairly conducted, in which all participants accept the election results. The disposition of the losers toward the outcome of founding elections is crucial to democratization. By acceding to the voters' verdict – an act that is harder for losers than for winners – participants signal tentative consent to a new set of participatory and competitive rules. This normative consensus is contingent on the understanding that losers will not be permanently dispossessed from political power and will enjoy regular subsequent opportunities to contest and win elections.

In this study, we considered that participants in founding elections, including the losers, signaled acceptance of the new democratic regimes by taking up any legislative seats they had won. In some places, they did so willingly – especially, as in Malawi and Niger, where minority parties won sizable blocs of seats and were poised to use parliament to influence governmental decision making. Elsewhere, acceptance was more grudging. In Mozambique and South Africa, for example, major opposition parties threatened electoral boycotts until just days before the poll (perhaps because they feared losing an open contest) but in the end had no choice but to accept a small share of legislative seats. In contrast to these democratic transitions, some free and fair elections were disrupted after the event when the losers rejected the results. The classic case was Angola, where Jonas Savimbi took his UNITA forces back to bush and reignited an intensified civil war when it became apparent that his bid to be elected national president had fallen short.[29] The Angolan case and the opposition's dismissal of Ethiopia's regional elections of June 1992 point to an important lesson: Warring factions that are not disarmed in advance of elections have the potential to overturn outcomes that they find objectionable.[30]

The likelihood that all parties would become stakeholders in a new democratic order was powerfully shaped by the quality of founding elections. Almost invariably, losing parties were more likely to accept official vote tallies when the elections had been certified as free and fair.[31] The installation of new governments went smoothly in Bénin and Zambia in large part because, to their credit, Kaunda and Kérékou bowed to the verdict of fair elections, gracefully conceded defeat, and stepped aside. In these and other countries that completed a democratic transition, newly elected legislative assemblies opened on time, unhampered by opposition boycotts or by anything more than minor skirmishes over election results in a few selected districts.

By contrast, elections that were marred by incumbent interference were usually followed by a period of heightened political conflict. In the October 1992 presidential elections in Cameroon, for example, the leading opposition candidate John Fru Ndi claimed that he had been rigged out of victory; Biya responded by placing Fru Ndi and supporters under house arrest and declaring a state of emergency in the English-speaking northwest province. Throughout this period, the Social Democratic Front (SDF), Cameroon's leading opposition party, maintained a boycott of legislative assembly elections and continued to call for a national conference and fresh presidential polls. Even in Ghana and Kenya, where observers could not agree among themselves about the fairness of elections, opposition leaders backed up charges of fraud with legislative boycotts. In Ghana, withdrawal from assembly elections proved to be a major miscalculation that marginalized the opposition from any share of power; in Kenya, where the oppo-

sition disputed official legislative election results, the losing parties at first refused to take up their seats. After symbolically staying away from the opening of
parliament, these minority legislators ultimately relented while continuing to
mount court challenges of election results for about one third of Kenya's electoral
districts. Thus, where the campaign and voting processes were flawed, elections
did not resolve the old regime's legitimacy crisis or create political stability.

As we have argued, a democratic transition does not require the ouster of a
sitting head of government; it leaves open the possibility that an incumbent
could be freely reelected. This eventuality came to pass in three African countries. In Guinea–Bissau, Mozambique, and Seychelles, the incumbent was returned and the losers did not question the fairness of the election. Nevertheless,
in Africa's personalistic regimes the fate of the strongman was the central issue
in founding elections, and prodemocracy forces were aligned solidly in favor of
the ouster of incumbents. Not unexpectedly, therefore, the losers' willingness to
accept election results was strongly influenced by the incumbent's fate. Where
incumbents lost, the opposition almost invariably went along with official results; where incumbents won, the opposition usually challenged the authenticity of the elections.[32]

It is not easy to judge whether, under these circumstances, the acceptance of
losers was motivated by rule-based calculations (like the integrity of election procedures) or by deeply felt personalistic considerations (as embodied in their attitudes toward the fate of the incumbent). For example, did challengers in Cameroon
and Kenya object to presidential elections because they were conducted imperfectly or because elections failed to get rid of unpopular strongmen? Precisely why did
losers behave as they did? We explored these questions with mutual controls on
each predictor variable for loser acceptance. In each case, the statistical strength and
significance of original bivariate associations were reduced, suggesting that together *both* the integrity of elections *and* the fate of the incumbent helped to shape
the behavior of losing parties.[33] In other words, participants in founding elections
accepted democratic rules for choosing leaders, not simply because electoral procedures delivered their preferred electoral outcomes but also because they valued the
rules themselves. Indeed, the data indicate that electoral integrity had a somewhat
greater impact on loser behavior than did incumbent ouster.[34] This suggests
(though hardly conclusively) that founding elections began to wean Africans away
from an attachment to personal political loyalties and toward new attachments to
democratic rules. The institutionalization of rule-governed politics is complete,
however, only when the fate of the incumbent becomes entirely irrelevant to the
willingness of losing parties to accept election results. Africa's founding elections
(1990–94) fell well short of this demanding standard.

PARTICIPATION AND COMPETITION

The outcomes of founding elections in Africa suggest that political elites were
often able to control the process of political competition so that they came out

on top. Even where elections resulted in the ouster of entrenched strongmen, new leaders quickly lapsed into the autocratic and patrimonial practices of their predecessors. Indeed, the victors in Africa's founding elections were often simply old-guard politicians who chose the right moment to break with the past. Thus, observers have charged that recent political changes in Africa have *"not directly involved many citizens* from outside the existing political elite ... the new power holders come, by and large, from the same political class."[35] In this vein, others have concluded that "the more things change the more they remain the same" and question whether "the second wind of change [is] any different from the first."[36]

We must therefore ask: How broad has the democratic movement been in Africa? Did the precedent of protest lead to other forms of political participation during transitions? How widely did ordinary citizens take part in founding elections? For political transitions in Africa to amount to more than a mere circulation of elites, leaders must be held accountable by their own constituents. Popular political participation is a *sine qua non* for "government by the people." Jane Mansbridge has identified political participation, which she describes as "the bottom-up practice of deliberative democracy," as an essential feature of democracy.[37] For Africa, Yves Fauré has commented, "One cannot really talk of an established democracy if elections do not enjoy the active support or enthusiasm of civil society."[38] This section discusses two key issues about popular participation in transition elections in Africa: Who participated? and, Why?

In founding elections, voters were offered a genuine choice among candidates from different political parties, often for the first time in a generation or, in the case of South Africa, in a lifetime. Thus one might predict that voter interest in these elections would be intense and that voter turnout at the polls would be correspondingly high. In fact, there was considerable variation in electoral turnout rates (see Table 8). In some places African citizens fulfilled the prediction of high participation by turning out at the polls with euphoric enthusiasm and at rates greatly exceeding those in mature Western democracies. For example, some 95 percent of registered voters were said to have participated in the poll of November 1989 in Namibia, followed by a reported 97.3 percent in Burundi in June 1993. On the other hand, in at least half a dozen of these elections, fewer than half the registered electorate exercised their right to vote: For example, just 16 percent turned out in Mali in April 1992 and approximately 30 percent in Nigeria in June 1993.

Why was political participation low in some founding elections? In places like Cameroon and Zambia, where elections were held without reopening voter registration lists, many eligible voters were deprived of their right to cast a ballot.[39] In places like Togo, voters stayed away from the polls because contestants used violence during the election campaign or threatened to do so on polling day.[40] More commonly, voters stayed at home because they perceived the election to be rigged, constrained, or otherwise predetermined. In Nigeria, for example, the electoral process was so circumscribed by military decrees – to limit

Table 8. *Participation and Competition in Founding Elections*

	Voter Turnout (% of registered voters)	Winner's Share (% of total votes)
Angola	91.5	49.6
Bénin	64.0	67.7
Burkina Faso	21.7	86.2
Burundi	97.3	64.8
Cameroon	71.9[b]	39.9
Cape Verde	59.0	73.5
Central African Republic	56.1	52.5[c]
Comoros	60.0[b]	55.1
Congo	61.1[b]	61.3
Côte d'Ivoire	60.0[b]	81.7
Gabon	86.3	51.8
Ghana	48.3[b]	58.3[c]
Guinea	78.5[b]	51.7
Guinea–Bissau	81.2	50.0
Kenya	68.0	36.4
Lesotho[d]	—	98.5
Madagascar	80.0[b]	66.7
Malawi	80.5	47.2
Mali	16.0[a]	69.0
Mauritania	51.7	61.6
Mozambique	90.0	53.3
Namibia[d]	95.0	56.9
Niger	38.0	54.8
Nigeria	30.0[b]	—
São Tomé	60.0[b]	81.8
Seychelles	86.0[b]	59.5
South Africa[d]	86.0	63.0
Togo	36.2[b]	96.5
Zambia	46.0	75.1
Mean	64.3	63.0

[a]Percentage of eligible voters (i.e., adults).
[b]Percentage base unspecified (i.e., whether registered or eligible voters).
[c]Percentage of valid votes.
[d]Data refer to legislative elections; all other data refer to presidential elections.

the number of contesting parties, to control the content of electoral debate, to repeatedly delay the dates of elections, and even to suspend results of earlier primaries – that many voters evidently concluded that they were unable to exercise a free choice. The low turnout in the Nigerian presidential contest can also be attributed to the confusion created by a lawsuit that secured an injunction against holding the election and was overturned on appeal only at the eleventh hour. The experiences of Angola and South Africa, where voter turnout was high, suggested that citizens who were set on voting were not deterred by threats from extremists. Violent intimidation apparently deterred participation only where voters perceived an election to be illegitimate; where a genuine choice was available, people were willing to take personal risks in order to exercise political rights.

Which brings us to political competition. The distinguishing mark of Africa's founding elections is their competitive character. What effect did the extent of political competition have on voter turnout? What light do these elections cast on the mutual linkages, if any, between the politico-institutional concepts of political competition and political participation?

On one hand, one could make the "horserace" argument that political participation rises as elections become more competitive. People are motivated to get involved as electoral choices widen, races become tighter, and electoral outcomes become more uncertain. From this perspective, we would expect political competition and political participation to be positively related. On the other hand, one could cite a "bandwagon" argument in which participation rises in the presence of dominant candidates who seem certain to win. People are motivated to turn out to vote for a sure winner, not least as a way of associating themselves with the spoils of victory. From this perspective we would expect competition and participation to be inversely linked.

The horserace argument derives from Western theories of democratic pluralism and would seem to reflect behavior in societies organized along individualistic and competitive lines. The bandwagon thesis is buttressed by organic-statist theories of national unity and seems better attuned to societies that value consensus and community. By this reasoning, one might be tempted to conclude that the introduction of multiparty competition into politics has different effects across world regions: In Western societies, political competition increases political participation, but in African societies, political competition reduces it. At face value, the finding of lower than expected participation rates in several founding elections would seem to support this thesis. As numerous incumbent African presidents have done, one might be tempted to conclude (though presumably for less self-serving reasons) that multiparty politics are not suited to Africa.

These claims were first weighed for Africa in Collier's groundbreaking work on regime change in the early postcolonial period, which uncovered no general connection between electoral participation and "the ability of a single party to achieve dominance over its competitors."[41] Instead, Collier posited that colonial heritage determined the effects of competition on participation at the time of pre-independence elections: Whereas dominant parties were able to mobilize mass electoral turnout in French colonies (the bandwagon effect), multiparty fragmentation led to high voter turnout in British colonies (the horserace effect). More recently, Fauré has advocated the bandwagon thesis for Côte d'Ivoire: "Competitive elections systematically register lower participation rates than elections organized under a single party."[42] With reference to Ivoirian electoral history, he found that voter turnout was lower both in periods of intense competition (i.e., 1946–57 and 1980–90) and in constituencies with several candidates (i.e., in the municipal elections of 1985 and the legislative elections of 1985 and 1990). This counterintuitive finding is held to "contradict ... doctrinal justifications of democratic pluralism." Fauré argues that it reflects "an ingrained political culture which values leadership and seniority" in which voters may be "irritated and indecisive when faced with a multiplicity of choice."[43]

Fortunately, such culturalist arguments can be tested. We doubted that participation in African elections was depressed by electoral competition. Table 8 presents data on the winner's share of the total votes cast in presidential elections, a measure that is a useful proxy for political competition: The lower the winner's share of the vote, the greater the degree of competition in the election.[44] By this criterion, the most competitive founding election in Africa was held in Kenya in December 1992, when incumbent President Moi squeaked back into office with a slim 36.4 percent plurality, similar to Biya in Cameroon. The least competitive election was in Togo in August 1993, where incumbent President Eyadéma claimed to have won an overwhelming 96.5 percent of the vote in a context where the opposition boycotted the election. (See also Campaoré in Burkina Faso.)

We found that the level of political competition was positively, strongly, and significantly associated with the rate of political participation in founding elections in Africa.[45] The sign of the relationship was in the predicted direction with voters turning out in greater numbers for more closely contested elections.[46] We concluded that although rates of popular political participation were sometimes low in founding elections, this was not generally due to a culturally embedded aversion to political competition. It was far more likely to be due to an inadequate electoral choice, resulting from either incumbent restrictions on the range of candidates or opposition boycotts that delegitimated the entire election. Contrary to Fauré's assertion, Africans were not threatened and immobilized by political competition; like voters anywhere, they were stimulated to participate by an open contest.

INTERPRETING MILITARY INTERVENTION

Voters were not the only political actors to determine the outcome of Africa's regime transitions. More powerful protagonists weighed in, especially during the middle to late stages of transitions when political conflicts escalated. Through their pervasive presence and repeated interventions in postcolonial African politics, military forces could be expected to play major roles.[47] Wherever soldiers held the reins of government, they were bound to figure centrally in any struggle to divide and distribute power. By the same token, leaders of civilian one-party states had long underpinned their regimes by threatening to deploy, or actually unleashing, the coercive instruments of state.

Above and beyond the military as an institutional pillar of the old regime, however, the actions of groups of military officers with political objectives constituted an unpredictable wild card in the game of regime transition. Whether military forces remained loyal to the incumbent or defected to the opposition had a decisive impact on the course of political events. We examined whether military forces chose to step in *during* any stage of the contemporary round of African regime transitions. Military intervention referred to independent political actions by the military (or elements within it) acting as a corporate group beyond civilian control. In its most extreme manifestation, military intervention took the form of a coup d'état in which the army or another branch of the armed forces took over the government in order to push the transition in one direction or another. Alternatively, soldiers opted for less sweeping but still consequential actions; for example, they disobeyed orders to shoot protesters or went on the rampage themselves. Whatever the action, the critical issue was the orientation of military forces: Did they intervene to push democratization forward or to hold it back?

Along with recording all instances when soldiers acted independently during the recent transitions, we coded intercessions as pro- or antidemocratic.[48] We found 13 instances of military action all told, seven of which (Bénin, Congo, Lesotho, Madagascar, Malawi, Mali, and South Africa) were supportive of democratic initiatives and six of which sought to stem the democratic tide (Cameroon, Nigeria, Rwanda, Sierra Leone, Togo, and Zaire). It is noteworthy that the disposition of the military was variable; the military did not always adopt a fixed institutional position as guardian of the *ancien régime*. In some countries, the military (or elements within it) reacted negatively to gains by the political opposition and rose to the defense of the incumbent; in other places the military abandoned the strongman when he lost political legitimacy. In a pioneering effort to encapsulate this variation, Michael Chege notes that although in some countries, "the disorganized and poorly disciplined soldiery who pass for the national army have attempted to sabotage the transition to democracy," elsewhere "the army may have been at least a partial accessory to political reform."[49]

The connections between military intervention and transition trajectories were among the most striking revealed by this study. The disposition of the military was strongly associated at high levels of statistical significance with the extent of democratization reforms by 1994.[50] Whether and how soldiers stepped in during regime transitions largely determined whether such transitions ultimately culminated in democratic outcomes.[51] Notably, all seven prodemocratic military actions resulted in the installation of freely elected governments.

In some cases, soldiers executed successful coups d'état that resulted in military takeovers of government during ongoing regime transitions. The frequency of military coups in Africa was lower in the first half of the 1990s than in previous decades, though whether this development was the beginning of a trend or merely a trough is not yet clear.[52] Importantly, the political transition in Algeria, initially seen in sub-Saharan Africa as a model of how to dismantle a single-party regime, was brought to an abrupt halt when, following electoral victories by the fundamentalist Islamic Salvation Front (FIS) in December 1991, the army canceled a second round of national elections. Through a higher state council, senior army and police officers banned the FIS, forced it underground, and plunged Algeria into a revengeful civil war. Shortly thereafter in Sierra Leone, a five-man military junta overthrew the government of the All Peoples' Congress (APC), driving incumbent president Joseph Momoh into exile in neighboring Guinea. The new strongman, army captain Valentine Strasser, embarked on "Rawlings-style housecleaning exercises ... to recreate a sense of public purpose and efficiency" and promised to speed up Momoh's announced introduction of a multiparty system.[53] But in practice Strasser was no democrat. He cracked down on the press and opposition parties and used an escalating war against rural insurgents as an excuse to delay handing government back to civilians.

Nigeria was the most important instance of a democratic transition ambushed by the military. Under the tutelage of head of state General Ibrahim Babangida, the governing armed forces of Nigeria embarked in 1986 on the most protracted and tightly managed restoration of civilian rule on the continent. Initially scheduled for 1990, the handover was repeatedly deferred until mid-1993, raising widespread suspicions about the sincerity of military intentions. Babangida asserted close personal control over the course and timing of events and over the military apparatus itself, demoting officers considered disloyal and executing suspected coup plotters. When it became apparent that Chief Moshood Abiola, a Yoruba publishing magnate, had won the climactic June 1993 presidential elections, the National Defense and Security Council declared the results invalid, citing widespread corruption and fraud.[54]

Still maintaining the fiction that he intended to surrender power, Babangida installed an interim national government headed by a civilian. This government was never accepted by the prodemocracy movement which, under the banner of the Campaign for Democracy, persisted with demonstrations and work stoppages aimed at installing Abiola as president. In November, the secretary of defense General Sani Abacha effected a "de facto palace coup" that displaced Babangida and led to the abolition of the full array of elected institutions painstakingly constructed at local, regional, and national levels, replacing them with military administrators.[55] For all intents and purposes – and notwithstanding Abacha's appointment of a sham constitutional conference – Nigeria's democratic transition had been blocked by an indefinite extension of military rule.

By contrast, a military coup promoted democratization in Mali.[56] Soldiers stepped into the political arena in order to move the transition forward when the incumbent government appeared to have second thoughts about democratic reform. President Traoré of Mali had tried to contain emerging partisan debate within the ruling party, demanding that new associations of lawyers and youth desist from political activity. His clumsy attempts to choke off newly granted rights of free expression, however, led to intensified protests, mass arrests, and a shutdown of educational institutions. In this polarized atmosphere, security forces in armored vehicles killed 100 and injured 700 in the course of quelling a violent demonstration in the streets of the capital in March 1991. The brutality of the crackdown alienated elements of the officer corps who balked at being used as tools to suppress their fellow citizens. Within days, a paratroop commander, Lt. Col. Amadou Toumani Touré (popularly known as "A.T.T."), announced a military takeover and arrested president Traoré and his wife as they tried to escape to the airport. Touré installed a transitional government, under military leadership but containing opposition representatives, to oversee a return to pluralism. He set in motion proceedings to bring to trial the former president and three top henchmen for "blood crimes." And he apologized to the Malian people for the past abuses committed by the military, acceding in the removal from the transitional government of colleagues implicated in the precoup massacre. Touré then essentially made good on promises to advance democratic gains by convening a national conference and a constitutional referendum, followed by municipal, legislative, and presidential elections. When the Konaré government took office in mid-1992, Touré retired from public life.

Unlike in Nigeria and Mali, military interventions during transitions did not always amount to full-blown coups and the displacement of sitting governments. Given strategic control of coercive resources, groups of officers took more modest actions to signal preferences and obtain objectives. Take the cases of Zaire and Malawi: Acting independently of civilian control but never actually seizing state power, military elements intervened to alter the course of events, though in sharply contrasting directions.

In Zaire, the political mood of military forces depended on whether they were being paid. By the 1990s, enlisted troops in the Zaire army earned under US$10 per month, less than a living wage whose value was continually eroded by inflation, which reached 3,000 percent in 1991. In September of that year, soldiers mutinied to protest late wage payments, sparking several days of looting and violence that destroyed what little remained of the country's modern productive and trading sectors. The suppression of the rebellion, which required intervention by French and Belgian paratroops, forced Mobutu to agree for the first time to share political power with the opposition. The resultant period of political cohabitation was highly unstable, however, because "Mobutu and his dwindling group of supporters control[led] the national treasury, the huge state security apparatus, and the armed forces ... and [Prime Minister] Tshisekedi ostensibly had the backing of the legislature, the High Council, which was dominated by the president's political opponents."[57] When Tshisekedi tried to deprive Mobutu of ready access to cash at the Central Bank, the latter dismissed the government and ordered loyalist troops to lock the prime minister and cabinet out of their offices.

A second military mutiny broke out in January 1993 when merchants, acting on the prime minister's orders, refused to accept a new high-denomination banknote (5 million zaires, worth about $2) issued on the orders of the president. Soldiers who had been paid with the new currency seized control of the parliament building and held several hundred lawmakers hostage.[58] Tshisekedi alienated the army by calling for foreign military reintervention to restore order, but Mobutu was able to bolster his political position by drawing the relatively well-paid presidential guard and civil guard around him. By March 1993, Mobutu had essentially restored the *ancien régime* by naming a rival government, reviving the old constitution, and reconvening the previous parliament. By mid-1994, "Mobutu's opponents in Kinshasa [were] too afraid of the military to march in protest down the main boulevard."[59]

The struggle for control of the military loyalties unfolded quite differently in Malawi. There, the principal instrument of state coercion was the police force, which the incumbent government deployed to detain and torture – even eliminate – opposition leaders. From the mid-1980s onward, the police were personally controlled by John Tembo, Minister of State in the Office of the President, the power behind the throne of ailing Life President Banda. The ruling clique enforced its will also through the Malawi Young Pioneers (MYP) – whose crimson shirts recalled Mao's Red Guards – a paramilitary movement attached to the Malawi Congress Party (MCP). Both the police (through its special branch) and the MYP performed political intelligence functions, using a dense network of informers. Compared with these much-feared units, the army never played an openly political or repressive role. On the contrary, key officers in the middle and junior ranks tacitly backed Malawi's growing opposition. By early 1992, army trucks accompanied student demonstrations in Zomba to provide protection from the police and the MYP. In the face of increased physical intimidation of citizens who attended prodemocracy rallies or joined opposition parties, the military struck. In November 1993, army units in Lilongwe burned the MYP headquarters, confiscated arms caches, and looted the houses of MYP members and government officials – actions that met with jubilant public support. The responsible officers forced the governing presidential council to order the disarming of the MYP and indicated that, henceforth, they were more inclined to take orders from an all-party National Consultative Council.[60] According to one commentator, by "making clear both the army's preference for democratic change and the ease with which it could block attempts to derail it, the military's action against the MYP played a critical role in ensuring the ultimate success of the political transition."[61]

How can we interpret these dissimilar forms of military intervention during regime transitions? Were they contingent events or a reflection of the institutional prominence of armies in a context of a generally weak array of political institutions? Huntington captures both aspects when he writes that "the military are the ultimate support of regimes ... if they withdraw their support, if they carry out a coup against the regime, or if they refuse to use force against those who threaten to overthrow the regime, the regime falls."[62]

One might expect that military interventions were contingent responses to the events of the transition. For example, soldiers may have been tempted to step in to restore political order in the face of persistent popular protest.[63] But the frequency of protest was entirely unrelated to subsequent interventions, leading us to conclude that military forces generally resisted a knee-jerk reaction to social unrest.[64] Yet, because soldiers' allegiances went unpredictably either way in relation to political reform, military actors clearly exercised the faculty of political choice. By upholding the rule of law in Malawi but by undermining it in Zaire, security forces determined the fate of the personal dictatorships of Banda and Mobutu. By seizing power in order to accelerate a planned electoral timetable in Mali – but to halt elections in Nigeria – army officers engineered democratization in one context while ensuring its collapse in another. In all these cases, the decisive factor was the disposition of military loyalties for or against the old regime.

Despite such advention, military intervention in Africa still displayed institutional features. At first we expected that the greater the strength and cohesiveness of military organizations vis-à-vis civilian political institutions, the more likely the army would act. Jenkins and Kposowa have proposed that "military centrality" is "the most consistent independent force" underlying interventionism.[65] We could not confirm this notion for midtransition military interventions in Africa using conventional predictors like the number of persons in the enlisted forces and the share of the public budget allocated to military expenditure.[66] Moreover, our research initially revealed no general relationships between the recent incidence of intervention and the previous experience of African countries with military coups or military rule.[67] This was largely because, in most coup–prone countries, relatively disciplined military forces already held the reins of government and were managing a return to civilian rule, thus reducing the need for fresh interventions.

It was nonetheless noteworthy that, when antidemocratic military strikes were examined alone, five out of the six cases were seen to occur in countries with a previous history of military coups and rule.[68] Similarly, of the 14 relevant cases within Africa where political transition was "precluded" or became "blocked," 12 occurred where the military had featured prominently in the country's regime history.[69] In short, an institutional legacy of military involvement in politics seemed to predispose security forces to intervene during transitions and to incline subsequent transition outcomes to fall short of democracy.

It must be noted, however, that the development of military institutions in Africa took distinctive neopatrimonial forms. African armies rarely resembled an idealized bureaucracy, molded into a cohesive organizational force by professional training, nationalistic sentiments, and shared *ésprit de corps*.[70] Instead, these institutions were riven by political factionalism based on the personal ambitions of would-be leaders within the officer corps and on ethnic solidarities in the ranks.[71] Because African armies "incorporate tensions characteristic of civilian elite society as a whole" their interventions in politics constantly reflected the ambitions of particular leaders and factions.[72] Certainly none of the armies under review acted as a unified force. The Nigerian army was splintered into "cabals within cliques" in which only a minority of top officers sought to retain political power, with the majority of soldiers agitating for a return to regular duties.[73] In Malawi, militant junior officers directly challenged the army commander, whom they considered too subservient to the strongman, by defying his orders to attack the Young Pioneers, and they ultimately secured his resignation. Even in Mali, where the army seemed most cohesive, the officer corps was split over the desirability of a return to multiparty elections.[74] The military was exceptionally fragmented in Zaire, where only the presidential and civil guards retained a semblance of discipline as they continued to follow sporadically the orders of their paymaster. The army for its part broke apart into armed bands, turning their guns on the citizenry in efforts to extort livelihood.[75]

Most distinctively, the behavior of military actors, including forays into transition politics, was propelled by struggles over coveted offices, rents, and graft. The factions within the military that resisted transferring power to civilians usually perceived political change as leading to a loss of privilege. For example, under Babangida in Nigeria, the top brass elevated rent-seeking to such unprecedented heights that individual officers came to fear "investigation of what happened to several petro-millions that are thought to have gone absent without leave."[76] Wherever it occurred, the acquisition of great wealth by senior officers fueled "resentment from those junior officers who [were] not recipients of the largesse and those who [found] corruption unacceptable in the face of continuously falling living standards."[77] In Sierra Leone, the grievances of disgruntled junior officers sparked political intervention. When a delegation of these officers demanded the payment of salary arrears and the improvement of battlefield logistics, "their protests turned into a coup when Momoh dismissed the soldiers as trouble makers, and troops he sent to quell the revolt joined the takeover."[78] And, during the 1993 pillage in Zaire, even Mobutu's elite troops joined the scramble for spoils, "grabbing their share and then summarily executing hundreds of rank and file looters."[79] These examples illustrate that antidemocratic military interventions were usually driven by a defense of existing material privilege by insiders in the patronage system or by the quest for such advantage by elements of the soldiery who felt themselves left out.

The military was least likely to countenance threats to institutional privilege if the incumbent political leader was their own ethnic patron. It is no accident that the cases of antidemocratic military intervention all fit this pattern. As Crawford Young notes, "The very nature of personal autocracy led rulers to build armies according to an ethnic security map."[80] In Nigeria, Islamic Hausa-Fulani elites had long dominated the army's officer corps, though the military as a whole was more ethnically and religiously diverse. A good part of Abacha's unwillingness to step aside was because his compatriots in the northern political establishment could not countenance ceding power to Abiola who, even though a Muslim, was a Yoruba from the south. In Rwanda, rogue units from Habyarimana's presidential guard, joined by other Hutu from the army and youth militia, sparked an anti-Tutsi carnage when it became evident that they would lose entitlements in an ethnically integrated army under a democratic regime. In Togo, the army – centered on Eyadéma's small Kabre ethnic group and including an inner core of immediate relatives – essentially vetoed further political reform after a national conference designated an independent prime minister. Similarly, as the security forces fragmented in Zaire, Mobutu fell back on a narrow base within the presidential guard whose inner core was composed of fellow tribalists recruited from his northern home area of Equateur Province. As Young comments, "Neutralizing imbalances [in military recruitment] constructed over [several] decades without triggering the army's intervention [is] an extraordinarily delicate task."[81]

Thus, military elements, typically acting in defense of institutionalized privilege, were decisive actors in regime transitions. Wherever the coercive apparatus remained intact and politically faithful to the incumbent ruler, repression of prodemocracy sentiment remained a real option. If the army split, and especially if senior officers sided with the opposition, then incumbents found difficulty in surviving politically. In short, as went the military, so went the transition. This finding has major implications for democratic prospects in Africa. Michael Chege has noted that "the issue of how to manage armies and paramilitary units in Africa's current liberalization drive ... is actually a greater priority than most advocates of democracy in the continent initially imagined."[82] Civilian protesters momentarily succeeded in setting the agenda for political change, but military forces retained a permanent and decisive role in African politics during later phases of transition. As of the mid-1990s, the fate of democracy on the sub-Saharan continent continued to rest in the hands of men with guns.

THE LEVEL OF DEMOCRACY

To conclude the analysis of regime transitions, we return to a statistical assessment of competing explanations. How can the extent of democratization and the level of democracy best be accounted for? The *extent of democratization* was measured as the change between 1988 and 1994 in an African country's political rights score, as catalogued in *The Comparative Survey of Freedom* (for further details and discussion see the Appendix). The *level of democracy* was measured as a country's score in 1994. The *Survey's* political rights indicator nicely captures the essence of democracy as "the right of all adults to vote and compete for public office and elected representatives to have a decisive vote on public policies."[83] The *Survey's* nine-point checklist of political rights includes, among others, the following questions:

Is the chief authority elected through free and fair elections?
Do people organize freely in different political parties?
Is there a realistic possibility that the opposition can gain power through elections?
Is political power decentralized to local governments?

By this index, a bare majority of African authoritarian regimes – 23 out of 42 – underwent some measure of democratization between 1988 and 1994 (see

Appendix, Table 12).[84] The attainment of democratic gains in about half of Africa's countries, however, did not herald a continental convergence around political norms. The ideology of liberal democracy had not decisively won the day. Indeed, the diversity of the types of political regimes in Africa increased rather than diminished as evidenced by the fact that standard deviation of country scores around the mean level of democracy in 1994 was higher than in 1988.[85] During the 1970s and 1980s, African leaders shared a normative consensus on political rules that restricted civil liberties and mandated single-party elections. Although that old hegemony had been broken by 1994, a new consensus in favor of liberal democracy or any other dominant ideology had yet to solidify.

Were there linkages between political liberalization and democratization? Although they are strongly associated,[86] these aspects of regime transition were not identical or mutually embedded. The reader will notice in Table 12 that fewer countries made gains on political rights (23, for a net gain across Africa of 4 countries) than on civil liberties (33, for a net gain of 24 countries). Moreover, only 16 of the 23 "democratizing" countries made sufficient gains by 1994 to actually complete a full-blown democratic transition by the end of 1994 (see Table 7). Quite clearly, therefore, across much of Africa liberalization occurred without democratization.

Interestingly, however, liberalization was an indispensable precondition for democratization. Without exception, the 23 African countries that advanced on political rights also made gains on civil liberties, with the latter invariably following the former over time. But the obverse did not hold. At least seven African countries made civil liberties gains during the period of transition without going on to hold free and fair elections. This confirms that, although political liberalization may be a necessary prerequisite, it is not a sufficient condition for democratization.

ECONOMIC FACTORS

Generally speaking, and now as expected, democratization in Africa was unrelated to any aspect of economic structure, change, or crisis. Until 1994, gains in political rights were statistically more likely in African countries with relatively high economic growth rates.[87] But when Mozambique managed to fulfill the minimal conditions for a democratic transition in November of that year, the positive general relationship between high growth and the installation of democracy disappeared. Not only was Mozambique the poorest country in Africa in 1989, but its post-independence economic growth rate was the lowest in our sample (GNP per capita, 1989 = $80, GNP growth rate, 1965–1989 = −8.2 percent). Moreover, apart from Mozambique, several other impoverished countries in Africa with negative growth rates also transited to democracy (e.g., Guinea–Bissau = −.3.0 percent, Niger = −2.4 percent, Madagascar = −1.9 percent).

We can only conclude that economic interpretations of political transitions in Africa are not supported by systematic empirical analysis. Widner's initial hunch is vindicated that "countries similar in resource endowment, in dependence on export agriculture, and in economic policies and performance show different political tendencies."[88] At least within the admittedly narrow band of low- and lower-middle-income African countries, we cannot confirm the assertion that "the level of economic development has a pronounced effect on political democracy ... GNP is the dominant explanatory variable."[89] Nor can we confirm the claim that "the correlation between wealth and democracy implies that transitions to democracy should occur primarily in countries at middle levels of development."[90] By 1995, almost a score of African political regimes, many of them located in desperately poor countries, had been tentatively transformed into fragile democracies.

Let us be clear. Unlike studies in the modernization tradition, the analysis in this chapter is concerned not with the correlates of stable or long-lived democracy but with the conditions under which successful efforts are made to *install* democratic regimes. Our findings do not challenge the conventional wisdom that stable democracies are most readily *consolidated* over the long run in advanced high-income economies (see Chapter 7). But we do contend that, regardless of subsequent regime sustainability, attempts at democratic *transition* can occur under a range of economic conditions and at any level of economic development.

INTERNATIONAL FACTORS

What about international influences? Was democratization driven from abroad? For the first time in our analysis, the level of aid dependence emerged as an explanatory variable.[91] The higher a country's relative level of aid flows, the more extensive were its democratization reforms.[92] Because aid-dependent countries were likely to be susceptible to political conditionalities, this result drew our attention back to the potential influence of international donor agencies in encouraging democratic reforms. The finding also survived statistical controls: for the size of the recipient country,[93] suggesting the observed effect was not limited to Africa's microstates; and for the timing of the onset of transition,[94] suggesting that the effect was not due simply to "ganging up" by donors over time.

But contradictory evidence (first seen when we discussed liberalization) must also be reviewed: If donors went so far as to impose explicit political conditions, then aid recipients undertook *less* democratization.[95] Stated differently, of the 25 cases of official political conditionality in Africa, only 8 ended in democratic transition, with the remaining 17 cases falling short: 8 became "blocked," 7 were "flawed," and 2 never got underway. In short, donor-driven transitions were problematic and led to ambiguous outcomes. Possible reasons were discussed in the previous chapter – namely, that many African leaders undertook "anticipatory reforms" before political conditions were formalized; and relatedly, donors reserved their hardest conditions for the "tough nut" regimes whose transitions were probably destined to fall short of democracy anyway. Beyond these considerations, Western donors may also have failed to discriminate adequately among domestic political situations in requiring universally that all African governments move to democratic elections. Some incumbent leaders or opposition movements were demonstrably unprepared to take such a step. In these cases — Rwanda and Angola stand out — donor demands for democratic procedures severely overestimated the willingness of the principal protagonists to genuinely embrace such reforms.

Instead, we should expect that international pressures will have interactive effects with domestic politics. This much became clear when we controlled the relationship between aid flows and democratization for the frequency of political protest: The partial correlation coefficient increased by almost half and gained considerable statistical significance.[96] This finding suggested that international aid dependence was most relevant to political transitions when it catalyzed or accompanied domestic political pressures. In other words, weak governments reformed politically not only because of their reliance on donor largesse but because this dependence increased and precipitated their vulnerability to popular resistance.

Thus, although international factors played an important part in explaining democratization, they remained secondary. The greatest weight of explanation had to rest elsewhere. Our comparative empirical analysis points in a clear direction: The search for the causes of democratization in Africa is more likely to be fruitful if focused on political rather than economic factors and on domestic as well as international factors. In a context of influence from abroad, democratization in Africa was driven politically from within. African regime transitions are primarily explicable in terms of domestic political struggles between incumbent state elites and opposition social movements in a context of inherited institutions. By way of conclusion, it is to such domestic political considerations that we again return.

DOMESTIC POLITICS

Democratic reforms in Africa were most extensive in political regimes with a distinctive institutional legacy that featured an *absence* of competitive elections and the *presence* of dominant parties.[97] These findings about democratization echoed and reinforced earlier results for liberalization (see Chapter 5). The greatest gains in democratization were recorded in countries — namely, Bénin, Cape Verde, Malawi, Mali, Mozambique, Niger, and São Tomé — that started from a very low base (scored 4 to 5) of democratic practice (see Table 12). Prominent in this group were single-party regimes that had previously held few elections. At the other end of the spectrum were countries that actually experienced declining levels of democracy between 1988 and 1994;[98] this group included Liberia, Nigeria, Rwanda, Sierra Leone, Sudan, and Zaire. Their political transitions stalled when incumbent leaders reneged on promises to convene elections and political com-

petition escalated into runaway violence. Significantly, all such countries had experienced frequent coups in the past, had endured long intervals of military rule,
and were governed by military-installed leaders at the time that transition began.
In these regards, the institutional heritage of preceding regimes shaped the outcome of transitions.

As we shall see, however, the effects of institutional legacies on the process
of democratization were more oblique than direct. Institutional precedents
played themselves out through the domestic politics of regime transitions by
lending structure to contingent choices and events. We established in Chapter 4
that the onset of transition through political protest was predominantly a function of the institutional heritage of previous regimes. Thus, when political
protests had impact of their own at later stages of transitions, they did so partly
as vectors for the institutional precedents on which they were founded. In this
way, institutional precedents were projected into transitions, structuring them in
patterned and predictable ways.

Of the 15 African countries that experienced extensive political protest, the
most common outcome (9 cases) was a transition to democracy.[99] Moreover, political protest was strongly and significantly related to the occurrence of competitive multiparty elections in the early 1990s.[100] Indeed, competitive elections almost always occurred wherever there was extensive protest (in 13 out of 15
cases[101]). At best, political protest prompted a full-blown democratic transition;
at minimum it allowed, through flawed elections, the installation of a liberalized
form of autocracy.[102] Notably, regime transition was rarely precluded or blocked
where extensive popular protests had occurred. Thus, even if democratization was
ultimately partial, transitions originating in political protest generally led by the
end of 1994 to regimes that were at least *somewhat* more democratic than the ones
that had gone before.

MULTIVARIATE MODELS

To estimate well-rounded models of democratization in Africa, we again used
OLS regression. Model D includes all the indicators with established bivariate
connections to the *extent of democratization* (see Table 9). We once more restricted
the model to eliminate the least effective variables. This procedure led us to drop
the only contending economic factor that still remained – namely, the number of
structural adjustment programs.

Which brings us to Model E, our best effort to explain the extent of democratization. It *carries two-thirds of the explanatory burden,* with just four variables. It
has three compelling attributes.

First, Model E suggests that regime transitions in Africa are *highly contingent
political processes.* The outcome of transitions depends greatly on the intercession
of military actors and mass protesters. Between them, these political protagonists
account for over 50 percent of the variance in democratization. The estimated
model indicates that the presence of protest and the support of the military great-

Table 9. *Multiple Regression Estimates of Democratization, 1988–1994*

Variable	Estimates		Signif-icance	Explained Variance
	(B)	(Standard-ized B)	(p-value)	
Model D				
Military Intervention	1.673	0.564	0.000	
Frequency of Political Protest	0.910	0.398	0.015	
Overseas Development Assistance	0.047	0.307	0.023	
Opposition Cohesion	0.919	0.233	0.060	
Percentage of Legislative Seats	0.006	0.137	0.231	
Number of Structural Adjustment Programs	−0.047	−0.106	0.381	
Number of Elections	−0.026	−0.051	0.724	
			Multiple R	0.865
			R Square	0.749
			Adj. R Square	0.673
			Standard Error	1.071
			F	9.828
			Sig. F	0.0000
Model E				
Military Intervention	1.750	0.590	0.000	
Frequency of Political Protest	0.833	0.364	0.006	
Overseas Development Assistance	0.043	0.281	0.026	
Opposition Cohesion	1.009	0.256	0.027	
			Multiple R	0.847
			R Square	0.717
			Adj. R Square	0.674
			Standard Error	1.070
			F	16.520
			Sig. F	0.0000

(n = 42)

ly enhanced the degree of democratization achieved. This corroborates our emphasis throughout this book on the widespread importance of protest action to all stages of regime transition in Africa and our exploration in this chapter of the more occasional, yet more decisive interventions of the military. We conclude that any explanation of democratization must incorporate the initiatives and interplay of purposive political actors. Any structural argument about the determinants of regime transitions must therefore be leavened with a strong antidote of political agency.

Second, the weight of our account of democratization rests on *domestic political factors*. Indeed, an adequate explanatory model could be constructed with reference to military intervention, political protest, and opposition cohesion alone, that is, entirely without reference to international or economic factors.[103] We interpret this as confirmation that, in the first instance, pressures for political change emanate from within the borders of affected countries and that regime transitions are propelled principally by a constellation of indigenous political actors and institutions. This is not to say that international factors are irrelevant; indeed, the fit of Model E to the data is improved by the inclusion of a measure of a country's dependence on foreign aid. But as always we see such international factors as more contextual than proximate; at minimum, they provide a setting conducive to domestic political action; at most, they help to precipitate it.

Third, and notwithstanding what has just been said, *institutions do matter.* To be sure, the direct effects of institutional legacies were too feeble to be included in an overall account of the *process* of democratization. Along with the economic variable, these were dropped in Model E. Instead, institutional effects were expressed *indirectly* through the actions of key political agents. We have already noted how political protests were structurally underpinned by the institutional heritage of the plebiscitary one-party state. And we have argued in this chapter that military intervention was a systematic effort by competing military factions to protect or obtain privileges in a context of the institutions of neopatrimonial rule. Moreover, the dynamics of transition generate new organizational forms such as opposition movements and national conferences, and the cohesion of the opposition remained a crucial factor in obtaining democratization. A strong and well-organized opposition movement led by a dominant leader helped to promote competitive elections, to ensure transparency in electoral administration, and to assemble a winning ruling coalition. And a cohesive opposition provided a vital institutional check on executive power, not only during the installation of democratic regimes but during their subsequent consolidation.

We therefore claim that democratization in Africa can be explained parsimoniously with a modest set of institutionally shaped political factors. This claim is considerably strengthened if we focus not on the extent of democratization but on the *level of democracy.* In many respects, the level of democracy is the most pertinent single measure of a country's regime status. By using this measure, we shift the target of explanation from tumultuous reform *processes* to more fixed regime *outcomes.* In Model F, the dependent variable is the level of democ-

Table 10. *Multiple Regression Estimates of Level of Democracy, 1994*

Variable	Estimates		Signif-icance	Explained Variance
	(B)	(Standard-ized B)	(p-value)	
Model F				
Military Intervention	−1.686	−0.479	0.000	
Number of Elections	0.161	0.314	0.019	
Frequency of Political Protest	−0.649	−0.275	0.046	
Percentage of Legislative Seats	−0.012	−0.250	0.038	
				Multiple R 0.724
				R Square 0.525
				Adj. R Square 0.474
				Standard Error 1.441
				F 10.218
				Sig. F 0.0000

(n = 42)

racy, operationalized as the absolute level of political rights present in African countries in 1994.[104] Unlike the extent of democratization, which was measured relatively against each country's own past political performance, the level of democracy is calibrated against an absolute standard as embodied in a definitive set of political rights. This formulation takes into account the fact that countries embark on transition from differing levels of political freedom, and it gives more weight to observations that did not undergo significant change during the period of transition. In these ways, it emphasizes historical continuities.[105]

Model F demonstrates anew the impact of inherited political regimes.[106] Again, we explain about half of the overall variation in the level of democracy with a small number of variables, each of which reflects specific institutional dynamics. The frequency of protest and the intervention of the military remain powerful explanatory factors, but familiar institutional variables now reappear in the analysis. *Political participation* (measured as the number of elections, independence to 1989) and *political competition* (measured as the largest party's share of legislative seats in 1989) are both significantly related to the level of democracy. Their institutional effects are direct, rather than obliquely mediated by political agents.

Importantly, participation and competition – the defining dimensions of political regimes – repeatedly recur as explanatory factors in successive multivariate models. We have shown that these variables constitute core elements in accounts of the incidence of protest, the extent of liberalization, and the level of democracy achieved during transitions. The ubiquity of these explanatory factors implies that the heritage of political institutions underpins the entire phenomenon of regime transition in rather fundamental ways. Manifestly, *the extent of both political participation and political competition in previous regimes* must be included in any analysis aimed at fully understanding regime changes, including their outcomes.

Note, too, that precedents of political participation have a positive impact on the level of democracy. Regimes that had featured regular elections in the past were likely to extend the availability of political rights during the period of transition. Thus, our model estimates that each election convened between independence and 1989 increased the level of democracy in 1994 by 0.16. Electoral precedents that were formative in getting to democracy are also likely to be helpful in consolidating participatory regimes over the long haul. And, notably, for the first time, precedents of political monopoly in the form of a dominant party were revealed as unconducive to high levels of democracy. This confirms that the presence of a capable opposition party or parties was necessary for installing viable democracies and that such parties will be required for the consolidation of democratic regimes. We turn to these and other institutional requirements of democratic consolidation in the next chapter.

ENDNOTES

1. A minimalist definition also addresses only the installation of democratic regimes; for consideration of the reversal, survival, and consolidation of democracy, see Chapter 7.
2. See Guillermo O'Donnell and Philippe C. Schmitter, *Transitions from Authoritarian Rule: Tentative Conclusions about Uncertain Democracies* (Baltimore: Johns Hopkins University Press, 1986), p. 57.
3. For an initial comparative analysis of the first of these contests, see John A. Wiseman, "Early Post-Redemocratization Elections in Africa," *Electoral Studies* 11 (1992): 279–91.
4. Indeed, these variables were almost as *un*related as they could possibly be: Spearman's r = −0.015, sig. = 0.927.
5. On the aftermath of Chad's national conference, see the following essays by Robert Buijtenhuijs: "Les Partis Politiques Africains ont-ils des Projets de Société? l'Exemple du Tchad," *Politique Africaine* (Decembre 1994): 119–36; and especially, "Une Conférence Nationale et des Massacres," in *L'Afrique Politique 1994: Vue sur la Démocratisation a Marée Basse,* ed. Patrick Quantin (Paris: Karthala, 1994).
6. Recall from Chapter 5 that the likelihood of different transition trajectories – via a national conference or direct to elections – was closely connected to a country's previous experience with plebiscitary or competitive single-party regimes.

7. Of the 22 countries that transited to elections without a conference, the following were in the francophone zone: Burkina Faso, Burundi, Cameroon, Côte d'Ivoire, Djibouti, Guinea, Madagascar, and Seychelles.

8. 0 = fragmented, 1 = cohesive.

9. The correlation between opposition cohesion and the number of registered political parties in 1994 has the correct (negative) sign, though the coefficient falls short of statistical significance (Spearman's r = −0.229, P = 0.145). Countries with fragmented oppositions averaged some 28 registered political parties compared to 17 in countries with relatively cohesive oppositions. This difference was magnified when only "effective" parties (measured as those those that won legislative seats in founding elections) were considered. Fragmented oppositions gave rise to an average of 8 parliamentary parties, versus 4.5 parties for relatively cohesive oppositions.

10. South Africa was scored as cohesive mainly because of the United Democratic Front, a preparty coalition that fell away when the African National Congress and other parties were relegalized.

11. Spearman's r = 0.356, sig. = 0.021.

12. For a useful summation, see Edward R. McMahon, "Lessons Learned from African Elections," in *The Democratic Challenge in Africa,* ed. Richard Joseph (Atlanta, Ga.: The Carter Center, May 1994), pp. 141–6.

13. On Ghana, see L. Cooper, F. Hayward, and A. Lee, *Ghana: A Pre-Election Assessment Report* (Washington, D.C.: International Foundation for Electoral Systems, 1992), which recommended a complete reregistration of all voters to correct defects in the existing register. See also Richard Jeffries and Clare Thomas, "The Ghanaian Elections of 1992," *African Affairs* 92 (1993): 331–6.

14. In addition to providing support for voter registration and electoral administration, the United Nations or Western donor consortia commonly underwrote the full costs of international and domestic election-monitoring efforts.

15. Governments placed obstacles in the path of international observer groups in Cameroon, Togo, and Kenya. Officials commonly stalled until the last minute in issuing credentials to domestic monitors. We found no record of an observer presence at elections in Djibouti and Comoros.

16. Benjamin Pogrund, "South Africa Goes to the Polls," *Elections '94 South Africa: The Campaigns, Results and Future Prospects,* ed. Andrew Reynolds (London: James Currey, 1994), 159–81.

17. McMahon, "Lessons Learned from African Elections," p. 142.

18. See Fred Hayward, *Elections in Independent Africa* (Boulder, Colo.: Westview, 1987), p. 12; also Naomi Chazan, "African Voters at the Polls: A Re-Examination of the Role of Elections in African Politics," *Journal of Commonwealth and Comparative Politics* 17: 136–58, (1979), p. 149.

19. Augustin-Maris-Gervais Loada provides a summary of the election and its aftermath in "Burkina Faso: Les Rentes de la Légitimation Démocratique," in *L'Afrique Politique 1995: Le Meilleur, le Pire et l'Incertain,* ed. Patrick Quantin (Paris: Karthala, 1995).

20. Free and fair elections from 1990 to 1994 were negatively related to the number of previous elections, independence to 1989, though at low levels of statistical significance (Spearman's r = −0.307, sig. = 0.087)(n = 29). Free and fair elections from 1990 to 1994 were positively related to the winning party's

share of legislative seats in the last election before 1989 (Pearson's r = 0.416, P = 0.018).

21. Although these relationships are potentially tautologous, they are still worth reporting since they demonstrate the consequences of the political choices made by key actors. Free and fair elections were negatively associated with the level of state repression during the transition (Spearman's r = −0.473, sig. = 0.007) (n = 29). Similarly, free elections were negatively related to the extent of rule manipulation by incumbents during transitions (Spearman's r = 0.558, sig. = 0.001). Even with a small sample size, both relationships were highly significant.

22. Free elections were positively related to opposition cohesion (phi = 0.406, sig. = 0.071) (n = 29).

23. The exception was Burkina Faso. Of the 14 other cases, 11 held fully free and fair elections ("Yes" in the third column of Table 7). The other three cases (Côte d'Ivoire, Ghana, São Tomé) scored "Yes?"

24. Michel Koyt, Maxime Faustin, M'Bringa Takama, and Pierre-Marie Decoudras, "République Centrafricaine: Les Vicissitudes du Changement," in *L'Afrique Politique 1995: Le Meilleur, le Pire et l'Incertain,* ed. Patrick Quantin (Paris: Karthala, 1995), pp. 235–52.

25. Patassé had won the election with 37.325 percent of the vote in the first round and 52.45 percent in the second. Kolingba came in fourth in the first round, with 12.1 percent of the vote. See Koyt et al., "Les Vicissitudes du Changement."

26. Spearman's r = 0.662, sig. =0.000; phi =0.719, sig. = 0.005.

27. Samuel P. Huntington, *The Third Wave: Democratization in the Late Twentieth Century* (Norman: Oklahoma University Press, 1991), p. 174.

28. David Throup, "Elections and Political Legitimacy in Kenya," *Africa* 63 (1993): 392; "Kenya: How Not to Win Friends and Influence People," *Africa Confidential* 34 (2 April 1993); and "Kenya: Donors Doubt," *Africa Confidential* 34 (19 March 1993).

29. Despite close United Nations supervision and approval of the September 1992 elections in Angola, Savimbi accused the government of election fraud and demanded suspension of the official announcement. The MPLA candidate for president, Marcelino dos Santos, won 49.6 percent versus Savimbi's 40.1 percent. But Savimbi declined to face dos Santos in a constitutionally mandated second-round runoff. See Christine Messiant, "Angola: Le retour à la Guerre, ou l'Inavouable Faillite d'une Intervention Internationale," in *L'Afrique Politique 1994: Vue sur la Démocratisation a Marée Basse,* ed. Patrick Quantin (Paris: Karthala, 1994), pp. 199–230.

30. See National Democratic Institute for International Affairs/African-American Institute, *An Evaluation of the June 21, 1992 Elections in Ethiopia* (Washington, D.C.: NDI/AAI, 1992).

31. In the 17 elections that were ruled free and fair, the losers accepted the results in 14 cases (phi = 0.699, sig. =0.004).

32. In 11 incumbent ousters, losers accepted the results in 10 cases (phi = 0.752, sig. = 0.002).

33. The association between free and fair elections and loser acceptance (Pearson's r = 0.669, P = 0.000) was slightly reduced when controlled for the ouster of in-

cumbents (Pearson's r = 0.487, P = 0.009). The association between incumbent ouster and loser acceptance (Pearson's r = 0.697, P = 0.000) was also reduced when controlled for free and fair elections (Pearson's r = 0.393, P = 0.039). Both relationships remained statistically significant.

34. See note 33. The control for free and fair elections has a larger statistical effect than does the control for incumbent ouster.

35. *Africa Confidential* 33 (1992): 1, emphasis added. See also Patrick Quantin, "Les Elites Politiques Face aux Transitions Démocratiques," in *L'Afrique Politique 1994: Vue sur la Démocratisation a Marée Basse,* ed. Patrick Quantin (Paris: Karthala, 1994), pp. 277–85.

36. See Peter J. Schraeder, "The More Things Change the More They Remain the Same: African Presidents and the Process of Democratization in Africa" (paper presented at the Transnational Institute, Cologne, Germany, November 13, 1993); also Masipula Sithole, "The African Political Scene: Is the Second Wind of Change Any Different from the First?" (paper presented at the African Studies Center, Michigan State University, East Lansing, Michigan, March 31, 1994).

37. Jane Mansbridge, "What Is Democracy?" in National Research Council, *The Transition to Democracy* (Washington, D.C.: National Academy Press, 1991), p. 11.

38. Yves Fauré, "Democracy and Realism: Reflections on the Case of Côte d'Ivoire," *Africa* 63 (1993): 324.

39. The turnout figures for registered voters reported in Table 8 must be corrected to take account of the generally low rates of voter registration in African countries. For example, Cameroon's 1992 turnout rate of 72 percent of registered voters drops to 54 percent when considered as a proportion of eligible adults and to 24 percent as a share of total population.

40. By contrast, Angolan voters turned out in huge numbers despite the fact that civil war combatants had not been fully disarmed, as did South African voters in the face of bomb threats from white extremists and a bitter campaign atmosphere of black-on-black violence.

41. Collier, *Regimes in Tropical Africa* (Berkeley: University of California Press, 1982), pp. 76–80.

42. Fauré, "Democracy and Realism."

43. *Ibid.,* 325–6.

44. We would have preferred to make the measure of political competition consistent with the one used earlier (i.e., the winning party's share of seats in the legislature). But because data on voter turnout was considerably more complete for presidential than legislative elections from 1990 to 1994, we chose to maximize sample size by basing all calculations on presidential elections.

45. Pearson's r = −0.499, P = 0.007 (n = 28). The association was even stronger for legislative elections (Pearson's r = −0.599) but due to small sample size (n = 6), the relationship was not significant.

46. Readers should not be confused by the negative sign on the correlation coefficient. Because the competition data are inverted, with a lower winner's share of total votes indicating a higher degree of competition, we would expect a negative statistical coefficient. But the relationship between the two underlying concepts is a positive one, with higher voter turnout rates (i.e., higher participation) being associated with lower winners' vote shares (i.e., higher competition).

47. For recent contributions, see Robin Luckham, "The Military, Militarization and Democratization in Africa: A Survey of Literature and Issues," *African Studies Review* 37 (1994): 13–76; Jendayi Frazer, "Conceptualizing Civil-Military Relations during Democratic Transitions," *Africa Today* 42 (1995): 39–48; and J. Craig Jenkins and Augustine J. Kposowa, "The Political Origins of African Military Coups," *International Studies Quarterly* 36 (1992): 271–92. With reference to Latin America, Alfred Stepan has criticized the "stunning" neglect in the transitions literature of the role of the military, whose role he regards as "fundamental to an analysis of the weakening of authoritarian regimes, of democratic transition, and democratic consolidation." *Rethinking Military Politics: Brazil and the Southern Cone* (Princeton: Princeton University Press, 1988), p. 21.

48. Prodemocratic intervention = +1, no military intervention = 0, antidemocratic intervention = −1.

49. Michael Chege, "The Military in the Transition to Democracy in Africa: Some Preliminary Observations," *CODESRIA Bulletin* (Dakar, Council for the Development of Social Science Research in Africa) 3 (1995): 13.

50. Spearman's r = 0.630, sig. = 0.000.

51. Phi = 0.646, sig. =0.006.

52. William J. Foltz, "Democracy, Development and the Military: Some Lessons from Africa" (paper presented at the annual meeting of the African Studies Association, Toronto, November 3–6, 1994), p. 5.

53. *Africa Confidential* 33 (October 1992).

54. According to partial results for 14 states released by the National Electoral Commission, Abiola was ahead in 11 states, including his presidential opponent's home state of Kano. The Campaign for Democracy, an activist front, later claimed that Abiola had won 19 states, and Tofa 11; significantly, Tofa did not dispute this claim.

55. For a useful summary of this case, see Peter M. Lewis, "The Politics of Democratic Failure in Nigeria," *MSU Working Papers on Political Reform in Africa* (East Lansing: Michigan State University, Department of Political Science, 1994): p. 65.

56. The Mali transition is reviewed in Richard Vengroff and Moctar Kone, "Mali: Democracy and Political Change," in *Democracy and Political Change in Sub-Saharan Africa,* ed. John Wiseman, (London: Routledge, 1995), pp. 45–70; and Nicolas van de Walle, "Economic Reform and the Consolidation of Democratic Rule: Three African Case Studies" (paper presented at the 1994 meetings of the International Political Science Association, Berlin, Germany, August 21–25, 1994).

57. *The New York Times,* 7 March 1992.

58. A virtually identical set of events occurred in Togo, where political cohabitation deteriorated into "a contest of brute force" and made it "almost seem as though Mobutu and Eyadéma were operating from the same manual." See editorial, *Africa Demos* 3 (1993): 15.

59. Cindy Shiner, "Mobutu Ascendant," *Africa Report* (May–June 1994): 46.

60. Richard Carver, "The Army Factor," *Africa Report* (Jan–Feb 1994).

61. Daniel N. Posner, "Malawi's New Dawn," *Journal of Democracy* 6 (1995): 139–40.

62. Huntington, *Third Wave,* p. 144.

63. Huntington notes that protest-led transitions are likely to attract military involvement: "in five out of six replacements (except Argentina), military dissafection was essential to bringing down the regime," *Third Wave,* p. 145.

64. Spearman's r = −0.003, sig. =0.986.

65. J. Craig Jenkins and Augustine J. Kpsowa, "Explaining Military Coups d'Etat: Black Africa, 1957–1984," *American Sociological Review* 55 (1990): 862, 867, 869. Military centrality concerns "the corporate interests and resources of the the military and [on] civil-military relations ... it emphasises the size, cohesion, and the budget claims of the military." From this perspective, interventionist armies tend to be large and to take up a sizable share of total government expenditure.

66. Axel Hadenius notes that "countries where a high proportion of the resources are assigned to the armed forces tend to have a low degree of democracy." *Democracy and Development* (Cambridge: Cambridge University Press, 1992): p. 148.

67. Military intervention by number of previous coups: Spearman's r = 0.038, sig. = 0.802; military intervention by number of years of previous military regime: Spearman's r = −0.067, sig = 0.671 (e.g., Burkina Faso, Ghana, Mauritania, and Uganda).

68. The one exception was Cameroon, where the military helped implement the state of emergency called by the government to fight the opposition's *villes mortes* campaign in 1991. The military would eventually take over the direct administration of 7 out of the country's 10 provinces. This was the culmination of a 10-year process for the Biya regime of growing dependence on the military to maintain his hold on power. Biya had purged the army following the attempted coup in 1984 by northern officers and had promoted southern elements whose loyalty had saved his presidency. Since then, the military had increasingly become an instrument of Beti and southern domination over the rest of the country. Biya would richly reward the army for its support, notably by maintaining their salaries even as the civil service accumulated months of salary arrears in 1992 and 1993, and – more significantly – by more than doubling the number of generals in the army by promoting eight officers to that rank in February 1993. By that point, the magazine *Jeune Afrique Economie* was describing the country as a "military regime with a civilian face." "Régime Militaire à Visage Civil," *Jeune Afrique Economie* 165 (March 1993): 118. See also Luc Sindjoun, "Cameroun: Le Système Politique Face aux Enjeux de la Transition Démocratique (1990–1993)," in *L'Afrique Politique 1994: Vue sur la Démocratisation a Marée Basse,* ed. Patrick Quantin (Paris: Karthala, 1994), pp. 143–65.

69. Even the exceptions help to make the point: Angola never had a military government, but it was governed by a militarized civilian regime that was on a permanent war footing; and civilian Tanzania's transition became "unblocked" after the closing date for this study, through a "flawed" election in October and November 1995.

70. For instance, see Eric A. Nordlinger, *Soldiers in Politics* (Englewood Cliffs, N.J.: Prentice-Hall, 1977); and Samuel E. Finer, *Man on Horseback,* 2nd ed. (Boulder, Colo.: Westview, 1988).

71. See Samuel Decalo, *Coups and Army Rule in Africa* (New Haven: Yale University Press, 1976 and 1991).
72. Foltz, "Democracy, Development and the Military," 5–6.
73. International Forum for Democratic Studies, "Nigeria's Political Crisis: Which Way Forward" (Washington, D.C.: National Endowment for Democracy, February 1995), p. 11.
74. *Africa Confidential* 31 (September 1990): 4–5.
75. Much the same was true in Sierra Leone, where "thousands of young men have been trained in the use of arms. They have become accustomed to the power that a gun gives them to treat those who don't have uniforms as second-class citizens" (*West Africa*, July-August, 1993).
76. *The Economist*, 19 June 1993. See also Peter Lewis, "From Prebendalism to Predation: The Political Economy of Decline in Nigeria," *Journal of Modern African Studies*, 34 (March 1997): 79–103.
77. *Africa Confidential* 32 (27 September 1991).
78. *Africa News* (May 11–24, 1992).
79. Bill Berkeley, "Zaire: An African Horror Story," *Atlantic Monthly* (August 1993): 28.
80. Crawford Young, "Democratization in Africa," in Jennifer Widner, ed., *Economic Change and Political Liberalization in Sub-Saharan Africa* (Baltimore: Johns Hopkins University Press, 1994): p. 241.
81. *Ibid.*
82. Michael Chege, "The Military in the Transition to Democracy in Africa: Some Preliminary Observations," *CODESRIA Bulletin* 3 (1995), p. 13.
83. Joseph E. Ryan, "The Comparative Survey of Freedom: Survey Methodology" (New York: Freedom House, 1993), p. 77.
84. If long-standing multiparty regimes are included, progress on democratization occurred in 24 out of 47 countries. This group of countries encountered more setbacks than advances from their relatively democratic starting points. Most strikingly, Gambia suffered a military coup in July 1994. And democratic practices were gradually eroded in Sénégal and Zimbabwe as a result of increased electoral intimidation and weakening opposition parties.
85. The standard deviation on political rights scores was 1.36 in 1988 and 2.03 in 1994.
86. Pearson's r = 0.615, P = 0.000.
87. Spearman's r = 0.316, sig. = 0.044.
88. Jennifer A. Widner, "Political Reform in Anglophone and Francophone African Countries," in *Economic Change and Political Liberalization in Sub-Saharan Africa*, ed. Widner (Baltimore: Johns Hopkins University Press, 1994), p. 49.
89. Kenneth Bollen and Robert Jackman, "Economic and Non-Economic Determinants of Political Democracy in the 1960s," *Research in Political Sociology* 1 (1985): 38–9. Against the objection that there is insufficient variation in economic variables within the sample, we would point to 1989 per capita GNP levels ranging from $120 in Ethiopia to $4,230 in Seychelles; economic growth rates in the 1980s ranging from minus 8 percent in Mozambique to plus 5 percent in Lesotho; and proportions of the labor force engaged in agricultural occupations from 18 percent in Mauritius to 93 percent in Rwanda.

90. Huntington, *Third Wave,* p. 60.
91. Measured as overseas development assistance as a percentage of GDP. The reader will recall that this variable was unrelated to either political protest or political liberalization.
92. Pearson's r = 0.337, P = 0.048 (n = 35). Note that the coefficient is barely significant.
93. Measured as the national population in millions. Pearson's partial r = 0.340, P = 0.049 (n = 32).
94. Measured as the time elapsed from January 1, 1988 to the first protest or first liberalization reform, whichever was the earlier. Pearson's partial r = 0.333, P = 0.073 (n = 28).
95. Spearman's r = 0.185, sig. = 0.242. Although the sign runs in the predicted direction, the association was weak and insignificant.
96. Pearson's partial r = 0.479, P = 0.007.
97. Pearson's r = 0.303, P = 0.038 and Pearson's r = 0.311, P = 0.045, respectively. The latter result only refers to the extent of democratization at the end of 1993; the result for 1994 was positive but not significant.
98. That is, these countries registered negative scores on Table 12.
99. Political protests were generally associated with democratic outcomes, at least at a simple bivariate level (Spearman's r = 0.341, sig. = 0.027).
100. phi = 0.446, sig. = 0.015.
101. The exceptions, major ones, being Nigeria and Zaire.
102. phi = 0.500, sig. = 0.005.
103. Multiple r = 0.684, adjusted r^2 = 0.426.
104. As measured in *The Comparative Survey of Freedom.*
105. Note that the sample of 42 African countries continues to exclude the five long-standing multiparty regimes of Botswana, Gambia, Mauritius, Sénégal, and Zimbabwe. Thus, the positive results of Model F cannot be attributed to the countries that were already relatively democratic.
106. Encompassing and diagnostic tests were used to assess the statistical validity of Models E and F. Competing models were compared using R-square, F-test, and standard error measures, but no significant differences were found. White tests failed to detect heteroskedastic disturbances, though the less robust Breusch-Pagan test suggested inconsequential levels of heteroskedasticity in Model F. Durbin-Watson statistics indicated that autocorrelation was absent from Model E but was inconclusive for Model F. However, since cross-national data were used and we had already tested for spatial relationships in this regression model, we do not interpret this result as a rejection of the null hypothesis of no autocorrelation.

7

THE PROSPECTS FOR
DEMOCRACY

In October 1993, Burundi's elected president Melchior Ndadaye was brutally murdered in the course of a military coup d'état, just four months after the country's first peaceful multiparty elections. Observers suggested that the Tutsi-led military had been unwilling to cede power to a government dominated by Hutu civilian politicians. In Gambia, another elected civilian regime – this one long-standing – was overthrown by the military on July 22, 1994.[1] The main justification claimed by the soldiers for their action was the Jawara government's inability to overcome the economic crisis facing the country. In Zambia, 1995 was marked by the political resurrection of former President Kenneth Kaunda, who came out of retirement to declare his intention to contest the presidency in the 1996 elections. President Chiluba, whose own popularity had dropped because of widespread corruption charges and a persistent economic downturn, proposed two constitutional amendments transparently designed to eliminate a challenge from his old nemesis.[2] In this strategy, Chiluba was only following the example set by President Bédié of Côte d'Ivoire, who earlier had changed legal codes to prevent Alassane Ouatara (who was half Burkinabe) from being allowed to run.

All across Africa, there are signs that the democratic gains of 1990 to 1994 that we examined in the preceding chapters are eroding. In a few countries, democratization has been reversed as military forces have overthrown elected governments, spelling an end to brief democratic experiments and a return to authoritarian rule. Elsewhere, new democracies survive, but elected rulers have lapsed back into manipulating political rules in order to consolidate their personal hold on power. In these states, *big-man democracy* is emerging, in which the formal trappings of democracy coexist with neopatrimonial political practice.

Given these signs, and under the weight of economic crisis and the weakness of pluralist institutional traditions, recent democratic gains may well be overturned in the coming years. Most observers agree that a host of structural socioeconomic factors conspire against stable democratic regimes in Africa. Does that mean that these fledgling democracies are all condemned? Although this book has focused principally on regime transitions, the present chapter analyzes the core issues of democratic consolidation in sub-Saharan Africa. We argue that some features of surviving African democracies resemble the imperfect regimes seen in Latin America and parts of Asia, where multiparty electoral regimes coexist with persistent authoritarian leadership tendencies and a shallow democratic political culture.

Whatever their merits, however, surviving democracies need to be clearly distinguished from the regimes that fail to consolidate and that revert to overtly authoritarian forms of governance – for example, through military takeovers. This chapter attempts to distinguish which new democracies are most likely to survive, thereby beginning the long process of consolidation, and which will soon suffer reversals. We again find that explanations based on socioeconomic structures take us only so far, though further than in explaining regime transitions. We therefore look instead to an explanatory approach that emphasizes political institutions and the extent of participation and competition embodied in them. We also emphasize the persistence of neopatrimonial rule, showing how newly elected political leaders continue to favor presidentialism and patronage.

Second, we posit that the "structured contingency" of regime transition also influences subsequent consolidation dynamics. Factors such as the length of the transition, the extent of negotiation and compromise, the degree of violence, and the nature of the opposition coalition all help to define the paths forged by newly democratic regimes. In short, along with the inherited institutional legacy, the mode of transition shapes the prospects for democracy.

REVERSAL, SURVIVAL, OR CONSOLIDATION?

Debates about democratic consolidation in low-income countries are often discourses about the meaning of consolidation itself. The first task is therefore to define consolidation precisely. Some scholars have adopted a procedural, minimalist definition: Huntington, for instance, defines a democratic regime as having been consolidated after two electoral turnovers – that is, when "the party or group that takes power in the initial election at the time of the transition loses a subsequent election and turns over power to those election winners, and if those election winners then peacefully turn over power to the winners of a later election."[3] The advantage of such a definition is its easy operationalization, as multiparty elections are discrete events that hold relatively little ambiguity, even though judging their "freeness and fairness" may in practice prove slippery.[4] On the other hand, to reduce democracy to the holding of regular elections is to risk the "fallacy of electoralism."[5] Regular multiparty elections may in fact be artificial exercises, that offer few meaningful choices to voters but that periodically legitimate hardline rulers. Elections may easily coexist, for instance, with systematic abuses of human rights or the disenfranchisement of large segments of the population.

As a result, scholars have increasingly adopted broader definitions of consolidation in which the criteria include the legitimation and institutionalization of democratic practices over time, buttressed by the widespread adoption of democratic values.[6] In this view, key political institutions, including political parties, the legislature, and the judiciary, need to function effectively and to successfully nurture broad-based pluralism. Some scholars even argue that the emergence of a democratic political culture is an essential component of consolidation.[7] Democracy, in other words, is not possible without democrats. Since the values and attitudes of people are unlikely to change quickly, this definition implies that consolidation is a long-term process, that is likely to take as much as several decades. Thus, even recent models of political learning, under which citizens change their attitudes about political institutions based on their own political experiences, still foresee a relatively lengthy interval before a critical mass of such conversions takes place.[8]

We draw a distinction between the consolidation of democratic rule and the mere survival of new democratic regimes. In our view, consolidation is the more or less total institutionalization of democratic practices, complete only when citizens and the political class alike come to accept democratic practices as the only way to resolve conflict. It requires that political actors so fully internalize the rules of the game that they can no longer imagine resorting to nonelectoral practices to obtain office. O'Donnell thus speaks of two separate transitions: a first, shorter passage from authoritarian rule to the installation of a democratic government and a second, longer, shift toward a democratic regime.[9]

Thus, emerging democracies may survive, in the sense of enduring without reversal to authoritarianism, without making much progress on the difficult process of consolidation. O'Donnell suggests that the conjunction of unfavorable socioeconomic characteristics and pressures brought on by inherited economic crises will militate against the full-blown consolidation of democratic institutions.[10] He predicts instead the mere survival of what he terms "delegative democracies." In these regimes, elected officials govern through direct populist appeals and resort to extensive use of patronage and clientelism, in the process undermining the judiciary, the legislature, and the institutions of civil and political societies. Indeed, over time, unchecked executive power may result in what he calls "the slow death" of democratic institutions.

Scholars like Przeworski and Di Palma have emphasized the role played by elite support for and observance of democratic rules.[11] If clientelist practices continue to dominate politics and if political elites are wedded to democracy only insofar as it enhances their power and influence, it is difficult to imagine much progress in the institutionalization and legitimation of democracy. Regular multiparty elections will change the form in which political actors pursue control of the state apparatus and its resources but not the logic of their behavior. Mechanisms of accountability and transparency will continue to be thwarted, while widespread clientelism, corruption, and patronage will undermine citizens' confidence in democratic institutions, leading to instability and the possibility of a return to more overt forms of authoritarian rule.

That the emerging democracies in the developing world will remain highly flawed is an article of faith in a literature that uses terms like "delegative democracies," "hybrid regimes," "democraduras," "facade democracies," and "patrimonial democracies" to describe emergent regimes.[12] Such terms capture the notion that the formal trappings of democracy – such as universal franchise, elections, and political parties – are superimposed on authoritarian practices and a clientelist political culture.[13] Multiparty elections of uncertain outcome may be regularly convened; but at the same time, civil and political rights are not fully respected between elections and various segments of the population are effectively coopted or intimidated. Moreover, formal democratic politics at the national level coexist with the informal, arbitrary, and clientelistic traditions at the local level.

In this chapter, we adopt the literature's preferred definition of democratic consolidation as a long-term process of legitimation and institutionalization. And we argue that, at least in the short run, various structural and contextual forces will conspire against democratic consolidation in Africa.[14] The more immediate and relevant issue, however, is whether these democracies will *survive at all,* or whether they will suffer reversals to authoritarian rule by executive coup or military takeover. Thus, we are concerned principally with the survival of democratic regimes, which we define minimally as the regular convening of multiparty elections, plus the basic respect for various political rights.

Is there a relationship between short-term survival and long-term consolidation? The two processes are sometimes portrayed as separate, as if democracies can endure without undergoing any consolidation.[15] We take the slightly different view that the longer democracies survive, the likelier is eventual consolidation. Over time, surviving democratic institutions will gain organizational strength and political constituencies. Democratic procedures will become routinized and win popular acceptance if not actual popularity, while nongovernmental actors will continue to apply pressures to extend and deepen democratic rights. In long-standing multiparty regimes like Sénégal or Botswana, we can see this process at work, however imperfectly and slowly.[16] By contrast, democratic rule will not survive if the new order does not enjoy either elite or popular backing, or if political elites manipulate democratic rules in pursuit of personal interests. It is only a matter of time before such regimes are overthrown, either because the powerful become tempted to dispense entirely with democratic niceties, or because a fresh cycle of popular unrest destabilizes and displaces the government.

Some observers have posited the existence of a *cycle* of democratic transitions followed by authoritarian restorations, themselves short-lived.[17] Countries that are prisoners of such cycles – as perhaps some in Latin America for much of the twentieth century, or African countries like Nigeria – find it difficult to consolidate any type of regime. Under the cyclical model, the impermanence of rules becomes a defining characteristic of political systems. Political elites limit their commitment to the present order and view democratic rules opportunistically, to be discarded as soon as they are no longer useful. Needless to say, such democracies are not in the process of being consolidated for the short time they survive. We can conclude that the less democracy is undergoing consolidation, the more unlikely it will survive at all and the more likely it will suffer reversal. Put another way, the cycle will be broken and the process of consolidation begun when the democratic phase leads to some institutionalization and legitimation of democratic rules.

The evidence from posttransition Africa suggests that democratic reversals are inevitable in some countries. How can one predict where these will occur? And which new African democracies will survive, thus beginning the arduous process of long-term consolidation? The rest of this chapter seeks to shed some light on these issues.

THE CONTEXT OF DEMOCRATIC CONSOLIDATION

Consistent with the theme of this book, we prefer to explain the prospects for democratic survival and consolidation in Africa in terms of the institutional legacy of neopatrimonial rule. Before addressing this topic, however, we briefly review the usefulness of competing frameworks in explaining posttransition problems.

SOCIOECONOMIC STRUCTURES

As argued earlier, approaches that start from the blueprint of social and economic structures are better suited to interpreting political situations of regime equilibrium than the conflictual and tumultuous intervals between regimes. By the same token, we expect that structural factors will obtain increased explanatory power as new political regimes settle down – initially as fragile democracies survive over the short term but especially as democratic political routines and institutions become consolidated.

It is difficult to dispute that the structural prerequisites of stable democratic rule are missing in Africa. Most countries are poor, with per capita incomes well below the levels commonly posited as the minimum necessary to sustain democratic rule.[18] A wide range of socioeconomic attainments that increase with national income correlate well with consolidated democracy, including a sizable middle class and private sector, for example, or high literacy rates. In each case, African countries are unambiguously deficient in these characteristics. According to the World Bank, the average African countries had a GNP per capita of $520 in 1993, and an adult literacy rate of 50 percent. Only a handful of states quali-

Table 11. *Socioeconomic Indicators for Selected African Countries*

	GNP per capita (US$, 1993)	Adult Literacy (1990)
Sub-Saharan Africa	520	50
Middle-Income States		
Seychelles	6,280	58
Gabon	4,960	61
Mauritius	3,030	83
South Africa	1,221	—
Botswana	2,790	74
Namibia	1,820	—
Congo	950	57
Cameroon	820	54
Sénégal	750	38
Other Regions		
Latin America, Caribbean	2,950	85
South Asia	310	46
East Asia and Pacific	820	76
Europe, Central Asia	2,450	95

Source: *The World Bank World Development Report (WDR), 1995*. (Washington, D.C.: The World Bank, 1995). Table 1, pp. 162–3. The latest available literacy figure for Mauritius is for 1985 (see *WDR, 1991*); the figures for Seychelles are drawn from *The CIA Fact Handbook* (Washington, D.C.: Central Intelligence Agency, 1995).

fy for the Bank's middle-income status, with GNP per capita of above $650 in 1991 terms. These countries are listed in Table 11. It should be noted that the January 1994 devaluation of the African Financial Community (CFA) franc has pushed the francophone states, except for Gabon, back below the middle-income threshold.

With the exception of South Africa, the African middle-income countries owe their status largely to mineral or oil resources, the revenues from which are unevenly distributed among the population; their literacy scores are perhaps more indicative of the prevailing socioeconomic characteristics of their populations. In any event, Table 11 shows clearly that other democratizing regions of the world, notably Eastern Europe and Latin America, enjoy considerably higher GNP levels and literacy rates. Of the new democracies in Africa, only Namibia, Seychelles, and South Africa appear economically prepared for democracy, with most African states falling below the $1,000 GNP level defined by Huntington as the bottom of the democratic "transition zone."

These structural characteristics undermine the independent sources of state accountability that are critical to the institutionalization of democratic rule.[19] The economic structure of most African countries gives rise to a weak private sector as well as small middle and professional classes that are likely to prove incapable of constituting an autonomous power base to balance and circumscribe state power. Instead, Africa's neopatrimonial political traditions are enhanced by these national economic patterns. In part because the economies in Africa are small and barely diversified, states play a predominant economic role and remain privileged vectors of accumulation. As argued in Chapter 2, this turns politics into a zero-sum game in which control of the state and its resources is the primary end of politics.

Neopatrimonial tendencies are exacerbated by the presence of subnational ethnic identities in a number of African states. Rustow has posited a sense of national identity as an essential prerequisite for stable democratic rule.[20] As many as 10 states in Africa probably do not fill this condition: The most egregious and tragic examples are Rwanda and Burundi, but one might also mention Chad or Mauritania. Yet, as argued in the introduction, a sense of national unity has been developed in most African states over the last 30 years, regardless of the arbitrary nature of the colonial boundaries and despite the simultaneous persistence of lineage, religion, and region-based identities.[21] In these states, although national unity is no longer questioned, political activity is still often organized around ethnoregional identities. Specific institutions like the military may be predominantly in the hands of specific groups, and ethnic and class categories may overlap. In each case, cultural pluralism is likely to sharpen politics by providing an additional cleavage around which conflict can ignite. Such conflict will be abetted when politics is widely perceived as an arena in which to pursue individual and group enrichment.[22]

The increase in political competition that necessarily results from democratization will indeed release long-suppressed conflicts, particularly where accumulation strategies are politically mediated.[23] In countries like Malawi, Congo, or Kenya, democratization has resulted in a reaffirmation of ethnic identities, with political parties emerging along ethnoregional criteria rather than ideological ones. Destabilizing ethnic conflict is not inevitable in the new democracies; political elites persistently pursue political arrangements and coalitions that will counter fragmentation and promote national unity.[24] At least some political elites understand that ethnic divisions must not be exacerbated and will seek to build political alliances across ethnic groups and regions, but the added potential for regime destabilization must be recognized.

ECONOMIC CONDITIONS

Karl's notion of "points of departure" draws attention to the immediate, as opposed to deep-seated, economic setting in which democratization takes place.[25] The African economic crisis will continue to undermine the legitimacy of any political regime, when incumbent governments receive blame for prevailing economic conditions. Democratic governments rarely rely for legitimacy on economic performance to the same extent as authoritarian governments do, but they too must improve material conditions on their watch. In a consolidated democracy, economic grievances are expressed through the ballot box and can lead to the replacement of one elected government by another; in a nonconsolidated democracy, however, the penalty for poor performance may well be the end of democratic rule itself and a return to authoritarianism.

Overcoming the economic crisis while simultaneously achieving democratization is a distinctive challenge facing African states. True, democratizing regimes in Latin America and Eastern Europe faced economic problems, but rarely was the crisis so severe and the means to overcome it so limited as in Africa.[26] Not only did democratic governments in Africa inherit a legacy of several decades of disastrous economic management; they also reached power after a period of political transition during which economic management had further suffered, in some cases leading to serious state decay.[27] As anywhere, elected governments enjoy an initial honeymoon during which they are not held responsible for economic conditions. Soon enough, however, populations forget previous hardships and come to associate their own well-being with the current government's policies and actions.

The condition of the economy thus typically poses a daunting challenge for Africa's fledgling democracies, but the challenges vary across our population of states. First, of course, some countries are richer than others or have a greater economic potential. In richer countries, with a more sophisticated economy or mineral wealth or both, the possibility is greater that the new government will be able to engineer a rapid economic recovery. Many experts believe that, given available levels of human capital and physical infrastructure, no country in Africa is capable of enjoying the kind of spurts of rapid, double-digit economic growth that have been witnessed in Asia and Latin America.[28] Others emphasize institutional obstacles to rapid growth. As Aron writes, "Africa's future growth prospects are overwhelmingly circumscribed by its institutional foundations. These encompass a broad range of state, legal, political and economic institutions, and private sector and business institutions."[29] Clearly, nonetheless, economic development poses a less daunting challenge in mineral-rich Namibia than in low-income countries like Malawi or the Central African Republic.

Second, the economic legacy of the previous regime varies, with the scope of the economic crisis being more severe in some countries than in others. One measure of the crisis is the size of the fiscal deficit: The average overall deficit excluding grants ranged from only 4.2 percent in Madagascar to a whopping 28.2 percent in Mozambique in 1991 to 1992.[30] Fiscal reform was clearly more urgent for incoming governments in countries with larger deficits. In Congo, the previous government had sold forward several years worth of oil production to pay for excessive expenditures throughout the 1980s, leaving incoming President Lissouba without access to the country's major source of revenues.

In addition, the process of economic stabilization and adjustment proceeded differentially during the 1980s. Some authoritarian governments implemented tough economic reform measures, sparing elected successor governments from at least some unpopular actions. In Zambia, after much hesitation, the Kaunda administration committed itself to a tough austerity package in 1989. Ironically, the democratic movement gained momentum from the protests that erupted as a response to the withdrawal of food subsidies in 1990. Although Kaunda backtracked and restored a part of the subsidy, his actions made it easier for the MMD government to permanently eliminate the subsidies soon after reaching power.[31] In Bénin, on the other hand, Kérékou essentially lost control of economic management in his last years in office, leaving the Soglo government with a central administration that had all but collapsed under fiscal and monetary pressures.[32]

THE INTERNATIONAL CONTEXT

Earlier, we cautioned against exaggerating the impact of international pressures on transitions, and similarly we do not believe that they will have a determinant effect on the survival of most new democracies. Nonetheless, the international context will provide some limited support for democratic governments.

In the post–Cold War world, Western diplomacy is generally intolerant of military intervention in new democracies. Thus, the 1993 coup in Burundi was greeted by the suspension of most foreign aid, as was the decision by the Nigerian military to annul the 1993 elections won by Moshood Abiola.[33] These precedents will have some deterrent effect for future military interventions, though more in small, aid-dependent countries than in large countries with a reliable export revenue base. Similarly, Western governments have discouraged elected leaders from manipulating political rules to their own partisan advantage. Thus, Western diplomats in Lusaka tried to dissuade Chiluba from barring Kaunda from running for president, and their counterparts in Abidjan and Nairobi openly criticized sitting presidents for playing the ethnic card in electoral campaigns.[34] In each case, the threat of Western sanctions raises the costs of antidemocratic behavior, even if the threats turn out to be largely empty.

Indeed, the importance the West attaches to the development of democracy in Africa should not be magnified. For some states, the support for democratization has been largely rhetorical. France's aid policies have contradicted the priorities favoring democratizing countries laid out by Mitterrand at the La Baule Franco-African summit of 1991. Democratic Bénin actually saw its French aid decline in the year following its transition, whereas recalcitrant authoritarian regimes in Togo, Cameroon, and Zaire all benefited from French aid increases during the same period.[35] Whatever their degree of attachment to democratic rule in Africa, all Western governments have other priorities in the continent. Foremost, they seek political stability, and when they must choose, they are likely to opt for stability over democratic rule. The West has proven unwilling to apply heavy pressure on behalf of democratization in Ghana and Uganda, the governments of which are making significant progress on painful economic reform. Where they have commercial interests, Western governments are also less likely to stand on principle. For example, the acquiescence of the British and

French governments to imperfect founding elections in Kenya and Cameroon, respectively, suggests that, even when they insist on electoral competition, they will be satisfied by an extremely weak standard of democratic performance.

In sum, the international environment on balance supports the survival of democratic forms, however superficially, but will have a lesser impact on consolidation. It raises the costs of obviously repressive practices and puts some pressure on executives to hold multiparty elections or to tolerate an opposition press; but it is difficult to believe that it will have much of an impact on the quality of democratic rule or prevent the "slow death" of democratic institutions.

INSTITUTIONAL LEGACIES

We are now ready to investigate the institutional dynamics that will likely dictate the success or failure of Africa's democratic experiments. We focus on specific institutions within the state, civil society, and political society. The capacity of agents within these organizations to shape the processes of democratic consolidation is largely determined by their status and resources before and during the transition. These institutional actors can thus be viewed as a product of the environment from which they spring, even if they have some facility to shape that environment in the long run.

Institutional legacies operate on two levels. First, political behavior is embedded in the informal traditions of neopatrimonial rule. The concentration of political power in the hands of all-powerful presidents is of course inimical to democratic practice and is likely to constitute a key problem of the consolidation phase. In countries where elected governments enjoy a legislative supermajority, presidents will find it hard to resist the temptation to change constitutional rules to their own benefit. Elected political executives will find it convenient to lapse into habits of centralized decision making, even as political actors in other branches of government and outside the state seek to maintain institutional pluralism. In addition, the systematic use of state resources to promote stability through clientelism is also likely to influence individual actions after the transition. For one thing, the disastrous economic heritage that the new democracies have to manage is largely the product of economic policies designed to facilitate clientelism and rent seeking. For another, the organizational imbalance between opposition and progovernment forces will continue to be politically mediated by access to state resources.

A second level of institutional legacies emanates from the specific regimes of competition and participation that developed in the postcolonial authoritarian period. The power of institutional actors to shape democratic consolidation after the transition is largely conditioned by the political spaces created beforehand. Political actors are constrained by the past roles of such institutions as the military, political parties, and interest associations. We will later examine these institutions, among others. If the notion of institutional continuity has any validity, then one would expect the prospects for democratic survival to be better in regimes with some previous experience with participation and especially competition.

Elsewhere in the world, most successful third-wave democratizations took place as a result of a second try following a failed previous attempt to install a democracy.[36] At first glance, however, the performance observed in Africa's past experiments with multiparty politics does not lead to optimism about future democratic consolidation. Democratization has been reversed following interludes of multiparty rule in Nigeria, Ghana, and Sudan. As Diamond argued earlier, "Democratically elected governments in Africa have generally performed quite poorly in respecting democratic norms and procedures."[37] The short democratic experiments in Ghana (under Limann) and Nigeria (under Shagari) at the end of the 1970s were foiled largely by the venality of elected officials who used their public offices to gain access to state resources, to plunder both in order to further partisan political advantages and to enrich themselves.[38] So completely had the civilian political class alienated the population that, in both countries, citizens welcomed the military coups that spelled the end of competitive politics.

Similar deficiencies are evident in the practice of democracy in the longest-standing African multiparty regimes. In Sénégal, the extension of political rights and the legalization of opposition parties has never been allowed to threaten the ruling Socialist Party's hold on the state,[39] or the cozy system of rural clientelism on which its power ultimately rests.[40] Botswana's political elites have deservedly enjoyed a better reputation for integrity and effective management of the development process.[41] But the country suffers from persistent social inequalities, weak civic organizations, and paternalism in state–society relations.[42] The electoral process has never led to the parliamentary defeat of the ruling party, so that at least one criterion of a consolidated democracy, the electoral alternation of leaders, remains unfulfilled. In sum, the continent's multiparty past points to a future for Africa of weakly institutionalized democracies. Among African countries by early 1996, only Mauritius and Bénin had met the minimal two-turnover test for democratic consolidation.

THE MILITARY

The first challenge for newly democratic regimes is to survive; only then does the possibility of consolidation arise. The role of the military is discussed first, because it poses the biggest and most immediate threat to the survival of young democracies. We argued in Chapter 6 that the trajectories and outcomes of African transitions were in large part a function of military interventions. This finding extends to the consolidation phase, given the military's unique and continuing institutional capacity to intervene with force in politics. We speculate that the role of the military in the *ancien régime* will condition its ongoing role.

Other analysts have posited that lasting transitions from military rule are hard to secure because the military retains the capacity to step back into politics long after returning to the barracks.[43] In the absence of assistance from the armed

forces, it is difficult to see how ousted authoritarian rulers can regain power unless legally through the ballot box. The initial decision of African militaries to
intervene in politics has been linked to a wide variety of factors, including corporate group interests, the idiosyncrasies of individual officers, the fragmentation
of party politics, and ethnic conflict.[44] The military is changed by its involvement in politics, however; a first intervention politicizes it and gives it a taste of
power and its prerogatives that officers may find difficult to surrender. Having
withdrawn, elements within the military sooner or later will develop a nostalgia
for the power they once wielded. A number of cross-country studies confirm that
the probability of a military coup is considerably enhanced by a past history of
them.[45] We have shown that the great majority of African states in which the democratization process was blocked or flawed between 1990 and 1994 are now or
were in the past ruled by military regimes.[46] By this logic, the military coups
that toppled the democratic government in Burundi in 1993 and in Niger in
1996 should be understood as part of a tradition of military intervention in the
politics of that country. The other new democracies in which there have been at
least two military coups in the past are Bénin, Congo, Central African Republic,
and Mali; all else being equal, they are all presumably at greatest risk.

The military's position in the neopatrimonial order can account for the decision to intervene during and after the transition. In the first place, the armed
forces often came to occupy a privileged position within the *ancien régime.* To keep
the soldiers content and under some semblance of civilian control, rulers granted to individual officers and the military units a generous array of perks, privileges, and rewards, including access to rents and commercial ventures. Transitions from authoritarian rule threaten these benefits, not only because the greater
transparency of a democratic regime may lead to pressures for the suspension of
privileges but also because the military must negotiate with a new and usually
less sympathetic political elite. In sum, the threat of losing various material benefits remains a powerful motive for intervention.[47]

The importance of military privileges varies in direct proportion to the importance of the role the armed forces played in the previous regime. The more
that a ruler relied on coercion, the higher price the military exacted for its support. The size of the official military budget was often a poor guide to the full
scope of the favors extended to a small number of key officers or to a reliable presidential guard. In Zambia in the late 1980s, for instance, the army received the
highest proportion of the national budget of any African country at peace, equivalent to over 3 percent of the GDP; at the same time, it did not play a significant part in Kaunda's system of personal rule, and consistently remained outside
of political life.[48] In Niger, on the other hand, the military was deeply involved
in national politics, to the enormous material benefit of individual officers, but
the military as a whole was starved of resources, with a budgetary allocation
under 1 percent of the GDP. Indeed, the threat of the military reintervention actually came to pass when president Ousmane was ousted at gunpoint in January
1996. This latest in a string of military coups in Niger was apparently motivat-

ed by army officer perceptions that civilian leaders, deadlocked in disputes between a weak presidency and a fragmented parliament, were unable to end decisively a Taureg secessionist movement in the north. In the past, there was no clear correlation between military intervention and the size of the military budget, and there is no reason to believe that will change after the transition.[49] In this regard, the Chiluba government was probably wise to resist donor and backbench pressures to reduce the military's generous budgetary allocations.[50] The risk of military intervention is most likely to increase when elected governments attempt to wean senior officers from the patrimonial benefits to which they have become accustomed.

In addition, whether the military forces are politically close to the old ruler influences their actions during and after the transition. In Cameroon, for instance, Paul Biya stacked the army with fellow Beti, and Kenya's army is increasingly commanded by Kalenjin.[51] These kinds of linkages enormously complicate the transition and its aftermath, for the military will not countenance threats to their patron; it is no accident that the cases in which the military intervened actively to protect the incumbent all fit this pattern. In cases in which a democratic transition occurred despite the close attachment of senior officers to the incumbent and his clique – notably in Niger and Central African Republic – a military-led end to democratic rule is probably likelier. Perhaps the most intractable cases involve ethnically divided countries in which the military has come to be clearly dominated by an ethnic minority, as was the case of the Tutsis in Burundi. There, Buyoya's managed transition and loss in a competitive election was perceived as a betrayal by many of his fellow officers. Democratization threatened not only the dominance of the minority Tutsis but also the military's patrimonial interests, which had been cemented over years of Tutsi dominance.

The ability of civilian institutions to assert control over the military also determines whether coups will lead to democratic reversal. Most notably in eastern and southern Africa, civilian strongmen have managed to keep the military under control with a neopatrimonial mixture of rewards, deprivations, and repression. To some extent democratic governments will benefit from such precedents, but they need to develop democratic mechanisms to assert a similar authority. These include civilian oversight of the military through a defense ministry, discretion over the defense budget, and senior promotions and professional training.[52] These moves are best initiated as soon as possible after the transition during the government's honeymoon. For example, in Bénin, as early as 1990, the government pushed through a reorganization of the discredited armed forces and devolved many of its political mobilization functions to civilian agencies. Partly as a result of these reforms, a coup attempt by a small group of pro-Kérékou officers in August 1992 was easily quashed.[53] One wonders how far similar efforts could have proceeded in Mali, where, after toppling the strongman, the military emerged from the transition with its reputation enhanced and prerogatives intact. Each difficulty of the civilian government in its first several years in power led to rumors in Bamako of the charismatic Lt. Col. Touré's imminent return to politics.

STATE INSTITUTIONS

The primary determinant of civilian control of the military – and the ability to forestall coups – is almost certainly the legitimacy, representativeness, and organizational strength of civilian regimes. We thus turn attention to the regimes' institutions. The more effective the permanent state apparatus, the greater its capacity to discipline the political class's patrimonial behavior and resist the latter's efforts to alter political rules to suit its own needs. Three institutions are particularly important: the legislature, the judiciary, and the civil service, all of which can potentially promote the accountability of the chief political executive. All three institutions encourage transparency in the affairs of state and thus undermine neopatrimonial practices, which thrive on its absence.

The Legislature

Some literature argues that stable democracies are more likely to last in parliamentary regimes than presidential ones.[54] Stepan and Skach conclude, for example, that "parliamentarianism is a more supportive constitutional framework" because of "its greater propensity for governments to have majorities to implement their programs; ... and its greater facility for removing a chief executive who does so; (and) its lower susceptibility to military coup."[55] This is a worrisome thesis in the African context, since all the new democratic regimes in Africa have adopted some form of presidentialism, and the only fully parliamentary regimes are Botswana, Lesotho, and Mauritius. But is the record as clear as the proponents of parliamentarianism imply? Shin notes that presidential democracies have fared considerably better in lower- than in higher-income countries, concluding that it is difficult to sustain the argument that parliamentary constitutions are more conducive to stable democracy.[56]

In Africa, presidential dominance was long overwhelming, and the weakening of the executive branch of government was an objective of the prodemocracy forces in every new constitution promulgated in the 1990s. To understand the prospects for strong legislatures, we focus on the patterns of executive-legislative relations in the 1970s and 1980s. Although presidentialism in Africa has often been antidemocratic, it has also fostered political stability.

The move toward presidential regimes in the years after independence followed one of two paths.[57] In a first category of countries, initial party fragmentation resulted in legislative instability, to which military intervention typically put an end. Military rule then eventually evolved to some form of presidentialism with a very weak or nonexistent legislature. Among the countries in this category, Bénin and Congo underwent democratic transitions in the early 1990s. In their second democratic experiments, neither of these countries chose a parliamentary constitution, preferring instead to maintain some form of presidentialism, but both initially sought to enhance the power of the legislature. For instance, Bénin's National Assembly was granted added constitutional prerogatives, including the power to make line-item modifications in the budget that the executive branch now has to submit for ratification.[58] Here, a reinvigorated parliament began to balance executive power, at least on the margins. More commonly, however, ethnic fragmentation quickly began to dominate the political process and weaken the democratic order. Within two years, Lissouba of Congo lost his working legislative majority, which was ravaged by ethnic disputes and personality-driven factionalism. In such conflictual polities, parliamentary rule was not a solution, because institutional effectiveness fell prey to political polarization and partisan pressures.[59]

In a second category of countries, the prospects for effective legislatures seemed better after the transition. In these states, strong party dominance after independence resulted in the progressive emergence of a single hegemonic party whose leader soon introduced some form of personal rule in the guise of presidentialism. These states enjoyed longer stretches of civilian rule, dominated by strong executives, with stable albeit extremely subservient legislatures. Presidents typically controlled backbenchers through a mixture of intimidation and clientelism. Several of these states also underwent transitions in the early 1990s, including Mali, Niger, Malawi, and Zambia. Here, too, the democratization process sought to strengthen the legislative branch and provide it with capacity to check the executive.

The prospects for effective legislatures seem better in these countries; legislative traditions were developed in the course of long stints of single-party civilian rule. The significant intraparty competition that existed in single party regimes like Kenya, Zambia, and Côte d'Ivoire have in part been transferred to a multiparty context. A smaller number of parties typically makes for a less chaotic legislative process and more stable presidential majorities.[60] Strikingly, however, it must be admitted that in each of these countries new legislatures have generally been unable to assert their institutional prerogatives. Either the president does not enjoy a stable working majority in the national assembly, as is the case for Konaré in an increasingly polarized environment in Mali; in a semipresidential system inspired by France's Fifth Republic, the president has had to rule by decree to prevent total government paralysis.[61] Or alternatively the president is essentially able to coopt the legislature within the context of clientelist relations to prevent it from playing an effective independent oversight role, as is the case in Gabon, Malawi, Côte d'Ivoire, and Zambia. In Zambia, for example, one third of the MMD members of parliament accepted positions with the government, typically as deputy ministers. In bestowing lucrative favors on backbenchers to keep them quiet, Chiluba was merely resuming a strategy his presidential predecessor had long perfected.

In sum, the prospects for effective legislatures that are able to monitor the executive and check the abuses of executive prerogatives appear to be better in countries in which a legislative tradition was built in the authoritarian *ancien régime*. The evident weakness of even these legislatures suggests that they will take time to develop as democratic institutions, but they will contribute to the stability of the new democracies, albeit within the context of age-old patrimoni-

al traditions. In this sense, they can be distinguished from parliaments in countries lacking legislative traditions in which polarization and party fragmentation
risk contributing to political instability and may even undermine the survival of
democratic politics.

The Judiciary

The judiciary is critical to the survival of the civil and political rights that
are the transition's most tangible gains. For example, it is a potential guarantor
of freedoms of association and expression if these come under assault. More generally, the judiciary disciplines and checks the executive by promoting the rule
of law and championing public accountability and transparency. Most directly, a
strong judiciary can play a critical role in the consolidation of democracy by
counteracting the presidential tendency to manipulate political rules for short-
term advantage. The judiciary may even arbitrate constitutional disputes between the executive branch and the legislature. For instance, President Soglo's refusal to accept the modifications to his budget made by Bénin's National
Assembly in mid-1994 led the latter to take the matter to the constitutional
court for a ruling. That body's decision to side with the legislature was a step in
the right direction for Béninois democracy.[62]

Under what circumstances will the judiciary offer such resistance? Again, we
speculate that the strength of the judiciary is largely tributary of its status at the
time of the transition. The organizational strength and independence of the judiciary varied across African states, as a function of professional norms, conditions of service, and the degree to which the executive branch had intimidated
and coopted the legal system over time. In some countries, the judiciary had been
thoroughly compromised by its subordination to executive power. In the most
personalized regimes, the courts were underfunded, legal training neglected, and
the profession of magistrate disregarded; in the worst, judgeships were prebendal sinecures handed out by the president with scant regard for legal expertise.
In Zaire, the court system was unambiguously subordinated to the prefect and
the local power elite, and judges were picked for their loyalty to Mobutu himself.[63] Only in situations where the judiciary was professionalized and the executive tolerant – as happened intermittently during civilian regimes in Ghana and
Sudan – did the judiciary begin to enjoy autonomy in the day-to-day running of
the legal system.

It is almost inevitable that in the first years of a young democracy, constitutional or legal disputes will arise on which the judiciary is asked to adjudicate.
To the extent that these are partisan disputes, the judiciary risks losing legitimacy in the process. This happened in Nigeria's Second Republic, for instance,
when the judiciary was repeatedly asked to settle electoral disputes between the
political parties.[64] The weakness of certain judges and the honest lapses in judgment of others endangered the integrity and credibility of the entire judicial
branch. Because such disputes are really struggles over the rules of the political
game, legal decisions are likely to have significant impact on the quality of

democracy. To emerge unscathed, the judiciary needs individual judges of national stature, with a reputation of integrity, backed by the legal establishment. No African bench escaped the years of authoritarian rule without some kind of accommodation and compromise with the executive, but judicial independence is more likely if the rule of law was allowed to operate before the transition.

The Civil Service

The role of the public bureaucracy in protecting democracy is perhaps less obvious. A capable civil service, after all, reinforces the power of the executive, and in other regions of the world, the civil service was an integral part of the bureaucratic-authoritarian coalition that undermined democracy.[65] We nonetheless argue that a strong state administration promotes democracy by strengthening the rule of law, by establishing impartial bureaucratic processes, and by undermining the arbitrary logic of personal power. There can be no executive accountability or transparency of policy making in the absence of information-based administration of state affairs. It is hard to see how nominally democratic governments in Congo or the Central African Republic will be able to avoid arbitrary governance given the near-total absence of bureaucratic capability within the central state apparatus. How can the judiciary or the legislature control the executive, if it had the inclination, when the state lacks the ability to characterize its own finances with any precision?[66]

In Africa, the civil service has been in an extremely ambiguous position throughout the postcolonial period. The civil service was privileged by authoritarian rule; at least until the mid-1980s, it was the main beneficiary of economic policies that promoted cheap food and overvalued exchange rates.[67] As patronage drove leaders to expand its ranks, it consumed ever-increasing shares of the national budget. Military governments in countries like Ghana and Nigeria, moreover, made prominent use of senior civil servants to manage the state apparatus.[68] Bienen shows how the Kenyatta regime in Kenya relied on the civil service to ensure social control and limit political participation.[69]

At the same time and despite the material interests of individual officials, the civil service as a whole was disempowered by neopatrimonial rulers who tended to undermine bureaucratic rationality in favor of personalized exchange. In many African states, little decision-making power was devolved to the most senior ranks of the civil service, as executives zealously centralized decisions and left for the former only limited implementation discretion. Civil servants resented the many parallel power structures that emanated from the president's own clientelist networks or the single party, and they undermined the effectiveness of the state apparatus. They felt frustrated by the absence of institutionalization and bureaucratic rationality.

At independence, the civil service contained few well-trained African administrators but, over time, fueled by donor support for training, the level of skills available to the civil service rose appreciably. A core of relatively professionalized and ambitious civil servants began to emerge across countries, albeit to varying degrees. They accommodated themselves to the realities of neopatrimonial rule, even benefited from them, but at the same time bridled at many of its features and deficiencies. In particular, the higher levels of the civil service were disheartened by the compression of public sector salaries during the 1970s and 1980s, made inevitable by the economic crisis and the government's own patronage policies. In the Franc Zone, salary levels were somewhat protected by low inflation, even if financially strapped governments stopped paying them regularly; in the other countries, it was not unusual for senior civil servants to have lost 90 percent of their real purchasing power over the course of the 1970s and 1980s.[70]

In sum, it should not be surprising that the civil service was typically a part of the alliance that promoted democratization or that in many countries the transition served to noticeably empower its technocratic core. Because the transition ushered in less personalized rule, it reinforced the power of existing bureaucratic structures, particularly in countries like Zambia and Bénin, where neopatrimonial rule had been combined with single-party control. There, the end of the single party's interference in decision making, coupled with the installation of more transparent, cabinet-driven government, sharply enhanced the power of ministerial staffs.[71]

Of course, the ability of the civil service to respond to new opportunities varies across countries and depends largely on its capacities and cohesiveness at the end of the transition. Some civil services were devastated by the economic crisis of the 1980s, suffering a tremendous erosion of their most skilled staff and a generalized loss of morale and discipline. Despite a small cadre of technocrats, they are unlikely to bring discipline to the state. In others, however, democratic empowerment could help the civil service make a difference. This is true for instance in Côte d'Ivoire, where, as Crook has convincingly argued, a fairly effective civil service has been developed within a neopatrimonial order.[72] Because state corruption was such a conspicuous characteristic of authoritarian rule, prodemocracy forces emphasized the need to strengthen instruments of administrative control, for instance the office of the auditor general, or the "inspection générale" in the francophone states.

The press and donor pressures can help to legitimate these technocratic controls on the state. In Kenya, revelations of high-level corruption in the 1994 annual report of the auditor general, generously advertised by the press, were deeply embarrassing to the state elite. That the Moi regime has never been able to fully muzzle such reports is a tribute both to the courageous civil servants and journalists who risk their careers to pursue these investigations and to long-standing professional traditions within the Kenyan civil service.[73] Thus, in a handful of posttransition countries, a relatively effective bureaucracy will contribute to internal discipline within the state and impede executive abuses by promoting rule-based governance. Ultimately, the extent to which the civil service is a force for democratic stability rather than merely a strong executive will depend on the presence of other forces promoting transparency and accountability, such as the press and the legislature.

POLITICAL SOCIETY

Political parties play a critical role in founding elections and in subsequent democratic politics. The key democratic function of parties is the aggregation and representation of individual interests; they give voice to people's grievances and channel political demands upward to the legislature. As Dix has noted, "Parties are typically major vehicles for the recruitment of political leadership, the structuring of electoral choice and peaceable political competition, and the framing of policy alternatives."[74] In turn, political parties communicate and legitimate the system's political processes back to the local level. Moreover, opposition parties espouse the accountability of those in power and provide choice to citizens.[75] Thus, the stability and long-term institutionalization of democratic politics in no small part depends on the ability of parties to meet these tasks. Two sets of factors are involved: first, the organizational strength and resource base of parties themselves and, second, the nature and dynamics of the party system that existed at the time of the transition. We look at each in turn.

The congenital weakness of African political parties was a major theme of the early literature on postcolonial politics.[76] Apart from dominant ruling monopolies in a few countries, political parties were often little more than collections of notables held together by clientelism and the promise of access to state resources; they were rarely effective at the grassroots and often lacked significant mobilizational capacity. These same features were very much in evidence in the majority of parties that appeared in the early 1990s. Indeed, the resurrection of many of the same parties that had competed for power in the early 1960s, but then more or less disappeared, was striking. In fact, they were often headed by the same leaders as before or by their relatives. There were other similarities. Once again, most party activity was in the capital and in a handful of regional centers. Parties were differentiated less by ideology or programmatic concerns than by the narrow interests of clientelist networks, typically organized around an individual. Beyond the imperative to criticize corruption, oust the dictator, and bring about democratic rule, founding elections were striking for the absence of policy debates. And the low election participation rates in founding elections in some African states were partly due to the limited capacity of parties to get out the vote.

Before 1989, political parties had often been based on ethnoregional loyalties, commonly leading to considerable party fragmentation. Few parties demonstrated the ability to gain a national constituency rather than a regional one, resulting in highly divided legislatures, in which polarization and parliamentary instability both were fueled by ethnic conflict and were its cause.[77]

What kind of party systems emerged from legislative elections held between 1990 and 1994? In fact, fragmentation of the party system was less problematic than might have been feared. True, a bewildering number of parties competed in elections, but a much smaller proportion actually won legislative seats. The extent of party fragmentation in the new African parliaments was little different from that in many European democracies. Out of 28 legislative elections examined, 17 resulted in parliaments with 4 or fewer parties represented, while 6 countries witnessed the election of 10 parties or more. Only four founding elections – in Bénin, Central African Republic, Malawi, and Niger – gave rise to governments that lacked parliamentary majorities. In all other cases, a majority party emerged that did not require a coalition partner in order to govern, though in South Africa, the majority ANC was temporarily bound by previous agreement to bring its opponents into a transitional government of national unity.[78] In sum, the danger of parliamentary instability was avoided in most African transitions.

On the other hand, many majority parties were little more than coalitions of smaller parties or party factions. In Mali, for example, the ADEMA grouping won 76 of the 116 seats contested in the March 1992 elections. Because nine other parties won seats and none had more than nine seats, ADEMA's majority would be thought to be secure. Yet, ADEMA itself was a loose coalition of small parties that had united to fight the Traoré regime.[79] Soon after the election, the coalition began to disintegrate, with the second biggest party, the PRMD, leaving in November 1993. Konaré's ability to push through his legislative agenda was thereby highly compromised. Similar points could be made about ruling parties in Madagascar, Niger, Bénin, and even Zambia, where the MMD suffered repeated defections following its electoral triumph.

Comparing parties and party systems across the new democracies does not lead us to note striking national differences. It is tempting to say that the reemergence of old parties in certain countries suggests the presence of resilient party traditions there, but these parties have exhibited little mobilizational or programmatic maturity in the 1990s. Their persistence seems to owe as much to the longevity of informal personal and lineage-based clientelist networks than to an organizational heritage. Indeed, the weakness of parties as organizations is a striking characteristic of almost all these transitions and bodes poorly for the consolidation of democracy, because elsewhere the weakness of parties has been associated with parliamentary instability, the persistence of clientelist politics, and an antidemocratic political culture.[80]

One striking distinction, however, concerns the capacity of varying single parties to survive and flourish under unfamiliar multiparty conditions. Thus, the PDCI in Côte d'Ivoire, the PS in Sénégal, and the CCM in Tanzania have emerged from ballot tests as relatively effective electoral instruments, whereas the UNIP in Zambia, the MCP in Malawi, and the RPDC in Cameroon were revealed to be exhausted and lacking popular legitimacy outside of a narrow ethnic base. Kenya's KANU and Gabon's PDG proved to be in an intermediate category, saved largely by a divided opposition.

Comparing the current global democratization wave with the last one, which followed World War II, O'Donnell notes that in Japan, Germany, and Italy the same party held power for more than 20 years.[81] In comparison, victories in more recent founding elections seem to have condemned winning parties to subsequent virtual eclipse in Spain, Portugal, Greece, Argentina, Bolivia, Brazil, Ecuador, Peru, Uruguay, Korea, and the Philippines. He attributes this latter difference to unfavorable economic and international environments. It is striking, however, that almost all these cases except the Philippines were elite-managed transitions. In Spain or Brazil, for example, the first elected governments were close to the previous regime and had benefited from various advantages, not the least of which was that the opposition had been muzzled for so long. Their disappearance in subsequent elections was as much a sign of a maturation process as it was of democratic instability.

It is too early to tell which pattern will develop in Africa. There is evidence from countries such as Congo, Madagascar, Malawi, and Mali of weak parliamentary governments that may well fail to retain power in the second elections, so brittle and shifting do their governing coalitions appear. On the other hand, in more than one third of founding elections, winning parties secured dominance by controlling more than 67 percent of assembly seats, which gave them unencumbered capacity to pass legislation and to amend constitutions. Moreover, evidence has begun to accumulate that dominant parties can survive a second round of competitive elections especially in situations where the dynamics of regime transition had been driven by cohesive opposition movements (see Chapter 6). For example, in Namibia, SWAPO increased its majority in the legislative elections of December 1994 (from 41 to 53 of the 72 legislative seats available), and in Côte d'Ivoire, PDCI again won big in November 1995, though its majority slipped slightly (from 163 to 147 of the 175 available parliamentary seats). One observer delegation ruled these elections in Côte d'Ivoire as more open than either the general elections of 1990 or the presidential poll of October 1995, the latter of which was boycotted by the opposition.[82] In South Africa and Zambia dominant parties show every prospect of winning second elections, perhaps even with increased majorities. These countries are most prone to the emergence of *big-man democracy,* in which ruling parties again make clientelist use of state resources to dominate electoral politics.[83] If dominant parties once more come to prevent political alternation at the polls, democratic rule will not even reach the minimal threshold for consolidation.

CIVIL SOCIETY

We showed earlier that the density of associational life varied across African countries and that civic groups were instrumental in transitions (see Chapter 4). The stronger and more diverse these institutions were, the likelier that transitions would be initiated by protest. After the transition, the fabric and organizational diversity of civil society is also likely to condition the success of democratic politics, albeit in fresh ways.

Religious groups, labor and professional associations, human rights groups, and the media play intermediary roles between state and citizen, provide public arenas for political participation, and promote the accountability of the political class.[84] Parties are likely to dominate political life during electoral periods, and civic associations to take a back seat. But between elections, particularly in countries with weak parties, these organizations can influence national politics and condition the quality of public life, each in its own way. Professional groups and unions defend the interests of segments of the population rather than general principles of national governance. They may well be less involved in national politics after the transition, or they may militate only on behalf of their members. At the same time, labor unions in particular have greater mobilizational capacity than other groups do and are more likely to be feared by the government, given their ability to orchestrate disruption.[85]

By contrast, churches and human rights organizations are more likely to defend the democratic order per se and serve as the conscience of the nation. But these organizations typically possess less mobilizational capacity and find it harder to take political positions because their legitimacy is derived from a reputation for nonpartisanship. Finally, the independent media are composed of for-profit businesses. They worry at least as much about their ability to keep selling newspapers and advertising space as about protecting the constitution. What the media lack in capacity to mobilize constituencies, however, they make up in their ability to form public opinion.

The parts these groups play during the consolidation phase will be determined by a number of factors. A primary one, of course, is their organizational strength and resource base coming out of the authoritarian era. The general pattern is that the richer and more industrialized states have a wider array of better organized groups. Nonetheless, most of these groups are typically weak in Africa, both because they were long repressed by authoritarian rule and because of the size and structure of national economies. Although their memberships and organizational skills increased impressively during the transition, they typically need time to gain experience.

The press provides a good example. As we have seen in previous chapters, the role of the independent press in mobilizing and sustaining protest should not be underestimated. At the same time, in most countries, the media are hurt by the paltry purchasing power of consumers, low levels of literacy, and an assortment of practical problems. A survey of the print press in Bénin noted that the cost of a newspaper is roughly equivalent to that of a good meal and so is accessible only to a relatively small proportion of the urban population.[86] In the countryside, poor education and communications ensure an exceedingly small readership: A survey of the cocoa belt of Cameroon in 1994 revealed that only 0.2 percent of households read newspapers on a regular basis, compared to 44 percent that listened to the radio and 5 percent that watched television.[87] The latter two remain under governmental monopoly in the overwhelming majority of countries. Once the excitement of the transition wears off, few newspapers can claim sales above 10,000 per issue. Many of the publications that popped up in the "political enthusiasm" of 1990 have since disappeared, and the surviving handful maintain a precarious existence.

In general, the institutions of civil society perform less well in the early stages of democratic consolidation than they do during transition. The reason lies in the deflation of popular political energy in the transition's aftermath. If a prodemocracy movement wins power, civic leaders are drawn into official positions in government and party hierarchies, thereby weakening voluntary organizations. Although such leaders are now poised to hold the political executive accountable, they are constrained from doing so by governmental norms of collective responsibility and by the economic inducements of office. Within civil society, political factions that united around the common goal of ejecting an authoritarian leader later rediscover differences of interest that can divide and incapacitate the voluntary sector. Among citizens, the intense levels of political engagement that were whipped up during the campaigns for founding elections cannot be sustained under normal conditions. Indeed, newly elected political elites deliberately seek to reduce the ebullience of their followers and dampen their often unrealistic expectations of immediate improvements in the conditions of life. Especially in the poorest countries, many of the people who became politically active during the transition choose to withdraw into the household realm in order to address pressing and neglected needs of economic survival.

In sum, the conclusion of a political transition can have demobilizing consequences for civil society. The reinvigoration of this sector as a force for democratic governance becomes a major item on the agenda for consolidation. Even so, a word of caution is in order. Following Robert Putnam,[88] the recent literature has sometimes assumed a simple positive correlation between the strength of associational life and the success of democratic government.[89] In fact, this positive link is far from certain, for associational groups may make demands on the state that it is incapable of processing, potentially leading to either repression or regime instability.

TRANSITION LEGACIES

So far, we have developed a chain of reasoning in which political institutions have powerful structuring effects on individual agency. It is important to understand, however, that political outcomes are subject to the historical evolution of the transitions themselves. Thus, in this final section, we focus on the mode of transition.[90] We seek to show that the choices and dynamics of transitions set precedents and paths, establish recurrent patterns of behavior, and shape the context for the survival and consolidation of political regimes.

THE LENGTH OF THE TRANSITION

Regime transitions in Africa occurred relatively swiftly, shortening opportunities for political learning and institution building. Some analysts argue that long transitions are more likely be successful in political terms because incremental processes favor accommodation by political elites.[91] And we have argued that rapid transition reduces the prospects that democratic institutions can take root.

But even protracted transitions can be problematic when they signal the presence of an intransigent strongman with access to sufficient resources to outlast and outmaneuver his opponents. A case in point is Zaire, where the transition was stretched over at least half a decade. Mobutu used personal control over the country's export revenues to feign political reform, buy off fragments of the army and the opposition, ingratiate himself with donors, and generally dissemble in order to hold onto office. Meanwhile in Nigeria, Cameroon, and Gabon the opposition had little option but to retreat in the face of strongmen who, bolstered in their grip on power by reliable flows of oil revenues, were determined to dig in for the long haul.

A logic favoring shorter transitions also holds in economic terms, at least for Africa. The economic cost of the transition varies as a direct function of the length of the transition, with lengthier transitions prolonging political uncertainty and confusion and hindering private investment and economic management. Desperate governments that were fighting for their political lives in election campaigns were not inclined to worry about fiscal prudence. Instead, several governments in their final months restored cuts in food subsidies, pumped up public spending (and promises thereof), and accorded large pay increases to civil servants.

The length of time during which there was no effective government is also critically important. In Zambia, the transfer of political power was swift and smooth, and economic management suffered little. At the other extreme, the transition in Madagascar was marked by an extended period of confusion and uncertainty: A full 22 months went by between the date that Ratsiraka agreed to figurehead status and the installation of a democratically elected government under President Zafy. The interregnum was devastating to the economy, with the breakdown of fiscal discipline and increases in corruption by government officials being added to the mess the democratic government would inherit. In several countries, the economy's evolution had led the IMF to put the country "off track," making it ineligible for multilateral assistance; long months of negotiation by the new government were necessary to resume the flow of resources. And by the time democratic governments were in place and ready to address complicated economic problems, their honeymoon was virtually over, and populations were ready to blame them for austerity measures.

Economic management will pose perennial problems for governments in Africa, because neopatrimonial pressures will result in slow economic growth and the generation of policy inefficiencies and recurrent fiscal crises. Nonetheless, our argument here is that transition dynamics will at least in part determine whether democratic governments get a good start on economic policy making, thus significantly enhancing their survival chances. If it is true that governments are best able to undertake economic reform early in their tenure, then long transitions may well prove to constitute a significant handicap for the survival of certain new democracies.[92] By the time a new government grasps the reins of power, the economic crisis will have spun out of control.

UNPACTED TRANSITIONS

A distinctive characteristic of democratic transitions in Africa, as compared with other world regions, is that most were initiated from below. To be sure, African strongmen sought to closely manage the transition process once it became inevitable, but incumbent rulers rarely embarked on change on their own accord or at the behest of a liberalizing impulse from within elite ranks. Instead, they tended to open up involuntarily in a more or less alarmed reaction to mass political protests. Consistent with this kind of start, transitions in Africa usually unfolded through confrontation: Outsiders escalated protest and insiders tried repression, making grudging concessions only under duress. Indeed, African countries usually embarked on founding elections in a context in which the participants could barely agree on electoral ground rules and in which the future division of power and spoils was highly uncertain.

Under these circumstances, regime transitions in Africa were rarely accompanied by bargaining or compromise; old regimes either survived largely intact or were abruptly displaced in sweeping opposition victories. This mode of regime transition offered few opportunities for participants to nurture the democratic art of give-and-take. Born out of polarized conflicts, new regimes were installed in a winner-take-all atmosphere in which the victors not only monopolized spoils but sometimes sought to punish the losers. In some cases, the search for retribution seemed justified, as when the incoming governments of Ethiopia and Rwanda convened tribunals to prosecute war criminals and the government of Malawi charged Banda and his cronies with the murder of political opponents. In other cases, however, the harassment of defeated strongmen seemed merely vindictive. In Zambia, for example, the new MMD government accused Kaunda of misappropriating public funds but never charged him with any crime, instead seeking to reduce his pension allowances as a former head of state. Other examples abounded of persistent political polarization. In Congo, President Lissouba, faced with irresolvable struggles within the ruling coalition over the allocation of cabinet posts, dissolved the national assembly and called for fresh elections. And throughout Africa the new leaders entered confrontational relationships with the free (and often wildly irresponsible) press, filing libel proceedings against journalists (à la Soglo in Bénin) or banning publications (as did Moi in Kenya).

We have remarked earlier on South Africa's exceptionalism, noting that its pacted transition was distinctly non-African. This mode of transition embodied distinct advantages for consolidation, imparting precedents of political compromise to the proceedings of the new regime. Mandela's wise appeals for moderation on all sides reinforced the prospects that negotiated solutions could be found to deep political conflicts. To be sure, his policy of national reconciliation will be

sorely tested as the government grapples with major challenges such as the allocation of power under a new constitution, the redistribution of economic assets
and incomes, and the prosecution of unrepentant military officials from the old
regime. But democratic procedures first established during the transition will
prove a valuable resource in resolving these challenges during the phase of regime
consolidation.

By contrast, unpacted transitions in the rest of Africa impair the prospects
for democratic survival and consolidation, a prediction consistent with observations in the literature. Karl has suggested that "*no* stable political democracy has
resulted from regime transitions in which mass actors have gained control" and
Stepan agrees that "society-led upheavals *by themselves* are virtually incapable of
leading to redemocratization."[93] Initially, a sweeping opposition victory may
seem to create many new opportunities for regime reform, but especially where
the incoming government is based on a poorly organized social movement with
limited experience at operating representative political institutions, the transition will be followed by a power vacuum. This vacuum is most readily filled, not
by the emergence of new, alternative forms of governance, but by reversion to
habitual behaviors and tried-and-true institutions.

BIG MEN

In Africa, transitions often found their denouement in the emergence – or, more
commonly, the *re*emergence – of big men. Africa's new governments were often
composed of individuals who had collaborated with the previous regime in the
not so distant past and who possessed no viable representative organization of
their own.[94] Among the new presidents, Lissouba (Congo), Patassé (Central
African Republic), and Trovoada (São Tomé) had previously served as prime
ministers under old regimes in their respective countries. Konaré (Mali) and
Zafy (Madagascar) had earlier served in the cabinet of the regimes they helped
to depose, but otherwise they were relatively obscure politicians who could
hardly claim a wide popular following. Soglo of Bénin had spent the decade before his election as a midlevel aid official in Washington and did not even take
up leadership of a political party until 1994. The emergence of these leaders
during the transition was in no small part the result of chance; being in the
right place at the right time was crucial.

There was also method in the machinations of would-be leaders, however.
Aspirants to office used promises of future patronage rewards to cobble together
winning coalitions.[95] They mobilized outsiders from the patronage system with
the prospect that they would become insiders once a new government was installed. To finance insurgent electoral campaigns, challengers either had to rely
on their own resources or turn to private business interests. It is difficult to imagine that Moshood Abiola in Nigeria or Bakili Muluzi in Malawi would have
emerged to lead opposition movements or would have won elections had they not

been able to pay for their own leadership campaigns. Even when successful businessmen ran and lost – as did Kenneth Matiba in Kenya – his followers still seemed to be attracted by the candidate's personal riches and his reputation as a big spender. Frederick Chiluba, whose labor-based movement had only limited finances of its own, apparently relied heavily on campaign contributions from leading business figures who later reemerged as influential figures within the Zambian cabinet.

The high degree of continuity between the political personnel of the old and new regime and their reliance on private patronage during the transition have implications for the consolidation of democracy in Africa. First, neopatrimonial politics will persist after the transition; both by habit and by necessity, the victorious politicians will resort to clientelism to consolidate their own power. Over time, these tendencies may well intensify. Because security of office is more tenuous in regimes where leaders are chosen in elections, incumbents will quicken the quest for personal gain while they still have the opportunity to do so. Against this tendency, the human rights and good government activists in the prodemocracy coalition can initially temper the corruption and clientelism of the new government. But over time, these activists are eclipsed when they come into conflict with the leadership over issues of political expediency and are purged by old-style politicians.

These dynamics are well illustrated in the Congo. The endemic corruption of the Nguesso regime has apparently been little affected by democratization. Blancq estimates that perhaps more than 30 percent of the national budget disappeared into personal hands in 1993 and 1994. Indeed, the political class continues to actively prevent any improvements in the transparency and professionalism of the budgetary process in order to continue to benefit from complex networks of reward that feed off of the state's resources. The official government accounts for 1990 and 1991 had still not been presented to the legislature in 1994, and the working 1992 budget incorporated less than 30 percent of foreseeable spending for that year, the rest being spent "off budget" and essentially not accounted for.[96] The democratic transition has not altered that.

Moreover, the weakness of political parties and civic organizations will ensure the continuation of executive dominance. Prodemocracy forces often promised to circumscribe executive power, notably in such forums as the national conferences, but ultimately the constitutions that emerged made few concessions to the legislature and judiciary.[97] Had the transition forces included several well-organized parties with legislative experience, or nongovernmental groups seeking to balance executive power, the constitutional engineering might have resulted in stronger legislatures. As it was, the transition process reflected both the relative strength of executive branch actors and the predilection of the politicians who were about to inherit the state. Under these circumstances, new strongmen could easily emerge who will continue to manipulate political rules and exercise unchecked power to their own advantage.

In sum, the internal dynamics of regime transitions set new patterns that will shape Africa's democratic political order. In many countries, neopatrimonialism will live on, albeit within the context of nominally democratic politics. In Africa's big man democracies, public life will continue to be dominated by executive presidents and their networks of personal loyalty. The prospects for the deepening of democracy will hinge on the strength of the permanent state apparatus relative to the ability of nongovernmental actors to exert countervailing powers. At the same time, the survival of these new regimes is by no means assured; their fates are likely to be just as divergent as prior regime forms and transition trajectories. Despite the striking changes of the early 1990s, new democracies are likely to coexist alongside familiar and reinvented forms of governance. As is already evident, some new democracies will succumb to military takeover, others will survive under the tutelage of a dominant political party, while a few will sustain, and perhaps begin to consolidate, regimes bases on multiparty electoral institutions.

ENDNOTES

1. See Ebrima Sall, "Gambia: Le Coup d'Etat de Juillet 1994," in *l'Afrique Politique 1995: Le Meilleur, Le Pire et l'Incertain* (Paris: Karthala, 1995).
2. One required all candidates to be Zambian citizens whose parents were both Zambians by birth, and the other disqualified any candidate who had already served two full terms in office. These rule changes eliminated Kaunda, whose parents were from neighboring Malawi, and who had served 27 years in office when he was defeated by Frederick Chiluba in 1991. See "Kaunda the Komeback Kid," *The New African* (September 1995); and "Police Order Zambia's Kaunda to Report to Them," Reuters Information Service, 18 October 1995.
3. Samuel P. Huntington, *The Third Wave: Democratization in the Late Twentieth Century* (Normal: University of Oklahoma Press, 1991), p. 267.
4. Gisela Geisler, "Fair? What Has Fairness Got to Do With It? Vagaries of Election Observations and Democratic Standards," *Journal of Modern African Studies* 31 (1993): 613–37.
5. See Terry Lynn Karl, "Dilemmas of Democratization in Latin America," *Comparative Politics,* 23 (1990): 1–22. See also Michael Bratton, "Are Competitive Elections Enough?" *Africa Demos* (Atlanta, Ga.: The Carter Center) 3 (1995): 7–8.
6. See the essays in Scott Mainwaring, Guillermo O'Donnell, and J. Samuel Valenzuela, eds., *Issues in Democratic Consolidation: The New South American Democracies in Comparative Perspective* (Notre Dame: University of Notre Dame Press, 1992).
7. See Robert D. Putnam, *Making Democracy Work: Civic Traditions in Modern Italy* (Princeton: Princeton University Press, 1992); Larry Diamond, "Introduction," in *Political Culture and Democracy in Developing Countries,* ed. Diamond (Boulder, Colo.: Lynne Rienner, 1994).
8. For example, Nancy Bermeo, "Democracy and the Lessons of Dictatorship," *Comparative Politics* 24 (1992): 273–92.

9. Guillermo O'Donnell, "Transitions, Continuities and Paradoxes," in *Issues in Democratic Consolidation: The New South American Democracies in Comparative Perspective*, ed. Scott Mainwaring, Guillermo O'Donnell, and J. Samuel Valenzuela (Notre Dame: University of Notre Dame Press, 1992), pp. 18–23.

10. Guillermo O'Donnell, "Delegative Democracy," *Journal of Democracy* 5 (1994): 55–69.

11. See Adam Przeworski, "Democracy as a Contingent Outcome of Conflicts," in *Constitutionalism and Democracy*, ed. Jon Elster and Rune Slagstad (Cambridge: Cambridge University Press, 1988); and Guiseppe Di Palma, *To Craft Democracies: An Essay on Democratic Transitions* (Berkeley: University of California Press, 1990).

12. See Terry Lynn Karl, "The Hybrid Regimes of Latin America," *Journal of Democracy* 6 (1995): 72–86; Guillermo O'Donnell and Philippe C. Schmitter, *Transitions from Authoritarian Rule: Tentative Conclusions About Uncertain Democracies* (Baltimore: Johns Hopkins University Press, 1986); Robin Luckham, "Dilemmas of Military Disengagement and Democratization in Africa," *IDS Bulletin* (Sussex, England: Institute for Development Studies) 26 (1995): 49–61; and Linda Beck, "Patrimonial Democrats: Incremental Reform and the Obstacles to Consolidating Democracy in Sénégal" (paper presented at the annual meetings of the American Political Science Association, Chicago, September 1995). Such examples could be multiplied several times: David Collier and Steven Levitsky, "Democracy with Adjectives: Strategies for Avoiding Conceptual Stretching" (Berkeley: University of California, Department of Political Science, September 1995, unpublished paper) compiles over 500 such terms.

13. See Jonathan Fox, "The Difficult Transition from Clientelism to Citizenship: Lessons from Mexico," *World Politics* 46 (1994): 151–84.

14. This pessimism is shared by a number of analysts. See among others Jean François Bayart, "La Problématique de la Démocratie en Afrique: La Baule, et Puis Après?" *Politique Africaine* 43 (1991): 5–20; Samuel Decalo, "The Process, Prospects and Constraints of Democratization in Africa," *African Affairs* 91 (1991): 7–35; and Richard Jeffries, "The State, Structural Adjustment and Good Government in Africa," *Journal of Commonwealth and Comparative Politics* 31 (1993): 20–35.

15. For example, J. Samuel Valenzuela, "Democratic Consolidation in Post-transitional Settings: Notion, Process and Facilitating Conditions," in *Issues in Democratic Consolidation: The New South American Democracies in Comparative Perspective*, ed. Scott Mainwaring, Guillermo O'Donnell, and J. Samuel Valenzuela (Notre Dame: University of Notre Dame Press, 1992), p. 59.

16. This point is made by Geoff Bergen in his interesting case study of Sénégal's labor movement, "Unions in Sénégal: A Perspective on National Development in Africa" (Ph.D. dissertation, University of California at Los Angeles, 1994), p. 775.

17. For example, Mitchell Seligson, "Democratization in Latin America: the Current Cycle," in *Authoritarians and Democrats: Regime Transition in Latin America*, ed. James M. Malloy and Mitchell Seligson (Pittsburgh: University of Pittsburgh Press, 1987).

18. *Ibid.*, p. 7. Also see Huntington, *Third Wave*, pp. 59–60, 270–3.

19. Barrington Moore, *Social Origins of Dictatorship and Democracy: Lord and Peasant in the Making of the Modern World* (Boston: Beacon Press, 1966). For an overview of capitalism's evolution in Africa, see Paul Kennedy, *African Capitalism: The Struggle for Ascendancy* (Cambridge: Cambridge University Press, 1988).
20. See Dankwart A. Rustow, "Transitions to Democracy: Toward a Dynamic Model," *Comparative Politics* 2 (1970): 337–63.
21. See for example the essays in Donald Rothchild and Victor Olorunsola, *State versus Ethnic Claims: African Policy Dilemmas* (Boulder, Colo.: Westview), 152–71.
22. See Nelson Kasfir, "Explaining Ethnic Political Participation," *World Politics* 31 (1979): 345–64; Jean Louis Amselle and Elikia M'Bokolo, eds., *Au Coeur de l'Ethnie: Ethnies, Tribalisme et Etat en Afrique* (Paris: la Decouverte, 1985); Jean François Bayart, *l'Etat en Afrique* (Paris: Fayard, 1989), pp. 65–86 and passim; and Marina Ottaway, *Democratization and Ethnic Nationalism: African and Eastern European Experiences,* Policy Essay No. 14 (Washington, D.C.: Overseas Development Council, 1994).
23. This is argued in René Lemarchand, "Uncivil States and Civil Societies: How Illusion Became Reality," *Journal of Modern African Studies* 30 (1992): 177–91.
24. See Jan Kees Van Donge, "Kamuzu's Legacy: The Democratization of Malawi," *African Affairs* 94 (1995): 227–57.
25. Karl, "Dilemmas of Democratization."
26. Among a huge literature, see William Easterly and Ross Levine, "Africa's Growth Tragedy" (Washington, D.C.: World Bank, November 1994, unpublished manuscript); World Bank, *Sub-Saharan Africa: From Crisis to Sustainable Growth: A Long Term Perspective Study* (Washington, D.C.: World Bank, 1989); World Bank, *Adjustment in Africa: Reforms, Results, and the Road Ahead* (Washington, D.C.: World Bank, 1994); and Giovanni Andrea Cornia, Rolph van der Hoeven, and Thandika Mkandawire, eds., *Africa's Recovery in the 1990s: From Stagnation and Adjustment to Human Development* (New York: St. Martin's Press, 1993).
27. See Nicolas van de Walle, "Political Liberalization and Economic Reform in Africa," *World Development* 22 (1994).
28. See Thomas M. Callaghy and John Ravenhill, eds., *Hemmed In: Responses to Africa's Economic Decline* (New York: Columbia University Press, 1993).
29. Janine Aron, "The Institutional Foundations of Growth," in *Africa Now: People, Policies and Institutions,* ed. Stephen Ellis (London: James Currey, 1996), pp. 93–118.
30. See Lawrence Bouton, Christine Jones, and Miguel Kiguel, *Macroeconomic Reform and Growth in Africa,* World Bank Policy Research Working Paper, no. 1394 (Washington, D.C.: World Bank, December 1994), Table B2.
31. See Nicolas van de Walle and Dennis Chiwele, "Democratization and Economic Reform in Zambia," *MSU Working Papers on Political Reform in Africa,* No. 9 (East Lansing: Michigan State University, 1994), and Carol Graham, *Politics, Markets and the Poor: Comparative Studies in Sustaining Reform* (Washington, D.C.: Brookings, 1994).
32. See Richard Westebbe, "Structural Adjustment, Rent Seeking and Liberalization in Bénin," in *Economic Change and Political Liberalization in Sub-Saharan Africa,* ed. Jennifer A. Widner (Baltimore: Johns Hopkins Press, 1994), pp. 80–100;

and Chris Allen, "Restructuring an Authoritarian State: Democratic Renewal in Bénin," *Review of African Political Economy,* (1992): 43–58.

33. On Nigeria, see "Nigeria: About Turn," *Africa Confidential* 36 (20 January 1995).

34. On Zambia, the information comes from several confidential sources; on Côte d'Ivoire, see "Ivory Coast's Bedie Plays the Ethnic Card," *The Financial Times* (London), 12 September 1995.

35. See Gordon Cumming, "French Development Assistance to Africa: Towards a New Agenda?" *African Affairs* 94 (1995): 383–98; and "Agir Ici et Survie," in *l'Afrique à Biarritz: Mise en Examen de la Politique Française* (Paris: Karthala, 1995).

36. See Huntington, *Third Wave* (1991), p. 42. He notes that "twenty-three of the twenty-nine countries that democratized between 1974 and 1990 had some prior democratic experience. Only a small number of countries that were non-democratic in 1990 could claim such experience" (p. 295).

37. Larry Diamond, "Introduction," in *Democracy in Developing Countries: Volume Two, Africa,* ed. Larry Diamond, Juan J. Linz, and Seymour Martin Lipset (Boulder, Colo.: Lynne Reinner, 1988), p. 15.

38. On Nigeria, see in particular the masterful accounts of these dynamics in Richard Joseph, *Democracy and Prebendal Politics in Nigeria: The Rise and Fall of the Second Republic* (Cambridge: Cambridge University Press, 1987); and Larry Diamond, "Nigeria: Pluralism, Statism and the Struggle for Democracy," in *Democracy in Developing Countries: Volume Two, Africa,* ed. Larry Diamond, Juan J. Linz, and Seymour Martin Lipset (Boulder, Colo.: Lynne Rienner, 1988). On Ghana, see Naomi Chazan, "Ghana: Problems of Governance and the Emergence of Civil Society," in *Democracy in Developing Countries: Volume Two, Africa,* ed. Larry Diamond, Juan J. Linz, and Seymour Martin Lipset (Boulder, Colo.: Lynne Rienner, 1988).

39. This is true even if one does not accept completely Robert Fatton's argument that the democratization of Senegalese politics in the late 1970s was pursued precisely to allow the ruling class to consolidate its hold on power. Fatton, *The Making of a Liberal Democracy: Sénégal's Passive Revolution, 1975–1985* (Boulder, Colo.: Lynne Rienner, 1987). See also Linda Beck, "Patrimonial Democrats"; Babacar Kanté, "Sénégal's Empty Elections," *Journal of Democracy* 5 (1994): 96–107; and Leonardo Villalon "Democratizing a Quasi Democracy: The Senegalese Elections of 1993," *African Affairs* 93 (1994): 163–93.

40. In addition to Fatton's work, see Momar Diop and Mamadou Diouf, *Le Sénégal sous Abdou Diouf* (Paris: Khartala, 1990); Crawford Young and Babacar Kante, "Governance, Democracy, and the 1988 Senegalese Elections," in *Governance and Politics in Africa,* ed. Goran Hyden and Michael Bratton (Boulder, Colo.: Lynne Rienner, 1991); Christian Coulon, *Le Marabout et le Prince: Islam et Pouvoir au Sénégal* (Paris: Editions Pédone, 1981); Christian Coulon, "Sénégal: The Development and Fragility of Semidemocracy," in *Politics in Developing Countries: Comparing Experiences with Democracy,* ed. Larry Diamond, Juan J. Linz, and Seymour Martin Lipset (Boulder, Colo.: Lynne Rienner, 1990), 411–48; Catherine Boone, *Merchant Capital and the Roots of State Power in Sénégal, 1930–1985* (Cambridge: Cambridge University Press, 1992).

41. See John D. Holm, "Botswana: A Paternalistic Democracy," in *Democracy in Developing Countries: Volume Two, Africa,* ed. Larry Diamond, Juan J. Linz, and Seymour Martin Lipset (Boulder, Colo.: Lynne Rienner, 1988); Stephen John Stedman, ed., *Botswana: The Political Economy of Democratic Development* (Boulder, Colo.: Lynne Rienner, 1993); and Patrick Molutsi and John Holm, "Developing Democracy When Civil Society is Weak," *African Affairs* 89 (1990): 323–40.

42. The extensive literature on elections in Botswana includes useful contributions by John Holm and Patrick Molutsi, eds., *Democracy in Botswana* (Gaborone, Macmillan, 1989); James Polhemus, "Botswana Votes: Parties and Elections in an African Democracy," *Journal of Modern African Studies* 21 (1983): 397–430; and Roger Charlton, "The Politics of Elections in Botswana," *Africa* 63 (1993): 330–69.

43. For example, Huntington, *Third Wave,* p. 120; and Robin Luckham, "Dilemmas of Military Disengagement and Democratization in Africa," 49–61.

44. Among a large literature, see Samuel Decalo, *Coups and Army Rule In Africa* (New Haven: Yale University Press, 1976); Henry S. Bienen, *Armies and Parties in Africa* (New York: Africana Publishing, 1979); Henry S. Bienen, ed., *The Military Intervenes* (New York: Russell Sage, 1968); Nicole Ball, "The Military in Politics: Who Benefits and How," *World Development* 9 (1981): 569–82; Cynthia Enloe, *Ethnic Soldiers: State Security in Divided Societies* (Athens: University of Georgia Press, 1980); and Robin Luckham, "The Military, Militarization and Democratization in Africa: A Survey of Literatures and Issues," *African Studies Review* 37 (1994): 13–76.

45. See John B. Londregan and Keith T. Poole, "Poverty, the Coup Trap and the Seizure of Executive Power," *World Politics* (1990): 151–83; see also Adam Przewroski, Michael Alvarez, José Antonio Cheibub, and Fernando Limongi, "What Makes Democracies Endure?" *Journal of Democracy* 7 (1996): 39–55.

46. See Luckham, "Dilemmas of Military Disengagement."

47. Similar arguments are presented in Michael Chege, "The Military in the Transition to Democracy in Africa: Some Preliminary Observations," *CODESRIA Bulletin* 3 (Dakar: Council for the Development of Social Science Research in Africa, 1995): 13–16.

48. See "Money in the Wrong Pockets," *Southern African Economist* (March 1995): 13–14. The spending figures are taken from the United States Arms Control and Disarmament Agency, *Annual Yearbook* (Washington, D.C.: United States Arms Control and Disarmament Agency, 1994).

49. For example, Robert Jackman, "The Predictability of African Coups d'Etat," *American Political Science Review* 72 (1978): 1262–75.

50. "Money in the Wrong Pockets."

51. For example, "Kenya: A Presidential Army," *Africa Confidential* 36 (28 April 1995).

52. See Alfred Stepan, *Rethinking Military Politics: Brazil and the Southern Cone* (Princeton: Princeton University Press, 1988).

53. René Lemarchand, personal communication, 1 March 1993.

54. See Juan J. Linz, "The Perils of Presidentialism," *Journal of Democracy* 1 (Winter 1990): 51–69; Alfred Stepan and Cindy Skach, "Constitutional Frameworks and Democratic Consolidation: Parliamentarianism versus Presidentialism," *World Politics* 46 (1993): 1–22; and Scott Mainwaring, "Presi-

dentialism, Multipartism and Democracy: The Difficult Combination," *Comparative Political Studies* 26 (1993): 198–228.

55. Stepan and Skach, "Constitutional Frameworks," p. 22.

56. Doh Chull Shin, "On The Third Wave of Democratization: A Synthesis and Evaluation of Recent Theory and Research," *World Politics* 47 (1994): 135–70, 159.

57. The following discussion is in part inspired by Ruth Collier, *Regimes in Tropical Africa* (Berkeley: University of California Press, 1982).

58. See Curt D. Grimm, "Increasing Participation in the Context of African Political Liberalization: The Bénin Budget Crisis of 1994 and Its Implications for Donors" (Washington, D.C.: United States Agency for International Development (USAID), January 1995, unpublished paper).

59. Throughout 1993 and 1994, Congolese politics were slipping into endemic ethnically based violence. See Kenneth B. Noble, "Democracy Brings Turmoil in Congo," *New York Times,* 31 January 1994; and Patrick Quantin, "Congo: Les Origines Politiques de la Décomposition d'un Processus de Libéralisation (Aout 1992-Décembre 1993)," in *l'Afrique Politique: Vue sur la Démocratisation à Marée Basse,* ed. Patrick Quantin (Paris: Karthala, 1994), 167–90. A more optimistic assessment of this period is provided by John F. Clark, "Elections, Leadership and Democracy in Congo," *Africa Today* 41 (1994): 41–62.

60. Mali is an exception to this last statement, because 10 parties were represented in the first session of the democratic parliament in 1992.

61. In Mali, throughout 1994 and 1995, Konaré could not rely on his governing coalition ADEMA to back his policies. In Niger, Mahamane lost his parliamentary majority in January 1995 and had to "cohabit" with a prime minister from the former single party, the MNSD. On Niger, see "Niger: Unhappy Cohabitation," *Africa Confidential* 36 (25 August 1995).

62. Personal communication, René Lemarchand; see also Grimm, "Increasing Participation."

63. See Thomas M. Callaghy, *The State–Society Struggle: Zaire in Comparative Perspective* (New York: Columbia University Press, 1984), 361–6. Many similar points are made in Cyprian Fisiy's study of the application of rural tenure law in Cameroon; see *Power and Privilege in the Administration of Law: Land Law Reforms and Social Differentiation.* (Leiden, Netherlands: African Studies Center, 1992).

64. This is well described by Richard Joseph, *Democracy and Prebendal Politics,* pp. 175–80.

65. See the essays in David Collier, ed., *The New Authoritarianism in Latin America* (Princeton: Princeton University Press, 1979).

66. As the Economist Intelligence Unit country report on the Central African Republic dryly noted (Third Quarter, 1995, p. 24), regarding Prime Minister Gabriel Koyambounou's promises to fight corruption, restoring "competent government" would be a major challenge, given the fact that "the culture of government as a competent provider of services and user of resources has been abused for decades."

67. This is the thesis of Robert H. Bates, *Markets and States in Tropical Africa: The Political Basis of Agricultural Policies* (Berkeley: University of California Press, 1981).

68. See Henry S. Bienen, *Armies and Parties in Africa* (New York: Africana Publishing, 1979).

69. Henry S. Bienen, *Kenya: The Politics of Participation and Control* (Princeton: Princeton University Press, 1974).

70. See David Lindaeur and Barbara Nunberg, eds., *Rehabilitating Government: Pay and Employment Reforms in Africa* (Washington, D.C.: World Bank, 1994).

71. For this phenomenon in Zambia, see van de Walle and Chiwele, "Democratization and Economic Reform."

72. See Richard Crook, "Patrimonialism, Administrative Effectiveness and Economic Development in Cote d'Ivoire," *African Affairs* 88 (1989): 205–28.

73. The professional norms and socialization of the Kenyan civil service are explored in a slightly different context in David Leonard, *African Successes: Four Public Managers of Kenyan Rural Development* (Berkeley: University of California Press, 1991).

74. Robert H. Dix, "Democratization and the Institutionalization of Latin American Political Parties," *Comparative Political Studies* 24 (January 1992): 488–511. See also Scott Mainwaring and Timothy R. Scully, eds., *Building Democratic Institutions: Party Systems in Latin America* (Stanford: Stanford University Press, 1995).

75. See Stephanie Lawson, "Conceptual Issues in the Comparative Study of Regime Change and Democratization," *Comparative Politics* 25 (1993): 183–205.

76. See Aristide Zolberg, *Creating Political Order: The Party States of West Africa* (Chicago: University of Chicago Press, 1966); Henry S. Bienen, *Tanzania: Party Transformation and Economic Development* (Princeton: Princeton University Press, 1967); and Arthur W. Lewis, *Politics in West Africa* (Toronto: Oxford University Press, 1965). Larry Diamond describes African parties as "fragile, shallow and weak" in "Introduction," in *Democracy in Developing Countries: Volume Two, Africa,* ed. Larry Diamond, Juan J. Linz, and Seymour Martin Lipset (Boulder, Colo.: Lynne Reinner, 1988), p. 19.

77. For example, Collier, *Regimes in Tropical Africa,* 154–61.

78. In Mozambique, the majority FRELIMO party offered cabinet seats to the defeated RENAMO.

79. See Richard Vengroff, "Governance and the Transition to Democracy: Political Parties and the Party System in Mali," *Journal of Modern African Studies* 31 (1993): 541–62.

80. See Scott Mainwaring, "Political Parties and Democratization in Brazil and the Southern Cone," *Comparative Politics* 21 (1988): 91–120; Frances Hagopian, "Democracy by Undemocratic Means? Elites, Political Pacts and Regime Transition in Brazil," *Comparative Political Studies* 23 (1990): 147–70.

81. O'Donnell, "Delegative Democracy," p. 63.

82. National Democratic Institute, *NDI Reports* (Washington, D.C.: NDI, Winter 1996), p. 15.

83. Bratton, "Are Competitive Elections Enough?" 7–8.

84. For a discussion of these themes, see Philippe C. Schmitter, "The Consolidation of Democracy and Representation of Social Groups," *American Behavioral Scientist* 35 (1992): 422–49.

85. See J. Samuel Valenzuela, "Labor Movements in Transitions to Democracy," *Comparative Politics* 21 (1989): 445–72.

86. See M. S. Frère, "Pluralism Médiatique au Bénin: l'Heure des Désillusions?" *Politique Africaine* 57 (1995): 142–9. Surveys of the press in Niger and Guinea reveal a similar pattern; see Seidick Mamadou Abba, "Les Problèmes de la Presse Independente au Niger," *Politique Africaine* 54 (1994): 156–9; and Benoit

Lootvoet and Jean-Marc Ecoutin, "Les Maux de La Presse Ecrite Guinéenne," *Politique Africaine* 51 (1993): 153–60.

87. Georges Courade and Véronique Alary, "Les Planteurs Camerounais ont-ils été Réévalués?" *Politique Africaine* 54 (1994): 74–87, especially p. 80.

88. Robert D. Putnam, *Making Democracy Work: Civic Traditions in Modern Italy* (Princeton: Princeton University Press, 1992).

89. For example, John R. Heilbrunn, "Social Origins of National Conferences in Bénin and Togo," *Journal of Modern African Studies* 31 (1993): 277–99; and Richard Sandbrook, *The Politics of Africa's Economic Recovery* (Cambridge: Cambridge University Press, 1992). This correlation is sometimes accepted uncritically by the donor community; see, for instance, European Centre for Development Policy, *Democratization in Sub-Saharan Africa: The Search for Institutional Renewal,* ECDPM Occasional Paper (Maastricht, the Netherlands: ECDPM, July 1992); and the United States Agency for International Development, *Democracy and Governance* (Washington, D.C.: USAID/Directorate for Policy, 1991).

90. The groundbreaking work for explaining democratic prospects in terms of the mode of transition was done by Alfred Stepan, "Paths Toward Redemocratization," in *Transitions from Authoritarian Rule: Comparative Perspectives,* ed. Guillermo O'Donnell, Philippe C. Schmitter, and Laurence Whitehead (Baltimore: Johns Hopkins University Press, 1986); and Karl, "Dilemmas of Democratization," especially pp. 8–12.

91. For example, Huntington, *Third Wave*, Chs. 4 and 5.

92. See Stephan Haggard and Robert R. Kaufman, "Economic Reform in New Democracies," in *Fragile Coalitions: The Politics of Economic Adjustment,* ed. Joan M. Nelson (Washington, D.C.: Overseas Development Council, 1989), pp. 57–78.

93. Karl, "Dilemmas of Democratization," p. 8, emphasis in original; Stepan, "Paths Toward Redemocratization," p. 79, emphasis in original.

94. The survival of the old political elites in the new democratic period is a theme of Henry S. Bienen and Jeffrey Herbst, "Authoritarianism and Democracy in Africa," in *Comparative Political Dynamics: Global Research Perspectives,* ed. Dankwart A. Rustow and Kenneth Erickson (New York: Harper Collins, 1991). Their analysis is updated in "The Relationship between Political and Economic Reform in Africa" (paper prepared for the U.S. Agency for International Development, Washington, D.C., 1995).

95. For other commentaries on the continuity of patronage relations before and after regime transitions, see Hagopian, "Democracy By Undemocratic Means?" 147–70; Paul D. Hutchcroft, "Oligarchs and Cronies in the Philippine State: The Politics of Patrimonial Plunder," *World Politics,* 44 (1992): 414–50; and Flemming Christiansen, "Democratization in China: Structural Constraints," in *Democracy and Democratization,* ed. Garaint Perry and Michael Moran (New York: Routledge, 1994), pp. 152–73.

96. Bernard Blancq, "Congo: Corruption et Résistance au Changement," in *l'Afrique Politique: Vue sur la Démocratisation à Marée Basse,* ed. Patrick Quantin (Paris: Karthala, 1994), pp. 191–8.

97. For example, Fabien Eboussi-Boulaga, *Les Conférences Nationales en Afrique Noire: Une Affaire à Suivre* (Paris: Karthala, 1993).

CONCLUSIONS: COMPARATIVE IMPLICATIONS

The political science literature is replete with arguments about the improbability of democratization in Africa. In this book, we have argued that democratization in Africa is a long-term institution-building project that is fraught with obstacles and constantly threatened with reversal. Nevertheless, in the early 1990s, political actors in more than a dozen African countries overcame objective handicaps in order to complete the minimal steps required for the installation of democratic regimes. Although most of these democratic experiments will fail, a handful of imperfect multiparty electoral systems could well survive.

Sweeping generalizations about Africa as a whole are too often derived from case studies of individual countries. Extrapolating from the case of Somalia, for example, one might be led to the unfortunate conclusion that political openings in Africa are bound to dissolve into clan warfare and collapsed states. Conversely, beginning with Bénin – as we did – one might be tempted to incorrectly project the likelihood of democratic transition onto countries where conditions are actually quite unfavorable. Although we have gained insights from many valuable case studies, we have tried to resist the temptation to overgeneralize from single cases. We have demonstrated, for example – the case of Zaire notwithstanding – that an economic crisis of hyperinflation is not the main catalyst of political reform in Africa. And, despite Kenya's experience with political conditionality, we have shown that political change is rarely driven by an ultimatum from the international donor community. We think that arguments along these lines are based on overly anecdotal evidence.

Instead, the diversity of paths and outcomes in Africa's regime transitions cries out for comparative analysis. Only through general tests of multiple cases can false propositions be eliminated. The rich array of contemporary African regimes can best be described by systematic juxtaposition of a large number of country examples; these range, after all, from the anarchy of civil-war Liberia to the flourishing multiparty democracy of Mauritius. In addition, only through detailed historical analysis of linked chains of events across countries – noting similarities and differences where they occur – can we appreciate the complex patterns of change recently forged by African political actors. Finally, only through cross-national comparison of indigenous institutional and transition legacies can one arrive at a general account of the reasons *why* democratic transitions have transpired in some African countries but not in others.

Indeed, comparative analysis is essential for understanding mixed outcomes, that is, where considerable variation occurs within the phenomenon to be explained. Like Huntington in *The Third Wave,* we have sought to analyze a cluster of regime transitions that occurred in a short time period, locating our explanation in the "complex, dense, and messy" terrain between elegant general theory and idiographic case histories.[1] But our approach departs from Huntington's in two respects. First, by including cases of *both* democratizing *and* nondemocratizing regimes within our sample, we have sought to avoid the methodological bias inherent in selecting cases on the dependent variable;[2] any explanation of regime transition constructed on the basis of a full population of cases should be more robust than one based on democratizing regimes alone. Second, we have attempted to move beyond summary accounts of national political histories by testing our explanation against prevailing theoretical frameworks. This chapter summarizes our claim to have devised a *politico-institutional explanation* of regime transitions with broad application within Africa and to other parts of the world where politics have neopatrimonial dimensions.

AFRICAN TRANSITIONS IN COMPARATIVE PERSPECTIVE

The thesis of this book is that the institutional heritage of neopatrimonial rule has shaped regime transitions in much of Africa. This heritage distinguishes Africa from world regions where authoritarianism took on more bureaucratic forms. In the institutional context of neopatrimonialism, regime change is more commonly driven from below through mass political protest than initiated by incumbent state elites. Moreover, the impetus for political liberalization does not originate in splits between moderates and hardliners among the rulers but from conflicts over access to spoils between insiders and outsiders to the state patronage system. Because the state's economic management discourages the accumulation of private capital, middle classes generally side with emergent movements of political opposition rather than buttressing the old regime. And because the stakes of political struggle are the state and its enormous resources, transition struggles are hard and bitterly fought, leading to zero-sum outcomes rather than compromises and pacts.

Most distinctively, the trajectory of regime transitions in Africa hinges on the way that personal rulers exercise power. Compared to incumbent elites in other political regimes, Africa's political big men are relatively unencumbered by legal restrictions on the scope of their decision making. The state and civil institutions that check personal power in more institutionalized systems are typically too weak to play such a role in Africa. Personal rulers are accustomed to making executive and policy choices, if not at will, at least with a considerable degree of arbitrary discretion, limited only by the low administrative and extractive capacity of the state. To the extent that regime transitions become struggles over the rules of the political game, they hinge on opposition challenges to this arbitrary monopoly of powers arrogated by the president and ruling party. In these struggles, strongmen vigorously resist changes to the battery of informal rules that buttress their authority. If they are forced to concede legal reforms, such leaders generally try to manipulate the process of rule making in such a way as to maintain their own best political advantage. In this way, the strategic choices made by neopatrimonial rulers have widely influential effects on the course and outcomes of transitions.

Other prime political movers undertake consequential choices and actions. For example, ordinary citizens, fueled by rage at entrenched incumbents, can intrude directly into politics through the drama of street demonstration. Out-of-power politicians decide to reenter the fray with calls for multiparty democracy and, in the process, impart direction to an otherwise leaderless protest movement. Military officers, disillusioned with the policy failures of an impotent government or disturbed by the prospect of losing privilege, leave the barracks in order to intervene to support or oppose a prodemocracy movement. Precisely because African opposition movements – and the states they confront – are not deeply institutionalized, their impact rests heavily on the caliber and effectiveness of leaders.

That political actors enjoy relative autonomy from formal political rules should not be taken to mean that neopatrimonial regimes are formless. Such regimes are marked by institutional regularities like the concentration of power in the hands of a president and political relationships based on personal loyalty, patronage, and coercion. These institutional precedents, in turn, shape the realm of the possible in the politics of transitions. Generally speaking, transitions from neopatrimonial regimes focus on the fate of the ruler, but they vary to the extent that strongmen had previously routinized their rule into military or one-party political institutions. For example, military oligarchs aim at orderly transition dynamics. They seek to regulate and graduate the pace at which *political participation* by civilians is reintroduced. To this end, they attempt to closely manage the process of political reform, albeit sometimes without any real intention of forfeiting power. By contrast, transitions from one-party regimes revolve around the issue of *political competition,* coming to a head when a national conference or founding elections challenge the long-standing monopoly of power enjoyed by incumbents.

The mobility and effectiveness of political actors during transitions also derives from underlying material structures. Neopatrimonial regimes are maintained by the regular flow of rewards from leaders to followers, that are used to cement political loyalty. Personal leaders themselves depend on access to reliable sources of public revenue from taxation, export revenues, or foreign loans and grants, among other sources. The room for maneuver of political executives is therefore severely confined in countries with a feeble export base, persistent budget crises, and overreliance on external finance, conditions that are widespread in Africa. Moreover, scarcities of resources for political distribution inhibit not only elite political actors but the participants in mass movements too. Opposition political organizations that emerge within neopatrimonial regimes are usually badly underfinanced, dependent on well-heeled patrons, and sustained by promises of future patronage rewards. And as we have shown, the cohesion of opposition forces was one of the more important institutional considerations determining whether a transition culminated in democracy.

Compared with most countries in other regions of the world, African countries are distinctive not only for their neopatrimonial legacy but also in terms of their substandard economic performance and dependence on the international system. While other regions traversed a period of economic crisis during the 1980s, the crisis was arguably more devastating for Africa's poorer and more vulnerable economies. The reliance on Western public finance to address fiscal and balance of payments shortfalls was certainly more pronounced. Perhaps these economic and international factors were formative in shaping Africa's transitions? This study established that – like neopatrimonial rule – economic crisis and financial dependency were ubiquitous background features with measurable degrees of variation across African countries. But their explanatory power was limited. Economic variables were *generally unrelated* to the specific dynamics of political change. International variables were somewhat more helpful, with political diffusion, donor conditionality, and aid dependence revealing *occasional connection* to one or other aspect of regime transition. By contrast, variations in institutional heritage – measured as the extent of political participation and political competition under previous regimes – were *repeatedly related* to a full range of transition indicators such as the frequency of protest, the extent of liberalization, and the level of democracy.

Substantively, we conclude that economic and international factors were contextually important and should not be excluded from overall explanations. To be sure, political protests in Africa were born out of the hardship engendered by long-term economic decline, and protesters sometimes lashed out at austerity policies. And it would be foolish to overlook the fact that African regime transitions were a post–Cold War phenomenon. Indisputably, international aid donors became major players in the game of regime transition after 1989, particularly when they began to wield the carrots and sticks of political conditionality. But we do not see these economic and international forces as decisive. They helped to create the conditions under which political change became possible, but they did not in and of themselves trigger or sustain regime transitions or determine the directions the transitions took.

Instead, the onset and subsequent trajectory of regime transition depended on the constellation of domestic political forces. What mattered most in African regime transitions was whether contending individuals and groups made use of the structure of opportunities and constraints embedded in inherited political institutions. Did the old regime allow civilian political competition? Was there a tradition of mass electoral participation? Was civil society organized into a plurality of associations? Were there latent opposition parties? Was there political protest? Did the opposition movement cohere around a single leader and organization? Did the incumbent concede a national conference? Did the military intervene? Political change was most likely where an emergent opposition leadership drew upon an institutional tradition of nonstate political organization. Political change was least likely where an incumbent leader maintained a tight grip over the material and coercive resources of a relatively well-endowed state. Between these extremes, a whole range of intermediate outcomes was possible, depending on the relative strength and cohesion of contending forces. Relevant too was the skill of leaders on both sides at seizing opportunities that came their way and at compensating for weakness and disorganization in their respective institutional bases.

Indeed, to the extent that economic and international factors were important to regime transitions, they were mediated by domestic political and institutional considerations. For example, economic crisis became salient to regime transition only when protesters transcended their own narrow corporate interests to call for the ouster of incumbents and for changes in political rules. Furthermore, donor political conditionality was most effective in promoting liberal and democratic reforms when preceded by popular protest led by organized groups in domestic society. As a final example, the dependence of African governments on international aid became relevant when it undermined political legitimacy: when, by caving in to donor demands for economic adjustment or free elections, governments exposed their previously hidden institutional vulnerabilities to full public view. In short, international and economic forces promoted regime transition in Africa mainly when manifested through domestic politics.

REVISING THEORIES OF REGIME TRANSITION

Under which domestic political conditions, then, is a transition to democracy most likely? By way of summary we select several further findings from our study that suggest extensions or refinements to regime transition theory.

In keeping with our emphasis on institutional legacies, a regime's starting point with respect to political rights is formative. Although we found that highly authoritarian regimes (like military oligarchies and plebiscitary one-party regimes in Africa) are likely to make seemingly substantial gains in democratization, they ultimately attain only modest absolute levels of democracy. By contrast, regimes with previous experience in respecting political rights (say through multiparty interludes or experience with competitive one-party institutions) commonly make less dramatic gains but end up with a greater measure of democracy. Thus, political reformers who start from a promising institutional foundation and aim at modest goals can expect to be most successful. Peering into the future, we expect that incremental, rather than dramatic gains in levels of democracy are likely also to prove most sustainable over time.

Which of the key dimensions that distinguish political regimes – participation and competition – is more critical in promoting democratization? Our results suggest the latter. Getting to democracy is easier from a regime in which competition is encouraged and the main challenge is to broaden participation; getting to democracy is much more difficult from a regime that has no tradition of political competition, however inclusive and participatory it may be. Whereas neopatrimonial regimes sometimes encourage mass rituals of political participation, they have rarely permitted competition, not least in civil society but especially between political parties. We regard intolerance of political competition as the fatal flaw of neopatrimonial regimes and a major reason why democratic transitions from such regimes are low-probability events. By this line of reasoning too, we conclude that democracy has more promising prospects in transitions from regime types, and in world regions, *other* than neopatrimonial ones.

If an *ancien régime* enjoys a legacy of political competition, through which institutions is it expressed? This study has conceptualized political competition as an attribute of both civil and political societies. Interestingly, we find that the legacy of political competition manifests itself distinctively depending on the phase of regime transition. Whereas dense and diverse civil societies help to bring about the onset of transition (see Chapter 4), democratic outcomes depend more upon pluralism in the party system and legislature (see Chapter 6). This makes sense once one recognizes that civil society is often the only arena for dissent and the only source of protest in authoritarian systems; once transitions get underway, however, democratization can only be consummated through political organizations that are capable of contesting elections and winning state power. Whereas, as transitions progress, opposition parties displace voluntary associations in counterbalancing the excesses of African presidents, both sets of institutions are required for the survival and consolidation of democracy.

Which brings us to the shifting weight of structure and contingency in successive phases of democratization. The comparative literature on this subject is bifurcated. On one hand, insightful accounts of *transitions to democracy* have propagated the influential view that the interval between regimes is comprehensible mainly by studying the choices of key political agents and the resultant cascade of political events. On the other hand, numerous empirical studies have confirmed the law-like generalization that the *consolidation of democracy* is most feasible in industrialized countries with a literate middle class, that is, in terms of favorable underlying economic and social structures. The emphasis on agency and the "crafting" of democracy in the transition literature on Latin America and Eastern Europe has recently given way to a renewed emphasis on structural explanations to predict the likelihood of long-term consolidation. Yet there is no overarching theoretical schema that bridges the divide between regime transition and regime consolidation, simultaneously explaining both. This inconsistency has been noted by theorists who consider that "the factors responsible for the end of a non-democratic regime may differ significantly from those that lead to the creation of a democratic one"[3] and that "the factors that keep a democracy stable may not be the ones that brought it into existence."[4]

We cannot claim to have elaborated a unified field theory of democratization; we doubt whether such is even feasible. Nevertheless, we have tried to take into account both structure and agency, both continuity and change, and both institutions and politics in this study of democratization. This study has demonstrated that contingent considerations become increasingly important as transitions progress. At the same time, the study affirms that trajectories of transition derive from the structure of the regime that went before. Far from being entirely uncertain, transition processes are patterned along knowable paths to an important degree. Thus our politico-institutional approach holds the key to a theoretical linkage between the dynamics of short-term transition and those of long-term consolidation. The same configuration of institutional forces that conditions the process of transition will regain saliency at increased levels during the consolidation phase as politics reenters more routinized and predictable patterns. By definition, institutions are resilient, and are likely to emerge little changed, at least in the immediate term, by the tumult of the transition.

It may seem odd to derive an institutional approach to regime transitions from a study of a continent where formal political institutions are notoriously weak. But just because politics is not bureaucratized in Africa does not mean that it is not institutionalized. Nor need analysts resort to formulations of personal rule that explain political outcomes solely in terms of the quirks of personality and skills possessed by history's "great men." On the contrary, we have argued that neopatrimonial regimes in Africa are marked by recurrent patterns of behavior – in short, by institutions – to which all political participants are attuned and which impart structure to political life. Although these informal, partially hidden, and extralegal institutions – like presidentialism, prebendalism, and clientelism – are sometimes difficult to observe, they are nonetheless concrete and consequential. Clustered together, these institutions are expressed as neopatrimonial regimes, which themselves vary according to routinized patterns of political participation and competition constructed by personalistic rulers.

If our institutional approach is relevant for Africa, then it should be largely transferable to other parts of the world – like selected countries in Central Asia, Central America, and the Caribbean – where neopatrimonial rule is the norm. The dynamics of the recent democratization process in Haiti, for example, bear several striking similarities to those described here; there too, the transition was driven by popular protest in the context of economic crisis, and its outcome conditioned by the weakness of political parties and civic associations. Today, democratic consolidation in that country is undermined by traditions of corruption and administrative debility while the survival of multiparty politics has been intermittently threatened by violence from elements in the military linked to the previous regime.[5]

A revised institutional model should be even more useful in settings where political institutions have been formalized and legalized. A pressing challenge for political science is to explore the general and specific effects on democratization of preexisting forms of bureaucratic authoritarian rule. Institution-based comparisons should help to cast light, for example, on the similarities and differences among political transitions from bureaucratic military oligarchies in Latin America and Southern Europe on the one hand and Leninist one-party regimes in the former Soviet Union and East Europe on the other. Accounts of the Third Wave of democratization focusing on these regions have so far taken institutional traditions largely for granted. Perhaps because of the apparent similarities in political institutions within these regions, frameworks for explaining transitions have focused on other factors, which were viewed as exhibiting greater cross-national variation. More truly comparative analyses of democratic transitions, especially if these had included African cases, would have been more likely to note the impact of political traditions. African cases help to demonstrate that many of the findings of the transitions literature do not travel well, in part because they are artifacts of the distinctive configuration of political institutions in Latin America and Southern Europe. This is particularly true of political pacts, for instance, widely argued to be central to Third Wave transitions, but absent from most of Africa.

Existing research already suggests the potential dividends from extending a politico-institutional approach to other democratic transitions. Mainwaring's study of party traditions in Brazil, for example, the Colliers' analysis of the influence of labor organizations on Latin American politics, or Roeder's institutional analysis of the fall of the Soviet Union are just a few examples of the kind of research we have in mind.[6] In these cases, the focus on political institutions establishes their structuring impact on political change and makes clear the excessive voluntarism of analyses that put the full weight of explaining transitions on individual agency and historical serendipity.

In recommending institutionalism, we wish to avoid its dry and deterministic attributes. A major weakness of the prodigious institutional literature on the state – and the slim institutional literature on civil society – is that it tends to leave politics out. In other words, institutional studies too often emphasize the fixed edifices of public life – like laws, organizations, and offices – at the expense of the dynamics of interests and identities, domination and resistance, compromise and accommodation. A *politico*-institutional approach brings politics back in. As Thelen and Steinmo argue, "The emphasis on institutions as patterned relations that lies at the core of an institutional approach does not replace attention to other variables – the players, their interests and strategies, and the distribution of power among them. On the contrary, it puts these factors in context, showing how they relate to one another by drawing attention to the way that political situations are structured."[7]

At its core, a politico-institutional approach contributes to the study of regime transitions by emphasizing "the reciprocal influence of institutions and politics."[8] It examines the ways that the uncertainties of politics interact with persistent institutional structures, portraying regime transitions as a process of *structured contingency*. By way of conclusion, we revisit the three dimensions of structured contingency proposed earlier (see Chapter 1) in the light of what we have learned about African regime transitions.

The first aspect of structured contingency is that inherited rules and institutions impose limits on the range of alternatives available to political actors, predisposing them to opt for certain courses of action.

For example, why were African regime transitions significantly more likely to begin with political protest than transitions in other regions? We have argued that protest was a function of a structure of opportunities and constraints born in the institutional setting of the plebiscitary one-party state, which by 1989 was postcolonial Africa's commonest regime form. Previous plebiscitary rulers had suppressed political competition, creating a pent-up demand for more open politics; on the other hand, they had allowed stage-managed elections that at minimum created opportunities for political participation. By contrast, the option of engaging in mass protest was largely unavailable to disgruntled citizens of military regimes due to the ever-present threat of state coercion; in these cases, the institutional constraints were too strong to allow spontaneous political action. In more competitive regimes, however, citizens forewent the protest option or used it only sparingly because they enjoyed, at least nominally, existing institutional opportunities for the expression of alternative political views. Thus we explain, in largely institutional terms, the political actions that launched the onset of regime transitions in Africa.

Similarly, inherited rules and institutions penetrated the transition process itself and there shaped the behavior of political principals. We argue that, even after their onset, transitions unfolded distinctively according to the nature of the previous political regimes. Military regimes were most likely to give rise to closely controlled transitions in which army-led governments set the terms and timetable for a return to civilian rule, and then micromanaged implementation. Plebiscitary one-party regimes were more likely to spawn transitions via national conferences, in large part because the characteristics of this distinctively African institution were consonant with the expectations about plebiscites that both incumbents and oppositions brought to the table. Lastly, competitive one-party regimes set up institutional circumstances under which contesting parties agreed, more readily and rapidly than in any other type of regime, on the need to resolve political disputes through a general election.

The second aspect of structured contingency is as follows: Contingent events, although seemingly random, harbor regularities and patterns of their own.

Processes that are apparently random have underlying structure. This notion is discussed at two levels. We begin broadly, with reference to the full set of African regime transitions. These processes were far from open-ended and not particularly numerous. Early in the book, we proposed several transition paths in the form of a tree diagram with forks identifying three main phases and with eight logical transition outcomes (see Chapter 3, Figure 6). It is striking that, of the eight potential paths African countries could have explored within this framework, only five were actually taken. And because one of these was a cul-de-sac in which transitions were precluded, the empirical record can be economically summarized with reference to just four alternative routes. The implication is that, far from being highly contingent processes with wildly proliferated consequences, African regime transitions were in reality fabricated along comprehensible lines. From a broader perspective still, if transitions were singular occurrences, they would not occur in waves.

At a narrower level, we also found micropatterns between key events within the extended excursion of regime transitions. Unlike the scattered reaction of billiard balls on a pool table, the behavior of actors in response to political stimuli did not careen in multiple directions. Predictable results were engendered by specific actions. For example, we showed that the choice by incumbent rulers to engage in state repression during transitions was a systematic response to foregoing political protest. Similarly, some political events were underpinned by prerequisite actions. We showed, for example, that free elections were consummated only where liberalization reforms, such as the relegalization of political associations, had come before. Indeed, liberalization was a necessary precondition of democratization. Thereby, a set of reform actions at one time helped to forge a later path of transition.

Third, structure and contingency connect by conflict, as well as by continuity. Generally, the notion of path dependency implies that institutions reproduce themselves through time. But path dependency should also allow that existing organizations may suffer from such weak performance capacities or internal contradictions that they cannot propagate, instead spawning demands for the introduction of new sets of rules and institutions.

In Africa, we found that, during the transition period, regimes that had previously experienced only limited levels of political participation and political competition moved furthest down the roads of *liberalization* and *democratization*. These seemingly counterintuitive findings have profound theoretical and practical implications. They cast doubt on deterministic arguments that political institutions are self-perpetuating; they draw attention instead to the conflicts and contradictions engendered by established practices. Thus, we find that by the 1990s, the African plebiscitary one-party state – which combined high levels of political participation with low levels of political competition – helped to generate the mass protest that contributed to its own demise. The African quest for democracy was driven fundamentally by mass disillusionment with misrule by personalistic leaders. It was a reaction *against* the authoritarian institutions that these leaders constructed to keep themselves in power.

We also found that, as regime transitions progressed, certain institutional factors incurred contrary results. For example, precedents of *political participation* made a positive contribution in *getting transitions started* – typically through protest – but subsequently *inhibited progress toward democracy*. Protest movements that emerged as a reaction against an entrenched regime did not necessarily have an alternative institution-building program in mind. Protesters expressed demands for political rights, but they had little experience with competitive politics and few precedents of pluralism on which to build. In the international and economic context of Africa in the early 1990s, mass political demands may have been enough to tip the balance in favor of multiparty elections and the installation of new governments, but protest-led reform did not necessarily lay a firm foundation for the subsequent institutionalization of democratic regimes. Indeed, African protest movements forged in the crucible of plebiscitary politics had limited democratic potential. This helps us to understand how popular efforts for political reform in Africa often started with great enthusiasm but soon fizzled out. It also leads us to expect that experiments to construct stable democracies in countries with little or no institutional heritage of political competition will be fragile, possibly transitory, and constantly threatened by reversal.

Finally, a politico-institutional analysis helps us to understand why the prospects for the consolidation of democracy in Africa are quite limited. Current political situations are national permutations on a theme of regime change in a context of neopatrimonial continuity. As latecomers to the third wave of democratic transitions, African citizens have only recently begun to demand political accountability from state elites. Yet already elected leaders have made it clear that they wish to govern along lines etched during previous regimes. About Bénin – which we portrayed at the outset as Africa's prototypical democratizer – Allen writes that "the present political system is uncomfortably similar to the post-independence system whose own internal contradictions created the preconditions for the installation of the Kérékou regime." The big men who hold power continue to "eat," much as the goat does, "where it is tethered."[9] The institutional logic of patronage and clientelism is alive and well. Only where political actors can solidify, revive, or create institutional traditions of political participation and competition will democracy in Africa thrive.

A consolidated democracy requires that democratic institutions are not only built but also valued. Democracy can be installed without democrats, but it cannot be consolidated without them. Political actors may initially see a founding election as the "least worst" alternative to solve an intractable political standoff or induce political movement in an ossified regime. Democracy may even survive in the short run under the force of these kinds of strategic calculations, but democracy will truly last only when political actors learn to love it. Until elites and citizens alike come to cherish rule by the people and exhibit a willingness to stand up for it, in Africa as elsewhere, there will be no permanent defense against tyranny.

ENDNOTES

1. Samuel P. Huntington, *The Third Wave: Democratization in the Late Twentieth Century* (Norman: University of Oklahoma Press, 1991), p. xiii.
2. See Barbara Geddes, "How the Cases You Choose Affect the Results You Get: Selection Bias in Comparative Politics," in *Political Analysis,* vol. 2, ed. James A. Stimson (Ann Arbor: University of Michigan Press, 1990), 131–50; see also Stanley Lieberson, "Small N's and Big Conclusions: An Examination of the Reasoning in Comparative Studies Based on a Small Number of Cases," *Social Forces,* 70 (1991): 307–20.
3. Huntington, *Third Wave,* p. 35.
4. Dankwart A. Rustow, "Transitions to Democracy: Toward a Dynamic Model," *Comparative Politics* 2 (1970): 346.
5. On the Haitian transition, see Anthony Bryan, "Haiti: Kick Starting the Economy," *Current History,* 94 (1995); Suzy Castor, "Democracy and Society in Haiti: Structures of Domination and Resistance to Change," *Social Justice* 19 (1992): 126–38; and Robert Fatton, "From Predatory Rule to Democratic Governance: The Ambiguities and Paradoxes of Haiti's Extrication from Dictatorship," (paper presented at the annual meeting of the American Political Science Association, Chicago, August 31–September 3, 1995).
6. Scott Mainwaring, "Political Parties and Democratization in Brazil and the Southern Cone," *Comparative Politics* 21 (1988): 91–120; Ruth Berins Collier and David Collier, *Shaping the Political Arena: Critical Junctures, the Labor Movement, and Regime Dynamics in Latin America* (Princeton: Princeton University Press, 1991); and Philip G. Roeder, *Red Sunset: The Failure of Soviet Politics* (Princeton: Princeton University Press, 1993).
7. Kathleen Thelen and Sven Steinmo, "Historical Institutionalism in Comparative Politics," in *Structuring Politics: Historical Institutionalism in Comparative Politics,* ed. Thelen, Steinmo, and Frank Longstreth (Cambridge: Cambridge University Press, 1992), p. 13.
8. *Ibid.,* p. 14.
9. See the Cameroon proverb quoted by Jean-François Bayart on page vxii of this book.

APPENDIX

THE DATA SET

The data set used in this study contains information for all 47 countries in sub-Saharan Africa on 99 variables. It is divided into two parts. The first contains information (63 variables) on the characteristics of political regimes and institutions from independence to December 31, 1989. The second part (36 variables) refers to the dynamics of regime transitions for the five-year period from 1990 to 1994.[1]

In order to characterize the old regimes, we drew primarily on established sources. Economic indicators were drawn largely from the World Bank's *World Development Report* (1991), which reported on the state of African economies in 1989. Social indicators – on characteristics like ethnic or religious fragmentation – were drawn together from a more disparate range of standard compendia.[2] Our principal aim was to add value to the existing stock of knowledge about the *political* characteristics of authoritarian regimes in Africa. For this reason, we compiled a listing of every national election in Africa from 1960 to 1989, for totals of 106 presidential and 185 parliamentary contests.[3] We assembled indicators on the numbers of political parties, associational groups, and media outlets in 1975 and 1989.[4] And we classified countries by type of political regime, noting the duration of each regime in years, and the number and mode of previous regime transitions for all 47 countries up to 1989.

For the second part of the data set, we generated new data to describe the contemporary round of regime transitions. First we created a standardized framework that identified and categorized the key events and features of political transitions. Of greatest interest were landmark events such as political protests, liberalization reforms, elections, and changes of government in each country. We also summarized the characteristics of national conferences, military interventions, and external influences, among other features of political transitions. Using *Africa South of the Sahara* (1994, 1995) as a consistent source, we then gathered qualitative accounts and quantitative facts about each of these aspects of the transition and deposited these narratives under the headings of the framework.[5] In addition, we assembled a complete set of standard election results for every multiparty contest in Africa between 1990 and 1994, along with information on whether observers ruled the vote as free and fair, whether incumbents were ousted, and whether losers accepted the results.[6] Research assistants exhaustively recorded details of all these designated features of regime transitions, and we systematically checked the accounts for reliability.

From this depository of information, we constructed a matrix of 36 quantitative indicators concerning the nature of regime transitions. It covered the 42 African countries that had authoritarian regimes on January 1, 1990, thus excluding long-standing multiparty systems. Each author and one assistant independently coded or counted the data from the information bank in order to enter numerical values into the cells of the matrix. In instances of intercoder disagreements (about 15 percent of all values), we jointly reviewed the available facts about the case until consensus could be established. Where the primary source was silent or apparently incomplete, we made reference to other publications of record, to journalists' reports, or to our knowledge of particular countries.

A word of caution is in order about the limitations of the regime transitions data. We have most confidence in those variables that are underpinned by objective indicators – for example, the occurrence of a national constitutional conference or a presidential election. We nonetheless concede that there is an element of subjectivity in the coding of a few variables. For some variables, such as whether an election was free and fair, we had to rely on the judgment of others, as reflected in the written reports of official election observers. In other cases (for about a dozen variables), the coders relied on their own judgment after reviewing the available evidence on the case. How else can one determine whether a government employed a little or lot of "repression," or whether an opposition was "cohesive" or "fragmented"? Because of such constraints, we did not attempt to gauge all regime transition variables at an interval level of measurement. Indeed, many transition variables (14 out of 36), were coded into ordinal or nominal categories, and a few of these (5 out of 14) were dummy variables with just two categories.

At all times we tried not to manipulate questionable data beyond the point that we judged they could reasonably bear. And the study from which this paper is drawn is supported with evidence adduced by eclectic methods, not by aggregate quantitative data analysis alone. It is fleshed out with critical case studies whose selection was facilitated with reference to extreme or typical values on particular variables within the data set.

MEASURING REGIME TRANSITION

As a first step in systematic comparison, operational definitions were established for key concepts, beginning with regime transition. Regime transition is a shorthand label for a composite process. It refers to an intricate series of changes of political rules, processes, and institutions that may occur simultaneously but are more often spread over a measurable period. For this reason, the loose macroconcept of regime transition was disassembled into more precise operational parts in order to render it usable for analysis.

Three component concepts together capture the substantive core and watershed events of regime transitions: (1) political protest, (2) political liberalization, and (3) democratization. These three concepts are the principal dependent variables in our analysis. In addition, we derived from these concepts several measures of the timing of transitions, including (4) the onset of transition, (5) the end of transition, and (6) the duration of transition. These concepts and their operational definitions are discussed below.

POLITICAL PROTEST

Political protest is defined as the frequency of mass actions directed at political goals. Qualifying for inclusion were street demonstrations, boycotts, strikes, and riots.[7] A mass action had a political purpose when protesters made explicit demands for changes of political rights or rulership, thereby distinguishing political protests from mass actions driven exclusively by economic grievances.

The frequency of political protest was measured by the number of these events occurring in each country during the 10-year period between 1985 and 1994. The source of data was *Africa South of the Sahara* (annual, 1985–95). Within this period, the average annual frequency of protests varied between a low of 16 in 1986 (in eight countries) and a high of 81 events in 1991 (in 28 countries). This measure was used when political protest was treated as a dependent variable.

In addition to this interval-level variable, we devised a three-category ordinal scale of protests (none, some, or many) for the years from 1988 to 1992. The period was chosen because it bracketed the beginning of the upsurge in political protest and the peak of liberalization reforms. In cases in which protests were infrequent but particularly widespread or violent, we allowed special consideration for the intensity of protest by coding these events as "many." This measure was used when political protest was treated as an independent variable.

POLITICAL LIBERALIZATION

Political liberalization is defined as the reform of a regime by the relaxation of governmental controls on the political activities of citizens. Often described as a political opening, liberalization occurs when the authorities grant previously denied liberties to individuals and groups in society. Liberalization reforms cover a wide gamut of substantive rights, from the lifting of censorship on independent newspapers to the repeal of constitutional provisions permitting the existence of only one political party.

To assess trends in political liberalization and democratization, we must first ask: "Compared to what?" What is the appropriate baseline against which to measure a country's performance at guaranteeing basic freedoms or open elections? Several standards are possible:

An absolute standard – for example, a universal model of democratic rights.
An empirical standard, one that actually prevails in other countries in the region or the world.
A self-anchoring standard derived from the country's own past performance.

Obviously, any judgment about whether change is occurring will be colored by the standard chosen.

This study takes a pragmatic approach to liberalization and democratization. The operational indicators of these concepts are measurements against each country's initial regime conditions. At minimum, this approach provides a common-sensical assessment of whether a regime is opening up politically or becoming more democratic, regardless of how open or democratic it was to begin with.

We operationalized political liberalization from an existing data set used frequently by social scientists to measure the openness of societies. *The Comparative Survey of Freedom* published by Freedom House (FH) monitors civil liberties and political rights on an annual basis for all countries and territories in the world. Freedom House reports scores for a country's compliance with standard lists of civil liberties (13 items) and political rights (9 items) as estimated by a panel of expert reviewers. It summarizes the quality of different regimes on a seven-point scale, with 1 representing the "most free" and 7 the "least free." In practical terms, the survey provides the best coverage of any data set on liberties and democracy currently available. The data are derived in a reasonably systematic manner, presented in quantititive form, and are complete, both cross-sectionally (for 186 countries) and over time (from 1973 to the present). The *Survey's* rankings are professional judgments based on a research team's empirical observations of governmental performance in respecting civil liberties and political rights.[8] Importantly, the concept of liberalization used in this book accords closely to the FH definition. What we mean by liberty is well captured by the FH's index of civil liberties, which includes protection from torture, media independence, and freedom of association and assembly. Our political liberalization indicator was the change in an African country's civil liberties score from 1988 to 1992.[9]

DEMOCRATIZATION

One of the most important questions about regime transitions concerns their denouement. Does the transition reach completion? And what is the nature of the resultant regime? We applied these questions to the status of regime transitions in Africa as of December 31, 1994. As a first cut, we created a variable called "transition outcome" for which each country was coded into one of four categories ordered to represent an ascending scale toward democracy.

The first possible outcome was that a regime transition never began. Either the authoritarian ruler was so obdurate that he refused to countenance reform, or the internal security situation was so uncertain due to civil war that reform efforts could not get underway. In either case, a transition was *precluded*. A common regime outcome, especially in the presence of civil war, was a form of anarchy. Second, there were countries in which a transition began but was soon *blocked*. Here the incumbent was never sincere about adopting a reform agenda, or the military as a corporate group intervened to foreshorten the reform process. These transitions led essentially to the reimposition of strict authoritarian rule. Third, there were *flawed* transitions to liberalized forms of authoritarianism in which incumbent strongmen conceded multiparty elections but managed to retain political power, usually by manipulating the electoral process. The fourth and last possible outcome was a *democratic* transition that culminated in the installation of a new government as a result of a free and fair election in which the loser accepted the election results. The resultant democracies were invariably fragile.

In addition to this ordinal scale of transition outcome we again drew on *The Comparative Survey of Freedom* for an interval measure of the extent of democratization.[10] What we mean by democracy is fairly represented by the *Survey's* index of political rights, which include open elections for the chief authority and legislative representatives, fair electoral laws, and political party competition. A score for each African country was derived by calculating the change in its political rights score between 1988 and 1994. The positive correlation between the measure of transition outcome and the measure of democratization was very strong and significant (Spearman's $r = 0.682$, sig $= 0.000$), suggesting that the concept of transition outcome is constructed robustly and can represent the actual extent of democratization.

As a third and final measure we used the level of democracy. Operationalized as a country's FH score on political rights in 1994, this measure captured attainments in terms of democracy as opposed to the process of democratization. It portrayed not how far a country had come in relation to its own political past, but against universal standards. It was an absolute, rather than a relative, measure.

THE ONSET OF TRANSITION

The onset of regime transition is the political event that "sets the ball rolling" in terms of replacing existing political rules with new ones. Conventionally, writers on democratization have marked the onset of political transitions by the first liberalization reform introduced by the existing authoritarian regime. But because, as argued in this book, regime transitions may also be started by political pro-testers, we generated an alternative measure of the onset of transition. For coun-tries where protesters initiated a transition (n = 28), we noted the date of the first protest. For countries where political elites took a preemptive liberalization ini-tiative (n = 12), we recorded the date of the first reform. And for all countries that embarked on transition (n = 40), we combined these variables into a single indicator for the onset of transition, depending on whether a protest or reform event occurred first. The sequence of events was measured as the number of months elapsed after January 1, 1988, an arbitrary moment prior to the first protests and reforms in the current round of African political transitions. In two cases, South Africa and Namibia, political protests against the incumbent regime broke out before January 1, 1988. And in the case of São Tomé and Principe, the first liberalization reform occurred in October 1987. To avoid overweighting, es-pecially for South Africa, where protest can be traced back to 1976, 1960, or even earlier, all such cases were anchored with a score of zero to indicate that the event occurred before 1988.

THE END OF TRANSITION

The indicator for the end of regime transition measured the number of elapsed months from January 1, 1988 to the date of the installation of a new government. If no new government had been installed by December 31, 1994, the score was 84 (for 84 months from the baseline date).

THE DURATION OF TRANSITION

The duration of transition was calculated by subtracting the onset score from the end score.

The scores for each African country on protest, liberalization, democratiza-tion, democracy, and transition outcome are reported in Table 12.

ENDNOTES

1. For information on access to the published data set see Introduction, note 5.
2. For example, for ethnic fragmentation we used scores from Donald G. Morrison, Robert C. Mitchell, and John N. Paden et al., *The Black Africa Handbook,* 2nd ed. (New York: Paragon House, 1989); the percentage of the population adher-ing to various religions came from the Central Intelligence Agency, *CIA World Factbook* (Washington, D.C.: Central Intelligence Agency, 1988); data on church-run schools and medical facilities is found in David B. Barrett, ed., *World Christian Encyclopaedia* (Oxford: Oxford University Press, 1982).
3. For example, *Africa Research Bulletin: Political, Social and Cultural Series* (Oxford: Basil Blackwell, annual).

Table 12. *Indicators of Regime Transition, Sub-Saharan Africa, 1990–94*

Country	Frequency of Political Protest[a]	Extent of Liberal-ization[b]	Extent of Democra-tization[c]	Level of Democ-racy[d]	Transition Outcome[e]
Angola	0	1	0	7	1
Bénin	17	4	5	2	3
Botswana	—	1	−1	2	—
Burkina Faso	2	1	2	5	2
Burundi	7	1	1	6	1
Cameroon	19	1	0	6	2
Cape Verde	3	4	4	1	3
Central African Republic	9	1	3	3	3
Chad	12	1	0	6	1
Comoros	13	4	2	4	2
Congo	6	3	3	4	3
Côte d'Ivoire	20	2	0	6	2
Djibouti	2	0	0	6	2
Equatorial Guinea	3	1	0	7	2
Ethiopia	2	3	1	6	1
Gabon	16	2	1	5	2
Gambia	—	1	−4	7	—
Ghana	6	1	1	5	2
Guinea	10	1	1	6	1
Guinea–Bissau	2	2	3	3	3
Kenya	16	1	0	6	2
Lesotho	6	2	2	4	3
Liberia	4	−1	−1	7	0
Madagascar	19	1	3	2	3
Malawi	5	0	4	2	3
Mali	14	3	4	2	3
Mauritania	11	0	0	7	2
Mauritius	—	0	1	1	—
Mozambique	1	3	4	3	3
Namibia	5	1	2	2	3
Niger	26	2	4	3	3
Nigeria	26	0	−2	7	1
Rwanda	0	1	−1	7	1
São Tomé	2	2	5	1	3
Sénégal	—	1	−1	4	—
Seychelles	0	2	3	3	3
Sierra Leone	4	−1	−2	7	1
Somalia	4	0	0	7	1
South Africa	16	2	3	2	3

Table 12 *(cont.)*

Country	Frequency of Political Protest[a]	Extent of Liberalization[b]	Extent of Democratization[c]	Level of Democracy[d]	Transition Outcome[e]
Sudan	8	−2	−3	7	0
Swaziland	7	1	−1	6	2
Tanzania	2	1	0	6	1
Togo	20	1	0	6	2
Uganda	1	−1	0	5	1
Zaire	22	2	−1	7	1
Zambia	12	2	3	3	3
Zimbabwe	—	2	−1	5	—
Summary					
Mean	—	1.28	1.00	4.66	—
Standard deviation	—	1.30	2.13	2.02	—
Missing Data	5	—	—	—	5
Frequency	0: 3 1–3: 10 4–10: 13 11+: 16	+ 37 (33[f]) − 10 (9[f])	+ 24 (23[f]) − 23 (19[f])	1–2: 10 3–5: 15 6–7: 22	0: 2 1: 12 2: 12 3: 16

[a]Total number of popular protests aimed at political goals, 1985–1994, as reported in *Africa South Of the Sahara* (1986 through 1995).
[b]Change in civil liberties score, 1988–1992, *Comparative Survey of Freedom* (1989 and 1993).
[c]Change in political rights score, 1988-1994, *Comparative Survey of Freedom* (1989 and 1995).
[d]Political rights score, 1994, *Comparative Survey of Freedom* (1995).
[e]0 = precluded transition, 1 = blocked or incomplete transition, 2 = flawed electoral transition, 3 = democratic transition (all data as of December 31, 1994).
[f]n = 42; figures exclude countries with multiparty regimes before 1990.

4. *Africa South of the Sahara* (London: Europa Publications, annual).
5. *Africa South of the Sahara,* 24th ed. (1994).
6. *Ibid.,* plus multiple country case sources.
7. Our operationalization is consistent with standard constructs of political protest used in Charles L. Taylor and David A. Jodice, eds., *World Handbook of Political and Social Indicators* (Ann Arbor, Mich.: Inter-University Consortium for Political and Social Research, 1983); and Arthur S. Banks, ed., *Cross-Polity Time-Series Data* (Cambridge: Massachusetts Institute of Technology Press, 1971). See also Ekkart Zimmerman, "Macro-Comparative Research on Political Protest," in *Handbook of Political Conflict,* ed. Ted Robert Gurr (New York: Free Press, 1980).

8. Despite efforts at objectivity, the methodology of the survey is not beyond reproach. The Freedom House data have been criticized over the years. See in particular Kenneth Bollen, "Liberal Democracy: Validity and Method Factors in Cross-National Measures," *American Journal Of Political Science*. 34 (1993) 1207–30. In the past, Freedom House displayed a Cold War bias that favored Western liberal democracies and their allies against the former Soviet bloc. The post–Cold War spread of liberal democratic values at least partly defuses the criticism that it represents only one narrow worldview. Calling the Freedom House data the "most widely used" indicators of liberalization and democratization, Edward Muller and Mitchell Seligson find "good reliability as suggested by very high correlations between them and other measures available for particular years only (cf. Bollen 1986, 588; Banks 1986; Coppedge and Reinecke 1991)." See Muller and Seligson, "Civic Culture and Democracy: The Question of Causal Relationships," *American Political Science Review* 88 (September 1994): 637. We too find *The Comparative Survey of Freedom* quite serviceable for purposes of broad, cross-country comparisons of trends in liberalization, democratization, and levels of democracy.

9. Because the later score was subtracted from the earlier score, a positive number indicates an advance in liberalization and a negative number a setback.

10. Precluded = 0, blocked = 1, flawed = 2, democratic = 3.

SELECTED BIBLIOGRAPHY

Ake, Claude. 1993. "The Unique Case of African Democracy." *International Affairs* 69: 239–44.

———. 1996. *Democracy and Development in Africa.* Washington, D.C.: The Brookings Institution.

Anyang' Nyong'o, Peter. 1987. *Popular Struggles for Democracy in Africa.* London: Zed Books.

Ayittey, George. 1992. *Africa Betrayed.* New York: St. Martin's Press.

Bach, Daniel C., and Anthony A. Kirk-Greene, eds. 1993. *Etats et Societés en Afrique Francophone.* Paris: Economica.

Bakary, Tessy. 1992. "Une Autre Forme de Putsch: La Conférence Nationale Souveraine." *Géopolitique Africaine* 15 (Sept.–Oct.).

Baloyra, Enrique A., ed. 1987. *Comparing New Democracies: Transitions and Consolidation in Mediterranean Europe and the Southern Cone.* Boulder, Colo.: Westview Press.

Barongo, Yolamu, ed. 1983. *Political Science in Africa: A Critical Review.* London: Zed Press.

Bates, Robert H. 1995. *Democratic Transition in Africa: A First Report on an Empirical Project.* Development Discussion Paper, no. 514. Cambridge: Harvard Institute for International Development.

Bayart, Jean-François. 1989. *L'Etat en Afrique: la politique du ventre.* Paris: Fayard.

———. 1995. "Réflexions sur la Politique Africaine de la France." *Politique Africaine* 58 (June): 41–50.

Berg-Schlosser, Dirk. 1984. "African Political Systems: Typology and Performance." *Comparative Political Studies* 17: 121–51.

Berman, Bruce, and Colin Leys, eds. 1994. *African Capitalists in African Development.* Boulder, Colo.: Lynne Rienner Publishers.

Bermeo, Nancy. 1990. "Rethinking Regime Change." *Comparative Politics* 22 (April): 359–77.

Bienen, Henry S. 1979. *Armies and Parties in Africa.* New York: Africana Publishing.

Bienen, Henry S., and Mark Gersovitz. 1986. "Consumer Subsidy Cuts, Violence, and Political Stability." *Comparative Politics* 19: 25–44.

Bienen, Henry S., and Jeffrey Herbst. 1991. "Authoritarianism and Democracy in Africa." *Comparative Political Dynamics: Global Research Perspectives.* Edited by Dankwart A. Rustow and Kenneth P. Erickson. New York: Harper Collins.

Bienen, Henry S., and Nicolas van de Walle. 1991. *Of Time and Power: Leadership Duration in the Modern World.* Stanford: Stanford University Press.

Bollen, Kenneth, and Robert Jackman. 1985. "Political Democracy and the Size Distribution of Income." *American Sociological Review* 50: 438–57.

Boone, Catherine. 1992. *Merchant Capital and the Roots of State Power in Sénégal, 1930–1985.* Cambridge: Cambridge University Press.

Boulaga, F. Eboussi. 1993. *Les Conférences Nationales en Afriques noire.* Paris: Editions Karthala.

Bourgi, Albert, and Christian Castern. 1992. *Le Printemps de l'Afrique.* Paris: Hachette.

Bratton, Michael. 1989. "Beyond the State: Civil Society and Associational Life in Africa." *World Politics* 41: 407–30.

Bratton, Michael, and Nicolas van de Walle with Kimberly Butler, Soo Chan Jang, Kimberly Ludwig, and Yu Wang. 1996. "Political Regimes and Regime Transitions in Africa: A Comparative Handbook." For machine-readable format see University of Michigan, International Consortium for Political and Social Research, 1996; for hard copy see Michigan State University, *MSU Working Papers on Political Reform in Africa,* no. 14. East Lansing: Department of Political Science, Michigan State University.

Buijtenhuijs, Rob, and Céline Thiriot. 1995. *Democratization in Sub-Saharan Africa, 1992–1995: An Overview of the Literature.* Leiden, The Netherlands: African Studies Centre.

Callaghy, Thomas M., and John Ravenhill, eds. 1993. *Hemmed In: Responses to Africa's Economic Decline.* New York: Columbia University Press.

Caporaso, James A., and David Levine. 1992. *Theories of Political Economy.* New York: Cambridge University Press.

Carothers, Thomas. 1991. *In the Name of Democracy: U.S. Policy Toward Latin America in the Reagan Years.* Berkeley: University of California Press.

Cartwright, John R. 1983. *Political Leadership in Africa.* London: Croom Helm.

Chabal, Patrick, ed. 1986. *Political Domination in Africa.* Cambridge: Cambridge University Press.

Chafer, Tony. 1992. "French African Policy: Towards Change." *African Affairs* 91: 37–51.

Charlton, Roger. 1983. "Dehomogenizing the Study of African Politics: The Case of Interstate Influence on Regime Formation and Change." *Plural Societies* 14: 32–48.

Chazan, Naomi. 1979. "African Voters at the Polls: a Re-examination of the Role of Elections in African Politics." *Journal of Commonwealth and Comparative Politics* 17: 136–58.

Chazan, Naomi, Robert Mortimer, John Ravenhill, and Donald Rothchild. 1988. *Politics and Society in Contemporary Africa.* Boulder, Colo.: Lynne Rienner Publishers.

Chege, Michael. 1995. "Between Africa's Extremes." *Journal of Democracy* 6: 44–51.
   1995. "The Military in the Transition to Democracy in Africa: Some Preliminary Observations." *CODESRIA Bulletin* 3:13. Dakar, Sénégal: Council for the Development of Social Science Research in Africa.
Clapham, Christopher, ed. 1982. *Private Patronage and Public Power: Political Clientelism in the Modern State.* London: Pinter.
   1985. *Third World Politics: An Introduction.* Madison: University of Wisconsin Press.
   1996. *Africa and the International System: The Politics of State Survival.* Cambridge: Cambridge University Press.
Clapham, Christopher, and George Philip, eds. 1985. *The Political Dilemmas of Military Regimes.* London: Croom Helm.
Clark, John C., and David Gardiniers, eds. 1997. *Political Liberalization in Francophone Africa.* Boulder, Colo.: Westview Press.
Clough, Michael. 1992. *Free At Last? U.S. Policy Toward Africa and the End of the Cold War.* New York: Council on Foreign Relations.
Cohen, Ronald, Goran Hyden, and Winston P. Nagan, eds. 1993. *Human Rights and Governance in Africa.* Gainesville: University of Florida Press.
Collier, David, and Steven Levitsky. 1995. "Democracy with Adjectives: Strategies to Avoid Conceptual Stretching." Paper presented at the annual meeting of the Latin American Studies Association, Washington, D.C., October 1995.
Collier, Ruth. 1982. *Regimes in Tropical Africa.* Berkeley: University of California Press.
Cornia, Giovanni Andrea, Rolph van der Hoeven, and Thandika Mkandawire, eds. 1993. *Africa's Recovery in the 1990s: From Stagnation and Adjustment to Human Development.* New York: St. Martin's Press.
Cumming, Gordon. 1995. "French Development Assistance to Africa: Towards a New Agenda?" *African Affairs* 94: 383–98.
Dag Hammarskjold Foundation. 1992. *The State in Crisis in Africa: In Search of a Second Liberation.* Uppsala, Sweden: Dag Hammarskjold Foundation.
Dahl, Robert A. 1971. *Polyarchy: Participation and Opposition.* New Haven: Yale University Press.
   1989. *Democracy and Its Critics.* New Haven: Yale University Press.
Dahl, Robert A., and Edward R. Tufte. 1973. *Size and Democracy.* Stanford: Stanford University Press.
Decalo, Samuel. 1976 and 1991. *Coups and Army Rule in Africa.* New Haven: Yale University Press.
   1992. "The Process, Prospects and Constraints of Democratization in Africa." *African Affairs* 91: 7–35.
Dia, Mamadou. 1993. *A Governance Approach to Civil Service Reform in Sub-Saharan Africa.* World Bank Technical Paper, no. 225. Washington, D.C.: World Bank.
Diamond, Larry. 1992. "Economic Development and Democracy Reconsidered." *American Behavioral Scientist* 35: 450–99.
   Ed. 1993. *Political Culture and Democracy in Developing Countries.* Boulder, Colo.: Lynne Rienner Publishers.
Diamond, Larry, Juan J. Linz, and Seymour Martin Lipset, eds. 1988. *Democracy in Developing Countries: Volume Two, Africa.* Boulder, Colo.: Lynne Rienner Press.

DiPalma, Guiseppe. 1990. *To Craft Democracies: An Essay on Democratic Transitions.* Berkeley: University of California Press.

Dix, Robert H. 1992. "Democratization and the Institutionalization of Latin American Political Parties." *Comparative Political Studies* 24: 488–511.

Downs, Anthony. 1957. *An Economic Theory of Democracy.* New York: Harper & Row.

Eisenstadt, Samuel N. 1972. *Traditional Patrimonialism and Modern Neopatrimonialism.* London: Sage.

Ellis, Stephen. 1995. *Democracy in Sub-Saharan Africa: Where Did It Come From? Can It Be Supported?* ECDPM Working Paper, no. 6. The Hague, The Netherlands: European Centre for Development Policy Management, 7 September 1995.

    1996. *Africa Now: People, Policies and Institutions.* London: James Currey.

Elster, Jon, and Rune Slagstad, eds. 1988. *Constitutionalism and Democracy.* Cambridge: Cambridge University Press.

Ergas, Zakis, ed. 1987. *The African State in Transition.* New York: St. Martin's Press.

European Centre for Development Policy. 1992. *Democratization in Sub-Saharan Africa: The Search for Institutional Renewal.* ECDPM Occasional Paper. Maastricht, The Netherlands: ECDPM, July 1992.

Faringer, G. I. 1991. *Press Freedom in Africa.* New York: Praeger.

Foltz, William J. 1994. "Democracy, Development and the Military: Some Lessons from Africa." Paper presented at the annual meeting of the African Studies Association, Toronto, November 3–6, 1994.

Friedman, Edward, ed. 1995. *The Politics of Democratization: Generalizing East Asian Experiences.* Boulder, Colo.: Westview Press.

Gasiorowski, Mark J. 1995. "Economic Crisis and Political Regime Change: An Event History Analysis." *American Political Science Review* 89: 882–97.

Geddes, Barbara. 1994. *Politician's Dilemma.* Berkeley: University of California Press.

Gibbon, Peter, Yusuf Bangura, and Arve Ofstad. 1992. *Authoritarianism, Democracy and Adjustment.* Uppsala, Sweden: Nordiska Afrika Institutet.

Hadenius, Axel. 1992. *Democracy and Development.* Cambridge: Cambridge University Press.

Haggard, Stephen, and Robert R. Kaufman. 1992. *The Politics of Economic Reform.* Princeton: Princeton University Press.

    1995. *The Political Economy of Democratic Transitions.* Princeton: Princeton University Press.

Haggard, Stephan, and Steven B. Webb, eds. 1994. *Voting for Reform: Economic Adjustment in New Democracies.* New York: Oxford University Press.

Harbeson, John W., Donald Rothchild, and Naomi Chazan, eds. 1994. *Civil Society and the State in Africa.* Boulder, Colo.: Lynne Rienner Publishers.

Hayward, Fred M. 1987. *Elections in Independent Africa.* Boulder, Colo.: Westview.

Healey, John, and Mark Robinson. 1992. *Democracy, Governance, and Economic Policy: Sub-Saharan Africa in Comparative Perspective.* London: Overseas Development Institute.

Held, David. 1987. *Models of Democracy.* Stanford: Stanford University Press.

Huntington, Samuel P. 1968. *Political Order in Changing Societies.* New Haven: Yale University Press.

    1991. *The Third Wave: Democratization in the Late Twentieth Century.* Norman: University of Oklahoma Press.

1993. "The Clash of Civilizations?" *Foreign Affairs* 72: 22–49.

Hyden, Goran. 1983. *No Shortcuts to Progress: African Development Management in Comparative Perspective.* Berkeley: University of California Press.

Hyden, Goran, and Michael Bratton, eds. 1992. *Governance and Politics in Africa.* Boulder, Colo.: Lynne Rienner Publishers.

Inkeles, Alex, ed. 1991. *On Measuring Democracy: Its Consequences and Concomitants.* New Brunswick, N.J.: Transaction Publishers.

Jackman, Robert. 1978. "The Predictability of African Coups d'Etat." *American Political Science Review* 72: 1262–75.

Jackson, Robert H. and Carl G. Rosberg. 1982. "Why Africa's Weak States Persist." *World Politics* 35: 1–24.

1982. *Personal Rule in Black Africa: Prince, Autocrat, Prophet, Tyrant.* Berkeley: University of California Press.

Jacquette, Jane. 1994. *The Women's Movement in Latin America: Participation and Democratization.* Boulder, Colo.: Westview.

Jeffries, Richard. 1993. "The State, Structural Adjustment and Good Government in Africa." *Journal of Commonwealth and Comparative Politics* 31: 20–35.

Jenkins, J. Craig, and Augustine J. Kposowa. 1992. "The Political Origins of African Military Coups: Ethnic Competition, Military Centrality, and the Struggle over the Postcolonial State." *International Studies Quarterly* 36: 271–91.

Jones, Mark P. 1995. *Electoral Laws and the Survival of Presidential Democracies.* Notre Dame: University of Notre Dame Press.

Joseph, Richard. 1992. "Africa: The Rebirth of Political Freedom." *Journal of Democracy* 2: 11–25.

Ed. 1994. *The Democratic Challenge in Africa.* Atlanta, Ga.: The Carter Center.

Kaplan, Robert D. 1994. "The Coming Anarchy: How Scarcity, Crime, Overpopulation, Tribalism, and Disease are Rapidly Destroying the Social Fabric of Our Planet." *The Atlantic Monthly* 273 (February): 44–65.

Karl, Terry Lynn. 1990. "Dilemmas of Democratization in Latin America." *Comparative Politics* 22: 1–20.

Kasfir, Nelson. 1976. *The Shrinking Political Arena.* Berkeley: University of California Press.

Kennedy, Paul. 1988. *African Capitalism: The Struggle for Ascendancy.* Cambridge: Cambridge University Press.

Keohane, Robert, Joseph Nye, and Stanley Hoffman, eds. 1993. *After the Cold War: International Institutions and State Strategies in Europe, 1989–1991.* Cambridge: Massachusetts Institute of Technology Press.

Krieger, Winfried Jung Silke, ed. 1994. *Culture and Democracy in Africa South of the Sahara.* Mainz, Germany: V. Hase and Koehler Verlag.

Lawson, Stephanie. 1993. "Conceptual Issues in the Comparative Study of Regime Change and Democratization." *Comparative Politics* 25: 183–205.

Lemarchand, René. 1992. "Uncivil States and Civil Societies: How Illusion Became Reality." *Journal of Modern African Studies* 30: 177–91.

1993. "Africa's Troubled Transitions." *Journal of Democracy* 3: 98–109.

Levine, Daniel. 1988. "Paradigm Lost: Dependence to Democracy." *World Politics* 40: 377–94.

Levine, Victor T. 1967. *Political Leadership in Africa.* Stanford: Stanford University Press.

Linz, Juan J. 1978. *The Breakdown of Democratic Regimes: Crisis, Breakdown and Reequilibration.* Baltimore: Johns Hopkins University Press.

Linz, Juan J., and Arturo Valenzuela. 1995. *The Failure of Presidential Democracy: Comparative Perspectives.* Baltimore: Johns Hopkins University Press.

Lipset, Seymour Martin. 1960. *Political Man: The Social Basis of Politics.* New York: Doubleday.

Londregan, John, and Keith Poole. 1990. "Poverty, the Coup Trap and the Seizure of Executive Power." *World Politics* 42: 151–83.

Lowenthal, Abraham F., ed. 1991. *Exporting Democracy: The United States and Latin America.* Baltimore: Johns Hopkins University Press.

Luckham, Robin. 1994. "The Military, Militarization and Democratization in Africa: A Survey of Literature and Issues." *African Studies Review* 37: 13–76.

———. 1995. "Dilemmas of Military Disengagement and Democratization in Africa." *IDS Bulletin* 26: 49–61. Sussex, England: Institute for Development Studies.

Lutz, J. 1989. "The Diffusion of Political Phenomena in Sub-Saharan Africa." *Journal of Political and Military Sociology* 17: 99–104.

Macpherson, C. B. 1973. *Democratic Theory: Essays in Retrieval.* Oxford: Clarendon Press.

Mainwaring, Scott, Guillermo O'Donnell, and J. Samuel Valenzuela, eds. 1992. *Issues in Democratic Consolidation: The New South American Democracies in Comparative Perspective.* Notre Dame: University of Notre Dame Press.

Malloy, James M., and Mitchell Seligson. 1987. *Authoritarians and Democrats: Regime Transition in Latin America.* Pittsburgh: University of Pittsburgh Press.

Mamdani, Mahmood, and Ernest Wamba-dia-Wamba, eds. 1995. *African Studies in Social Movements and Democracy.* Dakar, Sénégal: Council for the Development of Social Science Research in Africa (CODESRIA).

Mansbridge, Jane. 1991. "What is Democracy?" In National Research Council. *The Transition to Democracy.* Washington, D.C.: National Academy Press.

Markakis, John, and Michael Waller. 1986. *Military Marxist Regimes in Africa.* London: Frank Cass.

Mbembe, Achille. 1985. *Les Jeunes et L'Ordre Politique en Afrique Noire.* Paris: L'Harmattan.

———. 1988. *Afriques Indociles.* Paris: Karthala.

Médard, Jean François, ed. 1994. *Etats d'Afrique Noire: Formation, Mécanismes et Crises.* Paris: Karthala.

Michaels, Marguerite. 1993. "Retreat from Africa." *Foreign Affairs* 72: 93–108.

Migdal, Joel. 1988. *Strong Societies and Weak States: State–Society Relations and State Capabilities in the Third World.* Princeton: Princeton University Press.

Monga, Célestin. 1995. "Civil Society and Democratization in Francophone Africa." *Journal of Modern African Studies* 33: 359–79.

———. 1994. *Anthropologie de la Colère: Société Civile et Démocratie en Afrique Noire.* Paris: l'Harmattan.

Moore, Barrington Jr. 1966. *The Social Origins of Dictatorship and Democracy: Lord and Peasant in the Making of the Modern World.* Boston: Beacon Press.

Mosley, Paul, Jane Harrigan, and John Toye. 1991. *Aid and Power: The World Bank and Policy-Based Lending in the 1980s.* London: Routledge.

Moss, Todd J. 1995. "U.S. Policy and Democratization in Africa: The Limits of Liberal Universalism." *Journal of Modern African Studies* 33: 189–209.

Muller, Edward N. 1988. "Democracy, Economic Development, and Income Inequality." *American Sociological Review* 53: 50–68.

Munslow, Barry. 1993. "Democratization in Africa." *Parliamentary Affairs* 46: 483.

North, Douglass C. 1990. *Institutions, Institutional Change, and Economic Performance.* New York: Cambridge University Press.

O'Donnell, Guillermo. 1973. *Modernization and Bureaucratic Authoritarianism: Studies in South American Politics.* Berkeley, Calif.: Institute for International Studies.

O'Donnell, Guillermo, Philippe C. Schmitter, and Laurence Whitehead. 1986. *Transitions from Authoritarian Rule.* Baltimore: Johns Hopkins University Press, 4 vols.

Owusu, D. Maxwell. 1992. "Democracy and Africa: A View from the Village." *Journal of Modern African Studies* 30: 369–96.

Oyugi, Walter. O., ed. 1988. *Democratic Theory and Practice in Africa.* London: James Currey.

Packenham, Robert A. 1973. *Liberal America and the Third World: Political Development Ideas in Foreign Aid and Social Science.* Princeton: Princeton University Press.

Perry, Garaint, and Michael Moran, eds. 1994. *Democracy and Democratization.* New York: Routledge.

Pridham, Geoffrey, ed. 1991. *Encouraging Democracy: The International Dimension of Democratization in Southern Europe.* Liecester: Liecester University Press.

Pridham, Geoffrey, Eric Herring, and George Sandford, eds. 1994. *Building Democracy? The International Dimension of Democratization in Eastern Europe.* London: Liecester University Press.

Przeworski, Adam. 1991. *Democracy and the Market: Political and Economic Reforms in Eastern Europe and Latin America.* New York: Cambridge University Press.

Przeworski, Adam, and Fernando Limongi. 1993. "Political Regimes and Economic Growth." *Journal of Economic Perspectives* 7: 51–69.

Putnam, Robert D. 1992. *Making Democracy Work: Civic Traditions in Modern Italy.* Princeton: Princeton University Press.

Quantin, Patrick, ed. 1994. *l'Afrique Politique, 1994: Vue sur la Démocratisation à Marée Basse.* Paris: Karthala.

Remmer, Karen L. 1986. "Exclusionary Democracy." *Studies in Comparative International Development* 20: 64–85.

———. 1991. "New Wine or Old Bottlenecks? The Study of Latin American Democracy." *Comparative Politics* 23: 479–98.

———. 1993. "The Political Economy of Elections in Latin America, 1980–1991." *American Political Science Review* 87: 393–406.

Rimmer, Douglas, ed. 1994. *Action in Africa: The Experience of People in Government, Business and Aid.* London: James Currey.

Roberts, Brad, ed. 1990. *The New Democracies: Global Change and U.S. Foreign Policy.* Cambridge: Masachusetts Institute of Technology Press.

Robinson, Pearl. 1994. "The National Conference Phenomenon in Francophone Africa." *Comparative Studies in Society and History* 36: 575–610.

Roth, Guenther. 1968. "Personal Rulership, Patrimonialism, and Empire-Building in the New States." *World Politics* 20: 194–206.

Rothchild, Donald, and Naomi Chazan, eds. 1988. *The Precarious Balance: State and Society in Africa*. Boulder, Colo.: Westview Press.

Rothchild, Donald, and V.A. Olorunsola, eds. 1982. *State versus Ethnic Claims: African Policy Dilemmas*. Boulder, Colo.: Westview Press.

Rueschemeyer, Dietrich, Evelyne Huber Stephens, and John D. Stephens. 1992. *Capitalist Development and Democracy*. Chicago: University of Chicago Press.

Rustow, Dankwart A. 1970. "Transitions to Democracy: Towards a Dynamic Model." *Comparative Politics* 2: 337–63.

Sandbrook, Richard. 1986. *The Politics of African Economic Stagnation*. Cambridge: Cambridge University Press.

⸻. 1992. *The Politics of Africa's Economic Recovery*. Cambridge: Cambridge University Press.

Schatzberg, Michael G. 1993. "Power, Legitimacy and 'Democratisation' in Africa." *Africa* 63: 445–61.

Schmidt, Steffen W., James Scott, J. Guasti, and C. Lande, eds. 1976. *Friends, Followers and Factions: A Reader in Political Clientelism*. Berkeley: University of California.

Schmitter, Philippe C. 1992. "The Consolidation of Democracy and Representation of Social Groups." *American Behavioral Scientist* 35: 422–49.

Schmitter, Philippe, and Terry Lynn Karl. 1991. "What Democracy Is ... And Is Not." *Journal of Democracy* 2: 75–88.

Schraeder, Peter J. 1994. *United States Policy Toward Africa: Incrementalism, Crisis and Change*. New York: Cambridge University Press.

Schumpeter, Joseph A. *Capitalism, Socialism, and Democracy*. 1942. Reprint, London: Allen and Unwin, 1976.

Shin, Doh Chull. 1994. "On the Third Wave of Democratization: A Synthesis and Evaluation of Recent Theory and Research." *World Politics* 47: 135–69.

Shugart, Matthew S., and John M. Carey. 1992. *Presidents and Assemblies: Constitutional Design and Electoral Dynamics*. Cambridge: Cambridge University Press.

Sklar, Richard L. 1983. "Democracy in Africa." *African Studies Review* 36: 11–24.

Smith, Tony F. 1986. "The Underdevelopment of the Development Literature: The Case of Dependency Theory." In *The State and Development in the Third World*. Edited by Atul Kohli. Princeton: Princeton University Press, 25–66.

⸻. 1993. "Making the World Safe for Democracy." *The Washington Quarterly* 16: 197–214.

Snyder, Richard. 1992. "Explaining Transitions from Neopatrimonial Dictatorships." *Comparative Politics* 24: 379–400.

Stepan, Alfred. 1988. *Rethinking Military Politics: Brazil and the Southern Cone*. Princeton: Princeton University Press.

Stepan, Alfred, and Cindy Skach. 1993. "Constitutional Frameworks and Democratic Consolidation: Parliamentarianism versus Presidentialism." *World Politics* 46: 1–22.

Thelen, Kathleen, Sven Steinmo, and Frank Longstreth, eds. 1992. *Structuring Politics: Historical Institutionalism in Comparative Analysis*. Cambridge: Cambridge University Press.

Theobold, Robin. 1982. "Patrimonialism." *World Politics* 34: 548–59.

United States Agency for International Development (USAID). 1990. *The Democracy Initiative*. Washington, D.C.: USAID.

Valenzuela, J. Samuel. 1989. "Labor Movements in Transitions to Democracy." *Comparative Politics* 21: 445–72.

van de Walle, Nicolas. 1994. "Political Liberalization and Economic Reform in Africa." *World Development* 22: 483–500.

Walton, John, and David Seddon. 1994. *Free Markets and Food Riots: The Politics of Global Adjustment*. Oxford: Blackwell.

Widner, Jennifer A. 1994. *Economic Change and Political Liberalization in Sub-Saharan Africa*. Baltimore: Johns Hopkins University Press.

Wiseman, John A. 1986. "Urban Riots in West Africa, 1977-1985." *Journal of Modern African Studies* 24: 509–18.

1992. "Early Post-Redemocratization Elections in Africa," *Electoral Studies* 11: 279.

Wiseman, John A, ed. 1995. *Democracy and Political Change in Sub-Saharan Africa*. New York: Routledge.

World Bank. 1989. *Sub-Saharan Africa: From Crisis to Sustainable Growth: A Long Term Perspective Study*. Washington, D.C.: World Bank.

1993. *Adjustment in Africa: Reforms, Results and the Road Ahead*. Washington, D.C.: World Bank.

Young, Crawford. 1982. *Ideology and Development in Africa*. New Haven: Yale University Press.

1994. *The African Colonial State in Comparative Perspective*. New Haven: Yale University Press.

Young, Tom. 1993. "Elections and Electoral Politics in Africa." *Africa* 63: 299–312.

Zartman, I. William, ed. 1995. *Collapsed States: The Disintegration and Restoration of Legitimate Authority*. Boulder, Colo.: Lynne Rienner Publishers.

Zolberg, Aristide. 1968. "The Structure of Political Conflict in the New States of Tropical Africa." *American Political Science Review* 62: 70.

INDEX